THE PAPERBACK
APOCALYPSE

ROBERT M. PRICE

THE PAPERBACK

APOCALYPSE

How the Christian Church
WAS LEFT BEHIND

Prometheus Books
59 John Glenn Drive
Amherst, New York 14228-2119

Published 2007 by Prometheus Books

Inquiries should be addressed to
Prometheus Books
59 John Glenn Drive
Amherst, New York 14228–2119
VOICE: 716–691–0133, ext. 210
FAX: 716–691–0137
WWW.PROMETHEUSBOOKS.COM

11 10 09 08 07   5 4 3 2 1

Library of Congress Cataloging-in-Publication Data

Price, Robert M., 1954–
    The paperback apocalypse : how the Christian church was left behind / by Robert M. Price.—1st American pbk. ed.
        p. cm.
    Includes bibliographical references and index.
    ISBN 978–1–59102–583–2
    1. Apocalyptic literature—History and criticism. 2. End of the world. I. Title.

BS646.P75 2007
236'.9—dc22

2007027087

Printed in the United States on acid-free paper

For the Prophet Koganiah,
Dr. Michael S. Kogan,
Mentor and Example,
a Father and a Friend

CONTENTS

INTRODUCTION

The Beginning of Sorrows

"The mythical eschatology is untenable for the simple reason that the parousia of Christ never took place as the New Testament expected. History did not come to an end, and, as every schoolboy knows, it will continue to run its course."

—Rudolf Bultmann, "New Testament and Mythology"[1]

Popular evangelical/fundamentalist eschatology has for some time been all the rage. For example, though the *New York Times* was too embarrassed to include it on the best seller list, Hal Lindsey's *The Late Great Planet Earth*, which predicted the coming of the Rapture and the Antichrist by 1988, would have ascended to the top and stayed there through the whole decade of the 1970s. I had been a born-again Christian for about five years when Lindsey's book and several others like it (especially Salem Kirban's novel *666*) appeared. Christian eschatology was totally new to me. I had always believed in what theologians call "individual eschatology," the individual's destiny in heaven or hell. But I remember when I first heard about the truths of "corporate eschatology": the Antichrist, the Tribulation, and the Rapture. It all struck me as outlandish, though I trusted the church teachers who told me about it. Yet I could hardly believe Christian doctrine contained such extraordinary features. Jesus Christ, sure. But the *Anti*christ? What on earth? Where had *this* stuff come from? I was already a fan of fantasy and horror literature (Lovecraft, Tolkien, Robert E. Howard), so none of the new (to me) doctrines offended me. Just the reverse: I eagerly lapped it all up! End Times belief added vivid new colors to the Christian faith. So I read all the Last Days material I could get my hands on and eagerly imagined the end of the age happening in the near future. I must say I never went so far as others did, skipping college or career preparation because of the supposed proximity of the Rapture. And my fixation did not last long; I soon moved on to the more sober (as I thought then) area of apologetics.

But I must also confess a guilty pleasure. Once I read Kirban's awfully written attempt at a novel, I found myself hooked on End Times novels (and movies), seeking out earlier and better representatives of the genre. I absolutely loved *The Omen*. A few years later, I discarded belief in the End Times, and similar ideas, but that did not affect my enjoyment of the genre at all. Stephen King's *The Stand* towered above all the rest as the End Times epic par excellence—at least until many years later, when Tim LaHaye got his friend Jerry B. Jenkins to execute his vision for a gigantic exercise in edifying fiction, the now-famous *Left Behind* and its sequels. While no Stephen King, Jenkins proved himself quite the able writer, and his books are great fun. At least if you like End Times novels. As Abe Lincoln once commented, "For those who like this sort of thing, this is undoubtedly the sort of thing they like." And I like this sort of thing.

The hardiness of the notion of a soon-ish Second Coming (or, in the New Testament Greek, the Parousia) of Christ is evident by the fact that it continues to generate belief despite repeated disappointments, and equally by the fact that it produces epics of pop entertainment by and for both believers and nonbelievers. Secular moneymakers about the End Times include *The Omen* (plus its surprisingly many sequels, as well as its 2006 remake), *The Seventh Sign*, *Lost Souls*, and the Schwarzenegger shoot-'em-up, *End of Days*. There are even more Christian Rapture novels, but the *Left Behind* epic is virtually a genre unto itself. This series of adventure novels has morphed into films and, now, a violent video game in which the player may assume the role either of a Christian crusader filling the unrepentant full of holy holes or of a minion of the Beast persecuting Christians! Besides that, there is a series of prequels, filling in the backgrounds of the characters, as well as yet another sequence of kids' novels set during the Great Tribulation.

As Ludwig Wittgenstein said, those who find themselves outside the eschatological language game find themselves mystified by it.[2] They cannot even comment on it meaningfully, it is so alien to their frame of reference. This is not least evident in the case of secular politicos who seem to fear that any evangelical Christian president (or would-be president) of the United States must adopt the End Times scenario as official foreign policy. A world leader operating on such premises could be realistically expected to try to accelerate Armageddon in full confidence that the good guys would win and that a new and better world would follow. Ronald Reagan and George W. Bush have been so suspected, groundlessly, as I think. But Pat Robertson and Gary Bauer ran for president, too. And in their cases one would have to take such fears very seriously indeed. And there may well be more like them waiting in the wings.

All this means that outsiders and fair-minded insiders must be ready to take a searching second (or first!) look at the evangelical End Times phenomenon in order to assess its dangers and to realize how absolutely groundless it is, how very lacking in biblical support. For close scrutiny reveals that evangelical premillennialism (or whatever term by which one wishes to dignify it—à la Ed Norton calling himself a "subterranean sanitation engineer") is about as "biblical" a doctrine as its cousin creationism. Both rest upon a highly selective, artificial reading of the Bible and both result in the same sort of arbitrary treatment of evidence, in the one case scientific, in the other historical.

The Paperback Apocalypse examines the theological framework of popular eschatology, comparing it with the texts to which it erroneously appeals. It goes further, demonstrating that the New Testament promise of the Second Coming of Jesus Christ has long since fallen victim to a self-imposed statute of limitations. That is, this pseudo-event was never predicted as happening *someday*, in the sweet by-and-by; rather, it was always mentioned with the promise of a swift fulfillment in the ancient readers' *own day.* That promise failed, and there is as much reason to postpone it, still expecting it, as there is to hold onto one's ticket from a defunct airline. It will not be honored, and it is high time to make some alternate plans. I will reinforce this point with a historical survey of disappointed eschatological expectation.

In the process of all this refutation, I offer the reader a genuine scholarly inventory of items of lore such as the Antichrist, the Tribulation, the Rapture, and so on, and their origins and original meanings. For instance, as John A. T. Robinson and others have argued, the Gospel predictions of the Second Coming have been taken out of the context in which they originally referred to the impending fall of Jerusalem. I will track the evolution of the tradition. I even make bold to set forth altogether new theories as to the origin of the Rapture and the Antichrist.

My task also gives me the glad opportunity to review the various evangelical fictions on the End Times, especially the LaHaye/Jenkins *Left Behind* series, and to analyze the psychological appeal of the genre, which is essentially to salve the wound of constant disappointment at the failure of the Rapture to come on schedule. So, in short, I want to explain the appeal, the danger, and the baselessness of the evangelical End Times enthusiasm. I intend no derision or contempt for those who buy into it. They can't be expected to know better—until they read this book. Nor am I one of those who disdain the book of Revelation and all apocalyptic elements. They are an incredible source of mischief, true, but also irreplaceable as symbolism. Apocalypticism forms a wonderful example of the utility of the demythologizing of religious symbols. Rudolf Bultmann rejected the approach of rationalist Liberal Protestantism that sought to amputate all the now-unbelievable mythology and cling to whatever might be left, usually moral exhortation. No, there is more to both mythology and religion than that. The thing about powerful myths (and not all of them are) is that they use a symbol to convey something that cannot be conveyed in straight, rational terms. Something will be lost. To avoid reductionism, one must demythologize: *interpret* myth instead of rejecting it. A particular mythic symbol may speak to us even more loudly and deeply than it did when we once believed it literally, as is the case with what Tillich calls the "broken myth."[3] And so with apocalyptic. I find it hard to deny that Hitler was the Antichrist, the Beast from the Abyss. Saddam Hussein, too. Of course, not literally. When they passed, the world did not end. History did not issue in the millennium. Nothing supernatural was involved in their reigns of evil. And yet there is a depth and gravity to their very human evil that cannot be adequately conveyed if we do not hurl abusive mythological epithets against them. We would run the risk (and we will again in any analogous situation) of domesticating and underestimating the evil Hitler represents if we try to characterize it entirely in terms of national politics and militarism, scapegoat strategies, or the aberrant psychology of the individual. We need the myth.

Or take a different example. It is not hard to imagine that in the near future the government might seek to implement a security program that would require each citizen to receive a subcutaneous chip featuring credit and medical information and allowing the government to track one's whereabouts. If this happened, would fundamentalists be proven correct? Would such a development herald the rise of the Antichrist? Yes and no. It would not be the fulfillment of a clairvoyant prediction from the past, but it would mean that the sort of invasive tyranny that gave rise to the myth originally had now manifested itself again in a particularly insidious form. And familiarity with the myth of the mark of the Beast from the book of Revelation would enable us to grasp the full, ominous implications. Those implications would not include the literal belief that Satan had incarnated himself and would soon be picking a fight with Jesus Christ on the plain of Megiddo. But they would include "the big picture," the overweening hubris of a humanmade system that has gone out of control, become a reified monster demanding we serve it instead of it serving us. The myth of the mark of the Beast would be useful in galvanizing us as to the stakes we were playing. It might cost everything to resist such a system, but it might be worse if we played along. German citizens were faced with the mark of the Beast when they had to decide between helping persecuted Jews or quietly leaving them to their fate. Such terrible moments do sometimes come upon us, and we need the old myths to reveal their gravity.

And that makes the literalism of fundamentalists doubly ironic. It is the very power of myth that they risk missing as long as they take Revelation as a script for things to come, a one-to-one prediction. For that means that, if a tyrant's name cannot be computed out to 666, then we may mistakenly think we face only a mundane situation not requiring a genuine test of the soul. Otherwise, how can we explain how Chilean Pentecostals largely supported General Pinochet? He did not ask anyone to take a literal mark of loyalty. He did not try to suppress the Protestant Church. So he must have been okay. But he wasn't. They should have recognized the Beast in yet another garb. The Antichrist came at a moment they did not expect, and they were caught flat-footed. They missed the utility of myth.

NOTES

1. Rudolf Bultmann, "New Testament and Mythology" in *Kerygma and Myth: A Theological Debate*, ed. Hans Werner Bartsch, trans. Reginald H. Fuller (New York: Harper & Row, 1961), p. 5.

2. Ludwig Wittgenstein, *Lectures and Conversations on Aesthetics, Psychology and Religious Belief*, ed. Cyril Barrett (Berkeley and Los Angeles: University of California Press, 1966), p. 53: "Suppose someone were a believer and said: 'I believe in a Last Judgement,' and I said: 'Well, I'm not so sure. Possibly.' You would say that there is an enormous gulf between us. If he said 'There is a German aeroplane overhead,' and I said 'Possibly, I'm not so sure,' you'd say we were fairly near. It isn't a question of my being anywhere near him, but on an entirely different plane, which you could express by saying: 'You mean something altogether different, Wittgenstein.'" With the answer to the question about the German bomber, Wittgenstein's dissent is within a frame of reference he shares with the questioner, whereas when it comes to the Last Judgment, they share no such framework. Wittgenstein's dissent is not like that of

the posttribulationist dissenting from the opinion of the pretribulationist about the coming of the Day of Judgment, but, rather, Wittgenstein finds himself in a different ballpark altogther, playing a different game.

I once found myself in a similar situation with local Montclair, New Jersey, New Age guru Jyoti Chrystal over lunch. "Don't you think so-and-so is a result of good karma? Isn't this or that a sign we're in the cusp of the New Age?" I was utterly at a loss for words. She framed everything she said in such a way that I simply could not begin to respond, being completely outside her frame of reference. She is a wise person and an effective leader; I don't mean to criticize her. That's exactly my point: because of the total incommensurability between our perspectives, I could not even agree or disagree with her, and I think that's what Wittgenstein had in mind.

3. Paul Tillich, *Dynamics of Faith* (New York: Harper & Row, 1957), pp. 50–54.

Chapter One

THE EVOLUTION OF APOCALYPTIC

"Everything that has a beginning has an end."

—*The Matrix Revolutions*

"The disciples say to Jesus, 'Tell us what our end will be.' Jesus says, 'Have you found the beginning, that you ask about the end? For where the beginning is, there, too, shall be the end. Blessed is the one who shall stand at the beginning, for he shall know the end, and he shall not taste death.'"

—Gospel of Thomas, saying 18

BEGINNINGS OF THE END

The Greek word for *revelation* is *apocalypse*. Thus it is all the same whether one refers to the last book of the Bible as "the Revelation of John" or "the Apocalypse of John." They mean exactly the same thing. And the noun *apocalypse* has lent itself to a whole genre of books like Revelation, which also claim to set forth visions of (as Swedenborg put it) "heaven and its wonders and hell." The standard features of these writings as well as the unique, enigmatic style of them are both dubbed "apocalyptic." Apocalyptic documents usually take the form of visionary journeys starring this or that famous ancient hero, together with the secrets they have brought back and are now entrusting to the reader. Such secrets include, primarily, the scheduled events of the future—usually the immediate future, which is also the end of history as we know it, and the makeup of the physical universe including the machinery of weather, the motions of the stars and planets, and the proper calendars based on them.

Apocalyptic language is cipher language, an avoidance of straight description. Such texts abound in descriptions of monsters that are half this and half that: twelve-winged eagles, seven-headed dragons, and so on. The fortunes of earthly empires and mundane populations are somehow conveyed in the form of heavenly battles, angels, and stars. There are two likely reasons for such elusive language and such an abundance of symbols. First, apocalypses sometimes functioned as *samizdat*, underground handbills to encourage the members of a persecuted community, reassuring them that the evil powers' days were numbered and that the readers' redemption was drawing nigh. In such cases, the apocalypses must not fall into the wrong hands. If the Gestapo were to burst in and confiscate your sacred writings, and they discovered gleeful predictions of the demise of their regime, it would go much worse for you and your compatriots. So better to write in cipher language that they can never make sense of. Heck, you're in enough trouble already!

But most apocalypses do not seem to have been the product of persecution, nor were they occasioned by it. And here the clue for the explanation of the symbol language lies in the fact that apocalypses were the creations not of prophets but of scribes, the kind of people most interested in forecasting the future, speculating on the afterlife, and charting the stars and the calendars. What such language suggests is that the apocalypses were puzzles designed to force their readers to prove their acumen by making them work for the answers. It is exactly the same as when a teacher tells a parable, a figurative story, and caps it off with "He who has ears, let him hear." Even so, Revelation teases its readers with the name of the Beast but leaves it in a cipher: "Let him who has wisdom reckon the number of the Beast, for it is the number of a man. His number is six hundred sixty-six." Get it? The object was not to cast one's pearls of wisdom before swine. Such wisdom was not for everyone. In the same way, the rabbis forbade Jews to study the mysterious Lore of Creation until they were forty years old.

ROYAL VISIONS

As Paul D. Hanson suggests, we may discover "the dawn of apocalyptic" (his book's title) in the religio-political struggles of the Jewish aristocrats returning to Palestine after the Babylonian Exile in the fifth century BCE. But first we must take a step back for a brief look at the ideologies of the prophets and the monarchy in preexilic Judah.

The institution of the monarchy in Israel was an importation from the surrounding countries, as 1 Samuel, chapter 8, makes clear. Hitherto, rule was by charismatic judges, if at all. When the institution of kingship was introduced, the accompanying royal ideology came along with it. As everyone knows, traditionally all kings claimed "the mandate of heaven" for their regime. They reigned at the pleasure of God or the gods. The "divine right of kings" meant that the king was the earthly servant, mouthpiece, and vicar of God. If you wanted to know God's will, ask the king. He tried cases and set national policy. The welfare of the nation as well as the fertility of its crops and the bounty of its harvests were bound up with the king. The energy of nature seemed to run out in the fall as days became shorter and vegetation died away. This implied that the monarchy, too, had in some way run out of steam and required rebirth, reinvigoration, rehabilitation. Perhaps the year's end entropy had to do with the king's declining powers or with his possible unfaithfulness to God's commands. So the thing to do was to recall the primordial time when the gods/God created the earth and the king of gods rose to power via the creation. Each ancient culture in the Near East (and beyond) had a yearly ritual in which it ceremonially reenacted creation and thus sought to reinvigorate both the world of nature and the power of the monarchy.

The ritual, of which we know a good deal, mainly from Babylon but consistently echoed in the adjacent civilizations, contained many interrelated elements, all reenacting the local myth of creation. In Babylon, the story was that the gods cringed before the power of the titan Kingu and the dragon Tiamat. Neither the divine warrior Anu nor the warrior goddess Astarte availed against Tiamat. But then Marduk, the warrior and storm god, son of the king of gods, Ea, stood forth and proposed that he would vanquish the monster if in return the gods would agree to crown him king in his father's stead. The others were happy to agree to this, since such a victory would demonstrate Marduk's right to the universal throne. Marduk did indeed prevail, but not easily and not at once. He was devoured/imprisoned by the powers of darkness and killed. Rising from the dead, however, he defeated and destroyed Tiamat.[1] Then he dismembered her corpse and used the pieces to construct the heavens (i.e., the dome of the firmament) and the earth.

The elements of this story varied, as one might expect, from kingdom to kingdom, but the basic pattern was the same. Each version included a generational conflict, just as Kingu was the father of the gods and Zeus was the son of the titan Kronos, whom he must defeat to prove his kingship. And usually the monster represented the dreadful, unknown depths of the sea or else the devastating power of the flood. Thus Aliyan Baal, son of El, fights not only the death-spirit Mot but also against Yamm ("the Sea") and Lotan, the seven-headed dragon, the personification of the Litani River in Syria, with its many tributaries.[2] Hercules combats the seven- (or nine-) headed Hydra ("Water"). The Vedic god Indra, warrior and thunder wielder, also fights a dragon, Vritra, who hoards the water and parches the earth. Indra takes over the monarchy from the elder god Varuna, but he does not so much create the world as save it from death by bringing back the rains. But these differences are mere local variations on a theme.

In all versions, the New Year festival featured the king dressed in glorious raiment, posturing and pantomiming a ritual reenactment of the god defeating the dragon (no doubt a bunch of slaves under a big dragon suit, like marchers in a Chinese New Year parade). He would stride up the steps to the gate of the temple, where the high priest would remove his crown and tweak his nose or ears and slap him in the face, accusing him of sin, the ostensible cause of the expiry of the divine mandate as the year declined. But he would protest his innocence, turning the weight of responsibility back upon his subjects. Then, vindicated, he would retrieve his crown and receive the acclamation of the worshiping crowd. Following this, he walked into the temple, into whose inner recesses no one but the king and the priests might enter. There he (supposedly) arose into heaven for his annual glimpse of the heavenly Tablets of Destiny, which informed him of the events fated for the new year, as well as Marduk's plans for dealing with them. This meant that his subjects need never question his wisdom. Whatever came up, the king had been forewarned and even had God's advice on the matter. By the same token, no matter how badly things might seem to be going, it would be not only impious but insane to question the orders of the king. What, do you know better than God Almighty? Not likely.

ACCORDING TO THE HEBREWS

It was the same in Judah, where each new king represented Yahve, the warrior and storm god who won the kingship from (or the coregency with) his father, El Elyon ("God Most High") by defeating the sea (Yamm) and/or the dragons Leviathan (Lotan), Rahab, or Tiamat. That the Bible contains such a myth is news to most readers (who have naturally never heard a sermon on such texts) and requires a bit more than mere assertion.

Note first that, according to ancient belief, Yahve was not the only or even the highest Israelite deity. Rather, he was one of the seventy sons of the Most High God (El Elyon), who created enough nations for each of his sons (and daughters?) to have a people to rule:

Remember the days of old,
consider the years of many generations;
ask your father, and he will show you,
your elders, and they will tell you.
When the Most High gave to the nations their inheritance,
when he separated the sons of men,
he fixed the bounds of the peoples
according to the number of the sons of God.
For Yahve's portion is his people,
Jacob his allotted heritage. (Deut. 32:7–9)

In what follows, please note the juxtaposition of the three crucial elements: Yahve defeats the dragon(s), creates the world, and establishes his throne (hence the link to the Davidic monarchy). I have emphasized in boldface the relevant lines.

I will sing of your steadfast love, O Yahve, for ever;
with my mouth I will proclaim your faithfulness to all generations.
For *your steadfast love was established for ever,*
your faithfulness is firm as the heavens. [creation of the heavens]
You have said, "I have made a covenant with my chosen one,
I have sworn to David my servant:
'I will establish your descendants for ever,
and build your throne for all generations.'" [The Davidic king is God's
      vicar.]
Let the heavens praise your wonders, O Yahve,
your faithfulness in the assembly of the holy ones!
For who in the skies can be compared to Yahve?
Who among the heavenly beings is like Yahve,
a God feared in the council of the holy ones,
great and terrible above all that are round about him?
O Yahve Sabaoth,
who is mighty as you are, O Yahve, [Yahve's elevation as king of gods]
with your faithfulness round about you?
You rule the raging of the sea;
when its waves rise, you still them. [He defeated Yamm.]

You crushed Rahab like a carcass, [He defeated Rahab.]
you scattered your enemies with your mighty arm.
The heavens are yours, the earth also is yours;
the world and all that is in it, you have founded them.
The north and the south, you have created them;
Tabor and Hermon joyously praise your name. [He created the earth.]
You have a mighty arm;
strong is your hand, high your right hand. [He is a mighty warrior.]
Righteousness and justice are *the foundation of your throne*;
steadfast love and faithfulness go before you.
Blessed are the people who know *the festal shout*,
who walk, O Yahve, in the light of your countenance,
who exult in your name all the day,
and extol your righteousness. [a reference to the kingship renewal]
For you are the glory of their strength;
by your favor our horn is exalted.
For our shield belongs to Yahve,
our king to the Holy One of Israel.
Of old you spoke in a vision
to your faithful one, and said:
"I have set the crown upon one who is mighty,
I have exalted one chosen from the people.
I have found David, my servant;
with my holy oil I have anointed him;
so that my hand shall ever abide with him,
my arm also shall strengthen him.
The enemy shall not outwit him,
the wicked shall not humble him.
I will crush his foes before him
and strike down those who hate him.
My faithfulness and my steadfast love shall be with him,
and in my name shall his horn be exalted.
I will set his hand on the sea
and his right hand on the rivers.
He shall cry to me, 'You are my Father,
my God, and the Rock of my salvation.'
And I will make him the first-born, [Judah's king is God's son.]

the highest of the kings of the earth.
My steadfast love I will keep for him for ever,
and my covenant will stand firm for him.
I will establish *his line* for ever
and his throne as the days of the heavens.
If *his children* forsake my law [The dynasty, and neither David nor a
    future messiah is in view.]
and do not walk according to my ordinances,
if they violate my statutes
and do not keep my commandments,
then I will punish their transgression with the rod
and their iniquity with scourges;
but I will not remove from him my steadfast love,
or be false to my faithfulness.
I will not violate my covenant,
or alter the word that went forth from my lips.
Once for all I have sworn by my holiness;
I will not lie to David.
His line shall endure for ever,
his throne as long as the sun before me.
Like the moon it shall be established for ever;
it shall stand firm while the skies endure." (Pss. 89:1–37)

Yet **God my King is from of old**, [foundation of the divine throne]
working salvation in the midst of the earth.
You **divided the sea** by your might; [He defeated Yamm, splitting him
    as Marduk did Tiamat.]
you **broke the heads of the dragons on the waters.**
You crushed the heads of Leviathan, [He killed the dragons, even
    seven-headed Leviathan.]
you gave him as food for the creatures of the wilderness.
You cleft open springs and brooks;
you dried up ever-flowing streams.
Yours is the day, yours also the night;
you have established the luminaries and the sun.
You have fixed all the bounds of the earth;
you have made summer and winter. [Creation] (Pss. 74:12–17)

Yonder is the sea, great and wide,
which teems with things innumerable,
living things both small and great.
There go the ships,
and Leviathan which you formed to sport in it. (Pss. 104:25–26)

Awake, awake, put on strength,
O arm of Yahve;
awake, as in days of old,
the generations of long ago.
Was it not you who cut Rahab in pieces,
who pierced the dragon?
Was it not you who dried up the sea,
the waters of the great deep;
who made the depths of the sea a way
for the redeemed to pass over? (Isa. 51:9–10)

The crossing of the Sea of Reeds/Red Sea in Exodus is seen here as a replay of the primordial defeat of Yamm, the Sea.

In that day Yahve with his hard and great and strong sword will punish Leviathan the fleeing serpent, Leviathan the twisting serpent, and he will slay the dragon that is in the sea. (Isa. 27:1)

Here, as we will see again later, Yahve's primordial victory over the sea dragon is expected to occur again in the future, as in Revelation.

By his power he stilled the sea;
by his understanding he smote Rahab.
By his wind the heavens were made fair;
his hand pierced the fleeing serpent. (Job 26:12–13)

Can you draw out Leviathan with a fishhook,
or press down his tongue with a cord?
Can you put a rope in his nose,
or pierce his jaw with a hook?

Will he make many supplications to you?
Will he speak to you soft words?
Will he make a covenant with you
to take him for your servant for ever?
Will you play with him as with a bird,
or will you put him on a leash for your maidens?
Will traders bargain over him?
Will they divide him up among the merchants?
Can you fill his skin with harpoons,
or his head with fishing spears?
Lay hands on him;
think of the battle; you will not do it again! (Job 40:25:1–8)

What a picture! Yahve is shown having fished up the dragon from the sea, after spearing him with harpoon after harpoon! Dragging him back to the docks, the divine fisher is accosted by merchants who are desperate to buy his catch. But Leviathan has pleaded for mercy, and Yahve has agreed to tame him as a pet for his children, the gods and goddesses!

Daniel said, "I saw in my vision by night, and behold, the four winds of heaven were stirring up the great sea. And four great beasts came up out of the sea, different from one another. The first was like a lion and had eagles' wings. Then as I looked its wings were plucked off, and it was lifted up from the ground and made to stand upon two feet like a man; and the mind of a man was given to it.

And behold, another beast, a second one, like a bear. It was raised up on one side; it had three ribs in its mouth between its teeth; and it was told, 'Arise, devour much flesh.' After this I looked, and lo, another, like a leopard, with four wings of a bird on its back; and the beast had four heads; and dominion was given to it.

After this I saw in the night visions, and behold, a fourth beast, terrible and dreadful and exceedingly strong; and it had great iron teeth; it devoured and broke in pieces, and stamped the residue with its feet. It was different from all the beasts that were before it; and it had ten horns." (Dan. 7:2–7)

Here the author of the book of Daniel has taken over an old creation account in which the process begins, precisely as in Genesis 1:2 ("a mighty wind was moving over the face of the ocean depth"). Then the sea monsters emerge. Yahve, the young warrior, one like a son of man (i.e., humanoid in contrast with the chimeralike monsters), having apparently vanquished them, rides his cloud chariot (as Baal did) to the throne of his aged father, El Elyon, who welcomes him as successor or coregent, and Yahve receives universal lordship, just as Baal, Marduk, and the others did upon their victories:

> I saw in the night visions, and behold, with the clouds of heaven
> there came one like a son of man,
> and he came to the Ancient of Days
> and was presented before him.
> And to him was given dominion
> and glory and kingdom,
> that all peoples, nations, and languages
> should serve him;
> his dominion is an everlasting dominion,
> which shall not pass away,
> and his kingdom one
> that shall not be destroyed. (Dan. 7:13–14)

Subsequently, in the wake of the monotheistic preaching of Jeremiah and Second Isaiah, Jewish theologians fused El Elyon and Yahve to create the impression that there had always been a single Hebrew God: "But Abram said to the king of Sodom, 'I have sworn to Yahve El Elyon, maker of heaven and earth, that I would not take a thread or a sandal-thong or anything else from you, lest you should say, "Abram owes his wealth to me"'" (Gen. 14:22–23).

And the rest of the gods, the sons of El? According to one version, they were consigned to Sheol, the Hebrew netherworld, for mismanagement:

God has taken his place in the divine council;
in the midst of the gods he holds judgment:
"How long will you judge unjustly
and show partiality to the wicked?
Give justice to the weak and the fatherless;
maintain the right of the afflicted and the destitute.
Rescue the weak and the needy;
deliver them from the hand of the wicked."
They have neither knowledge nor understanding,
they walk about in darkness;
all the foundations of the earth are shaken.
I say, "You are gods,
sons of Elyon, all of you;
nevertheless, you shall die like men,
and fall like any prince."
Arise, O God, judge the earth;
for to you belong all the nations! (Pss. 82: 1–8)

Perhaps this is a vision of Yahve's condemnation and overthrow of the subordinate gods in the future, as most of the Bible continues to picture God convening his council of heavenly beings (Job 1:6; 2:1; 1 Kings 22:19–22; Pss. 89:5). These entities would eventually be designated as angels, beings heavenly but not quite divine. Even so, their original role as deputy gods ruling the nations survived in Daniel 10:13, where one of them is the prince behind the throne of Persia, just as Rimmon had been the god of Syria (2 Kings 5:18). They survive into the New Testament, too, as the Principalities and Powers, the twenty-four elders who surround the divine throne in Revelation 4:4.

Whatever became of the dragons? Why are they so unfamiliar to modern Bible readers, where once they were apparently so important? Well, at first they were gods with worshipers and priests of their own. Psalm 40:4 warns pious Israelites not to worship the dragons: "Blessed is the man who makes Yahve his trust, who does not turn to the Rahabs, to those who go after false gods!" Job knows of sorcerer priests who invoke the divine dragon, "who are skilled to rouse up Leviathan" (Job

3:8). Under the name or title Nehushtan ("Serpent"), no doubt the patron of the seraphim (flaming, winged serpents), Leviathan was worshiped in his own chapel in the Jerusalem temple and offered incense (2 Kings 18:4). But King Hezekiah forbade his worship and cast his image forth from the temple. And so commenced a campaign of suppression of his myth. First, for Nehushtan, represented by a bronze serpent, to retain as much as a toehold in Israel, he had to be given an alternative origin, hence the tale of Moses creating his image as a totem to cure snakebite (Num. 21:6–9). Second, his priests, the Levites, were demoted to temple flunkies because of their previous allegiance: "And the Levites who are gone away far from me, when Israel went astray, who went astray away from me after their idols; they shall even bear their iniquity" (Ezek. 44:10). You see, *Levi* also means "serpent," and "Levia*than*" is the equivalent of "Nehush*tan*," both meaning "serpent" with the same added honorific suffix.[3]

And though the creation myth of Yahve killing the dragon could never be completely expunged from the hymnbook (Psalms), it was downplayed and reinterpreted in Genesis. For instance, in the priestly creation story (the six-day creation in Genesis, chapter 1), Tiamat, the chaos dragon of the sea, and Behemoth, the earth monster, have been abstracted into the initial prime matter (*tohu-wa-bohu*, "without form and void") from which Elohim formed the earth. *Tohu* is the singular for "Tiamat" (a plural denoting the fullness of majesty), while *bohu* is the singular of "Behemoth."[4] Again, Tiamat the sea dragon becomes merely "the *tehom*," the ocean depth, in Genesis 1:2. Dragons do appear in the priestly creation story, as "the great sea monsters" in Genesis 1:21, mere creatures, no longer divine rivals. And, if I am not mistaken, I believe I spot old Nehushtan in the wise serpent of Eden (in Genesis 3, the Garden of Eden story of the Yahvist, or "J" account). Have you ever noticed how the Edenic serpent plays a role exactly parallel to the Greek Prometheus? It is he, not Yahve Elohim, who tells the man and the woman the truth: if they eat the fruit Yahve has peevishly forbidden them, they will not die on the spot as he has warned them but will instead instantly gain godlike knowledge, as Yahve Elohim afterward admits, with a note of panic, to his fellow deities in Genesis 3:22 ("He has become like one of us, knowing good and evil!"). Even as the titan Prometheus was, the serpent is severely punished for daring to share the perquisites of the gods with mere mortals, but he is no less a hero for that. I feel quite sure that the story was told by a demoted Levite priest, forced to repudiate his interdicted god. He could hardly deny that Yahve had prevailed, but he could still say who he regarded as the heroic friend of mankind, and who the villain.

The New Year's festival reenacted the primordial victory of the god Yahve over the sea monster Yamm/Leviathan/Rahab and his subsequent exaltation over the rest of the gods (the "sons of God") as king of gods and mortals. The king of Judah was his son (Pss. 2:7: "I will tell of the decree of Yahve. He has said to me, 'You are my son. Today I have begotten you.'" Also Pss. 89:26–27, above) and anointed or "messiah" (Pss. 2:2, 89:20), reigning at his right hand (Pss. 110:1). He could even be called "Mighty God" (Isa. 9:6) or be addressed as "O God" (Pss. 45:6). He sprang from the womb of the Jerusalemite dawn goddess Shahar, as had his predecessors, the Jebusite priest-kings of Jerusalem before David (Pss. 110:3). In this view of things, history was static and cyclical, ever returning, à la Mircea Eliade (*Cosmos and History: The Myth of the Eternal Return*), to be renewed by a yearly intersection with the primordial time of Creation. The heavens were simply an exalted projection of the earthly status quo, invoked to lend it the unalterable (but annually renewable) mandate of heaven.

The popular prophets Amos and Jeremiah opposed the monarchy and its mouthpieces, the ventriloquist court prophets. They did so in the name of a very different conception of God and history. They understood history as the theater of the acts of God not quite hidden behind apparently mundane events. It was the task of the prophets to discern the hand of God as he moved the chess pieces of the nations over the board of the world. The prophets had sacralized history or, alternately, secularized the acts of God by removing them from behind the rood screen of cult and myth.

MYTH SWAP

Things changed drastically once the Babylonian troops of King Neb-uchadnezzar destroyed the Judean monarchy. The common people were left to their own devices back home in Palestine, while among the deported aristocracy, sent off to Babylon, the priestly caste assumed what sovereignty it could in exile, hoping one day to take up the reins of power anew back in Jerusalem—they or their children, for whose sake they codified much of the lore of the Jews as they cooled their heels by the River Chebar (Ezek. 1:1; Pss. 137:1). They formulated what we call the Deuteronomic view of history, taking a leaf from the prophets' book. Jeremiah and his colleagues had long warned Israel and Judah that their sins would cause God sooner or later to withdraw his protective hand and surrender the chosen people to their heathen ene-mies. God was not to be made a fool of. One dared not presume him to be on one's own side. Rather, one had best try to make sure one was on God's side by repenting of sinful practices like idolatry and labor exploitation. The prophets and priests of Judah in King Josiah's time had written up Deuteronomy as a charter for national reform to fend off God's forsaking his people before it might be too late. But it was, and the pious Josiah died in battle against Egypt. It was not long before Nebuchadnezzar came knocking. As the people watched their priests and leaders being marched off to Babylon, they naturally blamed the aristocracy for the disaster that had crushed Judah. After all, had not the prophets excoriated the priests for their hypocritical liturgical floor shows? But in the priestly version, it was not their own sins that led to the Exile but those of the people, whose sins the priests saw themselves as vicariously bearing in exile. After all, had not the priests backed Josiah's reform program? It was hardly their fault that it proved to be too little too late.

The old language of the royal mythology (including the image of Yahve as warrior), of no further utility for the now-powerless priestly-aristocratic elite, was now free for the prophets' use. So on the eve of the end of the Exile, we find the Second Isaiah text employing it to describe the imminent historical purposes of God: the restoration to the Promised Land will be like the primordial victory of Yahve over Rahab. The nations will witness the return of the Exilic community and glorify the God of Israel. The old dragon-combat myth, once used to renew the divine right of kings every year, the royal status quo, now became the slogan for revolutionary change.

Ironically, once the return of the Exiles to the Holy Land was accomplished, there occurred a split among the priestly classes, between the Zadokite, or Aaronide, hierarchy on the one hand and, on the other, the Levites (once the attendants of Nehushtan and of the banned "high place" altars), Korahites, temple singers, local village priests (think of John the Baptist's father, Zacharias), and their sympathizers among the poor. These were the Jews who had never been to Babylon and were henceforth scorned by the returning Exiles as the *am-ha-arez*, "people of the land," a term once aimed at Canaanite riffraff. The latter group anticipated a glorious democratization of the holy, all Israel serving henceforth as a holy and priestly people, God dwelling freely in their midst, the temple restored and served by pagan kings and described in terms of mythic glory. They and their nonsacerdotal leaders, laymen like themselves, had conducted make-do worship amid the ruins of the Jerusalem temple (singing the Lamentations, for instance) during all the years of the Exile, and they found they could get along pretty well without the priests and their mumbo jumbo. But the returning priestly aristocrats, with the official backing of the Persian Empire, dug in and began to implement a more mundane, elitist, hardball agenda. For them, the community must be carefully segregated from the holy. Only the highest ranks of the priests might act as mediators between God and the people. The result was a colossal disappointment for the lower echelon, who now found themselves subject to a new group of oppressors, this time, fellow Jews.

The priestly party now found themselves heir to the old prophetic theology of history, which now resulted in the vindication of their own position as the righteous remnant of Yahve. God had brought them to their present state, just as he had once brought Moses and the children of Israel out of Egypt, so who dared challenge them? What they had done was to change the old prophetic view of God's acts in ongoing history into its opposite: a new ideology to legitimate the status quo. We find the program of the priestly group in Ezekiel, chapters 40–48, the platform of their opponents in Third Isaiah (especially Isa. chapters 56–66) and in Deutero-Zechariah (Zech. chapters 9–14).

What was left for the lower-class group, now on the outs? They emulated Second Isaiah and appropriated the language of royal mythology, using it to predict a drastic change, an overthrow of the status quo. God would once again flex his mighty arm to defeat Leviathan, but this time the monster was identified with the priestly faction controlling the emerging temple state. But, though dynamic, this view was by no means as truly historical as that of the old prophets had been, since the new, postexilic prophets abandoned the old hope that God would make history go their way. His hand would no more be seen in the movements of kingdoms and armies. By contrast, the deliverance they expected would be the discontinuing of history, a drastic suspension of it from outside, a direct intervention by God on judgment day.

The old stock in trade of the prophets, oracles of salvation and doom, were reapplied. There was a bifurcation in Israel, and now the oracles of doom were directed not at the nations but rather at the corrupt Jewish leadership. The oracles of salvation, once aimed at the whole commonwealth, were now reserved for the popular prophetic faction.

Here we see the origin of the two main features of developing apocalyptic: the *dehistoricizing of history* (not exactly an otherworldly flight from history but a greater emphasis on direct divine intervention, snapping the links of historical causation, a replacement of providence with miracle) and a *division within Israel*. Traditionally, Israelites drew the line between themselves and the heathen nations. We have sectarian factionalism to thank for the new distinction between the "true," that is, faithful, Israelites versus the compromisers, the backsliders, or as the Dead Sea Scrolls called them, the "seekers after smooth things." This stridency ought to be familiar to us from the thunderings of John the Baptist, himself the very epitome of an apocalyptic prophet: "The axe is poised at the root of the tree! Every tree that fails to bear good fruit shall be chopped down and tossed into the fire! And don't go reassuring yourselves, 'We have a good Abrahamic pedigree,' for the truth is: God can conjure up children to Abraham from these rocks if that's all he wants!"

It was the ongoing seesawing of these factions that kept alive and available the ancient myth of Yahve the mighty man of war and his victory over the chaos dragon. It would come in handy again and again throughout the history of apocalyptic, as one oppressor after another would be targeted as the human embodiment of the dragon Leviathan. If Pharaoh's Egypt could be cast as Rahab, why not Antiochus Epiphanes, the Seleucid emperor? Or the Roman Caligula?

SATAN REVAMPED

There are other elements in the apocalyptic worldview that cannot be explained as arising from this struggle over the legacy of the Divine Warrior myth. The increased attention to Satan and the angels (good and evil), as well as the appearance of the resurrection doctrine (which we begin to see a bit later and by no means in all apocalypses), are in all probability derived from Zoroastrianism, the Persian religion encountered by Jews during the Exile.

As for Satan, he had originally played the role, in Israel's mythology, of God's servant, the master of security and sting operations, setting traps to discover whether God's ostensible servants really loved and trusted him. He is shown doing this in the cases of Job (Job chapters 1–2), David (1 Chron. 21:1), and the postexilic priest Joshua (Zech. 3:1–2). In fact, the very term *Satan* is just Hebrew for "adversary, prosecutor," a role he continues to play even in the New Testament (Mark 1:12–13; Matt. 4:1–11; Luke 4:1–13, 22:31; Acts 5:3; Rev. 12:10). By contrast, Persian Zoroastrianism was a pure dualism, positing two virtually equal deities, one good (Ahura Mazda), the other evil

(Ahriman). History was a long struggle between these gods, and every human deed counted as a blow struck on behalf of one side or another. The outcome was known in advance but not quite determined. Ahura Mazda, being good, possessed wisdom greater than that of his self-possessed rival, and so he must in the long run prevail. In the meantime, however, the ball was genuinely in play. God neither willed nor allowed tragedy and evil. He did everything he could to stop it, but the Evil One was no mere puppet. He got his licks in. It was his fault when bad things happened.

Jewish theology found much of this appealing. As Judaism had evolved toward strict monotheism, it found itself stuck with a single divine cause of all events, good and evil. Even this was no real problem as long as the divine holiness was understood as sheer *otherness*. But once the God-concept, under the influence of the prophets, became rationalized, which is to say *moralized*, God's "holiness" was reinterpreted as moral goodness, as today when religious people seek holiness.[5] They are not trying to become divine but rather morally mature. And once God was understood to be absolutely righteous, responsible for keeping a moral code like that which binds humans, then it would come in handy to be able to attribute evil and adversity to some other agent. Zoroastrian dualism provided that. But Jews were able to adopt the notion only inconsistently, because they did not want to renege on monotheism by positing two gods. Thus the evil force had to be a subordinate, derivative entity, a created being.[6] Jewish theology drafted Satan for the job.

But now Satan was reinterpreted along the lines of the Persian Ahriman, the origin of evil. Of course, making the evil Satan subordinate to an all-powerful God kind of defeated the whole point, since presumably God would be able to stop Satan's efforts any time he wanted, so why doesn't he? Apocalyptic thinking didn't spend much time on that aspect of the problem; it was rendered moot by the simple fact that (they thought) God would soon put a stop to Satan's schemes for good. Once things were right again, who would really care how they had first gone wrong?[7]

SCRIBES AS SEERS

The universal practice of pseudonymity in apocalypses begins with the anonymity of the prophets whose work we now find in Trito-Isaiah and Deutero-Zechariah. The priestly group had begun to form (and thus close) a canon of scripture. While there was not yet a normative collection of the prophets, if any new claimants of the prophetic mantle appeared, they were not to be heeded but rather stoned to death. The doctrine of the cessation of prophecy was not after all a lamentation over some mysterious shortage of new prophets but rather an attempt to clamp the lid on new prophecy. Thus the postexilic prophets who belonged to the priestly elite (Zechariah, Haggai, Malachi) were admitted to the canon with no difficulty, but the popular prophets managed only to hang tenuously onto the margins under the names of the pro-priestly prophets—precisely for the same reason the later apocalypses had to be written under the names of inspired and venerable figures like Moses, Daniel, Baruch, and Enoch. They had lived before the latter-day ban on new words from God. It is no accident that these apocalyptic pseudonyms were all associated with the Torah and with scribalism: the real authors were clearly scribes and sages, a class attached to the lower echelons along with Levites, choristers, and doorkeepers. It was, accordingly, scribes and sages who redacted and compiled the Psalms for use in the postexilic temple for Levites to sing.

Gerhard von Rad and Jonathan Z. Smith have established the scribal/sapiential character and origin of apocalyptic vision literature.[8] The scribes indulged in natural philosophy (i.e., pretechnological scientific speculation) and they preserved their star maps in several of the apocalypses, in which astrological imagery abounds and which portray sages taking guided trips through the starry heavens. Fourth Ezra (2 Esdras) also wrestles with the problem of theodicy, the suffering of the innocent, as do great pieces of wisdom literature including Job and Ecclesiastes. First Enoch recounts the myth of personified wisdom (otherwise found in sapiential works like Proverbs, Wisdom of Solomon, and Sirach) descending from heaven to earth, receiving the cold shoulder, and returning to heaven. Christopher Rowland (*The Open Heaven*) shows the great extent to which the ancient Jewish apocalyptic writers overlapped the later esotericism of the rabbis (the Lore of Creation and Merkabah, or Throne Chariot, mysticisms). Joachim Jeremias seems to have been correct in theorizing that apocalyptic represented the secret doctrine of the scribes, even though their successors, the rabbis, thought it best to put a damper on all such speculation after the disastrous defeat of messiah Simon bar-Kochba in 136 CE.[9]

Ironically again, once the hierocratic party was brutally driven from power during the crisis of Hellenization in the second-century BCE (the persecution of Antiochus IV Epiphanes), they recapitulated the very same shift their opponents, the popular prophets, had made two and a half centuries before! In the Dead Sea Scrolls, the product, at least some of them, of a dissenting group of displaced Zadokite priests, we find them yearning for the day God will vindicate them with angelic armies from the sky. In short, they, too, revived the Divine Warrior myth.

Apocalypticism, with its apparent quietism combined with rooting for the overthrow of the evil powers, may be understood as the impotent response (born of *ressentiment*) of the retainer class (e.g., scribes).[10] The ruling class (the Boethusian Sadducees) sees no crisis at all, since they profit from collaborating with the occupying power. The lower classes and the dispossessed are less literate and more pragmatic. Less likely to be satisfied living in a world of religious dreams and abstractions, they paid little heed to written apocalypses and instead fielded actual, living political messiahs. The retainers (scribes, lower-level priests, etc.) instead merely dream of a better day. Their response to the crisis may be best understood in terms borrowed from sociologists Peter L. Berger and Thomas Luckmann (*The Social Construction of Reality*), social psychologist Robert J. Lifton (*Boundaries*), and New Testament scholar John G. Gager (*Kingdom and Community*). What we are seeing in written apocalypses are scripts for a kind of play, a miracle play or mystery play, a "finite province of meaning" in the "'as if' mode."[11] An apocalypse creates an experience for the reader or hearers (Rev. 1:3,

"Blessed [is] he that readeth, and they that hear the words of this prophecy") like that of a stage show, a television drama, a religious pageant, and so on, in which we enter a different state of mind and play as if we live by different assumptions or in a better world—until the lights come up. It is a compensatory zone of imagining in which "time and death vanish"[12] and "abreaction," a release of our pathological tensions, occurs through undergoing psychodrama. These insights are easy to apply to what must count as modern apocalypses: the Rapture movies and novels that allow frustrated fundamentalists to experience vicariously the End Time events they long to see but that never seem to happen on schedule in the real world.

NOTES

1. Geo Widengren, *Mesopotamian Elements in Manichaeism. (King and Saviour II) Studies in Manichaean, Mandaean, and Syrian-Gnostic Religion*, Uppsala Universitets Arsskrift 1946:3 (Uppsala, Sweden: A. B. Lundequistska Bokhandeln, 1946), pp. 64–67.

2. See Michael D. Goulder, *The Psalms of Asaph and the Pentateuch. Studies in the Psalter, III, Journal for the Study of the Old Testament* Supplement Series 233 (Sheffield, England: Sheffield Academic Press, 1996), pp. 68–71. For the nature and function of the combat myth, see Hermann Gunkel, *Creation and Chaos in the Primeval Era and the Eschaton*, trans. K. William Whitney Jr. (Grand Rapids, MI: Eerdmans Publishing, 2006) and Mary K. Wakeman, *God's Battle with the Monster: A Study in Biblical Imagery* (Leiden, Netherlands: E. J. Brill, 1973).

3. Ignaz Goldziher, *Mythology among the Hebrews and Its Historical Development*, trans. Russell Martineau (1877; repr., New York: Cooper Square Publishers, 1967), pp. 183–86.

4. Robert Graves and Raphael Patai, *Hebrew Myths: The Book of Genesis* (New York: Greenwich House, 1983), p. 31.

5. Rudolf Otto, *The Idea of the Holy: An Inquiry into the Non-rational Factor in the Idea of the Divine and Its Relation to the Rational*, trans. John Harvey (London: Oxford University Press, 1924), pp. 5–6.

6. C. S. Lewis, *Mere Christianity* (New York: Macmillan, 1952), pp. 48–50.

7. Peter L. Berger, *The Sacred Canopy: Elements of a Sociological Theory of Religion* (Garden City, NY: Doubleday Anchor, 1969), p. 69.

8. Gerhard von Rad, *Old Testament Theology Volume II: The Theology of Israel's Prophetic Traditions*, trans. D. M. G. Stalker (New York: Harper & Row, 1965), pp. 306–307; Jonathan Z. Smith, "Wisdom and Apocalyptic," in *Map Is Not Territory: Studies in the History of Religions* (Chicago: University of Chicago Press, 1993), pp. 67–87.

9. Joachim Jeremias, *The Eucharistic Words of Jesus*, trans. Arnold Ehrhardt (Oxford: Basil Blackwell, 1955), pp. 75–78.

10. Max Scheler, *Ressentiment*, trans. Lewis B. Coser and William W. Holdheim (Milwaukee: Marquette University Press, 1994).

11. Peter L. Berger and Thomas Luckmann, *The Social Construction of Reality: A Treatise in the Sociology of Knowledge* (Garden City, NY: Doubleday Anchor, 1967), p. 25.

12. Robert J. Lifton, *Boundaries: Psychological Man in Revolution* (New York: Random House/Vintage Books, 1970), p. 23.

Chapter Two

MESSIANIC PROPHECY

"His disciples say to him, 'Twenty-four prophets spoke in Israel, and every one of them predicted you!' He said to them, 'You have disregarded the Living, who is right in front of you, to prattle on about the dead!'"

—Gospel of Thomas, saying 52

B oth nonfiction and fiction books written by fundamentalists on the End Times make a running start toward eschatological prophecy by surveying prophecies already fulfilled, especially the predictions fulfilled in Jesus as the Messiah. The idea is to build the reader's confidence in the track record of biblical writers and their prognostications. If they had a poor-to-mediocre batting average when it came to past prophecies, why trust their guidance for the future? But if they had proven to be sure guides (albeit unheeded Cassandras) in the past, why, then, leave the driving to them?! What driving? Why, that along the "Tribulation road map" as some of the handy-dandy prophecy charts are called. The *Left Behind* books take this approach, too. And it is not just to reassure the reader that the Bible should be their guide. In addition to this, there is the belief of fundamentalist Protestants that the Last Days will witness a massive conversion of Jews to the Christian faith. And, not unreasonably, such a turnabout would almost have to involve a lot of Jews becoming convinced that Jesus of Nazareth was indeed the intended target of the ancient Hebrew prophecies. One of

Jerry Jenkins's major characters in *Left Behind* is orthodox rabbi Tsion Ben-Judah, a scholar commissioned by the State of Israel to make an exhaustive study of the scriptures and their possible messianic prophecies so that faithful Jews may know whom and what to look for as the End Times draw near. The rabbi appears on satellite television to announce that the goyim are right: Jesus is after all the predicted Messiah of the Jews. How plausible is this?

BEN-JUDAH'S FOLLY

For many centuries, indeed from the first century on, Christians have urged as proof of their faith that certain aspects of the life of Jesus corresponded to the predictions of ancient prophets in such a way as to rule out either coincidence or human design. Critical study of the Bible has made such an apologetic highly implausible for many and at the same time provided a floodlight of new clarity on the texts involved. The result is ironic: those who want nothing more than an accurate grasp of the biblical text rejoice in the great advances in understanding both Old and New Testaments, while those who profess to love the Bible most while merely using it as a proof text for a particular theological position have been deprived of one of their main rhetorical tools. As I will try to show in this chapter, defenders of the fundamentalist Christian faith, real-life counterparts to Tsion Ben-Judah, have in fact lost the luxury of an easy appeal to fulfilled prophecy even if they remain stubbornly oblivious of the advances of modern biblical scholarship; this is because biblical scholarship has thrown their appeals to the "proof from prophecy" so seriously into question that their task is now to defend it rather than use it as a powerful defense for something else, for example, the true Messiahship of Jesus. Any appeal to "proof from prophecy" today lengthens the line of defense rather than shortening it. I think I can make my point most clearly by a brief survey of the high points of Tsion Ben-Judah's exegetical report as summarized in *Tribulation Force*.

Born-again adventurer Buck Williams shows a sure grasp of the obvious as Dr. Ben-Judah's recital commences: "It didn't appear the rabbi was going to use the New Testament to convince his first and primary audience, the Jews."[1] Yet, as we will see, that is actually what he does. For in every case, the character, the mouthpiece for Tim LaHaye's sectarian exegesis of scripture, presupposes Christian, New Testament reinterpretations of Old Testament texts that have absolutely nothing to do with the Messiah. In the end, Ben-Judah is only parroting New Testament ventriloquism of the Old Testament.

Ben-Judah starts out endorsing the absurd claim of Victorian evangelical Alfred Edersheim that the Hebrew Bible contains some 456 messianic predictions. Then he shares what we must assume are the best ones, the big guns. First comes what appears to be an implicit conflation of Genesis 3:15 ("I will put enmity between you and the woman, and between your seed and her seed; he shall bruise your head, and you shall bruise his heel") and Isaiah 7:14 ("Behold, a woman shall conceive and bear a son, and shall call his name Immanuel"). Ben-Judah infers that "seed of the woman" implies a virginal conception without male semen, when in fact all it need mean, and all any ancient reader could have thought it meant, is that the woman's descendants, all subsequent humans, would never get along with future snakes. The Genesis context demands that what we are reading is an etiological story to explain why humans and snakes do not get along, one always lying in wait for the other. Where in the Genesis 3 context does it say *anything at all about a Messiah?* I know popular preaching makes Genesis 3:15 a prophecy of Jesus crushing the head of Satan. But who said anything about the Edenic serpent being Satan, much less the "seed of" Satan? Is that somebody *else* Jesus is supposed to defeat? Any thought of literal interpretation of the Bible has flown out LaHaye's window.

Isaiah 7:14 may incorporate earlier material dealing with the birth of the royal Judean heir from the virgin dawn goddess Shahar (see below), but the present context of Isaiah applies the oracle instead to the impending birth of a child to a woman contemporary of Isaiah and the king whom he is addressing. As the context makes absolutely clear,

young Immanuel is to be born to an *almah*, a "young woman," not necessarily a virgin (as any Hebrew scholar will tell you). And the "sign" is
not a miraculous birth but rather the fact that the child will grow only
so old (old enough to turn up his nose at baby food he does not like)
before the Syrian-Samaritan alliance threatening Judah has been wiped
off the map by Assyria. In the nature of the case, the prophecy cannot
possibly be referring to anything or anyone over seven centuries in the
future from Isaiah's time. It has nothing to do with any Messiah,
whether Jesus or anybody else. Where does it say otherwise? What
would make any Jewish reader (or indeed any reader not already poisoned by fundamentalist apologetics) see any reference to messianic
prophecy here?

"'Messiah, according to the prophet Micah, must be born in Bethlehem.' The rabbi turned to the passage in his notes and read, "'But you,
Bethlehem Ephrathah, though you are little among the thousands of
Judah, yet out of you shall come forth to Me the One to be Ruler in
Israel, whose goings forth are from of old, from everlasting.'"[2] Is the Messiah even mentioned here? Not that I can see. The text does, of course,
refer to a ruler whose coming is anticipated, so maybe it's close enough
to call it a messianic prophecy. So is the Messiah to be born in Bethlehem? One might read Micah 5:2 that way, as some Jews did (though we
have no pre-Christian attestation of such a Jewish belief), but it is hardly
a necessary inference. Why isn't the reference to Bethlehem, where
David grew up, just a piece of metonymy for the Davidic dynasty, like
the frequent references to "the root of Jesse," David's father? Either way,
the point would seem to be simply that the next or future king belongs to
the unbroken dynasty stretching all the way back to Jesse and/or to Bethlehem, in other words, to David. This king had no more need to be born
in Bethlehem personally than he did to be Jesse's direct offspring.

But even if Micah did mean to place a future king's birth in the
very town of Bethlehem rather than indicating his dynastic origins, can
we be so sure that Jesus was actually born there? The Gospel accounts
of the birth of Jesus in Bethlehem notoriously contradict each other.[3]
And there will never be any way of proving that early Christians did

not simply begin from the *assumption* that, being the Messiah, Jesus *must* have been born in Bethlehem. Mere assertion of the contrary will not make it so, nor will it win any arguments, if that's what we want to do.

But suppose Jesus was born in Bethlehem. The seventeenth-century messianic claimant Sabbatai Sevi was born on the ninth of Av (or so our sources tell us), the date that later messianic speculation stipulated for the Messiah's nativity. Does that mean Sabbatai Sevi was the Messiah? In both cases we might simply have a coincidence that helped fuel the fire of speculation that eventually elevated two possible candidates to Messiahship in the eyes of their followers. Stranger things have happened.

"Rabbi Ben-Judah continued. 'As a child, Messiah will go to Egypt, because the prophet Hosea says that out of Egypt God will call him.'"[4] Hold on, Ben-Judah! Hosea 11:1 says *nothing of the kind!* As the context makes absolutely clear, the reference is to God's "son" Israel coming out of Egypt at the time of the Exodus. Even since those days, the prophet says, Israel has given God nothing but trouble despite his fatherly care and affection. Neither LaHaye or his intranarrative counterpart Tsion Ben-Judah would ever think the text had any messianic reference at all if they read it as part of the book of Hosea. They would only treat it the way they do if they came across it first where it is quoted grossly out of context as a prediction of Jesus in Matthew's Gospel (2:15). (How did Matthew wind up treating the text this way? He had a reason LaHaye does not have, as we will see below.) LaHaye and Ben-Judah are really quoting from the New Testament, not the Old.

"Isaiah 9:1–2 indicates that Messiah will minister mostly in Galilee."[5] Oh, does it, now? The text is "But there will be no gloom for her that was in anguish. In the former time he brought into contempt the land of Zebulun and the land of Naphtali, but in the latter time he will make glorious the way of the sea, the land beyond the Jordan, Galilee of the nations.

> The people who walked in darkness
> have seen a great light;
> those who dwelt in a land of deep darkness,
> on them has light shined."

Where do we find any mention, any hint, any faint intimation that the Messiah is in view here? LaHaye regards it as messianic only because Matthew makes it messianic retroactively in Matthew 4:15–16. Plainly, as an interpreter of Hebrew scripture, "Rabbi" Ben-Judah is a hack who doesn't know his sanctified ass from his elbow.

"One of the prophecies we Jews do not like and tend to ignore is that Messiah will be rejected by his own people. Isaiah prophesied, 'He is despised and rejected by men, a Man of sorrows and acquainted with grief. And we hid, as it were, our faces from Him; He was despised, and we did not esteem Him.'"[6] Do you see the word "Messiah" anywhere in that passage, or in the chapter-and-a-half Servant Song in which it is contained? For one thing, it speaks of some sufferer *in the past tense.* There is just no messianic significance associated with the text—until we get to the New Testament (Acts 8:32–33). Again Rabbi Tsion LaHaye is quoting from the New Testament, not the Old, though he doesn't seem to know the difference.

"Isaiah and Malachi predict that Messiah will be preceded by a forerunner." Is that so? One supposes Ben-Haye is thinking of Isaiah 40:3–5.

> A voice cries:
> In the wilderness prepare the way of Yahve,
> make straight in the desert a highway for our God.
> Every valley shall be lifted up,
> and every mountain and hill be made low;
> the uneven ground shall become level,
> and the rough places a plain.
> And the glory of Yahve shall be revealed,
> and all flesh shall see it together,
> for the mouth of Yahve has spoken.

Now, in context, the prophet is plainly speaking of the impending return of the surviving exiles from Babylon to Jerusalem. There is no reference at all to Messiah, only to Yahve as the leader of the community who will soon lead his people to the Promised Land as he once led them there from Egypt. The only reason Ben-Haye thinks it speaks of Messiah's forerunner is that Mark so quotes it (out of context) in Mark 1:2–3.

Malachi 4:5 says, "Behold, I send you Elijah the prophet before the great and terrible day of Yahve comes." Again, it is God himself who is preceded by another, not the Messiah who is not so much as mentioned. Of course the New Testament (and probably contemporary Judaism) expected Elijah to precede Messiah, but Ben-Haye is telling us that the prophet Malachi already makes such a connection, and the plain fact is that he does not.

"The Psalmist said Messiah would be betrayed by a friend." Apparently the text LaJudah has in mind this time is Psalm 41:9: "Even my bosom friend in whom I trusted, who ate of my bread, has lifted his heel against me." But this is not even a prophecy, much less a messianic one! It is rather a typical Lament Psalm (see just below on Psalm 22).

"Zechariah said that he would be betrayed for thirty pieces of silver. He adds that people will look on the one whom they have pierced." You guessed it: Zechariah 11:12 makes no reference to the Messiah but speaks only of his own rejection, his dismissal as a shepherd with measly severance pay. It is only Matthew (26:15), in the New Testament, who rips the verse out of context to supply the figure for Judas Iscariot's bounty fee. Zechariah 12:10 reads as follows: "And I will pour out on the house of David and the inhabitants of Jerusalem a spirit of compassion and supplication, so that, when they look on him whom they have pierced, they shall mourn for him, as one mourns for an only child, and weep bitterly over him, as one weeps over a firstborn." I admit, I am not exactly clear on what this passage is about. But that it should refer to the Messiah is pretty much impossible. Notice that it is the Davidic dynasty, that is, the Davidic heir, the king of Judah, who will be doing the mourning—that is, for someone *else.*

"The Psalmist [in Psalm 22:17–18] prophesied that people would 'look and stare at Me. They divide My garments among them, and for My clothing they cast lots.'" No. No, I'm afraid not. Not if you have any regard for the original context. And if you don't, it's like the old joke where the guy says, "Hey, did you know the Bible teaches atheism?

Right here in Psalm 53:1 it says, 'There is no God.'" Of course, the context is "The fool has said in his heart, 'There is no God,'" which kind of throws a whole new light on the matter. Same here. As the greatest scholars on the ancient Psalms, Hermann Gunkel and Sigmund Mowinckel demonstrate, Psalm 22 is simply a member of the larger category of lament psalms.[7] For examples, see Psalms 3, 4, 5, 6, 7, 10, 11, 12, 13, 14, 17, 25, 26, 28, 31, 35. These were essentially scripts of suffering and prayers for vindication, pledging to return to the temple to provide a sacrificial feast to which the poor should be invited, to celebrate Yahve's deliverance. On that occasion, "a new song," one of the Thank-offering Psalms (e.g., 9, 30, 32, 33, 34), would be sung instead of the present gloomy plaint. The "Everyman" character of the lament psalm is evident from the vagueness and symbolism with which the envisioned trials and tribulations are described: wild dogs nipping at one's heels, strong bulls and lions, waters rising up to one's neck. Fill in the blanks as appropriate. "They have pierced my hands and feet" (22:16b), cited by apologists as a reference to the nail wounds of crucifixion, make more sense in context as bite and claw wounds incurred by the sufferer as he tries to fend off the wild animals snapping at him (22:16a), the symbols of his real-life dilemmas. What/who were these? Creditors? Political enemies? Romantic rivals? Vendetta avengers? Legal plaintiffs? The business about dividing up the sufferer's garments just means, "They've given me up for dead." It could apply to anybody in the same straits. That was the whole idea. Psalm 22, more than any other lament psalm, is no prophecy of any kind, no prediction of anything, much less of the crucifixion of Jesus. One can, on the other hand, easily imagine Jesus taking such a Psalm as a fitting prayer in his hour of desperation, as Mark seems to imply he is doing, by having him quote the first lines of it, "My God, my God, why hast thou forsaken me?"

"Isaiah says 'they made His grave with the wicked; but with the rich at His death, because He had done no violence, nor was any deceit in His mouth.'" Here we are, back at Isaiah 53, a passage that nowhere mentions the Messiah. So, Tim Ben-Judah, save all your fustian about Joseph of Arimathea and his tomb.

"The Psalms say he was to be resurrected." Do they? Our only clue is that LaJudah is thinking of those psalms taken out of context in the New Testament book of Acts as predicting the resurrection of Jesus. Decide for yourself whether they do. Acts 2:22–32 reads:

Men of Israel, hear these words: Jesus of Nazareth, a man attested to you by God with mighty works and wonders and signs which God did through him in your midst, as you yourselves know—this Jesus, delivered up according to the definite plan and foreknowledge of God, you crucified and killed by the hands of lawless men. But God raised him up, having loosed the pangs of death, because it was not possible for him to be held by it. For David says concerning him, "I saw the Lord always before me, for he is at my right hand that I may not be shaken; therefore my heart was glad, and my tongue rejoiced; moreover my flesh will dwell in hope. For you will not abandon my soul to Hades, nor let your Holy One see corruption. You have made known to me the ways of life; you will make me full of gladness with your presence." Brethren, I may say to you confidently of the patriarch David that he both died and was buried, and his tomb is with us to this day. Being therefore a prophet, and knowing that God had sworn with an oath to him that he would set one of his descendants upon his throne, he foresaw and spoke of the resurrection of the Christ, that he was not abandoned to Hades, nor did his flesh see corruption. This Jesus God raised up, and of that we all are witnesses.

Sorry, Pete (actually, Luke), but Psalm 16:8–11 speaks of God's favorite evading death, being delivered from it rather than dying and being resurrected. The whole thing is a prayer not to be left to die. Maybe Rabbi LaHaye will have better luck with Psalm 2:7, quoted as a resurrection prophecy in Acts 13:32–33:

"And we bring you the good news that what God promised to the fathers, this he has fulfilled to us their children by raising Jesus; as also it is written in the second psalm, 'You are my Son, today I have begotten you.'"

But no dice. As we have seen already, this one is a coronation Psalm, sung at the enthronement of every new king of Judah, denoting that he has entered upon his special relationship with God simply by taking the throne, as his fathers before him did.

Finally,

> According to one of the greatest of all Hebrew prophets, Daniel, there would be exactly 483 years between the decree to rebuild the wall and the city of Jerusalem "in troublesome times" before the Messiah would be cut off for the sins of the people. . . . Exactly 483 years after the rebuilding of Jerusalem and its walls, Jesus Christ offered himself to the nation of Israel. He rode into the city on a donkey to the rejoicing of the people, just as the prophet Zechariah had predicted: "Rejoice greatly, O daughter of Zion! Shout, O daughter of Jerusalem! Behold, your King is coming to you; He is just and having salvation, lowly and riding on a donkey, a colt, the foal of a donkey."[8]

For one thing, Daniel is by no means considered one of the greatest Hebrew prophets. Rather, he is one of the first apocalyptists, a post-prophetic phenomenon, as we have seen. Had he actually been a prophet and preached during the Exile, as he is fictively made to do in the second-century BCE writing that bears his name, he would have made it into the Nebi'im, the section of the Hebrew scriptures called, simply, "The Prophets." As it is, he was squeezed into the late "Miscellaneous" section, "The Writings," which means he came along too late, after the door was shut.

Be that as it may, Tim Ben-Judah seems to be privy to information no historian has, namely, certain exact dates. No one knows for certain exactly which Persian decree Daniel intends. There are a few possibilities. In addition, no one knows the year in which Jesus is supposed to have died. Thus no one knows whether this figure of 483 years is anywhere near correct.

But he's got the wrong anointed one anyway. The text certainly refers, and in minute detail, to the events of the persecution of Antiochus IV Epiphanes and of the ensuing Hasmonean revolt. The actual writer of Daniel was a witness to these events, which is how he is able to describe them so minutely, whereas his descriptions of life in ancient Babylon, centuries before, are vague and confused. The passage in question is Daniel 9:26, "And after the sixty-two weeks, an anointed one shall be cut off, and shall have nothing; and the people of the prince who is to come shall destroy the city and the sanctuary. Its end shall come with a flood, and to the end there shall be war; desolations are decreed." The anointed one is the high priest Onias III, killed during the depredations of Antiochus. Rabbi LaHaye has his chronology hopelessly mixed up.

Zechariah 9:9, alone of all those quoted in Ben-Judah's sermon, may be plausibly taken as messianic. The trouble here is that our earliest Gospel version of the Triumphal Entry story, Mark 11:7–10, makes no reference to Jesus offering himself as a king, or of the adoring crowds hailing him as one. They welcome him with the traditional festal entrance liturgy, "Blessed is he who comes in the name of the Lord," namely, any and every pilgrim, precisely as in Psalm 118:26, on which the gospel scene is largely based. And riding a donkey was a common mode of entry. It hardly marked one as messianic royalty. The subsequent evangelists, rewriting Mark, have added the note of messianic acclaim to Mark's simple "Blessed is the kingdom of our father David that is coming!" Matthew changes it to "Hosanna to the son of David!" Luke makes it "Blessed is the king who comes in the name of the Lord!" John has "Blessed is he who comes in the name of the Lord, even the king of Israel," this last phrase obviously being his own explanatory comment. Moreover, John tells us that no one on the scene had any idea Jesus was supposed to be fulfilling Zechariah's prophecy; it only occurred to the disciples in retrospect (John 12:16). That is enough to sink the idea that Jesus was offering himself as the messianic king.

Did he ride a donkey into Jerusalem? He might have, like thousands of other people. The claim that he fulfilled this prophecy fails to understand the point of Zechariah's prediction, namely, that the messianic king would not have to fight his way to the throne, since, in the providence of God who shakes the thrones of kingdoms, the Persian Empire would shortly collapse under its own weight, leaving Jews free to reassert their national sovereignty as, say, little Moldova did after the fall of the Soviet Union. And since the Triumphal Entry stories do not issue in Jesus being inaugurated as king of an earthly kingdom, the question of how he came to that throne, violently or peacefully, does not even arise.

"Buck wanted to say that a legitimate study of messianic prophecies could lead only to Jesus."[9] But of course poor Buck has no idea of how to study the Bible in any historically realistic way. He is simply a man of the world lately converted to fundamentalism and taught by some untutored youth pastor. We cannot expect anything but such assertions of pious ignorance from a guy like him. But the notion that an Orthodox rabbi, familiar with the Hebrew scriptures, could undertake a systematic study of the texts and come up with the raft of stale, text-twisting Christian arguments for Jesus as the Jewish Messiah is laughable and cringe-inducing. Tsion Ben-Judah would be about as likely to find a recipe for ham sandwiches in Leviticus as he would to find scriptural proof that Jesus was the Jewish Messiah. Perhaps more than anything else in the book, this feature reveals the degree to which LaHaye and Jenkins are living inside the bubble of fundamentalist sectarianism. Indeed, what else are the *Left Behind* books but an exercise in theological daydreaming? "Wouldn't it be great if the real world were actually like the one we pretend we live in while we are in church?"

WHAT WAS MESSIANIC PROPHECY?

If we are to examine the Old Testament evidence for a predicted Messiah, we must reframe Ben-Judah's question. Rather than accepting his question-begging query "Did Jesus fulfill all these messianic prophecies?" we have to go back and ask first *what a messianic prophecy was*. As we will see, a great number of the texts LaHaye and company deem messianic predictions are actually passages taken completely out of context and matched up with gospel events by means of fortuitous word associations. These Old Testament texts, in other words, become messianic prophecies only in the New Testament, not in the Old. This is a vital point simply because the "proof from prophecy" presupposes that Jesus managed the humanly impossible task of meeting the requirements of messianic prophecy already established and long recognized. It would be quite a different thing, though by no means a bad one, if he had instead created, or prompted the creation of, a whole new way of viewing old texts, which is what I think he did. But in this event, there can be no question of evidence and proof.

It appears that the hope of a "Messiah," or anointed king, appeared first in ancient Judah (not Israel, for which we lack evidence, given the Judean perspective of the eventual compilers of the Bible), after the destruction of the Davidic monarchy by the Babylonian conquerors in 586 BCE. Jeremiah made this crisis understandable by announcing that the conquest was the result of God punishing his people for their failure to live up to Josiah's Deuteronomic Covenant. No, the people continued to worship the Baals and reneged on their pledges to free their slaves. Such disobedience would cost them their independence. While most Jews remained in their homeland, their aristocracy and priesthood were deported to Babylon. King Zedekiah lived under house arrest in the Babylonian court. For centuries Jews, whether under foreign rule in their own land or among the Diaspora, longed for the return of national sovereignty. Since their monarchy was restricted to Davidic rulers, unlike in the North (the Kingdom of Israel), a return to national sovereignty meant a return to Davidic rule. Second Samuel 2:11–16, repeated in Jeremiah 33:14–18, served as the dynastic charter for the house of David.

In the cold dawn of the Babylonian conquest, the hope for a restored dynasty of David began to express itself in prophecies like that in Isaiah 10:33–12:6, in which Yahve is said to have taken an ax to the roots of the Davidic monarchy, but hope is nonetheless expressed that eventually he will relent and allow a tender shoot of new life to emerge from the old, apparently dead stump of the royal family tree: a new Davidic heir. "The stump of Jesse" (Isa. 11:1) refers to the moribund monarchy of David, Jesse being David's father. Some scholars have suggested that the point of the prophecy is to abandon David's lineal descendants (perhaps because they might all have been eradicated in a purge) and claim credentials for a related, collateral line also descending from the same clan; hence the reference to Jesse rather than David. In this case, the prophet would be picking up the pieces, saying that God would go back to the same source. The interpretation has much to be said for it, but who knows? The reference to Jesse rather than to David himself may, as I suggested above, merely be a piece of metonymy, allowing the source to stand for the product, father for son.

It may be significant that in Isaiah 11:10, the beginning of a prose section (the preceding portion being verse, hence a different source), we read of the "root of Jesse," a metaphor lacking the crucial element implied by the "shoot and stump" metaphor, namely, the idea of a restoration of a failed dynasty, a resumption after a severing of the thread. In other words, this part of the Isaiah text may have referred originally to the projected glories of a reigning, not a future, king.

Another text apparently treating a future restoration of the monarchy of David is Micah 5:2–4, which speaks of a future ruler with ancient origins, "from of old," namely from Bethlehem, the town of David. Again, while early Christians took this verse to mean the Messiah would be born literally in Bethlehem, it may well be another piece of metonymy, this time using David's hometown, rather than his father, as a metonymic substitute for his name. The point would be that God would return to the same place for a Judean king, not, as in Israel to the north, beginning again with a new dynasty. It seemed important to point this out because of the status Second Samuel 7 enjoyed as a prophetic guarantee of the rights of David's line. Witness the problems that arose centuries later when the Levitical Hasmonean dynasty took over after winning independence for Judah. They were not Davidic, so they had a lot of explaining to do.

A third "messianic" text would be Zechariah 9:9, where we are told that the monarchy will be reinaugurated in peace time, denoted by the conveyance of the donkey, rather than a stallion appropriate to triumph in war. The point would seem to be to make the hoped-for restoration a providential gift of God rather than the hard-won product of bloody conflict.

Ezekiel 34:22–24, 37:24, has in view the return of the leaders of Judah from the Babylonian Exile and, again, it envisions a restoration of the Davidic monarchy. Whereas Isaiah 11 uses the apparent metonym "Jesse" and Micah uses the metonym "Bethlehem," Ezekiel uses the name of "David" himself to stand for the restored monarchy. Then again, can we rule out a literal belief on Ezekiel's part that David himself would return, just as Malachi seems to have predicted a literal return of Elijah? We cannot say for certain.

It is crucial to note that in all these cases, what we read of is an expectation, a promise, of the resumption of Judean independence under the Davidic dynasty. What we do not read of is the coming of one immortal, divine man who will reign forever. This element will eventually appear in later Judaism, for example, in 4 Ezra 7:28–29, where we read that the Messiah will reign for four centuries. But we are interested not so much in the history of messianic speculation as we are in what the Old Testament prophets actually say concerning a Davidic Messiah.

To understand some of the language of the relevant texts we need to remind ourselves again of the "royal ideology" of the Davidic monarchy that exalted the king's authority to that of a god on earth. The propaganda value of this is obvious: what would Richard Nixon not have given for such an aura of absolute power? This is why the king could actually be addressed as God (Pss. 45:6–7, a royal wedding song) or as the earthly son of God (Pss. 2:7, a birth oracle or coronation song—see below)—just like the Egyptian pharaohs, whose names denoted their divine parentage: Thutmose (Son of Thoth), Ramses (Son of Ra). When each new king was crowned, he came into possession of his divine status or nature, and hopes were expressed for a reign of perfect righteousness, universal justice and amnesty to prisoners, even peace among animals. We find the same pattern attested for the sacred kings of ancient Iran. Finally, we ought to note that all Judean kings were "Messiahs," anointed with oil as a symbol of consecration to their office.

Now we are in a position to recognize that several passages that were reinterpreted by New Testament writers as predictions of a Messiah were first intended as birth or enthronement oracles, or as coronation anthems, for contemporary kings of Judah. The "Messiah" and "son" of Yahve in Psalm 2 is every new king of Judah, as the song was ritually performed by king and Levitical singer each time a new king came to the throne. Psalm 110 makes pro forma predictions for military victories by the new sovereign and secures for him the hereditary prerogatives of the old Melchizedek priesthood (taken over by David when he annexed Jebusite [Jeru-]Salem and made it his capital). Psalm 110:3 also makes him, like the king of Babylon (Isa. 14:12), the son of the Semitic dawn goddess Shahar (translated incorrectly as a common noun, "dawn," in most Bibles). Isaiah 9:2–7 is either a coronation oracle or a birth oracle in honor of a newborn heir to the throne, depending on whether "unto us a child is born, unto us a son is given" (verse 6) refers to the literal birth or to the adoption as Yahve's "son" on the day of coronation ("this day I have begotten you," Pss. 2:7). The epithets bestowed on the king in Isaiah 9:6, "Wonderful Counselor, Mighty God, Everlasting Father [cf., 1 Kings 1:31: "May my lord King David live forever!"], Prince of Peace," are the divine titles of Pharaoh and have been borrowed directly from Egyptian court rhetoric.

Isaiah 61:1–4 is apparently yet another piece of inauguration liturgy (much like the inaugural oath sworn by the president of the United States, hand on Bible), pledging universal justice and amnesty to prisoners (which may or may not actually have been granted!).

Isaiah 7:14 may perhaps have been a similar birth oracle, casting the newly conceived or newborn royal heir in the role of the son of the virgin goddess Anath (equivalent to Shahar as in Pss. 110), though if so, it has been reapplied by the writer/redactor of Isaiah 7 as a reference to one of Isaiah's own sons, whom he named after his prophecies so as to remind people of his words once they came to pass (as if he had named his son Mark, to stand for "Mark my words!"), as he also does in Isaiah 8:1–4, similar in other important details to 7:14 as well.

It now becomes easy to recognize two other pieces of supposed "messianic prophecy" as birth/coronation oracles of this type, and thus as ornamental court rhetoric, not as genuine predictive prophecies at all, or at least not predictions of distant events. The first of these is Jeremiah 33:14–18, where the "righteous branch" (notice: nothing about a cut-off stump this time) seems certainly to be Zedekiah ("Yahve is Righteous"), the Judean king carried off into exile, whose ignominious fate thus belied the early hopes expressed on his behalf. If this optimistic appraisal of Zedekiah seems barely to comport with Jeremiah's dim view of this king expressed elsewhere in the book (contrast also 33:18 with 7:22; 8:8), it may come as no surprise to find that these verses do not appear in the Septuagint version of Jeremiah and thus may be later interpolations.

The other possible birth/coronation oracle is Isaiah 11:1–9, to which we have already given some attention. Now let us consider the possibility that in this case an old birth/coronation oracle has been reapplied as a prediction of an eventual restoration of the monarchy. All that would have been necessary is the reinterpretation of a reference to a branch of Jesse's line as a shoot from Jesse's stump. Remember that 11:10 speaks of the "root" of Jesse, implying perhaps that the reference is to a currently reigning king, not some future successor. If this reinterpretation has occurred, it would be a very instructive one, for it would be the beginning of the otherwise post–Old Testament tendency to reinterpret royal texts as future-restoration texts, in other words, messianic texts in the traditional sense.

By my reckoning, there remain a pair of other messianic texts in the Old Testament, but these, too, are more in the nature of enthronement oracles, royal propaganda. They are Haggai 2:20–23 and Zechariah, chapter 4 and 6:9–13a, which are postexilic and presuppose civil war in the Persian Empire, which these prophets supposed would lead to the fall of Persia and the restoration of Jewish sovereignty. Haggai and Zechariah were great champions of Zerubbabel and Joshua, the former a Davidic descendant appointed governor of Judea by the Persian overlords, the latter the current high priest. These two had seen to the rebuilding of the temple, and for this Haggai and Zechariah decided they must both be anointed Messiahs, one royal, the other priestly. (Here we can observe the beginning of the two-Messiah doctrine traceable through the Dead Sea Scrolls, the Testaments of the Twelve Patriarchs, and the rabbinic expectation of Messiah ben-David and Messiah ben-Joseph.)

Haggai and Zechariah, then, do not so much predict the future coming of some Davidic successor; they are already unstoppering the anointing oil! They have a candidate in mind! For them, Zerubbabel was the Davidic Messiah. Sadly, they were a bit premature. And this casts a somewhat different light on the business in Zechariah 9:9 about the messianic entry into Jerusalem: is this even a predictive prophecy if the point was to call attention to the supposed messianic advent of a contemporary figure?

What about Isaiah 52:13–15, 53:1–12? Nothing in the text suggests any connection with the hope of a coming Messiah. And though it seems to have had nothing to do with birth or coronation oracles, it does represent an aspect of the royal ideology of the ancient Judean god-king. This time, as Ivan Engnell and Helmer Ringgren show, we are dealing with a fossil of the ancient New Year's Festival, which, like its prototype in Babylon, renewed the heavenly mandate of the monarchy by having the king undergo, in ritual drama, the fate of the ancient gods whose kingship he represented on earth.[10] The king ritually assumed the burden of the fertility of the land and the sins of his people. Then came a ritual humiliation, as the high priest publicly removed the king's crown, tweaked his ears, and slapped his face. Protesting his innocence, the king would don his robe and crown again and rise to full power once more, redeeming his people in a ritual atonement in which he himself had played the role of scapegoat. Isaiah 52:13–15, 53:1–12 seems to reflect the Hebrew version of the same liturgy, which gave way after the Exile (with no king on the throne any longer) to the familiar Yom Kippur ritual.

But what is the function of the text in its present context, the announcement of glad tidings of the impending return of the exilic community of aristocrats and priests to the Holy Land? The old text has been updated, reapplied to a new situation. As Morna Hooker (*Jesus and the Servant*) argues, the text as we now read it functions as part of an apologetic for the returning exiles who sought to enhance their position in the eyes of their contemporaries who had remained in the homeland all this time and had ascribed the deportation of their leaders to the leaders' sinfulness, not their own.[11] The so-called Servant Song of Isaiah 52–53 attempts to turn the tables by insisting that it was the innocent minority (or righteous remnant) that was taken away to punishment not because of their own sins but in the place of those who actually did the sinning, the reprobate who remained behind! Thus did they theologize the privilege accorded them by their royal Persian patrons. We are not surprised to learn in Ezra and Nehemiah of severe tensions between the newly returned leaders, with their arrogant "take-charge" attitude, and the people of the land who had never left. So Isaiah 52–53 in its present context represents a secondary reinterpretation whereby the returning exiles are the suffering servants of Yahve, once mistakenly blamed for their own punishment when in fact, from their own viewpoint, they were taking it on behalf of the very upstarts who despised them as sinners. It is they who, having suffered on behalf of sinners, will be exalted to the glory due them (in their own estimation, anyway).

Some would see Psalm 22 as part of the same royal-divine humiliation liturgy, seeing that various sections of the Psalms (all of which had a ritual setting in the temple—none were private lyric poems) are written just for the king's use and that the psalm does share Isaiah 52–53's pattern of shameful suffering giving way to final (if only implied) vindication.[12] That may be, but I tend rather to go with Gunkel and Mowinckel (see above).

When we see what sort of ancient meaning-contexts gave rise to the several texts that Christian apologists claim as messianic prophecies, we can readily see many points of correspondence between the ancient texts and the gospel story of Jesus. But the connection is not as the apologists imagine, that Old Testament prophets made predictions and Jesus fulfilled them. Rather, the texts, very few of them prophecies at all, contain potent mythemes that recur in the Hellenistic Jewish milieu of early Christianity: the divine king, the dying and rising savior, the atoning suffering of the innocent on behalf of the guilty who blame him, and so on. So the New and the Old Testament texts share common roots: the rich mulch of religious and mythical ideas of the ancient Mediterranean world. It is by no means necessary to posit divine prediction to explain the correspondences. Once Christians believed Jesus was the Messiah, it seemed natural to dust off the old court rhetoric of Judah and to use it to describe him.

WHAT WERE MESSIANIC FULFILLMENTS?

We have seen that the apologists' notion of messianic prophecy has precious little to do with the apparent intentions of the Old Testament scriptures they cite. Now we shall see how little their notion of the fulfillment of messianic prophecy has to do with the New Testament concept of fulfillment. First, what do the apologists seem to have in mind? They seem to mean that there was a raft of predictions of things that would happen to God's anointed one, things no mortal could engineer on his own initiative. The predictions, supposedly, were there on the books for anyone to read, much like the legend of the sword in the stone: He who draws the sword shall be king of all England. Many try to dislodge the blade Excalibur, but all fail till young Arthur tries and succeeds. Thus there was a publicly understood prophecy functioning as a credential or condition for a coming king, and someone met that condition, proving himself the rightful king. A similar story is told of Alexander the Great cutting the Gordian Knot ("He who undoes the knot shall be ruler of all Asia"). But is this what the New Testament writers meant when they affirmed that Jesus had fulfilled Old Testament prophecy? I think not. Of all the New Testament writers, Matthew provides us with the clearest idea of what such an early Christian appeal to prophecy meant.

Matthew appears to have shared the hermeneutical assumption of the scribes of the Dead Sea Scrolls Habakkuk Commentary, namely, that old texts were full of hitherto hidden cipher-allusions to events transpiring in the life of his particular sect. The idea was that specific predictions had long ago been "smuggled in" by divine inspiration underneath any discernible, straightforward reading of the text. One could most certainly not have read the Old Testament texts to determine beforehand what would happen. Rather, it was only in retrospect, once the secretly predicted events had come to pass, that the initiated reader could, by means of striking, punlike verbal associations, tune in to the esoteric meaning of the text. In this manner, the Dead Sea Scrolls sectarians read any reference to "the righteous" as predicting some aspect of the life and work of their guru, the Righteous Teacher.[13]

Such an approach to "fulfilled prophecy" was the very opposite of the popular Christian notion that reading publicly, literally understood predictions should have led any Bible reader to faith in Jesus as Messiah, since anyone could have seen that he fulfilled them, for example, by being born in the right place.[14] The idea was not that the publicly discernible correspondence between predictions and events in the life of Jesus would lead one to faith (the apologists' own aim to "demand a verdict"), but rather that, once one had Christian faith, old texts took on a new layer of meaning that hitherto, before the "prophesied" fact and before one accepted faith in Jesus, could never have been recognized as a prophecy in the first place! It was not that if you refused to hear the voice of prophecy you weren't entitled to be part of Jesus' flock. Rather, you could only hear the voice of prophecy if you were already part of that flock. Faith provided a new and esoteric hermeneutical perspective. Exoteric, publicly available exegesis did not lead to faith. You came to faith in Jesus first on other grounds, the simple preaching of the Gospel, and then Christ began to open the scriptures to your wondering eyes. Only then did your heart begin to burn within you.

As I say, Matthew appears to have been operating with this sort of understanding. His programmatic statement is to be found in Matthew 13:52, where we read of the distinctive role and prerogative of the Christian exegete, the "scribe trained for the kingdom of heaven." He is like a householder who is able to display out of his storehouse treasures old and new. The treasury of a scribe is certainly the scriptures. The old goods he brings forth from there are the literal, conventional interpretations, while the new items are new readings made possible by the new esoteric key he possesses as a Christian, thanks to the charismatic illumination of the Holy Spirit. This understanding is borne out by Matthew's treatment of Old Testament scripture throughout the rest of his Gospel, notably the series of "formula quotations."[15] Matthew has a number of stories that he says happened in order that the word of the Lord through the prophet might be fulfilled. In virtually every case, the fulfillment works only if one completely disregards the Old Testament context.

One example would be Isaiah 7:14, which Matthew sees as predicting the birth of Jesus. Yet, as a simple reading of the whole chapter of Isaiah makes unmistakably clear, that prophecy of Isaiah dealt with contemporary events many centuries before: the birth of a child who would not be old enough to spit out food he didn't like by the time the threatening coalition of Israel and Syria had been wiped off the map by the Assyrian Empire. The original, literal relevance of the passage was long ago exhausted, save as a testimonial to God's faithfulness to Judah. Matthew certainly knew this; no one could miss it. By the same token, Matthew could never have invoked the Isaiah passage as a proof in the manner of subsequent apologists, that is, as a straightforward prediction of Jesus' birth; any skeptics would immediately dismiss the citation, understood literally. Matthew would only be inviting ridicule.

Similarly, when he cited Hosea 11:1, "Out of Egypt I have called my son," and referred it to the return of the Holy Family from Egypt after the death of Herod the Great, he just cannot have thought he was reproducing the literal, historical intent of Hosea, which rather has to do with Israel emerging from Egypt at time of the Exodus. No reader of Hosea could possibly think it meant anything else, nor could Matthew have expected him to. In both cases (and in many others), it seems much more likely that Matthew was interpreting scriptural passages as the Qumran sectarians did. The references to events in King Ahaz's day and the time of the Exodus were the exoteric, universally recognized "old treasures" available to any reader, to the old scribe and the new. But the references perceived in these verses to the nativity of Jesus are examples of the new goods available only to the scribe trained for the kingdom of heaven, trained, that is, in esoteric exegesis. Matthew gives no sign of rejecting the old, conventional interpretations (which have nothing to do with the Messiah); he merely adds levels of meaning newly available to the eye of Christian faith.

WHENCE THE PROOF FROM PROPHECY?

In all this, there is nothing of the apologetical appeal to public, long-standing messianic claims. Matthew was not aiming at the same thing subsequent Christian apologists like Tim LaHaye are. Why the change? Why did apologists, ancient (I would include Luke) and modern, shift over to an incredible appeal to Old Testament proof texts as if the Christian *re*interpretation represented the *original* intentions of the prophets to predict Jesus? I think it is because very shortly, the vast majority of Christians, and Christian scholars, were Greek-speaking gentiles who were accustomed to reading only the Greek Septuagint and reading it with only a Christian application in mind. They viewed the Old Testament dispensation simply as the time of waiting for the Christ, and the Old Testament characters as pretty much "Christians before Christ" (to borrow Justin Martyr's term for Socrates and other Greek spokesmen for the Logos). They read the Old Testament anachronistically, made it into a Christian book, and began to suppose that Isaiah had nothing in mind but predicting Jesus Christ. Here and there one catches an early Christian voice protesting that the Old Testament author could not have had Jesus in mind—Marcion of Pontus, Theodore of Mopsuestia, who held out for a literal, nonmessianic reading of most or all of the Old Testament—but these, obviously, are the exceptions that prove the rule.

Even if most did read the Old Testament as a Christian document even on the surface, Christian hermeneutics did not theoretically demand this. Most exegetes held in common with Origen some sort of multisense hermeneutic, whereby the surface, literal sense was often not even the most important one. One could still find the messianic sense in one of these esoteric levels of meaning, and many of the supposed "messianic" predictions that Tim LaHaye, Hal Lindsay, and others today seem to take as the surface meaning the ancients regarded as secondary, nonliteral interpretations. The crisis really came at the time of the Protestant Reformation, when to rule out Catholic appeals to nonliteral meanings on behalf of the papacy or the sale of indulgences, Martin Luther rejected, on principle, any but the straightforward, surface sense of any text as recoverable by means of the grammatico-historical method. At the same time, it did not occur to him to break with traditional appeals to Old Testament prophecy to prove that Christians were right and Jews were wrong about Jesus. This double standard is what created the intolerable bind in which fundamentalist apologists find themselves today (though they seem oblivious of the difficulty, one suspects because they share the same merely opportunistic interest that ancient Christians had in the Old Testament as a source of Christian proof texts).

If you do not believe there is a secret zone of subtle, esoteric meaning in scripture, placed there (or placed in the mind of the Christian reader) by the Holy Spirit, if you insist that what the Bible says, it can say only by grammatico-historical interpretation, and you are hellbent on finding Jesus in the Old Testament, you are inevitably going to assume that all of Matthew's Old Testament citations represent the literal, authorial intention of the Old Testament writers. And since any straightforward reading of the Old Testament texts makes it apparent that no such reference to Jesus was in view, the appeal to prophecy becomes something quite different from what it was either for Matthew (who sought to prove nothing by it) or for ancient and medieval apologists who had completely lost sight of the historic meaning of the Old Testament texts or were more interested in imaginary "deeper" levels of meaning. Now you had the spectacle of exegetes who insisted on the literal, grammatico-historical meaning of the Old Testament text as well as the New Testament text—and who had their work cut out for them since the two seldom seemed to agree. This means, in short, that the appeal to prophecy had passed from the offensive to the defensive: to square the Old Testament "prediction" with the New Testament "fulfillment," you had to try to show they agreed despite appearances. In other words, the proof from prophecy had become but another case of harmonizing apparent contradictions in the text.

And harmonized contradictions can never be the basis of appeal for assertions as dubious as they themselves are. You cannot get very far appealing to something as evidence that you have just admitted does not look like evidence but may be read that way if you try hard enough.

Though I have never run across an apologist (certainly there may be some) who is even aware of the original contexts and meanings of the passages I have reviewed above, I can imagine the strategy of such an apologist would be to charge that scholars have just invented all these clever categories ("birth oracles," "lament psalms," etc.) to evade the force of messianic prophecy. Why anyone would do that is beyond me. In any case, such a desperate suggestion has to come to grips with the wider utility of the categories. That is, if these form-critical categories are mere exegetical phantoms invented to make mischief for apologetics, why do they, how can they make so much sense in illuminating the sense of many other similar Old Testament texts that are irrelevant to the apologetics debate? The categories in which I have placed most of the major "messianic" texts do not exist for the sake of denying the texts to apologetical use. They exist as an interpretive tool for a much broader selection of texts in their own right.

But we can recognize a familiar style of apologetical argumentation here: to argue for the uniqueness of an item the apologist wants, for dogmatic reasons, to privilege. In the same way, creationists go to any imaginable lengths to deny that humans evolved from apelike ancestors despite the fact that the two seem so much alike. The strong, apparently "family" resemblances between reptiles and amphibians, for example, would seem to imply a common descent, but, no, the fundamentalist wants to have it that God simply made a lot of similar things discretely at different times, that he just happened to like the basic design and kept repeating parts of it. If ancient myths of dying and rising gods, of miracle-working divine men, of world-drenching floods, and of saints walking on water seem so close to biblical stories as to imply a common membership in a body of myth and folklore, the fundamentalist will insist that the resemblances are illusory, or that in the particular case he has a vested interest in, "myth became fact."[16]

Tillich saw the urgency here: religion never easily allows itself to be subsumed as one of a larger species, under a larger category, for this takes away the uniqueness, the ultimacy, and the absolute explanatory power religion likes to claim as a divine revelation discontinuous with mere human speculation and therefore superior to it.[17] The Grand Inquisitor never wants his divine truth to be revealed as being no less a human creation than that of the rivals he persecutes. The Wizard of Oz never wants to have anyone pay attention to the man behind the curtain.

There is something inherently grotesque about the very idea of seeking verification by appeal to clairvoyant predictions. Verification of what? What on earth would such proof, even if possible, have to do with, for example, the contents of the Sermon on the Mount? Is one's conscience likely to take such sayings more seriously if one can prove their author to have been predicted in advance by ancient seers? Does not the felt need to secure such "verification" demote and demean the self-evident power of the spiritual truths at issue? We do not need miraculous proofs to force us to take the truths of the Gospel seriously, nor can we be taking those truths very seriously if we still feel the need to seek afar for some supernatural warrant for heeding them. The teaching of scripture does not need and will not be helped by proofs from miracle. The continued insistence on such paranormal props only invites the suspicion that for fundamentalism, moral and spiritual wisdom is not enough, that in their case religion has gone offtrack and degenerated, like the modern New Age movement, with its pyramids and channelers, into a crass hankering after signs and wonders. Let us learn instead from the Old Testament prophets that all else is a snare and a delusion save for doing justly and walking humbly with a clear conscience.

All I can say is, if Tim LaHaye's grasp of the predictions made in the Old Testament is any guide to his acuity in interpreting End Times prophecy, I think we would be a lot better off playing Pin the Tail on the dispensational chart.

NOTES

1. Tim LaHaye and Jerry B. Jenkins, *Tribulation Force: The Continuing Drama of Those Left Behind* (Wheaton, IL: Tyndale House, 1996), p. 391.

2. Ibid., pp. 392–93.

3. Robert M. Price, *The Incredible Shrinking Son of Man* (Amherst, NY: Prometheus Books, 2003), pp. 51–52.

4. LaHaye and Jenkins, *Tribulation Force*, p. 394.

5. Ibid.

6. Ibid.

7. Hermann Gunkel, *An Introduction to the Psalms: The Genres of the Religious Lyrics of Israel*, ed. Joachim Begrich, trans. James D. Nogalski. Mercer Library of Biblical Studies (Macon, GA: Mercer University Press, 1998); Sigmund Mowinckel, *The Psalms in Israel's Worship*, trans. D. R. Ap-Thomas (New York: Abingdon Press, 1962).

8. LaHaye and Jenkins, *Tribulation Force*, pp. 395–96.

9. Ibid., p. 107.

10. Ivan Engnell, *Studies in Divine Kingship: Critical Essays on the Old Testament* (Nashville: Vanderbilt University, 1969), p. 230; Helmer Ringgren, *The Messiah in the Old Testament*, Studies in Biblical Theology series, no. 18 (London: SCM Press, 1956), pp. 46–53.

11. Morna Hooker, *Jesus and the Servant: The Influence of the Servant Concept of Deutero-Isaiah in the New Testament* (London: SCM Press, 1959), pp. 45–48.

12. Engnell, *Studies in Divine Kingship*, pp. 41, 119, 122; Ringgren, *Messiah in the Old Testament*, pp. 54–57.

13. For an excellent discussion of this "pesher" technique and its use by the New Testament writers, see *Biblical Exegesis in the Apostolic Period* (Eerdmans, 1975) by Richard Longenecker, a veteran evangelical New Testament scholar.

14. Hal Lindsey with C. C. Carlson, *The Late Great Planet Earth* (New York: Bantam Books, 1973), pp. 20–21.

15. See Krister Stendahl, *The School of St. Matthew and Its Use of the Old Testament* (1954; repr., Philadelphia: Fortress Press, 1968).

16. C. S. Lewis, "Myth Became Fact," in *God in the Dock: Essays on Theology and Ethics*, ed. Walter Hooper (Grand Rapids, MI: Eerdmans, 1970), pp. 63–67.

17. Paul Tillich, *What Is Religion?* ed. and trans. James Luther Adams (New York: Harper & Row, 1969), pp. 27, 127.

Chapter Three

THE GOSPEL OF THE ANTICHRIST

"Every one of us harbors within us a streak buried fathoms deep, below the apparently placid normality of our everyday appearance— a streak of rapt fascination for the Prince of Darkness and all his works."

—Christopher Lee[1]

Who or what is the Antichrist? The title is ambiguous, overfull of meaning. It seems to imply both "Opponent of Christ" and "False Christ." And, though both terms can be understood naturally as overlapping, they are at first sight distinct notions. For instance, one might understand the Antichrist to be the opposite number to the Christ, focusing on the notion of the Christ as God incarnate or God's son. Then the Antichrist's salient feature would be his diabolical origin and empowerment. He would be Satan's son or Satan himself in human form. And neither would have to have anything to do with pretending to be a Jewish Messiah. One might be a self-aggrandizing Caesar or another secular tyrant and still be the Antichrist. But then again a counterpart to Jesus as Messiah might not have to have any Jewish reference at all: we could still picture the Antichrist to be a charismatic religious figure, an analogue to the Christ, one whose very success threatens to supplant Jesus Christ by pushing him into the shadow of history.[2] One might even speak of a tragic sense in which failed Messiahs are Antichrists as soon as they step onto the stage of history; that is because "the Messiah" is inherently a symbol and embodiment of *future hope.* For him to enter the corrosive atmosphere of history on earth is to tarnish him irreparably. The world will not assume the proportions of the millennium no matter what he or any other visionary does, and as soon as that becomes apparent yet again (for we quickly forget it), the momentary Messiah ("We had hoped he was the one to redeem Israel") passes rudely into the rogues' gallery of false Messiahs and Antichrists.

MANDRAGON

Originally the Antichrist was the chaos dragon Leviathan, and so he still appears in Revelation. He assumes the form of a man to repeat the primordial struggle with God at the end of the world, this time in political and military terms. At first that might seem an unnatural juxtaposition, a harmonization of two very different ideas. But it does stand clearly on display for us in Revelation, where the Beast arises from the sea in the spittin' image of the Satanic dragon but appears to play the role of a tyrant in human form. His identifying number, after all, "is the number of a man." One might possibly venture to imagine Revelation's Beast in literal terms, perhaps as a hydra like the one Hercules fought, or as the creature from the science fiction movie *Ghidrah the Three-Headed Monster,* who also possesses three waving tails and flies along on a massive pair of batlike wings. Toho Studios has more than once demonstrated that an effective apocalyptic scenario might feature such rampaging giants. It would not be much of a stretch for Toho to make John's Revelation into a movie, taking every bit of apocalyptic imagery quite literally. One hopes they will.

Whence this myth of transformation: the dragon of primordial times appearing in human form as a tyrant? Like so many other aspects of apocalyptic myth, this one seems to be a debt owed to Persian Zoroastrianism, the faith of Cyrus the Great, liberator of Jews from the Babylonian Exile and proclaimed God's "anointed" by the Second Isaiah (Isa. 45:1). In the paired deities Ahura Mazda and Ahriman, masterminds of good and evils respectively, Jewish theologians thought they could recognize Yahve and Satan. The angel attributes of Ahura Mazda became the seven archangels of Jewish lore, and the Saoshyans ("future benefactor") became, or became merged with, the Davidic Messiah, his eventual task to raise the dead and to judge the wicked. From Zoroastrianism Jews also derived their penchant to henceforth plot a course for history and to subdivide it into dispensations during which God and Satan contested for human souls. Last but hardly least was the myth of Azdahak (also Azi Dahaka), the "fiendish serpent." He represented Babylonian power in the region and was conceived of as Ahriman's kin, just as the Beast in Revelation is the dragon, Satan's protégé. Azdahak, too, appears as a web-winged dragon with three heads, and his wingspan covers the sky. Another myth says he had been a wicked king of Assyria who made a compact with Ahriman, who then planted two kisses on either side of his neck from which sprouted the stalks and spitting heads of a pair of living serpents. Already we have the chaos dragon taking the form of an evil tyrant. But it hardly ends there. In the End Times, Azdahak is to fight the noble warrior Atar (the Vedic fire god Agni) and be defeated by him. Atar will chain Azdahak to the boulders of Mount Demavand, where he will languish powerless until later in the final millennium, when he must shatter his chains and raven forth again, destroying fully one-third of humanity before another hero, Keresaspa, will destroy him in the flame-river of Ayohsust. It is evident that Azdahak has contributed the basic outline to the mythic careers of both Satan and his clone the Beast in Revelation 19:20; 20:1–3, 7–10.

Given its Zoroastrian origin, it is no surprise that the identification of a mortal tyrant with the ancient chaos dragon would appear in Jewish scripture just following the Exile, when we see it applied to Antiochus IV Epiphanes, megalomaniacal potentate of the Seleucid (Syrian) Empire, one of the superstates emerging from the conquests of Alexander the Great. Antiochus was the classic Oriental despot, believing fervently in his own divinity and eager to spread his own gospel. Having repudiated his ancestral god Tammuz/Adonis, Antiochus turned to the pantheon of the Greeks and decided that he was none other than (as his royal epithet implied) Zeus manifest on earth in human form.

> And the king shall do according to his will; he shall exalt himself and magnify himself above every god, and shall speak astonishing things against the God of gods. He shall prosper till the indignation is accomplished; for what is determined shall be done. He shall give no heed to the gods of his fathers, or to the one beloved by women; he shall not give heed to any other god, for he shall magnify himself above all. He shall honor the god of fortresses instead of these; a god whom his fathers did not know he shall honor with gold and silver, with precious stones and costly gifts. He shall deal with the strongest fortresses by the help of a foreign god. (Dan. 11:36–39a)

Most of his subjects could tolerate such theology without too much trouble, whether or not they actually believed in it (though, given the arbitrariness of all-powerful beings in mythology, certainly no king could be too tyranical to be plausible as a god!). Jews, of course, were an exception, at least enough Jews to stand up to the god-king and to frustrate him. Antiochus might have grudgingly tolerated Jewish non-cooperation had he not found in the Jews a convenient scapegoat on which to pour his frustrations when Rome blocked his expansionist attempts at adding the Ptolemaic (Egyptian) Empire to his own. The god on earth had been thwarted one too many times, and his hellish scorn erupted full force onto pious Jews in the Holy Land. The most notorious blasphemy of Antiochus was to have a sow sacrificed to Zeus on the altar of the Jerusalem temple.

Many Jews were willing to knuckle under, figuring "Better red than dead," but their accomodation only drove more militant Jewish traditionalists to the breaking point. The elderly priest Mattathias and his sons began making sure the compromisers among their people regretted their decision to hellenize, really, to apostatize, more than they'd have regretted risking Antiochus's wrath. The Hasmonean/Maccabean resistance was thus born. A fighting force resembling their eventual successors in Roman times, the Zealots, the Hasmoneans managed to take advantage of Seleucid woes on other fronts to expel the distracted empire from their borders. For the first time in centuries, Judea was ruled by Jewish rulers, though it would last only about a century until pathetic internecine struggles actually made Roman dominion seem a brighter option. At that time Judea, albeit still nominally independent, became a client state of the Roman Empire under the Roman lapdog Herod the Great.

These events are all chronicled for us in 1 and 2 Maccabees. Josephus, too, wrote them up at the end of the first century CE. It is one of the things that makes his histories so important for the student of the Bible. Another witness, however, stood even closer to the events, and that was the author of the book of Daniel. "Daniel" was the name of a very ancient sage in Canaanite mythology, but the character was updated to become a Jewish exile in Babylon whose visionary gifts made him an important adviser to the Babylonian kings. And among Daniel's visions (wonderful literary fictions like the rest of the book) are those chronicling "in advance" and in great detail the events of all parties to the Seleucid/Hasmonean struggle, amid which the author himself actually lived, despite his using a character from centuries before as his mouthpiece. So most of his "predictions" are summaries of what had already taken place in his recent past. As he wrote, things were hurtling toward their climax. He correctly anticipated the defeat of Antiochus and the vindication of dedicated Jews, but he did not get it quite right. He thought Antiochus would take over Libya to the west and Ethiopia to the south, upping the stakes, before dying on his way home, somewhere along the Mediterranean coast. And his death would signal the advent of the kingdom of God on earth, a millennial paradise. These last predictions, the only genuine predictions in the book, failed. But who was complaining? Antiochus did indeed perish, and Jewish independence dawned, at least for a century. Daniel's glass was half full.

Though not a god, Antiochus IV Epiphanes certainly did make himself a devil in the flesh, one of the great monsters of history. So it was no stretch for the apocalyptist Daniel to cast him in Azdahak's sinister role as the human incarnation of the chaos monster, as in Daniel 7:8, 24b–25: "I considered the horns, and behold, there came up among them another horn, a little one, before which three of the first horns were plucked up by the roots; and behold, in this horn were eyes like the eyes of a man, and a mouth speaking great things. . . . He shall speak words against the Most High, and shall wear out the saints of the Most High, and shall think to change the times and the law; and they shall be given into his hand for a time, two times, and half a time." Though the term *Antichrist* is not used here, it should be clear that we are seeing the first occurrence of that theme in the Bible.

Despite the confident boasting of fundamentalist authors that every biblical prophecy came true, it is obvious that often enough they did not. One must not ignore the fact that Daniel's glass was also half empty; the ancients certainly did not. If a prophecy of deliverance was left hanging, the ancients allowed for no statute of limitations. Some clever scribe, like apologists today, would find some novel construal to place upon the old words to make it possible to stretch them and come up with a new deadline that lay yet (un-debunked) in the future. The author of Daniel had already indulged in such exegetical machinations himself. Jeremiah had predicted a glorious restoration of the Judean monarchy seventy years after the Exile began. While history went Jeremiah one better, the Exile concluding after only fifty years, the return of the exiles was to a Judea constituted as a Persian province, from which it passed into the grasping hands of Alexander the Great, then of his Ptolemaic and Seleucid successors. The promised return to national glory and sovereignty never arrived. The author of Daniel sought to fill this embarrassing gap between prophecy and reality by the expedient of interpreting Jeremiah's seventy years as seventy *heptads* of years. If that had been what Jeremiah had wanted the wise to understand, that would mean the kingdom of the holy ones of the Most High should be dawning very shortly, in the very generation for whom Daniel wrote, his own in the second century BCE.

TWO STEPS FORWARD, ONE STEP BACK

What wonder, then, when still later scribes smuggled extra flexibility into Daniel's own schedule? Future-oriented Jews saw that the End had been in motion: the prophecies of Daniel had advanced quite far and begun their fulfillment. But then the machine had stopped. They did not regard the persecution of Antiochus and the victory of the Hasmoneans as a dress rehearsal, much less a false alarm. They believed that the process had begun but been suspended, God alone knew why. Soon, they figured, the machine would crank up again, and, just as the latest book in a series of novels recaps the cliff-hanger from the previous book before carrying the action further (each *Left Behind* volume does just this, for instance), so the climax would replay, rebuild, and then the denouement would ensue. So it did not surprise anyone when, in 40 CE, history seemed on the verge of repeating, then fulfilling, itself. Another like Antiochus had appeared: the Roman emperor Caligula. He, too, regarded himself as Zeus, even troubling to replace the sculpted heads on all statues of Zeus with images of himself. One such statue he ordered erected in the Herodian temple for the benefit of his Jewish subjects, a favor they hastened to decline with threats of an agricultural strike if the plan should proceed. Must not Caligula be the Little Horn returned? A self-proclaimed divine being ready to defile the temple of God? It was the abomination of desolation all over again! And did that not presage the arrival, hitherto delayed, of the kingdom of God on earth? Sure it did! It must!

Only it didn't. Caligula's crony Herod Agrippa I finally convinced the emperor not to pursue the plan. The clock had stopped again, but the image of Antiochus Epiphanes had by now been firmly stamped upon the myth. Future candidates for the Antichrist could be expected to do what Antiochus had done and what Caligula had come so close to doing: performing the abomination of desolation. That is certainly the picture conveyed to us in the Synoptic Apocalypse, three versions of which survive in the Gospels: Mark 13, Matthew 24–25, and Luke 17:20–37, 21:1–36. The events of the End, at least of the end of

Jerusalem, include "the abomination of desolation." Mark 13:14 has "But when you see the abomination of desolation set up where it ought not to be (let the reader understand), then let those who are in Judea flee to the mountains." Matthew expands the text to explain it: "So when you see the abomination of desolation spoken of by the prophet Daniel, standing in the holy place (let the reader understand), then let those who are in Judea flee to the mountains" (Matt. 24:15–16). Luke 21:20 drops the apocalyptic cipher language altogether: "But when you see Jerusalem surrounded by armies, then know that its desolation has come near. Then let those who are in Judea flee to the mountains." In view in all three versions is a Roman siege of Jerusalem, culminating in the destruction of the temple. The Synoptic Apocalypse, then, carries forward the Antiochus scenario, merely updating it. If the destruction of 70 CE is in view here, then the Antiochus character is Titus, son of Vespasian and his successor. If the destruction of bar-Kochba's temple in 135 is meant, then the new Antiochus would presumably be the emperor Hadrian.[3]

The book of Revelation clearly continues the Antiochus tradition, this time with Nero and, superimposed upon him, Domitian, sharing the role. In recent history, Adolf Hitler (himself nominated as Antichrist) was such a storybook villain that the popular imagination could not let him go, cherishing survival myths, even imagining his masterminding the Falklands War in 1982. In just the same way, the first-century CE Romans could not really accept that they had seen the last of the capricious tyrant Nero. He had been killed (like Caligula before him) by his own guards who had had all they could take. But many believed the guards killed one of the emperor's doubles, and that the man himself had escaped east to Parthia, Rome's greatest enemy, whence he would one day come to exact vengeance upon Rome for spurning him.[4] As time went on, it became necessary, if one were to maintain this urban legend, to suppose that Nero, who could not have survived so long, was killed by his guards, but that he had meantime risen from the grave and would return.

This latter version, that of Nero Redivivus, occurs in the Revelation as a way of extending and reusing the Antiochus myth. That is why the number of the Beast is 666, which "happens" to work out to the numerical equivalent of "Neron Caesar." Some manuscripts have 616, but that is only because someone realized it was all right to leave off the last letter of the name, yielding "Nero Caesar," just as we commonly shorten "Platon" to "Plato," "Paulon" to "Paul." The Nero resurrection myth also explains the business about one of the Beast's heads having been mortally wounded, yet being alive (13:3), as well as the scene in which the Beast's hordes cross dryshod over the Euphrates (16:12; 17:15–18) to overwhelm the Harlot seated on the seven hills: Rome. That another "Antiochus," Caligula, has left his indelible mark on the tradition is evident from the fact that Revelation's Beast has a statue of himself that all must worship (13:14–15).

If Irenaeus, bishop of Lyons (writing about 180 AD/CE) was correct in placing the Revelation in the reign of Domitian, that clears up something else: Domitian was viewed as a revived Nero in all but name. This, in turn, is why the Beast is an eighth king yet also one of the previous seven (17:11). Some have objected against this identification by pointing out there is precious little evidence that Domitian ever staged a persecution against Christians. But that doesn't matter: Revelation clearly expects that someone *soon will.* The time of trial is *about to* come upon the earth (3:10). The author might have jumped the gun. After all, he also insisted Jesus would very shortly return to destroy the Beast, and that was nineteen centuries ago.

Jews, too, had no difficulty updating the neo-Antiochus figure to make him a Roman. Not pausing to get hung up on specific names and individuals, they called him simply "Armillus," or, Romulus. Any Roman persecutor could fill the role, and several already had.

It is tempting to interpet 2 Thessalonians 2:3–8, like all these other texts, as presupposing the recurrence of Antiochus's blasphemies:

> Let no one deceive you in any way; for that day will not come, unless the rebellion comes first, and the man of lawlessness is revealed, the son of perdition, who opposes and exalts himself against every so-

called god or object of worship, so that he takes his seat in the temple of God, proclaiming himself to be God. Do you not remember that when I was still with you I told you this? And you know what is restraining him now so that he may be revealed in his time. For the mystery of lawlessness is already at work; only he who now restrains it will do so until he is out of the way. And then the lawless one will be revealed, and the Lord Jesus will slay him with the breath of his mouth and destroy him by his appearing and his coming.

If he does refer to the Antiochus mytheme, and the temple reference initially inclines one to suppose so, then the suggestion of commentator A. S. Peake is apropos: "The mystery of lawlessness has already manifested itself in Caligula. At present it is held in check by Claudius, the reigning emperor of Rome. When he is 'taken out of the way', his successor will be the man of sin, carrying to a climax the impious tendencies already revealed by Caligula. The guarded language is much easier to understand if Paul identified the man of sin with the next Roman emperor."[5] The idea of the mystery of iniquity warming up, then getting stifled, only to be continued after a respite would be yet another delay after a disappointed expectation, in other words, that Caligula was the Antiochus-Antichrist about to bring things to a conclusion.

But I wonder. Is the writer of 2 Thessalonians confusing the abomination of desolation (which he does not mention specifically) with Antiochus's delusions of grandeur? Or are we? His blasphemous megalomania is one thing; his desecration of the Jerusalem temple is another. And 2 Thessalonians speaks only of self-deification. And what sort of deification is that, pray tell? Antiochus believed he was Olympian Zeus. Caligula believed he was the very incarnation of the spirit of the Caesars. None of these could be construed as "God" in a Jewish or Christian context such as underlies 2 Thessalonians. Nor does the original Daniel passage, quoted above, say that Antiochus, the Little Horn, claimed to be Yahve. So I wonder if 2 Thessalonians means to make reference to the Antiochus tradition after all. There is another, better candidate. More in a moment.

THE SECOND BEAST

Why does the book of Revelation double the Antichrist figure? Why is there a second Beast that rises from the land (of Israel?), not from the sea (the Mediterranean, whence the pesky gentiles come)? They are different in kind, the first Beast being our familiar Antiochus-analog, the second being more of a prophetic figure. Greg Jenks distinguishes between two Antichrist personae, the older "Endtyrant" figure and the False Prophet. Of the two, only the second looks anything like a counterfeit Messiah, that is, someone who might be taken, by way of deceit, for the Jewish Messiah. George Beasley-Murray calls attention to the fact that, for Mark 13, the abomination of desolation (a hallmark, remember, of the Antiochus-type) does not involve a Jewish False Messiah or prophet, for Mark has these come out of the woodwork at a later stage (Mark 13:22: "False Christs and false prophets will arise and show signs and wonders, to lead astray, if possible, the elect").[6]

Jenks traces the second figure back to the Deuteronomic warnings (chapter 13) against false prophets in general: those who either proselytize for alien gods or make failed predictions in Yahve's name. It is much more intelligible that such a figure could be a Jew. By contrast, it goes against the grain for a new Antiochus figure, much less a Roman Caesar, to be a Jew. Think of the Roman procurator's words: "Am I a Jew?" It is equally incongruous to envision a gentile posing as the Jewish Messiah. Those modern novelists who do (including Jerry Jenkins) seem to have lost sight of the Jewish origin and character of the Messiah, thinking instead of "Christ" as being synonymous with Jesus, a figure with a much wider range of cultural and theological associations. When they think of a "false Christ," they are probably thinking of an analogous leader or figurehead from some non-Christian religion, like Muhammad or the Buddha. But ancient Jews would never have made such a connection. For them, a pretend-Messiah would pretty much have to be a Jew.

It is obvious what catalyzed the bogeyman figure of the Endtyrant: the appearance and reappearance of historical figures like Antiochus.

As such, this species of Beast was a living reality. But what would have brought to imaginative life the textbook phantom of the False Prophet? Why should Christian faith have made a place for him at all? There is nothing much the second Beast does in Revelation that the first could not have done in his own name. Nor is the redundancy of Beasts peculiar to Revelation. The two versions of Antichrist have been more than once harmonized by Christians. A Jewish Sibylline Oracle (7:16), followed by Lactantius (*Institutiones Divinae* 7:10ff); Commodian (*Carmen Apologeticum* vv. 791–911); and St. Martin of Tours (preserved in Sulpicius Severus, *Dialogue* 2:14), has two Antichrists giving way to one, the Neronic one succumbing to the Jewish one.[7]

Where did the Jewish pseudo-Messiah version come from? It is here that I wax bold to add a new note to the discussion. I rejoice to set forth a new proposal, namely, that the Christian picture of an Antichrist as a false prophet represents the unwitting Christian borrowing of the Jewish view of *Jesus of Nazareth* as a false prophet and seducer of Israel. Christians heard of the Jewish parody of Jesus, which we find in several versions of the *Toledoth Jeschu*, the Jewish satire of the Christian Gospels. Tertullian and Celsus attest to the early circulation of various features of the Jewish "Jesus Pandera" caricature. I am proposing that some Christians knew the story simply as that of a Jewish false Messiah, therefore an Antichrist, and they added it onto the ancient Antiochus/Azdahak model as a second Antichrist. Consider the parallels.

The fourth-century Pseudo-Hippolytus tells us that the Antichrist is to be born of a whore. Jewish polemic identified Mary Magdalene and Mary the mother of Jesus, taking "Magdalene" to represent the Aramaic *m'gaddla*, "the hair curler," a euphemism for a brothel madam, since elaborate hairstyling was regarded as the mark of a prostitute. The whole thing is either a parody of the virgin birth story or a reflection of a real scandal that the virgin birth doctrine sought to cover up.

As per 2 Thessalonians 2:3–8 (and many later writers), the Antichrist magnifies himself as God in the temple. Antiochus, though he believed himself to be Zeus on earth, is never said to have personally set foot in the Jerusalem temple, much less to have claimed to be Yahve. Nor did Caligula. But in John 8:19, 58; 10:30 (cf. verse 33), Jesus seems to claim identity with God, a blasphemy for which pious Jews seek to stone him on the spot. In the *Toledoth Jeschu*, the false prophet Jesus secretly enters the temple to secure knowledge of the divine Name, which he goes on to employ as a magical talisman.

Antichrist appears as the Jewish Messiah and poses as a friend of Jews, making a covenant with them for three and a half years. Before we chalk this up to the influence of Daniel 9:27a ("And he shall make a strong covenant with many for one week [of years]; and for half of the week [of years] he shall cause sacrifice and offering to cease"), let us recall that the length of Jesus' ministry in John's Gospel and in Christian tradition generally is a bit over three years, culminating in the establishment of a new covenant (by his death), which does away with temple sacrifices (as per the Epistle to the Hebrews). Nor is his covenant making restricted to the end of the three-year period, since Matthew already depicts Jesus at the beginning of his ministry as a new Moses legislating from a high mountain.

Then the Antichrist is to turn on his erstwhile protégés, the Jews, and begin persecuting them. This reflects the Christian persecution of Jews after Jews rejected Jesus and the Christian Gospel.

It almost goes without saying that the Jewish Pseudo-Christ dazzles his followers by performing miracles through magical or even diabolical means. That is exactly how the scribes and Pharisees are said to view the miracles of Jesus of Nazareth in Matthew 12:24 and elsewhere. But the most spectacular miracle attributed to the Antichrist is flying through the air, upheld by invisible demons (in the employ, after all, of the Prince of the Power of the Air). The Pseudo-Hippolytus (*About the End of the World, and about the Antichrist, and on the Second Coming of our Lord Jesus Christ* 29:111:10) predicts this feat, but fundamentalist scholar Arthur W. Pink independently inferred that the Antichrist will be able to fly on the basis of Daniel 9:27b ("and upon the wing of abominations shall come one who makes desolate, until the decreed end is poured out on the desolator").[8] The same feat is famously attributed

also to Simon Magus in his miracle contest with Simon Peter before
Nero in the Acts of Peter. Most strikingly, however, the Jewish gospel-
satire *Toledoth Jeschu* has Jesus fly through the air in combat with Judas,
a heroic agent of the Sanhedrin. The parallel between the Christian
False Prophet Antichrist and Jesus of Nazareth as Jews saw him holds
good even here, at what might be judged its most far-fetched point.

What might seem at first to be a gap in the parallel I am drawing is
the absence of any resurrection ascribed to the False Prophet. If that
character really is the Jewish Jesus spoof, Jesus Pandera, why does he
not rise from the dead? Simply because the Jewish Jesus parody did not
include the resurrection: the disciples stole his body.

I say, Christians picked up this version, not knowing it was about
Jesus, seeing in it only a Jewish account of a seductive and deceptive
False Jewish Messiah. They added it alongside the traditional Endtyrant
character. But this does not quite account for a few features of the
Christian myth of Antichrist, for instance, the notion that the False
Messiah would overthrow Rome, regather the Jews to the Holy Land,
and rebuild a temple for them there. But the origin of these items, too,
is not far to seek. These features come from positive Jewish messianic
expectation, which Christians viewed with the same jaded eye as Jews
viewed the Christian Messiah Jesus. Where the Christian Antichrist
does not sound like Jesus from a Jewish standpoint, it is because Christians have simply added (and vilified) the Jewish messianic expectation:
after Rome falls, the Jewish Messiah will rise to power. He will regather
the lost tribes and rebuild the temple. None of these expectations have
any positive value in terms of Christian expectation. Jesus or the
Church has become their temple. Christians increasingly cultivated
Roman favor, eager to scapegoat Jews for the death of Jesus, eventually
canonizing Pontius Pilate as a saint. And of course Christianity officially took the place as the state religion.

Things had changed since John had cast Domitian as the Beast in
Revelation. Subsequent Christians, friendly to Rome, came to view
Rome as the final bulwark against the eruption of evil in the End
Times. Rome must fall before the Antichrist could come to power.

Rome was, Tertullian and others believed, the restrainer mentioned in
2 Thessalonians 2:6–7. So the notion of a Messiah who would destroy
Rome was not a welcome one to Christians. Where then did they get it?
From a group who was still on the outs with Rome and relished the day
"Armillus" would fall, to be succeeded by a Jewish Messiah who would
regather his people and restore their temple. Yes, what in the Christian
Antichrist doctrine does not come from the Endtyrant legend (the first
Beast) or the Jewish caricature of Jesus (the second Beast) came from
contemporary Jewish messianism. The Jewish Messiah was ipso facto
the Christian Antichrist.

What Jews expect their Messiah to do, Christians admit, he will do;
only it won't be Jesus, hence it will be a false Messiah: Antichrist. Marcion, too, allows that the Jewish Messiah will come and do what Jews
expect him to do, but Tertullian correctly sees that this ought to make
the Jewish Messiah the Antichrist. Tertullian's speculation is quite
revealing: "According . . . to Marcion's view, it is really hard to know
whether he [Antichrist] might not be the Creator's Christ; because
according to him He is not yet come."[9]

What we wind up seeing is Jews and Christians each demonizing
the other's Messiah concept as Antichrist. Jews deem Jesus of Nazareth
a false prophet and Antichrist. Christians, unaware it is their Jesus, add
this character to their own eschatology. Christians view the Jewish messianic expectation as a false rival to Jesus, the Christian Messiah, so they
make the Jewish Messiah the Christian Antichrist, too, adding together
the Jewish parody of Jesus with the Christian vilification of the Jewish
Messiah. And the second Beast, the second Antichrist, is the result.

IN THE PINK

The version of the Antichrist we see in the *Left Behind* series definitely
falls in the Endtyrant (Azdahak/Antiochus) trajectory. The closest parallel to Jesus Christ is Nicolae Carpathia's resurrection, but that, too, as
we have seen, comes from the Antiochus/Nero tradition, a function of

explaining how Nero could still be available to conquer Rome so many years after his disappearance. It did not originate as an attempt to parallel Jesus. By contrast, LaHaye and Jenkins can think of little role for the second Beast, the False Prophet, except as comedy relief. He is a bumbling sycophant.

So closely does Nicolae match Antiochus Epiphanes that he finds himself having to fight the kings of the south and of the west as minor distractions from the main attraction at Armageddon. These are ciphers for the kings of Ethiopia and Libya whom Daniel expected Antiochus to have to battle. Here LaHaye and Jenkins are following closely in the footsteps of the evangelical premillenarian tradition, which sees in Daniel's blow-by-blow account of Antiochus's adventures the career of his End Time counterpart. "Thus from v. 21 to the end of the [eleventh] chapter we have a continuous history of the Antichrist" (Arthur W. Pink).[10] We have already seen how from ancient times Jewish apocalyptic interpreters looked back on the circumstances of Antiochus's downfall, expecting them to repeat themselves as a run-up to a reenactment that would, this time, not be mysteriously aborted before the kingdom of God appeared. Thus there would again be a desecration of the temple, and so on. Dispensationalists like Pink have taken this approach much further than the ancient scribes and apocalyptists ever thought of doing: the whole business of Antiochus's military movements, as well as his establishment and cancellation of a covenant with Jews, and so forth, has to happen all over again. And if there is no temple for him to defile, then, by God, there will be another one. If he is to suspend Levitical sacrifices, then these sacrifices will have to be revived in the meantime. If he is to overthrow the Roman Empire, then there will have to be a new one in place for him to kick over like a sand castle when he comes.

Whether it ever occurred to Pink that he was throwing out the Protestant Reformation's insistence upon a single, literal sense of scripture (something ostensibly more important to dispensationalists than any other group), we do not know. But Pink was forthright in claiming he could discern multiple fulfillments of prophetic texts beyond the original, historical, literal meaning. "Many, if not the great majority of the prophecies—not only those pertaining to the Antichrist, but to other prominent objects of prediction—have at least a twofold, and frequently a threefold fulfillment. They have a local and immediate fulfillment; they have a continual and gradual fulfillment: and they have a final and exhaustive fulfillment."[11] "This is sometimes true with passages which contain prophecies concerning Christ. It is often the case in the prophets that the Holy Spirit is treating of something near at hand and then, without any warning, projects the view into the distant future."[12] Pink knew Daniel was concerned with Antiochus Epiphanes, and that that book was closed. But since the kingdom of God did not come to round off the story, why, then, the story would just have to be retold, this time including the proper ending. We will see in the next chapter how important it is to the dispensationalist view of prophecy to take it all as literally as possible, as distinct from Calvinists and Catholics, who interpret the old prophecies figuratively (as referring to the Christian Church, not the nation of Israel). And yet, to vindicate the Bible's prophetic accuracy, dispensationalists are forced to resort to hermeneutics like the following: "During the age of the church, God's prophetic time clock has stopped. The church age is the great parenthesis that exists between the sixty-ninth and seventieth week of Daniel's time prophecy in 9:24ff."[13] "The prophetic clock will begin to tick off the last week of the times of the gentiles, under similar geographical boundaries and political circumstance[s] to those which prevailed in Europe and the Near East when the time clock stopped over two thousand years ago."[14] "The age of the church intervenes between verses 8 and 9 of Matthew 24."[15]

Pink, thus allowing himself almost infinite freedom to chop and splice the text, proceeds with a virtually Kabbalistic creativity, midrashically expanding the Antichrist tradition even as he thinks merely to exegete it. To hear him tell it, the Bible speaks (to those with ears to hear) almost as much of Antichrist as it does of Christ. LaHaye and Jenkins have followed him in this, or at least in the results: much that Tsion Ben-Judah surmises of the exploits of the Antichrist about to transpire have no visible connection at all to any biblical text read literally. LaHaye and Jenkins do not seem to understand how Pink arrived at such conclusions, which they have inherited. LaHaye's counterpart, Ben-Judah, still thinks he is interpreting prophecy in a literal and straightforward manner, as when Jeanne Dixon predicted JFK's assassination. If LaHaye realized, as Pink (to say nothing of the evangelist Matthew) did, that any Jesus reference in the Old Testament texts must be an esoteric sense discernible only in retrospect by Christian believers, we would be spared the ludicrous charade of the good rabbi urging Jews to accept Jesus as Messiah by the chicanery of appealing to Old Testament texts ripped out of context.

DEFINING SHADOW

The utility of an "Antichrist" is that it defines one's concept of "Christ." If you can't tell what the Antichrist would be like, you don't have a Christ to define him against. We will see how the *Left Behind* books fail at just this point, for, in the end, their returning Jesus Christ bears an uncanny and disturbing resemblance to their Antichrist. Like Nicolae Carpathia, he is a tyrant who destroys his theological enemies, settles questions by mere fiat, and demands absolute and unconditional servility from everyone around him, even the whole human race— which he has ruthlessly decimated.

NOTES

1. Christopher Lee, ed., *Christopher Lee's Treasury of Terror* (New York: Pyramid Books, 1966), p. 5.

2. Arthur W. Pink, *The Antichrist* (Bible Truth Depot, 1923; repr., Minneapolis: Klock & Klock, 1979), p. 60.

3. Hermann Detering, "The Synoptic Apocalypse (Mar 13 par): A Document from the Time of Bar Kochba," *Journal of Higher Criticism* 7, no. 2 (Fall 2000): 161–210.

4. I think we can expect sooner or later to hear rumors that Saddam Hussein escaped the noose, that one of his many doubles was killed in his place, and some Saddam pretender will arise to lead Sunni insurgents.

5. Peake as cited in T. Francis Glasson, *The Second Advent: The Origin of the New Testament Doctrine*, 2nd rev. ed. (London: Epworth Press, 1947), p. 183. Johann Albrecht Bengel, *Gnomon*, commenting on 2 Thessalonians 2, cited in J. Stuart Russell, *The Parousia: A Study of the New Testament Doctrine of Our Lord's Second Coming* (London: T. Fisher Unwin, 1887; repr., Grand Rapids, MI: Baker Book House, 1983), p. 188, called it the belief of the ancients. By the way, this would mean the epistle is pseudepigraphical, as many other signs indicate. The next to come after Claudius was *Nero*, the antichrist *par excellence*. So this is all retrospective! It presupposes Nero's persecution, especially of Paul!

6. George R. Beasley-Murray, *Jesus and the Kingdom of God* (Grand Rapids, MI: Eerdmans, 1986), p. 329, cited by Gregory C. Jenks, *The Origins and Early Development of the Antichrist Myth* (New York: Walter de Gruyter, 1991), p. 205.

7. Wilhelm Bousset, *The Antichrist Legend: A Chapter in Christian and Jewish Folklore*, trans. A. H. Keane (London: Hutchinson and Co., 1896; repr., New York: AMS Press, n.d.), pp. 79–84.

8. Pink, *Antichrist*, p. 168.

9. *Against Marcion*, Ante-Nicene Fathers III, pp. 463–64, quoted in Jenks, *Origins and Early Development*, p. 73.

10. Pink, *Antichrist*, p. 157.

11. Ibid., p. 11.

12. Ibid., p. 140.

13. Walter K. Price, *The Coming Antichrist* (Neptune, NJ: Loizeaux Brothers, 1974; 2nd ed., 1985), p. 119.

14. Ibid., p. 177.

15. Ibid., pp. 111–12.

Chapter Four

THE SECOND COMING

"Jesus' moral teachings must be understood as a mere 'interim ethic'—designed and appropriate only for the interim, which Jesus firmly believed to be quite brief, before the kingdom of God would come with power. Schweitzer's result implies not only that Jesus' ethic is inapplicable today but that it has never *been applicable and that Jesus' most central conviction was wrong."*

—Walter Kaufmann, *The Faith of a Heretic*[1]

How did the early Christians first come to imagine that Jesus Christ would return to judge the world he once came to save? The obvious and traditional answer is that Jesus himself taught such an expectation, and at some length. But as with many obvious and traditional answers, this one would be wrong, as I hope to demonstrate in this chapter.

PARABLES OF CRISIS

Are there not a number of parables in which Jesus emphasizes the duty of his disciples to be busy about their assigned tasks, running the Church, until he may come to evaluate their performance? These would certainly count as predictions of the Second Coming of Jesus Christ, would they not?

It is like a man going on a journey, when he leaves home and puts his servants in charge, each with his work, and commands the doorkeeper to be on the watch. Watch therefore—for you do not know when the master of the house will come, in the evening, or at midnight, or at cockcrow, or in the morning—lest he come suddenly and find you asleep. (Mark 13:34–36)

Then the kingdom of heaven shall be compared to ten maidens who took their lamps and went to meet the bridegroom. Five of them were foolish, and five were wise. For when the foolish took their lamps, they took no oil with them; but the wise took flasks of oil with their lamps. As the bridegroom was delayed, they all slumbered and slept. But at midnight there was a cry, "Behold, the bridegroom! Come out to meet him." Then all those maidens rose and trimmed their lamps. And the foolish said to the wise, "Give us some of your oil, for our lamps are going out." But the wise replied, "Perhaps there will not be enough for us and for you; go rather to the dealers and buy for yourselves." And while they went to buy, the bridegroom came, and those who were ready went in with him to the marriage feast; and the door was shut. Afterward the other maidens came also, saying, "Lord, lord, open to us." But he replied, "Truly, I say to you, I do not know you." Watch therefore, for you know neither the day nor the hour. (Matt. 25:1–13)

For it will be as when a man going on a journey called his servants and entrusted to them his property; to one he gave five talents, to another two, to another one, to each according to his ability. Then he went away. He who had received the five talents went at once and traded with them; and he made five talents more. So also, he who had the two talents made two talents more. But he who had received the one talent went and dug in the ground and hid his master's money. Now after a long time the master of those servants came and settled accounts with them. And he who had received the five talents came forward, bringing five talents more, saying, "Master, you delivered to me five talents; here I have made five talents more." His master said to him, "Well done, good and faithful servant; you have been faithful over a little, I will set you over much; enter into the joy of your master." And he also who had the two talents came forward, saying, "Master, you delivered to me two talents; here I have made two talents more." His master said to him, "Well done, good and faithful servant; you have been faithful over a little, I will set you over much; enter into the joy of your master." He also who had received the one talent came forward, saying, "Master, I knew you to be a hard man, reaping where you did not sow, and gathering where you did not winnow; so I was afraid, and I went and hid your talent in the ground. Here you have what is yours." But his master answered him, "You wicked and slothful servant! You knew that I reap where I have not sowed, and gather where I have not winnowed? Then you ought to have invested my money with the bankers, and at my coming I should have received what was my own with interest. So take the talent from him, and give it to him who has the ten talents. For to every one who has will more be given, and he will have abundance; but from him who has not, even what he has will be taken away. And cast the worthless servant into the outer darkness; there men will weep and gnash their teeth." (Matt. 25:14–30)

Peter said, "Lord, are you telling this parable for us or for all?" And the Lord said, "Who then is the faithful and wise steward, whom his master will set over his household, to give them their portion of food at the proper time? Blessed is that servant whom his master when he comes will find so doing. Truly, I say to you, he will set him over all his possessions. But if that servant says to himself, 'My master is delayed in coming,' and begins to beat the menservants and the maid-servants, and to eat and drink and get drunk, the master of that servant will come on a day when he does not expect him and at an hour he does not know, and will punish him, and put him with the unfaithful. And that servant who knew his master's will, but did not make ready or act according to his will, shall receive a severe beating. But he who did not know, and did what deserved a beating, shall receive a light beating. Every one to whom much is given, of him will much be required; and of him to whom men commit much they will demand the more." (Luke 12:41–48)

As they now stand, that is, in the redactional contexts into which the evangelists Mark, Matthew, and Luke have placed them, the parables do indeed warn Christians to "look alive" in case the Second Coming of Christ should occur unexpectedly, as in the old Lenny Bruce joke in which Jesus Christ strolls into Saint Patrick's Cathedral and the priest on duty hurries to the office of the cardinal and breathlessly exclaims, "Your Holiness, that's Jesus Christ out there! What should we do?" His superior replies, "Look busy!"

In C. H. Dodd's great book *The Parables of the Kingdom*, he suggests these parables might originally have had a very different point, one preserved in other parables that were never reinterpreted as dealing with a future, Second Coming of Jesus.[2]

> And he began to speak to them in parables. "A man planted a vineyard, and set a hedge around it, and dug a pit for the wine press, and built a tower, and let it out to tenants, and went into another country. When the time came, he sent a servant to the tenants, to get from them some of the fruit of the vineyard. And they took him and beat him, and sent him away empty-handed. Again he sent to them another servant, and they wounded him in the head, and treated him shamefully. And he sent another, and him they killed; and so with many others, some they beat and some they killed. He had still one other, a beloved son; finally he sent him to them, saying, 'They will respect my son.' But those tenants said to one another, 'This is the heir; come, let us kill him, and the inheritance will be ours.' And they took him and killed him, and cast him out of the vineyard. What will the owner of the vineyard do? He will come and destroy the tenants, and give the vineyard to others." (Mark 12:1–9)

> But he said to him, "A man once gave a great banquet, and invited many; and at the time for the banquet he sent his servant to say to those who had been invited, 'Come; for all is now ready.' But they all alike began to make excuses. The first said to him, 'I have bought a field, and I must go out and see it; I pray you, have me excused.' And another said, 'I have bought five yoke of oxen, and I go to examine them; I pray you, have me excused.' And another said, 'I have married

a wife, and therefore I cannot come.' So the servant came and reported this to his master. Then the householder in anger said to his servant, 'Go out quickly to the streets and lanes of the city, and bring in the poor and maimed and blind and lame.' And the servant said, 'Sir, what you commanded has been done, and still there is room.' And the master said to the servant, 'Go out to the highways and hedges, and compel people to come in, that my house may be filled. For I tell you, none of those men who were invited shall taste my banquet.'" (Luke 14:16–24)

These last two parables, those of the wicked tenants and the great supper, as they are usually called, face the hearer with a challenge to read the signs of the times around him *right now*, or in the day of Jesus' public ministry. It is obvious in the case of the wicked tenants that Jesus means to challenge the stewardship over the Jewish commonwealth exercised by the priestly and scribal establishments. They have failed to render God his due crop of repentance and faithful service at the time he has come demanding it. The great supper chides the same groups for their indifference to the preaching of John the Baptist and/or Jesus: God's invitation to repent and gain salvation has met with the cold shoulder on the part of those complacent sophisticates who can no longer recognize their own mediocrity. Much the same point is made in Revelation 3:15–19 and Matthew 3:7–10. *Now* is the day you did not think would come so soon, or at all. *Now* you are held accountable. And in precisely the same way, Dodd suggested, the other parables of faithful and unfaithful servants were originally aimed at awakening Jesus' contemporaries to their danger. But what was the implicit threat if they still did not repent? Probably the wrath of Rome, which eventually did fall like the headman's ax.

And as for the parable of the talents (Matt. 25:14–30, see pp. 90–91), the focus need not go beyond the responsibility of each individual before God. Is any other interpretation so natural and striking as the one whereby the servants stand for three possibilities for your own efforts to make something of your life while you still have it to invest in something? Before the loan of it is called in by the God who entrusted you with seventy years—or if by reason of strength, eighty—see that you take the risk to make something of yourself! This need have nothing at all to do with a future coming of Christ or any apocalyptic scenario. The departure and return of the boss is just part of the narrative frame, the window dressing.

So, even if these sayings should chance to go back to a historical Jesus, they would not necessarily have predicted a Second Coming. And, on second thought, do any of the parables listed above require the framework of a future, Second Coming, either? Dodd's point was that they do not, and we have no business reading in later dogma. Yes, it is true that the Second Coming doctrine is held by the evangelists themselves, so we can hardly say it is alien to the context in which the parables now appear. But in terms of form criticism, we have to distinguish between what a parable may originally have meant, on its own terms, and what it came to mean later, to new readers or hearers. So when we isolate the parable from its current context, we have only the evidence of the parable itself to consider, not what the evangelist thought it meant or made it mean. After all, the parable of the lost sheep is placed in quite different contexts in Matthew 18:12–14, where it refers to pastoral care within the Christian congregation, and in Luke 15:1–7, where it defends Jesus' outreach to notorious sinners. Which of these is the original meaning, if either? (Even if Jesus himself told the parable twice in different circumstances, as apologists would have it, the point is the same, only it would be Jesus who has reapplied a parable that had an earlier meaning, and we would still have to try to decide which was original.) And there is nothing in those parables of vigilant stewards and prudential bridesmaids that requires a reference to the Second Coming. The point, as we read it in the Gospels' context, may well be to be vigilant for the long haul, but as self-contained stories, these parables seem to have a different time reference: Now is the time! Wake up!

SON OF MAN SAYINGS

There is a small group of sayings in which Jesus is heard predicting the coming of the Son of Man in judgment or to vindicate his followers. But it is extremely unlikely that any of these go back to a historical Jesus. For one thing, one must learn not to read the text in a facile way through the lenses of Christian faith, knowing the outcome of the story and assuming it would all be as clear to the characters on the scene as it is to the "clued-in" reader. Remember that, according to the story itself, the disciples were far from clear in their understanding about Jesus' future. The very notion of his coming arrest and execution seemed unthinkable, and when these events occurred, the men fled in terror, utterly unprepared. It does not read like they had a timetable of events in mind. Can we then imagine that they understood all (or any) of these sayings that presuppose a worked-out Christian eschatology? Did they grasp that Jesus would both die and rise and then return to earth to complete his messianic mission? The whole thing is anachronistic. The evangelists are talking theology to already Christian readers. The sayings make sense in that framework but hardly as quotes from a man in the historical circumstances of Jesus as the Gospels themselves describe them.

But there are other, more specific factors that rule out various of these sayings as authentic to a historical Jesus. Chief among them is the midrashic character of the sayings. They are composites of scripture verses, taken out of context atomistically, as was common in sectarian Jewish exegesis in ancient and medieval times. Such sayings, put into the mouth of the Jesus character, are the result of careful scribal labors. It is just absurd to imagine Jesus himself cribbing half lines from this and that verse and parroting them as his own spontaneous comments. In fact, such sayings would have the phony, flat effect of Jenkins's dud of a climax in *Glorious Appearing*, when Jesus comes down from heaven, breaking the silence of the ages—and all he does is drone Bible quote after Bible quote! Given the hypersensitive audience he knew he was writing for, Jenkins realized he dared not "presume" to have Jesus say anything new or bold, lest he offend the scruples of "nothin' but the Bible" readers. But surely if there was a living, breathing historical Jesus, he would have spoken his own thoughts in his own words, rather than a hash of scripture phrases. First, consider the reply of Jesus at his trial:

> And the high priest stood up in the midst, and asked Jesus, "Have you no answer to make? What is it that these men testify against you?" But he was silent and made no answer. Again the high priest asked him, "Are you the Christ, the Son of the Blessed?" And Jesus said, "I am; and you will see the Son of man seated at the right hand of Power, and coming with the clouds of heaven." (Mark 14:60–62)

The scene as a whole is a rewrite of a similar scene in 1 Kings 22:24–27, in which the maverick prophet Micaiah has announced that Yahve has sent a lying spirit into the mouths of the court prophets who have merely rubber-stamped the king's disastrous military plans. His words still sound blasphemous to modern readers: the very thought that God should send false prophecy! What happens?

> Then Zedekiah the son of Chenaanah came near and struck Micaiah on the cheek, and said, "How did the Spirit of Yahve go from me to speak to you?" And Micaiah said, "Behold, you shall see on that day when you go into an inner chamber to hide yourself." And the king of Israel said, "Seize Micaiah, and take him back to Amon the governor of the city and to Joash the king's son; and say, 'Thus says the king, "Put this fellow in prison, and feed him with scant fare of bread and water, until I come in peace."'"

John must have known the origin of the story, too, as he has borrowed a feature of it Mark didn't; he has a flunky of the high priest slap Jesus for his insolence (John 18:22). But note how Mark copies 2 Kings, having Jesus answer a question, as Micaiah did, beginning with the words "You will see . . ." And the interview comes to a precipitous conclusion, with orders for the rogue prophet to be taken away to the authorities. So the scene itself is artificial and fictitious. Now, as to the Son of Man saying, as Norman Perrin has shown,[3] it is a midrashic conflation of three scripture passages much loved by early Christians. The predicted "coming of the Son of man in the clouds of heaven" comes from Daniel 7:13:

> I saw in the night visions,
> and behold, with the clouds of heaven
> there came one like a son of man,
> and he came to the Ancient of Days
> and was presented before him.

His session at the right hand of God comes from the widely quoted Psalm 110:1 (see Mark 12:36; Acts 7:56; Rom. 8:34; Col. 3:1; Heb. 1:13):

> Yahve says to my lord:
> "Sit at my right hand,
> till I make your enemies your footstool."

The notion that the tables will be turned, that those who now condemn Jesus to death will soon behold him coming to take vengeance ("You will see . . .") comes from Zechariah 12:10b:

> When they look on him whom they have pierced, they shall mourn
> for him, as one mourns for an only child, and weep bitterly over him,
> as one weeps over a first-born.

The same passage is quoted in Revelation 1:7:

> Behold, he is coming with the clouds, and every eye will see him,
> every one who pierced him; and all the tribes of the earth will wail
> on account of him.

Matthew also adds it to his version of the Synoptic Apocalypse (or Olivet Discourse), combining it with Daniel 7:13:

> Then will appear the sign of the Son of man in heaven, and then *all the tribes of the earth shall mourn*, and they will see *the Son of man coming on the clouds* of heaven with power and great glory; and he will send out his angels with a loud trumpet call, and they will gather his elect from the four winds, from one end of heaven to the other. (Matt. 24:30–31)

Now let us compare two versions of a Son of Man saying and see how one appears to be a development of the other. The first is Mark's version:

> For whoever is ashamed of me and of my words in this adulterous and sinful generation, of him will the Son of man also be ashamed, when he comes in the glory of his Father with the holy angels. (Mark 8:38)

This one clearly does envision a coming of the Son of Man in judgment, *though not necessarily to the earth*. As Robinson points out, nothing in this verse goes beyond the parameters of Daniel 7:13, where the "coming of the Son of man" is *to* the throne of God. But the version drawn by both Matthew and Luke from the shared Q Document is significantly different.

> Every one who acknowledges me before men, the Son of man also will acknowledge before the angels of God; but he who denies me before men will be denied before the angels of God. (Luke 12:8–9/Matt. 10:32–33)

There is nothing about the anticipated judgment occurring on earth, much less about the Son of Man coming to earth from heaven. It looks as if the Markan version is the later, and that oral tradition (or Markan redaction) has added the circumstances of the judgment in order to satisfy Christian curiosity. Thus the Second Coming motif is not original to the saying even if Jesus did say it.

In both Markan and Q versions, the Son of Man is called as witness in the judgment. He is not the judge, as later sayings will make him, giving him a major raise in status. No, here the idea is merely that those who repudiated Jesus' words when things got hot will be disappointed if they think to appeal to Jesus as a character witness on that day. Note, too, that the angels are said to belong to the retinue of God, not of Jesus himself. But both these elements change in a set of sayings that appear only in Matthew.

> The Son of man will send *his* angels, and they will gather out of *his* kingdom all causes of sin and all evildoers. (Matt. 14:41)

> For the Son of man is to come with *his* angels in the glory of his Father, and then *he* will repay every man for what he has done. (Matt. 16:27)

> When the Son of man comes in his glory, and all the angels with him, then he will sit on *his* glorious throne. (Matt. 25:31)

The Son of Man is pictured here as king and judge (the same thing in ancient times), not merely as witness, and as possessing his own angelic host.[4] Matthew has heightened the Christology in these sayings of his own creation. Jesus did not say them.

Matthew is the only evangelist to include this very difficult saying:

> When they persecute you in one town, flee to the next; for truly, I say to you, you will not have gone through all the towns of Israel, before the Son of man comes. (Matt. 10:23)

Albert Schweitzer tried valiantly to make sense of this saying on the assumption that Jesus really did say it, and on the occasion reported in Matthew's Gospel: just before he sent out the twelve on their preaching tour in Galilee.[5] Schweitzer reasoned that Jesus must have privately expected to be supernaturally transfigured into a glorified body and to take the messianic throne during the following month or so, before the disciples could have finished their mission. He was much surprised and dismayed when they got back and little had changed. Virtually no scholars follow Schweitzer in this view. It seems much more likely that, since the Mission Charge (to which Matthew has added 10:23) was included in the Gospels (see also Mark 6:7–13; Matthew 10:1–23; Luke 9:1–6) as a handbook for Christian missionaries, anticipations, as it were, of the Great Commission, then Matthew 10:23 was aimed at early Christian missionaries contemporary with Matthew and the writing of his Gospel. Matthew simply placed the saying where he did *topically*, never thinking to imply Jesus had meant he would come in apocalyptic glory in the next couple of weeks! Surely that is the point, but it also means the saying does not go back to a historical Jesus. It merely represents the mission agenda of Jewish Christians who did not approve of preaching the Gospel to the gentiles (as in Acts 10–11): "Go nowhere among the gentiles, and enter no town of the Samaritans, but go rather to the lost sheep of the house of Israel" (Matt. 10:5–6) because you'll have your hands full missionizing the latter.

Matthew has redactionally manufactured yet another saying about the "coming of the Son of man," Matthew 16:28, "Truly I say to you, there are some standing here who will not taste death before they see the Son of man coming in his kingdom." But does the saying not have the ring of prior familiarity? Indeed it does, for we recall the original in Mark 9:1, "Truly, I say to you, there are some standing here who will not taste death before they see that the kingdom of God has come with power." This version, however, lacks the Son of Man reference. For Mark's original, it was the kingdom of God, not the Son of Man, whose coming the onlookers would witness.

Luke alone has a saying, again, clearly based on Daniel 7:13: "When the Son of man comes, will he find faith on earth?" (Luke 18:8). The trouble with this one is, it is not quite clear that it refers to a Second Coming at all. Rather it recalls the Q passage about the centurion's slave (Luke 7:2–10/Matt. 8:5–13), where Jesus announces, "I tell you, not even in Israel have I found such faith!"

THE SYNOPTIC APOCALYPSE

The most prominent teaching on the Second Coming of Jesus is the Synoptic Apocalypse, or the Olivet Discourse. With this one, the trouble starts when we notice the flagrant contradiction between the approach taken in this chapter and that ascribed to Jesus elsewhere. In Luke 17:20–21 we read:

> Being asked by the Pharisees when the kingdom of God was coming, he answered them, "The kingdom of God is not coming with signs to be observed; nor will they say, 'Lo, here it is!' or 'There!' for behold, the kingdom of God is within [or, possibly: "in the midst of"] you."

Granted, it is entirely possible that neither viewpoint was that of the historical Jesus (if there was one), but both cannot be.

Then there is the now familiar problem of Mark 13 being a cento of fragments from the Old Testament. That is precisely what we would expect of an apocalyptic tract, because all apocalypses were this way, with Revelation as the prime example (most of it is derived directly from Zechariah, Ezekiel, and Daniel). Remember, too, that all apocalypses were *pseudonymous*, and not by accident: they were all attempts to gain attention for the work by putting it forward under the name of some ancient worthy who had considerable clout. It is no use asking whether a prophet might write an apocalypse (and "write" is the word; they are all patently literary compositions, not transcripts of prophetic preaching like the Old Testament books of the prophets). A real prophet would simply have held forth in his own name—like John the Baptist did. The fact that we are reading an apocalypse at all means it is pseudonymous. Thus this one does not go back to Jesus. As for the dependence of Mark 13 upon the Old Testament, let's get specific.

> Mark 13:7, "And when you hear of wars and rumors of wars, do not be alarmed; this must take place, but the end is not yet," comes from Daniel 11:44, "But rumors from the East and from the North will dis-

turb him, and he will go forth with great wrath to destroy and anni-
hilate many."

Mark 13:8, "For nation will rise against nation, and kingdom against
kingdom; there will be earthquakes in various places, there will be
famines; this is but the beginning of the birth-pangs," comes from
Isaiah 19:2: "And I will stir up Egyptians against Egyptians, and they
will fight, every man against his brother and every man against his
neighbor, city against city, kingdom against kingdom" and/or from
2 Chronicles 15:6: "They were broken in pieces, nation against
nation and city against city, for God troubled them with every sort
of distress."

Mark 13:12, "And brother will deliver up brother to death, and the
father his child, and children will rise against parents and have them
put to death," derives from Micah 7:6: "For the son treats the father
with contempt, the daughter rises up against her mother, the
daughter-in-law against her mother-in-law; a man's enemies are the
men of his own house."

Mark 13:14, "But when you see the abomination of desolation set up
where it ought not to be (let the reader understand), then let those
who are in Judea flee to the mountains," is based on Daniel 2:11, "And
from the time that the continual burnt offering is taken away, and the
abomination that makes desolate is set up, there shall be a thousand
two hundred and ninety days," as well as Genesis 19:17, "And when
they had brought them forth, they said, 'Flee for your life; do not
look back or stop anywhere in the valley; flee to the hills, lest you be
consumed.'"

Mark 13:19, "For in those days there will be such tribulation as has not
been from the beginning of the creation which God created until
now, and never will be," comes from Daniel 12:1 "At that time shall
arise Michael, the great prince who has charge of your people. And
there shall be a time of trouble, such as never has been since there
was a nation till that time; but at that time your people shall be delivered, every one whose name shall be found written in the book."

Mark 13:22 warns that "False Christs and false prophets will arise and show signs and wonders, to lead astray, if possible, the elect." This is from Deuteronomy 13:2, "And if the sign or the wonder come to pass, of which he spoke to you, saying, 'Let us go after other gods alien to you, and let us serve them,'" and so on.

Mark 13:24, "But in those days, after that tribulation, the sun will be darkened, and the moon will not give its light," comes from Isaiah 13:10, "For the stars of the heavens and their constellations will not give their light; the sun will be dark at its rising and the moon will not shed its light."

Mark 13:25, "and the stars will be falling from heaven, and the powers in the heavens will be shaken," is taken from Isaiah 34:4 in the Greek Septuagint (LXX): "And all the powers of heaven shall melt, and the sky shall be rolled up like a scroll. And all the stars shall fall like leaves from a vine, as leaves fall from a fig tree." The original Hebrew would not make the required point: "All the host of heaven shall rot away, and the skies roll up like a scroll. All their host shall fall, as leaves fall from the vine, like leaves falling from the fig tree." Can we really imagine Jesus would be quoting the Greek translation of the Old Testament to fellow Aramaic-speaking Palestinian Jews?

Mark 13:26, "And then they will see the Son of man coming in clouds with great power and glory," comes, of course, from Daniel 7:13: "I saw in the night visions, and behold, with the clouds of heaven there came one like a son of man, and he came to the Ancient of Days and was presented before him."

Mark 13:27, "And then he will send out the angels, and gather his elect from the four winds, from the ends of the earth to the ends of heaven," comes from Zechariah 2:6 (LXX): "'Ho, ho, flee from the land of the North,' says the Lord: 'for I will gather you from the four winds of heaven, saith the Lord.'" Again, the original Hebrew, which the historical Jesus would have quoted, does not quite make the desired point: "'Ho! Ho! Flee from the land of the North,' says Yahve; 'for I have spread you abroad as the four winds of the heavens,' says

Yahve." Another source is Deuteronomy 30:4, "If your outcasts are in the uttermost parts of heaven, from there Yahve your God will gather you, and from there he will fetch you."

There is also a form-critical consideration to be brought against the authenticity of the Olivet Discourse. It begins as a private revelation to Jesus' inner circle: "And as he sat on the Mount of Olives opposite the temple, Peter and James and John and Andrew asked him privately, 'Tell us, when will this be, and what will be the sign when these things are all to be accomplished?'" (Mark 13:3–4). Why not all the disciples, or even the public, as Luke has it? This is a dead giveaway that we are reading a late text added to the common Gospel tradition, covering its tracks by means of the tired fiction that it was a private revelation to a few, only recently divulged, like the Transfiguration vision (Mark 9:9), or the empty tomb angelophany (Mark 16:8). "Uh, don't worry; it's the real thing, all right. It's only just now been declassified." That's the ticket. Numerous esoteric revelations in the Nag Hammadi texts start out the same way. The Apocryphon of James begins: "Since you asked that I send you a secret book which was revealed to me and Peter by the Lord, I could not turn you away or gainsay you, but I have written it in the Hebrew alphabet and sent it to you, and you alone. . . . [T]ake care not to rehearse this text to many—this that the Savior did not wish to tell to all of us, his twelve disciples."[6] Likewise, the book of Thomas the Contender: "The secret words that the Savior spoke to Judas Thomas which I, even I, Mathaias, wrote down while I was walking, listening to them speak with one another."[7]

And let the reader understand: though the Gospel of Mark is constantly having Jesus speak over the heads of his ostensible audience in the story, direct to the reader,[8] Mark 13:14 explicitly draws attention to itself *as a written text*: "When you see the abomination of desolation standing where it ought not to be (let the reader understand) . . ." This goes beyond anything of the kind elsewhere in Mark, but it sounds exactly like notes to the reader found in the text of Revelation: "This calls for wisdom: let him who has understanding reckon the number of the Beast, for it is the number of a man, its number being six hundred sixty six" (13:18). Thus it seems more likely that we are reading a text, composed as a text, not a transcript of a speech given orally and off the cuff.

So where did the Olivet Discourse come from? Timothee Colani figured it out.[9] He called attention to a hitherto puzzling comment in Eusebius's *Ecclesiastical History*:

> But the people of the church in Jerusalem had been commanded by a revelation, vouchsafed to approved men there before the war, to leave the city and to dwell in a certain town of Perea called Pella. And when those that believed in Christ had come thither from Jerusalem, then, as if the royal city of the Jews and the whole land of Judea were entirely destitute of holy men, the judgment of God at length overtook those who had committed such outrages against Christ and his apostles, and totally destroyed that generation of impious men. (3:5:3)

Mark 13:5–20 is that oracle of impending doom. And its import was that Jerusalem was about to be destroyed, not the whole world, as it now reads. As John A. T. Robinson showed, verses 24–27 have been added, some time after the fall of Jerusalem, in order to update the tract and give it new currency, expanding its horizons at a time when things looked grim, to make the apocalypse predict the end of the age.[10] The text flows better without that paragraph, and verses 24–27 drop the second-person address evident in the rest. Also, this section contains scripture quotes that make the required sense only in the Greek, which cannot go back to Jesus.[11]

I know some readers automatically stop listening once the suggestion is broached that this or that inconvenient verse is a later addition. They start cracking jokes about "surgical exegesis" and laugh the whole thing off. But I would remind such a reader that such treatment of the text of the Synoptic Apocalypse is no mere hypothesis, as we have superabundant evidence of it as soon as we cross-reference the versions of Matthew (chapters 24–26) and Luke (chapters 17 and 21). Both versions have chopped and spliced, rewritten and revised Mark's original. It should not seem odd to suggest that Mark had already begun the process. In fact, a consideration of what Matthew and Luke did to Mark's version makes you understand exactly what John was afraid of in Revelation 22:18–19: "I warn every one who hears the words of the prophecy of this book: if any one adds to them, God will add to him the plagues described in this book, and if any one takes away from the words of the book of this prophecy, God will take away his share in the tree of life and in the holy city, which are described in this book" (cf. Matt. 5:17–19).

In light of the addition of Mark 13:24–27, "the end" in verses 7 and 13 are now read as if referring to the end of the world, not to the end of Jerusalem as originally intended. Verse 10, about the universal preaching of the Gospel as a precondition for the end of the age, is secondary, as Henry Burton Sharman[12] saw—a new mission deadline, after they *did* finish with the towns of Israel (the earlier deadline preserved in Matt. 10:23). And this detail is of great interest for our dating of Mark's Gospel. Scholars (really, conservative apologists) like to date Mark as a whole just before or just after the fall of Jerusalem, given its prominence in Mark 13, but they err greatly in so doing. The impending fall of the city helps date only the Markan source, not the Gospel into which it has been grafted. And, again as per Sharman, the apocalypse of Mark 13 now presupposes *two* delays of the Second Coming (which itself represents a secondary stage in the document). The stipulation that the Gospel first be preached to all the towns of Israel (Matt. 10:23) already sounds like backpedaling: "I'll tell you why the return of Christ has been delayed: every Jew must have a chance to hear the Gospel before Jesus can bring the judgment; otherwise it wouldn't be fair. So let's stop griping about the delay and get busy! That way we can hasten it!" But then that goal was accomplished, and still nothing materialized. As Sharman says, the next expedient was to widen the scope, to make evangelism of all the nations a precondition for the Second Coming. It was an effort, not exactly to buy more time—as if one needed more time to accomplish a surprisingly difficult job—but rather to stall for time. "Look, I don't know *what's* keeping him, but I'm sure there's a very good explanation!" And how late must Mark be in that case? Nor is that the worst of it, as we shall see in the next chapter.

But let's not lose sight of the big picture: the Olivet Discourse does not go back to any historical Jesus. In any case, it was originally a prediction of the imminent doom of Jerusalem. It had nothing to do with the end of the world or the Second Coming of Jesus. That element entered the text *only once it was expanded with verses 24–27.* So we still have to ask: where did early Christians derive the notion that Jesus Christ would come a second time, if not from the teaching of Jesus himself?

"THE COMING OF THE LORD"

"The Jews did not speak of the *parousia* of the Messiah, they did not expect that he would descend with clouds from heaven. . . . [T]he first appearance of this idea in Judaism seems to be in Joshua ben Levi (c. 250 A.D.), who combines Dan. 7.13 with Zech. 9.9: 'If they (Israel) are worthy, he will come with the clouds of heaven; if they are not worthy, then lowly and riding on an ass.'"[13] So where did early Christians derive the idea of the (second) "coming" of Jesus Christ? As T. Francis Glasson showed, the Old Testament conception of the "coming of the Lord," of Adonai, or "the LORD" (Yahve), was reapplied to the "Lord Jesus."[14] Let us first follow Glasson in gathering some general "coming of the Lord" texts from the Old Testament, the language of which has plainly influenced the New Testament and other early Christian literature. Isaiah 2:10, 19, 21, reads,

Enter into the rock,
and hide in the dust
from before the terror of the LORD,
and from the glory of his majesty . . .

And men shall enter the caves of the rocks
and the holes of the ground,
from before the terror of the LORD,
and from the glory of his majesty,
when he rises to terrify the earth.

... to enter the caverns of the rocks
and the clefts of the cliffs,
from before the terror of the LORD,
and from the glory of his majesty,
when he rises to terrify the earth.

Surely this text has laid its stamp upon 2 Thessalonians 1:9: "They shall suffer the punishment of eternal destruction and exclusion from the presence of the Lord and from the glory of his might."

In Isaiah 40:3, "A voice cries: 'In the wilderness prepare the way of the LORD, make straight in the desert a highway for our God.'" In Luke 3:4–6 (and its parallels), the LORD Yahve has become the Lord Jesus: "As it is written in the book of the words of Isaiah the prophet, 'The voice of one crying in the wilderness: Prepare the way of the Lord, make his paths straight. Every valley shall be filled, and every mountain and hill shall be brought low, and the crooked shall be made straight, and the rough ways shall be made smooth; and all flesh shall see the salvation of God.'"

Two Isaiah texts will be used in order to cast the returning Jesus as the vengeful Yahve. Isaiah 42:13:

The LORD goes forth like a mighty man,
like a man of war he stirs up his fury;
he cries out, he shouts aloud,
he shows himself mighty against his foes.

Isaiah 63:1–6 asks,

Who is this that comes from Edom,
in crimsoned garments from Bozrah,
he that is glorious in his apparel,
marching in the greatness of his strength?
"It is I, announcing vindication,
mighty to save."
Why is your apparel red,
and your garments like his that treads in the wine press?
"I have trodden the wine press alone,
and from the peoples no one was with me;
I trod them in my anger
and trampled them in my wrath;
their lifeblood is sprinkled upon my garments,
and I have stained all my raiment.
For the day of vengeance was in my heart,
and my year of redemption has come.
I looked, but there was no one to help;
I was appalled, but there was no one to uphold;
so my own arm brought me victory,
and my wrath upheld me.
I trod down the peoples in my anger,
I made them drunk in my wrath,
and I poured out their lifeblood on the earth."

In Revelation 19:11–16, this vengeful Yahve has become a no longer meek and mild Lord Jesus:

Then I saw heaven opened, and behold, a white horse! He who sat upon it is called Faithful and True, and in righteousness he judges and makes war. His eyes are like a flame of fire, and on his head are many diadems; and he has a name inscribed which no one knows but himself. He is clad in a robe dipped in blood, and the name by which he is called is The Word of God. And the armies of heaven, arrayed in fine linen, white and pure, followed him on white horses. From his mouth issues a sharp sword with which to smite the nations, and he will rule them with a rod of iron; he will tread the wine press of the

fury of the wrath of God the Almighty. On his robe and on his thigh
he has a name inscribed, King of kings and Lord of lords.

In Isaiah, too, we find the origin of the apocalyptic imagery in 2
Thessalonians 1:8: "inflicting vengeance upon those who do not know
God and upon those who do not obey the gospel of our Lord Jesus."
Isaiah 66:15–18 reads:

> For by fire will the LORD execute judgment,
> and by his sword, upon all flesh;
> and those slain by the LORD shall be many.
> "Those who sanctify and purify themselves to go into the gardens,
> following one in the midst, eating swine's flesh and the abomination
> and mice, shall come to an end together," says the LORD.
> "For I know their works and their thoughts, and I am coming to
> gather all nations and tongues; and they shall come and shall see my
> glory."

Zechariah 14:3–5 says,

> Then the LORD will go forth and fight against those nations as when
> he fights on a day of battle. On that day his feet shall stand on the
> Mount of Olives which lies before Jerusalem on the east; and the
> Mount of Olives shall be split in two from east to west by a very wide
> valley; so that one half of the Mount shall withdraw northward, and
> the other half southward. And the valley of my mountains shall be
> stopped up, for the valley of the mountains shall touch the side of it;
> and you shall flee as you fled from the earthquake in the days of
> Uzziah king of Judah. Then the LORD your God will come, and all
> the holy ones with him.

Second Thessalonians 3:13 mines this passage:

> "so that he may establish your hearts unblamable in holiness before
> our God and Father, at the coming of our Lord Jesus with all his
> saints."

COMING FROM THE OLD TESTAMENT

Other Old Testament passages anticipating the coming of the Lord have also helped set the stage for the New Testament expectation of the return of Jesus Christ. These include Psalm 50:3–6:

> Our God comes, he does not keep silence,
> before him is a devouring fire,
> round about him a mighty tempest.
> He calls to the heavens above
> and to the earth, that he may judge his people:
> "Gather to me my faithful ones,
> who made a covenant with me by sacrifice!"
> The heavens declare his righteousness,
> for God himself is judge!

Psalm 68:1–8, originally a chant for the Levitical bearers of the Ark of the Covenant, is similar. And note the image of Yahve, a storm God, riding on the clouds like his Syrian counterpart, Baal Hadad. We must keep this image in mind when, in the New Testament, we read of the returning Christ "coming with the clouds."

> Let God arise, let his enemies be scattered;
> let those who hate him flee before him!
> As smoke is driven away, so drive them away;
> as wax melts before fire,
> let the wicked perish before God!
> But let the righteous be joyful;
> let them exult before God;
> let them be jubilant with joy!
> Sing to God, sing praises to his name;
> lift up a song to him who rides upon the clouds;
> his name is Yahve, exult before him!
> Father of the fatherless and protector of widows
> is God in his holy habitation.

God gives the desolate a home to dwell in;
he leads out the prisoners to prosperity;
but the rebellious dwell in a parched land.
O God, when you went forth before your people,
when you marched through the wilderness,
the earth quaked, the heavens poured down rain,
at the presence of God;
yon Sinai quaked at the presence of God,
the God of Israel.

From the ancient Hebrew New Year's enthronement festival comes Psalm 96:10, 13. Yahve's yearly enthronement has become the resurrection enthronement of the Lord Jesus at the right hand of God, from which he shall come in judgment:

Say among the nations, "Yahve reigns!
Yes, the world is established, it shall never be moved;
he will judge the peoples with equity."

Bow before the Yahve, for he comes,
for he comes to judge the earth.
He will judge the world with righteousness,
and the peoples with his truth.

It is well to ask oneself if the apocalyptic Jesus whose eyes are as a flame of fire can possibly be derived ultimately from the peaceful Socratic sage of Galilee who once dandled toddlers on his knee. No, the Jesus of New Testament apocalyptic comes "again," all right, but not from the Gospel. Rather, he "returns" from the Old Testament, where the war god Yahve issues forth upon humanity like a thundering cyclone. Consider these Isaiah passages:

Your dead shall live, their bodies shall rise.
O dwellers in the dust, awake and sing for joy!
For your dew is a dew of light,
and on the land of the shades you will let it fall . . .

For behold, Yahve is coming forth out of his place
to punish the inhabitants of the earth for their iniquity,
and the earth will disclose the blood shed upon her,
and will no more cover her slain. (Isa. 26:19, 21)

Say to those who are of a fearful heart,
"Be strong, fear not!
Behold, your God
will come with vengeance,
with the recompense of God.
He will come and save you." (Isa. 35:4)

For thus Yahve said to me,
"As a lion or a young lion growls over his prey,
and when a band of shepherds is called forth against him
is not terrified by their shouting
or daunted at their noise,
so Yahve Sabaoth will come down
to fight upon Mount Zion and upon its hill." (Isa. 31:4)

He saw that there was no man,
and wondered that there was no one to intervene;
then his own arm brought him victory,
and his righteousness upheld him.
He put on righteousness as a breastplate,
and a helmet of salvation upon his head;
he put on garments of vengeance for clothing,
and wrapped himself in fury as a mantle.
According to their deeds, so will he repay,
wrath to his adversaries, requital to his enemies;
to the coastlands he will render requital.
So they shall fear the name of Yahve from the west,
and his glory from the rising of the sun;
for he will come like a rushing stream,
which the wind of Yahve drives.
And he will come to Zion as Redeemer,
to those in Jacob who turn from transgression, says Yahve. (Isa. 59:16–20)

Behold, Yahve has proclaimed
to the end of the earth:
Say to the daughter of Zion,
"Behold, your salvation comes;
behold, his reward is with him,
and his recompense before him." (Isa. 62:11)

For behold, Yahve is coming forth out of his place,
and will come down and tread upon the high places of the earth.
(Micah 1:3)

"Sing and rejoice, O daughter of Zion; for lo, I come and I will
dwell in the midst of you," says Yahve. (Zech. 2:10)

THESSALONIAN THUNDER

Next, still following Glasson, let us compare some passages from the
apocalyptic sections of the Thessalonian epistles with their probable
roots in the Greek Old Testament. Keep in mind that, in our copies of
the Septuagint (LXX), the proper name "Yahve" is replaced with the
title "the Lord."

Second Thessalonians 1:7–8, "and to grant rest with us to you who
are afflicted, when the Lord Jesus is revealed from heaven with his
mighty angels in flaming fire, inflicting vengeance upon those who do
not know God and upon those who do not obey the gospel of our Lord
Jesus," seems clearly to be based on Isaiah 66:15 LXX: "For, behold, the
Lord will come as fire, and his chariots as a storm, to render his
vengeance with wrath, and his rebuke with a flame of fire."

Likewise, 2 Thessalonians 1:9, "They shall suffer the punishment of
eternal destruction and exclusion from the presence of the Lord and
from the glory of his might," must derive from Isaiah 2:10 LXX: "Now
therefore enter into the rocks, and hide yourselves in the earth, for fear
of the Lord, and by reason of the glory of his might, when he shall
arise to strike terribly the earth."

Second Thessalonians 1:12, "so that the name of our Lord Jesus may be glorified in you, and you in him, according to the grace of our God and the Lord Jesus Christ," comes from Isaiah 66:5 LXX: "Hear the words of the Lord, you who tremble at his word; speak, our brethren, to those who hate you and abominate you, that the name of the Lord may be glorified, and may appear your joy; but they shall be ashamed."

Second Thessalonians 1:10, "when he comes on that day to be glorified in his saints, and to be marveled at in all who have believed, because our testimony to you was believed," must reflect Isaiah 24:23 LXX: "And the brick shall decay, and the wall shall fall; for the Lord shall reign from out of Sion, and out of Jerusalem, and shall be glorified before his elders."

First Thessalonians 4:15–16, "For this we declare to you by the word of the Lord, that we who are alive, who are left until the coming of the Lord, shall not precede those who have fallen asleep. For the Lord himself will descend from heaven with a cry of command, with the archangel's call, and with the sound of the trumpet of God. And the dead in Christ will rise first," draws upon several Septuagint texts:

For, behold, *the Lord comes* forth out of his place, and *will come down*, and will go upon the high places of the earth. (Mic. 1:3 LXX)

And the sounds of the trumpet were waxing very much louder. Moses spoke, and God answered him with a voice. And *the Lord came down* upon mount Sina on the top of the mountain; and the Lord called Moses to the top of the mountain, and Moses went up. (Exod. 19:19–20 LXX)

And the Lord descended in a cloud, and stood near him there, and called the name of the Lord. (Exod. 34:5 LXX)

And *the Lord came down* in a cloud, and spoke to him, and took of the spirit that was upon him, and put it upon the seventy men who were elders; and when the spirit rested upon them, they prophesied and ceased. (Num. 11:25 LXX)

> *For thus said the Lord to me,* "As a lion would roar, or a lion's whelp over prey which he has taken, and *cry* over it, *until the mountains are filled with his voice,* and the animals are awe-struck and tremble at the fierceness of his wrath: so *the Lord of hosts shall descend* to fight upon the mount Sion, even upon her mountains." (Isa. 31:4 LXX)

This last passage with its apparent relation to 1 Thessalonians 4:15–16 raises an interesting question. Scholars debate whether the Thessalonian passage means to introduce its oracle of the Second Coming by reference to some prophecy of the Risen Jesus through a Christian prophet or rather a quotation from the historical Jesus. It may be neither one. Perhaps the Thessalonian author is merely reflecting in his phrase "This we declare to you by the word of the Lord" the Isaiah 31:4 text, "For thus said the Lord to me."[15]

First Thessalonians 3:13, "so that he may establish your hearts unblamable in holiness before our God and Father, at the coming of our Lord Jesus with all his saints," comes from Zechariah 14:5 LXX: "And the valley of my mountains shall be closed up, and the valley of the mountains shall be joined on to Jasod, and shall be blocked up as it was blocked up in the days of the earthquake, in the days of Ozias king of Juda; and the Lord my God shall come, and all the saints with him."

Finally, Glasson traces a whole set of theophany themes between Thessalonians and Septuagintal Isaiah, as follows:

The Lord's Coming:

Isaiah 26:21a LXX: "For behold, the Lord is coming forth out of his place to punish the inhabitants of the earth for their iniquity" finds numerous echoes throughout 1 Thessalonians, chapter 4, and 2 Thessalonians, chapter 1.

Judgment:

Isaiah 26:21 LXX: "For, behold, the Lord is bringing wrath from his holy place upon the dwellers on the earth; the earth also shall disclose her blood, and shall not cover her slain." Similarly, 2 Thessalonians 1:9: "Who shall be punished with everlasting destruction from the presence of the Lord, and from the glory of his power," as well as 2 Thessalonians 2:8: "And then the lawless one will be revealed, and the Lord Jesus will slay him with the breath of his mouth and destroy him by his appearing and his coming."

Resurrection:

Isaiah 26:19 LXX: "The dead shall rise, and they that are in the tombs shall be raised, and they that are in the earth shall rejoice: for the dew from you is healing to them: but the land of the ungodly shall perish" matches 1 Thessalonians 4:16: "For the Lord himself will descend from heaven with a cry of command, with the archangel's call, and with the sound of the trumpet of God. *And the dead in Christ will rise first.*"

The Last Trumpet:

Isaiah 27:13 LXX: "And it shall come to pass in that day, that they shall blow the great trumpet, and the lost ones in the land of the Assyrians shall come, and the lost ones in Egypt, and shall worship the Lord on the holy mountain in Jerusalem." We find the same elements in 1 Thessalonians 4:16: "For the Lord himself will descend from heaven with a cry of command, with the archangel's call, and *with the sound of the trumpet of God. And the dead in Christ will rise first.*"

Gathering of the Elect:

Isaiah 27:12 LXX: "And it shall come to pass in that day that God shall fence men off from the channel of the river as far as Rhinocorura; but you are to gather one by one the children of Israel." Compare 1 Thessalonians 4:17: "then we who are alive, who are left, shall be caught up together with them in the clouds to meet the Lord in the air; and so we shall always be with the Lord."

Pangs shall seize them on the Day of the Lord:

Isaiah 13:6, 8 LXX: "Howl, for the day of the Lord is near, and destruction from God shall arrive. . . . The elders shall be troubled, and pangs shall seize them, as of a woman in travail, and they shall mourn one to another, and shall be amazed, and shall change their countenance as a flame." A similar warning occurs in 1 Thessalonians 5:2–3: "For you yourselves know well that the day of the Lord will come like a thief in the night. When people say, 'There is peace and security,' then sudden destruction will come upon them as travail comes upon a woman with child, and there will be no escape."

Some have pointed out parallels between 1 and 2 Thessalonians and the Synoptic Apocalypse, as if to prove that the teachings of Jesus were already known to Paul when he wrote his earliest epistles. This claim is quite dubious. For one thing, the authorship of the Thessalonian letters has been in serious question ever since F. C. Baur in the nineteenth century.[16] For another, the Thessalonian parallels turn out on closer inspection to occur only with the secondary, redactional stages of Matthew's version: Jesus' "parousia," not that of the kingdom; *his* angels, not the Father's; his coming *to earth*, not just "in the clouds."[17]

WHO ARE YOU, LORD?

How did the Lord Yahve of the Old Testament passages come to be referred to as the Lord Jesus, who was consequently ascribed an apocalyptic advent of his own? That all depends upon the answer to a prior question: what did the early Christians mean by calling Jesus "Lord"?

One answer is provided by Wilhelm Bousset, the greatest scholar of the Antichrist tradition, to whose work I referred in the previous chapter. In Bousset's masterpiece *Kyrios Christos*, he argued very convincingly that once the Christian Gospel took root outside of Palestine, especially in places like Syrian Antioch, a church composed of ex-pagan gentiles and hellenized Jews, the Jewish Messiah Jesus came to be interpreted along the lines of the *Kyrioi*, "Lords," of the Mystery Religions. The Lords were savior deities subordinate in rank beneath the classical Olympian, Egyptian, and other elder gods. Such younger gods seemed nearer to hand to poor mortals and readier to come to their aid, at least according to their evangelists and their myths. Asclepius, Apollo's son, outdid his divine father in popularity because of his ubiquitous healing shrines. Mithras was more popular than Ahura Mazda, whom he had once served, because Mithras showed the way, through initiations, past the planetary gods to eternal bliss in heaven. Osiris had risen from the dead and could pass on the privilege to his own initiates. And so on. The classical, elder deities were the "gods," the younger tier the "lords," and both were worshiped, as 1 Corinthians 8:5–6 attests: "For although there may be so-called gods in heaven or on earth—as indeed there are many 'gods' and many 'lords'—yet for us there is one God, the Father, from whom are all things and for whom we exist, and one Lord, Jesus Christ, through whom are all things and through whom we exist." Jesus would have qualified as a Lord, his Father as a God. And Jesus, too, had bridged the gap between humanity and his divine Father. Like many of the Mystery Cult saviors, he had died and risen from the dead. He, too, offered salvation through rituals including a sacred meal and immersion. When these bilingual worshipers called Jesus "Lord" (whether the Aramaic *Mar*, as in the invocation *Maranatha*, or the Greek *Kyrios*, as in the Greek New Testament), this is what they would have meant. Once such Christians began paging through the Septuagint Bible, well beloved of their Jewish members, they would have begun reading the numerous references to "the Lord" (as the LXX rendered the divine Tetragrammaton) as if they referred to Jesus.

I remain convinced that Bousset's reconstruction of Christological evolution is quite sound.[18] But there are alternate possibilities.

Margaret Barker makes a strong case that the Deuteronomic attempt to streamline theology and reduce traditional Israelite polytheism to monotheistic simplicity never fully succeeded on a popular level. The old worship continued despite official disapproval, even if a few cosmetic adjustments were required. As I discussed in the first chapter, Israel had once worshiped a king of gods, El Elyon, "God Most High," a god "ancient in days," as well as his son Yahve, originally the patron deity of Israel and Judah but who had attained supremacy after killing the dragons Leviathan and Rahab and creating the world from their remains. In his battle with the chaos monsters, Yahve had, like Marduk, Tammuz, Baal, and others, died and risen from the dead, as ritually celebrated with the festal acclamation "Yahve lives!" (Pss. 18:46).[19] Barker suggests that the early Christians were Jews who cherished the old faith, long interdicted by the (hated) priesthood but surviving on a grassroots level.[20] For them, Jesus simply was a theophany, an earthly visitation of Yahve. When he spoke of his Father, he spoke of El Elyon. If he died and rose, that, too, was believed of Yahve. Thus there was not a "transfer" of Septuagintal "Lord" language from the Old Testament Yahve to the New Testament Jesus, for they were one and the same from the beginning. To be sure, Jesus was Yahve in human form, but, come to think of it, Yahve had always occupied human form, as when he used to walk with Adam and Eve in the garden shade or when he visited Abraham at his camp fire. Jesus simply *was* Yahve.[21] And thus, if Yahve had been expected to come in judgment, so would Jesus.

NOTES

1. Walter Kauffman, *The Faith of a Heretic* (Garden City, NY: Doubleday Anchor, 1963), p. 235.
2. C. H. Dodd, *The Parables of the Kingdom*, rev. ed., especially chap. 5, "Parables of Crisis" (New York: Scribner's, 1961), pp. 122–39.
3. Norman Perrin, "Mark 14:62: The End Product of a Christian Pesher

Tradition?" in Perrin, *A Modern Pilgrimage in New Testament Christology* (Philadelphia: Fortress Press, 1974), pp. 10–18.

4. John A. T. Robinson, *Jesus and His Coming* (Philadelphia: Westminster Press, 1957, 2nd ed., 1979), p. 55.

5. Albert Schweitzer, *The Mystery of the Kingdom of God: The Secret of Jesus' Messiahship and Passion,* trans. Walter Lowrie (1914; repr., New York: Schocken Books, 1964), pp. 88, 150, 208, 233.

6. Francis E. James, trans., in *The Nag Hammadi Library,* ed. James M. Robinson, 3rd rev. ed. (San Francisco: Harper & Row, 1988), p. 30.

7. John D. Turner, trans., in Robinson, *Nag Hammadi Library,* p. 201.

8. Robert M. Fowler, *Let the Reader Understand: Reader-Response Criticism and the Gospel of Mark* (Minneapolis: Fortress Press, 1991).

9. Timothee Colani, "The Little Apocalypse of Mark 13," trans. Nancy Wilson, *Journal of Higher Criticism* 10, no. 1 (Spring 2003): 41–47. Excerpted from Colani, *Jesus-Christ et les croyances messianiques de son temps,* 1864, pp. 201–14.

10. Robinson, *Jesus and His Coming,* pp. 119–21.

11. Ibid., p. 57.

12. Henry Burton Sharman, *The Teaching of Jesus about the Future according to the Synoptic Gospels* (Chicago: University of Chicago Press, 1909), p. 145.

13. Robinson, *Jesus and His Coming,* p. 22.

14. T. Francis Glasson, *The Second Advent: The Origin of the New Testament Doctrine,* chap. 18, "The Coming of the Lord" (London: Epworth Press, 1947), pp. 162–79.

15. Werner Kramer, *Christ, Lord, Son of God,* trans. Brian Hardy, Studies in Biblical Theology series, no. 50 (Naperville, IL: Alec R. Allenson, 1966), p. 160, comes very close to saying this, but he does not quite zero in on this particular passage as the source. Call me a nitpicker.

16. Ferdinand Christian Baur, *Paul the Apostle of Jesus Christ: His Life and Works; His Epistles and Teachings,* trans. A. Menzies, vol. 2, chap. 7, "The Two Epistles to the Thessalonians" (London: Williams & Norgate, 1875; repr., Peabody, MA: Hendrickson Publishers, 2003), pp. 85–97.

17. Robinson, *Jesus and His Coming,* p. 108.

18. Apologists have tried to refute Bousset's theory of the origination of "Lord/*Kyrios*" Christology from the hellenistic Mystery Religions by pointing out that the primitive eucharistic chant *Maranatha* (meaning either "O Lord, come!" or "Our Lord comes!") must stem from the earliest days of the

Jerusalem church and therefore proves that these early Jewish Christians were already calling Jesus their divine Lord in their own language before Christianity ever penetrated to gentile lands where Attis, Sarapis, and other Mystery Cult *Kyrioi* were invoked. But this is to ignore the importance of Antioch as an early center of bilingual Christianity where both Greek and Aramaic were common. Jesus as *Mar* may have originated in Syrian Mystery worship. Jerusalem was not the only place people spoke Aramaic!

19. Geo Widengren, "Early Hebrew Myths and Their Interpretation," in S. H. Hooke, *Myth, Ritual, and Kingship: Essays on the Theory and Practice of Kingship in the Ancient Near East and in Israel* (New York: Oxford University Press, 1958), pp. 191–94.

20. We ought to add Barker's sketch of popular religion maintaining elements banned as heretical by the priesthood to Hanson's description of the sturdy popular faith of the people left behind in the Holy Land during the Exile. See Paul D. Hanson, *The Dawn of Apocalyptic: The Historical and Sociological Roots of Jewish Apocalyptic Eschatology* (Philadelphia: Fortress Press, 1975). It must have been both populist and polytheist.

21. Margaret Barker, *The Great Angel: A Study of Israel's Second God* (Louisville, KY: Westminster/John Knox Press, 1992), pp. 221–31.

Chapter Five

THE SECRET RAPTURE

"Indeed, they say, Jesus blew a trumpet and took all his favorite people to heaven, leaving the rest of us lost sinners to suffer here on earth. I do not believe that accurately reflects the truth of Christianity as it was taught for centuries."

—Nicolae Carpathia in *Apollyon*[1]

"We believe that all Scripture teaches the secrecy as well as the suddenness of the rapture of the church."

—Sydney Watson, *In the Twinkling of an Eye*[2]

CHRIST THE RAPTOR

The most controversial part of fundamentalist eschatology is the doctrine of the Rapture of the Saints. *Rapture* means "catching up," as when a reptile or bird raptor seizes its prey, often from above. In an uncomfortable parallel with the beliefs of UFO cults that teach that true believers will soon be "beamed up" by the mother ship to escape alien catastrophes like the ones agents Mulder and Scully seek to avert on *The X-Files*, fundamentalists envision a day coming soon on which millions of people will vanish, seemingly into thin air, summoned by Jesus Christ at his Second Coming. (Since there will be no visible cause, the event is sometimes called "the Secret Rapture." It is Jesus Christ who will come, albeit not quite touching down, but no one will see him.) All these absentees will prove to have been born-again Christians and their instantaneous absence from airplane cockpits, the driver seats of cars and buses, and from operating rooms will cause the deaths of countless hapless thousands—who are hardly to be mourned, having made their beds by not converting to fundamentalism while they had the chance. After all, what was stopping them from soberly considering the reasoned urgings of Jack Van Impe, Jimmy Swaggart, and Pat Robertson? Whom do they have to blame but themselves?

Upon any kind of close examination, it is surprising, no, amazing just how little scriptural support there is for the Rapture doctrine anywhere in the pages of the New Testament. I will set aside the complexities of the intrafundamentalist debate over whether the Rapture is scheduled to occur before, after, or in the middle of the Great Tribulation. What I mean to say here is that *any* form of the Rapture doctrine is conspicuous by its absence in the very passages where one would most expect to find it. It is as if not only believers in the doctrine have been rapt up to heaven, but also that any biblical passages teaching it were sucked up along with them!

Wouldn't you think there would be some mention of the Rapture in the book of Revelation? But there isn't. In desperation, some have pointed to Revelation 3:10, "Because you have kept my command to patient endurance, I will keep you from the hour of trial that is coming on the whole world, to try those who dwell upon the earth." But this verse must be balanced against another in the same context. Revelation 2:10 says, "Do not fear what you are about to suffer. Behold, the devil is about to throw some of you into prison, that you may be tested, and for ten days you will have tribulation. Be faithful unto death, and I will give you the crown of life." Both passages form part of the collection of seven cover letters under which copies of the text were sent out to the seven churches under the Revelator's jurisdiction. It is plain that each promise from the Risen Lord applies to a particular one of his Asia Minor congregations, that in Philadelphia and that in Smyrna, respectively. Neither can be automatically taken to establish God's policy for all Christians living at the Time of the End.

Even more desperately, some point to Revelation 4:1 as a reference to the Rapture: "After this, I looked, and lo, in heaven stood an open door! And the first voice which I had heard speaking to me like a trumpet, said, 'Come up here, and I will show you what must take place after this.'" It is interesting that, as in 1 Thessalonians, there is the imagery of a trumpet blast followed by an ascension, but it is impossible to miss the fact that the heavenward voyage is restricted to the seer himself, like Enoch in Genesis 5:24, Elijah in 2 Kings 2:11, or Jesus in Acts 1:9. Nothing is said about his somehow standing for the whole of the elect.

What about Revelation 11:12, the assumption of the Two Witnesses? "Then they heard a loud voice from heaven saying to them, 'Come up here!' And in the sight of their foes they went up to heaven in a cloud." These witnesses are Moses and Elijah returned from heaven, whereunto each had ascended alive in the body according to the direct statement of 2 Kings 2:11 (Elijah) and contemporary inference from Deuteronomy 34:5–6 (Moses). This time they had to die first, but they ascended again. Nothing is hinted about Christians sharing their grand exit.

Finally, some have sought support for the Rapture in this verse: "And the Dragon stood before the woman who was about to bear a child, that he might devour her child when she brought it forth; she brought forth a male child, one who is to rule all the nations with a rod of iron, but her child was caught up to God and to his throne" (Rev. 12:4b–5). Another vain effort, alas, for the text plainly refers to the birth of Jesus Christ and God's providential preservation of the babe from his foes, as in Matthew 2:13–15, where Herod plays the role of the dragon. It is a very old mytheme, appearing as far back as Hesiod's *Theogony* 453–484:

> But Rhea was subject in love to Cronos and bare splendid children,
> Hestia, Demeter, and gold-shod Hera and strong Hades, pitiless in
> heart, who dwells under the earth, and the loud-crashing Earth-

Shaker, and wise Zeus, father of gods and men, by whose thunder the wide earth is shaken. These great Cronos swallowed as each came forth from the womb to his mother's knees with this intent, that no other of the proud sons of Heaven should hold the kingly office amongst the deathless gods. For he learned from Earth and starry Heaven that he was destined to be overcome by his own son, strong though he was, through the contriving of great Zeus. Therefore he kept no blind outlook, but watched and swallowed down his children: and unceasing grief seized Rhea. But when she was about to bear Zeus, the father of gods and men, then she besought her own dear parents, Earth and starry Heaven, to devise some plan with her that the birth of her dear child might be concealed, and that retribution might overtake great, crafty Cronos for his own father and also for the children whom he had swallowed down. And they readily heard and obeyed their dear daughter, and told her all that was destined to happen touching Cronos the king and his stout-hearted son. So they sent her to Lyetus, to the rich land of Crete, when she was ready to bear great Zeus, the youngest of her children. Him did vast Earth receive from Rhea in wide Crete to nourish and to bring up. Thither came Earth carrying him swiftly through the black night to Lyetus first, and took him in her arms and hid him in a remote cave beneath the secret places of the holy earth on thick-wooded Mount Aegeum; but to the mightily ruling son of Heaven, the earlier king of the gods, she gave a great stone wrapped in swaddling clothes. Then he took it in his hands and thrust it down into his belly: wretch! he knew not in his heart that in place of the stone his son was left behind, uncon-quered and untroubled, and that he was soon to overcome him by force and might and drive him from his honours, himself to reign over the deathless gods. (translated by Hugh G. Evelyn-White)

It is common to see the Q passage Matthew 24:40–41 ("Then two men will be in the field; one is taken and one is left. Two women will be grinding at the mill; one is taken and one is left." Cf. Luke 17:34) pressed into service as a mention of the Rapture. But Robinson is right: given the context, in which the eschatological catastrophe is compared to Noah's flood and the whelming of Sodom, the one "taken" must be the one destroyed, the one "left" the lucky survivor.[3] See also Genesis 7:23 ("He blotted out every living thing that was upon the face of the ground, man and animals and creeping things and birds of the air; they were blotted out from the earth. Only Noah *was left*, and those that were with him in the ark.") Luke had the disciples ask for clarification: "Where, Lord?" Luke has Jesus answer, "Where the body is, there the vultures will circle" (Luke 17:37).

Another would-be Rapture proof is found in 2 Thessalonians 2:3, "Let no one deceive you in any way; for that day will not come unless the rebellion comes first, and the man of lawlessness is revealed, the son of perdition." Again, if any reference to the Rapture is in there, it certainly is pretty secret! John F. Walvoord summarizes what he calls the "somewhat novel view" of E. Schuyler English (editor of *The New Scofield Reference Bible*):

> The expression "the rebellion" is the translation for the Greek word *apostasia*. It is normally considered a reference to doctrinal apostasy. English pointed out that the word is derived from the verb *aphistemi*, used fifteen times in the New Testament with only three of the references relating to religious departure. In eleven of the instances the word *depart* is a good translation. [In fact numerous early English-language translations do so translate the word in this verse.] He therefore suggested the possibility of rendering 2 Thessalonians 2:3 to the effect that the departure must "come first," i.e., the rapture of the church must occur before the man of sin is revealed. If this translation be admitted, it would constitute an explicit statement that the rapture of the church occurs before the Tribulation."[4]

But the context rules out such a clever redefinition. The concern of the Thessalonians addressed here is "When is the day of deliverance? Did we miss it?" "That day" and "the departure" would then refer to the very same event, and it would make no sense to comfort the Thessalonians with the news that the Rapture will not come until after the Rapture has come. And since the motif of "the apostasy" is so widespread in apocalyptic texts (e.g., 1 Timothy 4:1, "Now the spirit expressly says that in later times some will depart from the faith by giving heed to deceitful spirits and doctrines of demons"), it seems arbitrary to make "apostasy" mean something else in a context where it occurs cheek by jowl with the advent of the man of lawlessness and son of perdition.

A few verses down, some pretribulationists think to have struck gold in the mine of 2 Thessalonians 2:6–7, "And you know what is restraining him now so that he may be revealed in his time. For the mystery of lawlessness is already at work; only he who now restrains it will do so until he is out of the way." But it is fool's gold, for there is no natural way to make "what restrains" and "who restrains" refer to the Christian Church or the Holy Spirit as contained in the Church. Even if one granted this was even possibly the writer's intent, he did not make it nearly clear enough for us to claim this passage as attesting the belief that the Church must be removed from the earth before the Antichrist may appear. Gross ambiguity is not worth much as evidence for anything.

GATHERING THE ELECT

A better bet for a reference to the Rapture might be Mark 13:26–27: "And then they will see the Son of man coming in clouds with great power and glory. And then he will send out the angels, and gather his elect from the four winds, from the ends of the earth to the ends of heaven." But even this is not really referring to the bodily assumption of believers. Instead it embodies a more traditional Jewish hope, one that predates apocalyptic in the true sense but became a major feature of it.

Ever since the Assyrian conquest of Israel in 721 BCE, when the conquerors resettled much of the population elsewhere in the empire, followed by the deportation of the Judean aristocracy by Nebuchad-nezzar in 586 BCE, pious Jews always dreamed of the day when God would regather these displaced Hebrews, or their descendants, back home in the Promised Land. The Assyrian Exile gave rise to the myth of the "Ten Lost Tribes of Israel," as if they had vanished from sight and have been hiding out somewhere in Shangri-la, when in fact they simply intermarried with other Assyrian subjects, becoming irretrievably lost in the gene pool.[5] As for the Judean exiles, the decree of Cyrus the Great in 538 allowed any who wished to return. That year an initial wave did return, under the leadership of Sheshbazzar. Zerubbabel and the priest Joshua led a second wave under Darius from 521 to 485, followed by a third wave led by Nehemiah under the authority of Artaxerxes I from 464 to 423, and a fourth under Ezra, an agent of Artaxerxes II (404–358). But Jews had gotten along quite well in Babylon, and many decided not to return to the Holy Land. A major Jewish community continued to thrive there for centuries, eventually producing the Babylonian Talmud. Jews came to live all throughout the Mediterranean world, with a very important colony in the city of Alexandria. This was the Diaspora. In New Testament times, twice as many Jews lived outside Palestine as in. Many made pious pilgrimages to Jerusalem, and many resettled there in their declining years so they might die and be buried there. One day, the common belief went, God would bring all his people back there, even if it took angelic or messianic intervention to do it. Many, many texts document this important belief.

> In that day from the river Euphrates to the Brook of Egypt Yahve will thresh out the grain, and you will be gathered one by one, O people of Israel. And in that day a great trumpet will be blown, and those who were lost in the land of Assyria and those who were driven out to the land of Egypt will come and worship Yahve on the holy mountain at Jerusalem. (Isa. 27:12–13)

> If your dispersed are from one end of heaven to the other end of heaven, from there will the Lord gather you together. (Deut. 30:4 LXX)

> "As I live," says the Lord Yahve, "surely with a mighty hand and an outstretched arm, and with wrath poured out, I will be king over you. I will bring you out from the peoples and gather you out of the countries where you are scattered, with a mighty hand and an out-

stretched arm, and with wrath poured out; and I will bring you into the wilderness of the peoples, and there I will enter into judgment with you face to face. As I entered into judgment with your fathers in the wilderness of the land of Egypt, so I will enter into judgment with you," says the Lord Yahve. (Ezek. 20:33–36)

I will gather you together out of the four winds of heaven. (Zech. 2:6 LXX)

And it came to pass after this that I saw another host of wagons, and men riding thereon, and coming on the winds from the east, and from the west to the south. And the noise of their wagons was heard, and when this turmoil took place the holy ones from heaven remarked it, and the pillars of the earth were moved from their place, and the sound thereof was heard from the one end of heaven to the other, in one day. And they shall all fall down and worship the Lord of Spirits. (1 Enoch 57:1–3)

At once Israel shall be saved from among the gentiles and the Messiah shall appear to them and bring them up to Jerusalem with great joy. Moreover, the kingdom of Israel, gathered from the four quarters of the world, shall eat with the messiah. (3 Enoch 48A:10)

And then I will sound the trumpet out of the air, and will send my Elect One, having in him all my power in one measure, and he shall summon my despised people from all nations, and I will send fire upon those who have insulted them and who have ruled over them in this age. And I will give those who have covered me with mockery to the scorn of the coming age, and I have prepared them to be food for the fires of Hades, and perpetual flight through the air in the underworld, for they shall see the righteousness of the Creator, and those whom he now honours, and they shall be ashamed, for I had hoped that they would come to me in repentance, rather than loving strange gods, but they forsook the Mighty Lord, and went the way that they willed to go. (Apocalypse of Abraham 61)

Now I suppose, from the words of the righteous Enoch, that there will be also evil-doings among you: for you will commit fornication with the fornication of Sodom, and shall perish all save a few, and will multiply inordinate lusts with women; and the kingdom of the Lord shall not be among you, for forthwith he will take it away. Nevertheless the temple of God shall be built in your portion, and shall be glorious among you. For he shall take it, and the twelve tribes shall be gathered together there, and all the gentiles.
(Testament of Benjamin 9:1–2)

Gather together the dispersed of Israel, with mercy and goodness;
For your faithfulness is with us.
And though we have stiffened our neck,
yet you are our chastener;
Overlook us not, O our God,
lest the nations swallow us up,
as though there were none to deliver. (Psalms of Solomon 8:28–32)

Take off the garment of your sorrow and affliction,
O Jerusalem,
and put on for ever the beauty of the glory from God.
Put on the robe of the righteousness from God;
put on your head the diadem of the glory of the Everlasting.
For God will show your splendor everywhere under heaven.
For your name will for ever be called by God,
"Peace of righteousness and glory of godliness."
Arise, O Jerusalem, stand upon the height
and look toward the east,
and see your children gathered from west and east,
at the word of the Holy One,
rejoicing that God has remembered them.
For they went forth from you on foot,
led away by their enemies;
but God will bring them back to you,
carried in glory, as on a royal throne.
For God has ordered that every high mountain

and the everlasting hills be made low
and the valleys filled up, to make level ground,
so that Israel may walk safely in the glory of God.
The woods and every fragrant tree
have shaded Israel at God's command.
For God will lead Israel with joy,
in the light of his glory,
with the mercy and righteousness that come from him.
(Baruch 5:1–9)

Therefore, if you consider that you have now suffered those things for your good, that you may not finally be condemned and tormented, then you will receive eternal hope; if above all you destroy from your heart vain error, on account of which you departed hence. For if you so do these things, he will continually remember you, he who always promised on our behalf to those who were more excellent than we, that he will never forget or forsake us, but with much mercy will gather together again those who were dispersed. (2 Baruch 78:6–7)

And after this they will turn to me from amongst the gentiles with all their heart and with all their soul and with all their strength, and I will gather them from amongst all the gentiles, and they will seek me, so that I shall be found by them, when they seek me with all their heart and with all their soul. (Book of Jubilees 1:14)

If they feel shame throughout their whole soul, and change their ways, reproaching themselves for their errors, and openly avowing and confessing all the sins that they have committed against themselves with purified souls and minds, so as in the first place to exhibit a sincerity of conscience utterly alien from falsehood and concealing nothing evil beneath; and secondly, having their tongues also purified so as to produce improvement in their hearers, they will then meet with a favorable acceptance from their merciful savior, God, who bestows on the race of mankind his especial and exceedingly great gift, namely, relationship to his own word; after which, as its archetypal model, the human mind was formed.

For even though they may be at the very extremities of the earth, acting as slaves to those enemies who have led them away in captivity, still they shall all be restored to freedom in one day, as at a given signal; their sudden and universal change to virtue causing a panic among their masters; for they will let them go, because they are ashamed to govern those who are better than themselves.

But when they have received this unexpected liberty, those who but a short time before were scattered about in Greece, and in the countries of the barbarians, in the islands, and over the continents, rising up with one impulse, and coming from all the different quarters imaginable, all hasten to one place pointed out to them, being guided on their way by some vision, more divine than is compatible with its being of the nature of man, invisible indeed to every one else, but apparent only to those who were saved, having their separate inducements and intercessions, by whose intervention they might obtain a reconciliation with the Father. (Philo, *On Curses* 8–9)

The language used in Mark 13:27 is entirely of a piece with what we read here. Even the business about the trumpet blast is traditional, deriving from the great trumpet used to summon the people to convocations in Numbers 10:2–10; Joel 2:15, and so on. It is unreasonable to suppose that in Mark 13:27 the same language refers instead to an unprecedented notion of the Rapture of the elect en masse, as if they were all to share the fate of Enoch and Elijah of old. It seems evident that the Rapture doctrine somehow evolved from the expectation of the regathering of the Jewish Exiles, as the religious imagination magnified and supernaturalized that hope. I believe we can glimpse the beginning of that development in a text from the Testament of Moses.

For the Most High will arise, the Eternal God alone,
And he will appear to punish the gentiles,
And he will destroy all their idols.
Then you, O Israel, shall be happy,
And you shall mount upon the necks and wings of the eagle,
And they shall be ended.

And God will exalt you,
And he will cause you to approach to the heaven of the stars,
In the place of their habitation.
And you will look from on high and see your enemies in Gehenna
And you shall recognize them and rejoice,
And you shall give thanks and confess your Creator.
(Testament of Moses 10:7–10)

It appears that the writer of the Testament of Moses has literalized the metaphor of Exodus 19:4, "You have seen what I did to the Egyptians, and how I bore you on eagles' wings, and brought you to myself." (Perhaps also Isa. 40:31, "But those who wait on Yahve shall renew their strength; they shall mount up with wings as eagles; they shall run, and not be weary; and they shall walk, and not faint." Or maybe Isa. 60:8–9: "Who are these that fly like a cloud, and like doves to their windows? For the coastlands shall wait for me, the ships of Tarshish first, to bring your sons from far, their silver and their gold with them, for the name of Yahve your God, and for the Holy One of Israel, because he has glorified you.") Or perhaps the writer meant it metaphorically, as did his source texts, but someone took *him* literally. If so, we would be on our way to the Rapture: God not only regathering his people to the Holy Land but also whisking them up into the sky to share his Olympian view of the judgment of sinners.

As it is, however, 1 Thessalonians 4:16–17 ("For the Lord himself will descend from heaven with a cry of command, with the archangel's call, and with the sound of the trumpet of God. And the dead in Christ will rise first; then we who are alive, who are left, shall be caught up together with them in the clouds to meet the Lord in the air; and so we shall always be with the Lord") appears to be the *single, solitary* mention of the Rapture doctrine in the New Testament. And remember: there it is described as a sort of adjunct coincident with the End Time resurrection of the dead. Not only that, but note that there is no mention at all in this passage of Jesus or the raptured saints coming back down to earth to live in material bodies. If we were not in a rush to read elements from other Bible passages into this one, we might read this one as picturing the ascension of dematerialized, glorified persons to a permanent residence in heaven. After all, the Stoics (whose influence is so ubiquitous in the New Testament) spoke of the final rest of righteous spirits "in the air." Here in 1 Thessalonians 4:17, too, we read that the saved shall "meet the Lord in the air" and "so," in other words, *in this manner,* "we shall ever be with the Lord."

Thus there is simply *no* New Testament teaching concerning a Secret Rapture that will leave the majority of people puzzled over the sudden absence of certain fellows from their ongoing lives in the world, such as we find in virtually all Rapture novels and movies.

COSMIC DUNKIRK[6]

Absolutely central to the *Left Behind* books, as to fundamentalist eschatology in general, is the belief that the Rapture will occur before the Great Tribulation begins. In other words, the born-again Christians have nothing to worry about except getting a front-row seat to watch the fireworks from heaven. As comedian Dana Carvey's Church Lady character might say, "How convenient!" My old Sunday school teacher at Brookdale Baptist Church once admitted to me that he believed in pretribulationism over posttribulationism simply because he preferred to think he'd be escaping all the suffering. Maybe that's the real basis of the doctrine. At least deep down.

Even its advocates, like the erudite John Walvoord, freely admit that pretribulationism is not so much the result of inductive exegesis as it is a correlate of dispensationalist ecclesiology.[7] Dispensationalism is a system created in the nineteenth century by John Nelson Darby, former Church of Ireland (Anglican) priest and founder of the Plymouth Brethren family of sects. Darby, laid up for months following a riding accident, had plenty of time to read the scriptures and to reassess their teaching. He came to reject the classical approach of Catholics and Calvinists alike that the Christian Church had replaced Israel in the divine plan of salvation and that the promises and prophecies originally addressed to Israel now applied instead to the church. No, Darby reckoned, "the gifts and the call of God are irrevocable" (Rom. 11:29). Jews are right: scriptural promises made to the patriarchs and their progeny will certainly be fulfilled one day in a restoration of Israelite theocracy. It may come as something of a surprise when the Jewish Messiah turns out to be Jesus of Nazareth, but he will be sitting on the throne of David, not the chair of Peter.

Darby and dispensationalists divided sacred history into seven periods, or "dispensations," in each of which God has dealt with his people under different terms. First came the Dispensation of Innocence: Adam and Eve in the Garden of Eden. Of course this one lasted about five minutes before they ate the forbidden fruit. Second was the Dispensation of Conscience during which the ill-gotten Knowledge of Good and Evil had to serve as a makeshift moral compass. The third one began with Noah following the Flood, when God gave him a basic set of laws, ushering in the Dispensation of Human Government. The fourth period was the Dispensation of Promise, inaugurated when God made his covenant with Abraham, to give him descendants as numerous as the stars of heaven, as well as the land of Canaan to be their inheritance— some day. (For Darby, as for Paul, this promise also included the coming of Jesus Christ.) Not exactly superceding it but rather superimposed upon the age of Promise was the fifth period, the Dispensation of Law, begun by Moses on Sinai. (Meanwhile, the unwashed gentiles, who were not responsible to keep the Torah's 613 statutes, continued to live under the terms of Human Government.) The Day of Pentecost after the ascension of Jesus brought in the Sixth Dispensation, that of Grace. This period was a "parenthesis" undreamt of by the Israelite prophets, for it marked a new age in which God required only saving faith in the resurrected Christ as an atonement for sin. During the Dispensation of Grace, gentiles and Jews together were offered the gospel of faith in Christ, while the destiny of Jews/Israel was on hold, the prophetic clock having stopped for the time being. Individual Jews could jump on the Christian bandwagon (in fact, they had to in order to be saved!), but God's plan for Jewish theocracy was temporarily on hold.

This Dispensation must end when the Antichrist arises and opens the Tribulation by making a covenant with Jews, allowing them to build a new temple in Jerusalem and to reinstate animal sacrifices there. The focus has been restored to Jews, apparently with a temporary return to the Dispensation of Law, but after three and a half years (half of one of Daniel's heptads of years) it will soon become "the Time of Jacob's Trouble" as the Antichrist reveals his true colors, deifying himself in the temple and persecuting Jews who will yield to him no more readily than their ancient forebears had to Antiochus Epiphanes. However, their fidelity to Judaism will not save them. In fact, God will be both allowing the depredations of the Beast and strafing the earth with devastating plagues of his own in a last-ditch effort to hammer some sense into Jews, using "tough love" to get them to turn at last to Jesus. One hundred and forty-four thousand Jews are to be converted and then to act as miraculously effective evangelists, reaping an unprecedented harvest of Jewish converts. After another three and a half years in which the Tribulation kicks into high gear and can be called the *Great* Tribulation, the final coming of Christ occurs. The Antichrist and his promoter the False Prophet are thrown screaming into the Lake of Fire, and Satan, their patron, is imprisoned (like the Zoroastrian Antichrist, Azdahak) for a thousand years, which constitutes the seventh period, the Dispensation of the Millennium. In this period the theocratic promises to Israel are at last fulfilled. But Satan is scheduled for a last hurrah in which he will rally the nations of Gog and Magog, once imprisoned by Alexander the Great. They besiege the Holy City where a never-aging Jesus reigns, only to be incinerated by his grace. Then history ends, the heavens and the earth are destroyed by fire, and a new cosmos appears, in which God reigns at last on earth among humanity, Jesus having abdicated his throne so that God may reign unopposed.

Where in all this does the Rapture occur? Darby reasoned that the Christian Church, a separate and distinct "chosen people of God," has no role in God's plan during the Tribulation, since Christians (i.e., born-again fundamentalists) have already accepted the Gospel of Jesus.

Why make them sit through the remedial school of hard knocks along with the slow-learning Jews? Why should they get pounded along with Jews? Thus, dispensationalists argue, Christians must literally *leave the planet* during the Tribulation. It is a very shaky inference. (It may seem pedantic to enter into this debate here, but it is advisable for the simple reason that so much of *Left Behind* rests upon this theory, pretribulationism. Any attempt to critique the novels necessarily scrutinizes their major theological premise.)

For one thing, dispensationalism already allows for the overlapping of dispensations so that one group may sit out the action pertaining to another group, cooling their heels on the sidelines, like the gentiles observing the laws of Noah (thus continuing the Dispensation of Human Government) even while Jews are living under the Mosaic Dispensation. The Dispensations of Promise and Law overlap, too. So how can dispensationalists be so sure there is no place for Christians on the stage of history at all during the Tribulation? Why did God not park the Jews off on some asteroid somewhere while their theocratic-prophetic clock stopped and the Church age passed? Furthermore, what of those many gentiles who converted to Christ during the Tribulation? In what sense are they not the Church? They sure aren't part of theocratic Israel. To define such "Tribulation saints" as something other than the Christian Church is circular: they can't count as the Church only if the Church is defined as "those Christians raptured before the Tribulation," which one would only do for the sake of maintaining pretribulationism!

And remember, the Tribulation is not properly part of any of the seven dispensations anyway. What is it? The Church age, Grace? It is not yet the Millennium either. In such a dispensational no-man's land, one cannot be so sure that Christians must be vacuumed off the earth's surface.

Second, it is by no means difficult to suggest a role for Christians during the Tribulation. We have already seen that there is to be a major missionary effort among Jews during this time. And who's doing the evangelism? Newly converted Jews. (*Left Behind* has characters during the Tribulation frequently lament how all of them are greenhorns in theology and the Bible, since all the spiritual veterans were extracted at the Rapture.) Wouldn't it be more Christian to picture the born-again Christians as enduring the pains of the Tribulation precisely for the sake of evangelizing Jews and others during a very difficult time?

Third, I doubt seriously whether Darby's distinction between the Church and Israel as distinct peoples of God, the one indwelt by the Holy Spirit, the other not, will stand close exegetical scrutiny. It seems hard to deny that the great message of Romans 9–11, Galatians, Ephesians, and 1 Peter is that, through Christ, there is no more difference between Jews and gentiles, since all may approach God on the same footing. Dispensationalism seems to be committing Paul's cardinal sin: undoing the bridge-building work of Christ. One might even venture to say that if Christians and Jews really constitute two peoples of God instead of one, then Christ died in vain (Gal. 2:15–21), and that we have endeavored to rebuild the wall Christ's death demolished (Eph. 2:11–22). They are alike citizens of the commonwealth of Israel (Eph. 2:12). All of Walvoord's arguments for the continued separation of Christians and Jews as distinct peoples of God strike me as circular.[8] Time and again Walvoord argues that whatever may be said about the blessed state of theocratic Israel and of Christians, nothing is said about them not being separate chosen peoples. But I would urge that nothing is said about them *being* distinct elect peoples. The burden of proof is on the dispensationalist. Walvoord argues that A is said about the New Testament Church, not about Old Testament Israel, while B is predicated of Israel, not of Christians. But to divide the territory in this manner already takes for granted the very distinction he is supposed to be proving.

Walvoord and other apologists for pretribulationism do point to some biblical texts, but their appeal is a futile one. For instance, regarding 1 Thessalonians 4:14 ("For since we believe that Jesus died and rose again, even so, through Jesus, God will bring with him those who have fallen asleep"), pretribulationsts think that for Jesus to bring with him a host of deceased Christians (as he does in *Glorious Appearing*) implies that he has at some earlier point harvested the dead and brought them to join him in heaven. Thus there must have been a Rapture some time prior to the final appearance when living Christians will see their dead loved ones again. But surely Robinson is correct: "the assurance in v. 14 [is] that, as Jesus died and rose, so God, through Jesus, will bring with him those who have fallen asleep—not, that is to say, from heaven to earth, but from the grave to share his risen life."[9] The point is precisely the same as in 2 Corinthians 4:14: "knowing that he who raised the Lord Jesus will raise us also with Jesus and bring us with you into his presence."

TALKIN' ABOUT MY TRIBULATION

The major exegetical argument brought to bear by pretribulationists is their appeal to numerous New Testament passages where the readers are told to be ready at any moment for the coming of Christ. Such urgings, says Walvoord, must imply an initial Rapture before the Tribulation begins for the simple reason that otherwise, the warning would be to watch and prepare for the Tribulation. If the early Church believed the Rapture could occur only following a seven-year Tribulation, they could not expect the Rapture any time. How could the Son of Man "come at an hour ye expect not" if you could count it down from the beginning of a seven-year Tribulation? Thus they must have anticipated a Rapture at any moment, whether far or near, and *then* the Tribulation.[10]

The crucial assumption in this argument is that all the New Testament writers built into their system of belief the Danielic timetable of seventy heptads ("weeks") of years with a Tribulation occupying the seventieth. And we cannot be sure they did, even if in other respects they retained some of the elements of Daniel's Antiochus scenario. No Pauline epistle makes mention of this schedule. One might infer that 2 Thessalonians 2:3–4 presupposes it, since it mentions the Antichrist exalting himself as God in the temple of God. But remember, we could not be sure the reference was to the Antiochus figure after all. The remembered (and expected) Danielic abomination of desolation was defilement of the temple, not self-deification.

But does not the Synoptic Apocalypse make virtually explicit appeal to Daniel, even in Mark's slightly more reticent version? Yes, but in Mark 13:20, it clearly says God has decided to throw out his timetable! "And if the Lord had not shortened the days, no human being would be saved; but for the sake of the elect, whom he chose, he shortened the days." So much for the seventieth week business!

Revelation certainly retains the three-and-a-half-year duration for the Antichrist's rampage, but then this book does urge its readers to be ready, not for the Rapture, which it never mentions, but rather for the Tribulation, which it assumes its readers will face. Besides this, Revelation's agenda would seem to rule out the pretribulation Rapture, since it places the resurrection of the Tribulation martyrs coincident with the return of Jesus at the close of the Beast's reign (20:4–5). This it calls "the first resurrection." The second resurrection follows fully a thousand years later and it brings back the rest of the righteous dead as well as all the wicked dead, and they are variously judged by the ledger of their earthly deeds (20:12–15). But if LaHaye, Jenkins, Darby, and Walvoord are right, why are these two events not called the *second* and *third* resurrections? The first would be that of the Secret Rapture, before the seven years of the Beast. Even more absurd, the dispensationalist doctrine divides the Second Coming of Christ into *second* and *third* comings, seven years apart! Jenkins comes close to having his characters actually put it this way! "The prophecies seemed to deal more with the first coming of Christ than with the Rapture or the Glorious Appearing."[11] "'This is sure different from the last time Jesus came,' Naomi said. 'Besides that we weren't ready, it happened in the twinkling of an eye. Apparently God's going to play this one out for all it's worth.'"[12]

Radio host Walter Bjork used to quip that, while all theories have holes in them, the pretribulation Rapture theory was "all hole!" He was right. For me, the nail that shuts the coffin tight is 1 Thessalonians 1:4–10.

Therefore we ourselves boast of you in the churches of God for your steadfastness and faith in all your persecutions and in the afflictions which you are enduring. This is evidence of the righteous judgment of God, that you may be made worthy of the kingdom of God, for which you are suffering—since indeed God deems it just to repay with affliction those who afflict you, and to grant rest with us to you who are afflicted, when the Lord Jesus is revealed from heaven with his mighty angels in flaming fire, inflicting vengeance upon those who do not know God and upon those who do not obey the gospel of our Lord Jesus. They shall suffer the punishment of eternal destruction and exclusion from the presence of the Lord and from the glory of his might, when he comes on that day to be glorified in his saints, and to be marveled at in all who have believed, because our testimony to you was believed.

The author assures his readers, just then undergoing persecution, that they will shortly find relief and vindication when Christ returns with his retinue of angels and destroys the persecutors with the fires of judgment. The persecution they now endure is the one that will be brought to a close at the final and eschatological coming of Christ in judgment. There is no future Tribulation of seven years to wait for. This is it! And the final coming of Christ is the next item on the schedule. That's posttribulationism if you need a name for it.

But if that verse settles one question, as it does for me, ruling out any conception of a pretribulation Rapture as an early Christian option, it creates much bigger problems: does not the author take for granted that his generation is the last? I will take up that question in the next chapter.

NOTES

1. Tim LaHaye and Jerry B. Jenkins, *Apollyon: The Destroyer Unleashed* (Wheaton, IL: Tyndale House, 1999), p. 105.

2. Sydney Watson, *In the Twinkling of an Eye* (Los Angeles: Biola, 1921; repr., Old Tappan, NJ: Fleming H. Revell Company, 1933), p. 171.

3. John A. T. Robinson, *Jesus and His Coming* (Philadelphia: Westminster Press, 1957; 2nd ed., 1979), p. 75.

4. John F. Walvoord, *The Rapture Question*, rev. ed. (Grand Rapids, MI: Zondervan Publishing, 1979), pp. 67–68, referring to E. Schuyler English, *Rethinking the Rapture* (Travelers Rest, SC: Southern Bible, 1954), pp. 66–70.

5. Of course, as Luke 2:36 presupposes, there were still plenty of people in the Holy Land who cherished ancient tribal pedigrees; neither the Assyrians nor the Babylonians completely emptied Israel or Judah of all inhabitants.

6. I heard Fuller Theological Seminary Professor of Missiology Arthur Glasser refer to the Rapture this way in 1973 at the InterVarsity Christian Fellowship Urbana Missionary Conference. The reference is to what Winston Churchill called "the miracle of Dunkirk," the rescue of three hundred thousand British troops cornered on the beaches of Belgium by Nazi troops in May–June 1940. The Brits were rescued by a ragtag armada of private yachts, fishing boats, etc., as well as by ships from France, Belgium, the Netherlands, and Poland.

7. Walvoord, *Rapture Question*, p. 19: "In determining the question of whether the church will go through the Tribulation, a most important factor is the definition of the term church."

8. Ibid., e.g., pp. 28–29.

9. Robinson, *Jesus and His Coming*, p. 25.

10. Walvoord, *Rapture Question*, p. 73.

11. Tim LaHaye and Jerry B. Jenkins, *Desecration: Antichrist Takes the Throne* (Wheaton, IL: Tyndale House, 2001), p. 99.

12. Ibid., *Glorious Appearing: The End of Days* (Wheaton, IL: Tyndale House, 2004), p. 132.

Chapter Six

THE DELAY OF THE PAROUSIA

"Those who do not remember the lessons of history are doomed to repeat it."

—George Santayana, quoted on a placard above the throne
of the Reverend Jim Jones

DAYS OF FUTURE PAST

Most people who look forward to the speedy end of the age and the coming (Greek: Parousia) of Jesus Christ are no doubt at least vaguely aware that plenty of fellow believers in the past have had similar expectations dashed time after time. What lesson do they learn from that fact? Apparently the lesson is "If at first you don't succeed, try, try again." Hal Lindsey and others assured their readers more than thirty-five years ago that previous generations had no business expecting the coming of Christ in their immediate future because certain requisite signs of the end had not occurred. Certain prophecies (based, as we have seen, on the expectation that numerous events in the careers of Antiochus IV Epiphanes, Caligula, and Domitian must repeat themselves) presupposed the existence of a Jewish temple, a Roman Empire, and a functioning system of sacrifices. As long as these pieces remained on the chessboard, the ancients were justified in at least hoping to see the return of Christ. But after all alike were swept away by the tides of history, believers should have realized they must wait for the restoration, the resetting of the stage. And by Lindsey's day, all stood ready again, or could very soon. Lindsey and his colleagues, in books like *The Late Great Planet Earth*, tried to calculate the coming of the end, but the more impressive they made their predictions by tying them to specific news events, the more vulnerable to debunking they made them as history continued to march by, leaving their correlations behind.

I want to document and specify how fundamentalist End Times fans have again and again jumped the gun. My survey is largely borrowed and summarized from the excellent work of Dwight Wilson in *Armageddon Now!* His story commences in the nineteenth century. One might go back much further into history to demonstrate a virtually unbroken succession of false eschatological alarms. But many of these were based less on biblical exegesis than on new prophecies and visions, natural calamities and omens, and so on. I want to stick with false predictions that emerged from fundamentalism and by the same machinery that continues to generate them today. I will then move on to the apocalyptic expectation of the New Testament writers, examining their own tendency to set and reset dates for the end. It will become clear that present-day tendencies to jump the prophetic gun bear the same relation to that earlier eschatological embarrassment as neurotic symptoms do to a repressed trauma. Finally, I will address the recent revival of "Preterism" as a desperate and futile attempt to vindicate the accuracy of the New Testament writers by reinterpreting them almost beyond recognition.

PRINCIPALITIES AND CENTRAL POWERS

The modern history of "Pin the Tale on the Prophecy" may be said to begin with George Stanley Faber's 1809 work, *A General and Connected View of the Prophecies Relative to the Conversion, Restoration, Union, and Future Glory of the Houses of Judah and Israel; the Progress, and Final Over-*

throw, of the AntiChristian Confederacy in the Land of Palestine; and the Ulti-mate General Diffusion of Christianity. In this work, Faber pegged the emperor Napoleon as the Antichrist, perhaps because he had been hailed by the Jewish populace of Frankfurt as the Messiah. Napoleon's growing European possessions would count as the Revived Roman Empire that prophecy seemed to require. Great Britain, on the other hand, would oppose Napoleon's designs and see to it that Israel was restored to Palestine. (Already one can begin to surmise that the eventual promulgation of the Balfour Declaration may have been in large measure a case of self-fulfilling prophecy.) It was not mere patriotism but (supposedly) biblical prophecy that entrusted such a destiny to Britain, for must she not be the referent behind "the ships of Tarshish" (Isa. 60:9) and "the isles of the sea" (Isa. 24:15)? (Here we may see an anticipation of Damien Thorn's appeal to the apocryphal Book of Hebron and its prediction of messianic events in the British Isles; see chapter 9.) And there were other parts to be handed out: Russia would play the role of Daniel's King of the North (Daniel 11), Napoleon's ungodly ally.

The year 1855 saw the publication of a pair of books by Scottish National Church pulpeteer John Cumming, *The End: The Proximate Signs of the Close of the Dispensation* and *Signs of the Times, Or Present, Past, and Future*. He saw the eschaton "Cumming" in 1864, which was indeed pretty darn proximate. He understood Daniel's half week of 1,260 "days" (years) as the era of papal power extending from 530 (when the pope was granted temporal authority by the emperor Justinian) to 1790, the supposed decline of the papacy. Daniel's related figure of 1,290 days/years took him further, up to the fall of the Turks, whom Cumming identified with the Persian Empire of the Bible as well as the Little Horn of Daniel. The author also reported rumors that wealthy Jews were raising the needed funds to buy Palestine outright to turn it into a Jewish homeland and to erect a new temple. Of course, the poor fools little realized they were merely investing in the stage props for the Antichrist's command performance in defiling the structure.

Sometimes, obviously, the identification of a modern country with an ancient counterpart mentioned in the Bible was based simply on geographical proximity. But just as often speculative philology played a key role. Nineteenth-century philologist Wilhelm Gesenius had decided that Rosh (from Ezek. 38) must represent Russia. To modern scholars the link seems dubious to say the least: *rosh* is simply Hebrew for "head" or "chief," while Russia was named for the Nordic Rus people. Gesenius went on in the same vein, tagging Ezekiel's Meshech as Moscow and Tubal as Tobolsk, even though Meshech and Tubal, as a glance at any Bible atlas will show, were peoples living in Ezekiel's day adjacent to the Black Sea. (The people of Tubal were famous for their copper work, and that is why the book of Genesis makes their eponymous ancestor Tubal-Cain a forger of instruments of bronze and iron.) But it was Cumming who claims the honor of being the first prophecy maven to extend the list, identifying Hierapolis (the old bish-opric of Papias in the second century) in Asia Minor as Gog (based on Pliny the Elder), Magog as the Scythians (or so said Josephus), and the Muscovites as refugees from Pontus (as per Herodotus). Actually, Gog must be the mythical Gyges, king of Lydia, and Magog just means "land of Gog." Cumming also identified Ezekiel's Gomer (another con-temporary nation) with Germany, and he envisioned Gomer and Rosh (Germany and Russia) confederating to invade Palestine. Much of this survives into *The Late Great Planet Earth*.

Though apparently he wrote no book, Michael Baxter, a British preacher, spoke widely in America and Britain between 1861 and 1908. It was now too late for Napoleon Bonaparte to play Antichrist, but Baxter conferred the honor on the royal nephew, Louis Napoleon, or Napoleon III. If he knew about it, the emperor no doubt appreciated having his ambitions taken so seriously. Baxter, though history proved him wrong, was sure enough of his facts that he scheduled the end of the world between two-thirty and three PM on March 12, 1903. He must have had second thoughts when the day passed, but he kept on preaching.

Premillenarians were those fundamentalists who expected Christ to return before the dawn of the Millennial Kingdom rather than appearing only at its culmination as per the Puritan postmillennialists. They are also to be distinguished from the more mainstream Protestants, Calvinists, and Catholics who, with Saint Augustine, deem the whole Christian age, no matter its literal duration, as a spiritual millennium. These last were the amillennialists. It was the premillennialists alone who speculated on the End Times scenario. And they only speculated the more as history left their previous predictions in the lurch. Cyrus I. Scofield (editor of the enormously influential *Scofield Reference Bible*) was among many who believed World War I would culminate in the Battle of Armageddon. Some saw the prediction of Isaiah 19:23 ("In that day there will be a highway from Egypt to Assyria, and the Assyrian will come into Egypt, and the Egyptian into Assyria, and the Egyptians will worship with the Assyrians") fulfilled in the railroad built between Cairo and Jerusalem, funded by the Ottoman Empire and Great Britain. And when on December 9, 1917, Ottoman Jerusalem fell to British general Edmund Allenby, various fundamentalists proclaimed it as marking the end (or, more modestly, perhaps, the beginning of the end) of the "times of the Gentiles." Luke 21:23b–24 ("For great distress shall be upon the earth and wrath upon this people; they will fall by the edge of the sword, and be led captive among all nations; and Jerusalem will be trodden down by the Gentiles, until the times of the Gentiles are fulfilled.") took the long view of the aftermath of the Roman defeat of Jewish rebels (in either 70 CE or 135 CE), acknowledging it as the beginning of an indeterminate period when gentiles would tread Jerusalem underfoot, a Jerusalem empty of Jews. But such a time would reach its end just before the Second Coming of Jesus. That is what prophecy buffs believed had happened with Allenby's entry, with the strong implication that Jesus would be back very soon.

The flames of expectation were further fanned with the growing Russian victories over the Ottoman Turks, a scenario that could be without too much difficulty superimposed onto Daniel's prophecies. But as the Great War wound down, Russia's power waned, and this was a major setback for premillenarians who were following the same events as the rest of the waiting public but with an almost surreal agenda: how did this or that development bode for the end of the world? In a real sense, it was quite a relief to fundamentalist prophecy fans when the Bolsheviks came to power, for this cemented Russia's character as a larger-than-life, Bible-scale villain. And when the Brest-Litovsk Treaty of July 3, 1918, ceded large chunks of East European territory to Germany, premillenarians read this as an omen of the impending Gog-Gomer alliance. (Can you imagine pundits soberly considering these matters on *Meet the Press* or *Hardball*?)

As it turned out, however, fundamentalist interest in Russia as the End Time juggernaut soon began to give way to a new preoccupation with a Revived Roman Empire, a group of ten European kingdoms who would invite the rule of the Antichrist (little suspecting his true identity, of course). Various prophecy "experts" argued that either Revived Rome would thwart a Russian invasion of Jewish Palestine, securing its false pose as an ally of Israel or that Revived Rome would ally itself with Russia. And naturally the Balfour Declaration was greeted as a fulfillment of biblical prophecy, paving the way for the eschatological regathering of the Jews. Never mind that British premillenarians like Lord Shaftesbury had long influenced events to this end precisely in order to see that prophecy was fulfilled. Some Christians (as well as religious Jews) dismissed Zionism as a vain and doomed attempt to bring about by human strength a prophetic fulfillment that could properly occur only with the coming (first or second) of the Messiah (or by mass Christian conversion of Jews to Christianity). But after the official birth of the State of Israel, fewer and fewer raised these scruples, reminding one of the answer of Charles Haddon Spurgeon when a fan asked if he believed in infant baptism: "Be*lieve* in it? Why, man, I've *seen* it!"

Returning to the 1920s, there were two major candidates for the position of Antichrist: Benito Mussolini and the League of Nations. The latter seemed ideally made to be a Revived Roman Empire, but on the other hand, *Il Duce* was talking explicitly about reviving Rome and its imperial glory. As for the rebuilding of the temple, rumors circulated that the Mosque of Omar would be blown up and replaced by a Jewish temple, a construction project Jews were already supposed to be planning. Presumably they were believed to be leaving the mosque to divine providence, but they wanted to be ready when the coast was clear.

But already in 1922, Russia and Germany were beginning to attract new interest among prophecy buffs. The Rapallo Treaty restored cordial relations between the old enemies, providing for new economic and political cooperation. In 1939, the Nazi-Soviet Pact was greeted as a near-miraculous fulfillment of Bible prophecy, since in human terms it had seemed unlikely—given Hitler's hatred for "Jewish" Bolshevism—that the Third Reich and the USSR could ever get together—as prophecy said they had to!

But almost as soon as the rejoicing started, it stopped, when Hitler turned on his fellow dictator and invaded Russia. History is fickle that way, a lesson one might have thought prophecy buffs would have learned, but they had as short a memory for the past as they did a timetable for the future. Neither could be very long. But there was at least some consolation to be found in the accelerating arms race of the 1930s, which emboldened many fundamentalists to think that Armageddon must occur before the end of the decade. And one thing was for sure: Stalin was predicted, virtually by name, in Jeremiah 15:12: "Can one break iron, iron from the north, and bronze?" "Stalin," you recall, meant "steel."

Work continued on identifying all the names mentioned as Israel's doomed foes in Ezekiel 38. Assemblies of God pastor Thomas M. Chalmers was the first to spot verse 6's Riphath as Rumania, Togarmah as Turkey and Armenia (surely he didn't just think the ancient name combined the two modern ones?), and Ashkenaz as Germany. Another 1930s trend was a running debate over whether Russia would last long enough to participate in Armageddon. Would Revived Rome take Russia out before that? That's the way I learned it from Hal Lindsey, though LaHaye and Jenkins in *Left Behind* have Russia attack Israel and get trounced by miraculous weather phenomena. And if Russia did not have a place on the fight card, who would Revived Rome be fighting at Armageddon? Some began to suggest that Japan and China, both flexing new muscles, might wind up as the Kings of the East, back across the Euphrates, whose invasion is mentioned in Revelation 16:12.

As the once-promising Mussolini was eclipsed already during the 1930s, hopes for the revival of the Roman Empire shifted to the European Common Market and the United States of Europe proposed by Aristide Briand, prime minister of France. The Common Market remained the favorite steed in the race for another three decades, if not longer.

The biggest shot in the arm yet for prophetic speculators was the establishment of the State of Israel in 1948. Combined with the cold war, this event only poured gasoline on the fire. More temple rumors circulated for the occasion, and some saw NATO as the prophesied alliance of the Ten Kings preparatory to the New Rome. Others saw the emerging United Nations as a likelier prospect.

Already in the 1950s premillennialists were predicting that next must come an Israeli annexation of Old Jerusalem, and with it the destruction of the inconvenient Mosque of Omar. When, in the course of the Six Days' War, on June 5, 1967, Israeli forces did take the Old City, it was widely heralded as the definitive end of the times of the gentiles. The Mosque of Omar survived unscathed, though, leaving yet another delaying factor, but then that could be mitigated by hoping for a devastating earthquake, if not some terrorist incident. And the temple could be built on the same site pretty quickly if, as was inevitably rumored, builders used pre-fab modules already in the works. Dispensationalists saw no significant obstacle in the way of the Rapture, and their preaching and publishing in the late 1960s and the 1970s evidenced that.

The Yom Kippur War of October 1973 and the Persian Gulf War in 1990 both were good for some scare-preaching and a few more books. But fundamentalism as a whole has calmed somewhat in the last decades, especially as its followers have largely shed their former political indifference and adopted an implicitly postmillennialist "Christ Transforming Culture" model, forming groups like the Christian Coalition and the Moral Majority to advance old-time Christian values.[1] The result has been a greater this-worldly focus, though of course all fundamentalists still believe in the literal, personal, visible Second Coming of Christ, and probably sooner rather than later. Dwight Wilson's summation is worth quoting:

> The current crisis was always identified as a sign of the end, whether it was the Russo-Japanese War, the First World War, the Second World War, the Palestine War, the Suez Crisis, the June War, or the Yom Kippur War. The revival of the Roman Empire has been identified variously as Mussolini's empire, the League of Nations, the United Nations, the European Defense Community, the Common Market and NATO. Speculation on the Antichrist has included Napoleon, Mussolini, Hitler, and Henry Kissinger. The northern confederation was supposedly formed by the Treaty of Brest-Litovsk, the Rapallo Treaty, the Nazi-Soviet Pact, and then the Soviet Bloc. The "kings of the east" have been variously the Turks, the lost tribes of Israel, Japan, India, and China. The supposed restoration of Israel has confused the problem of whether the Jews are to be restored before or after the coming of the Messiah. The restoration of the latter rain has been pinpointed to have begun in 1897, 1917, and 1948. The end of the "times of the Gentiles" has been placed in 1895, 1917, 1948, and 1967. "Gog" has been an impending threat since the Crimean War, both the Czars and the Communists.[2]

Nor has there been a complete absence of doomsaying and date setting since Wilson wrote. Some notable recent predictions include the 1988 publication of *88 Reasons Why the Rapture Is in 1988*, by Edgar C. Whisenant, a North Carolinian.[3] The fateful year passed. I recall watching the seconds tick by on the fateful day along with my students in class at Mount Olive College. I was not too surprised when I heard no trumpet and none of the students disappeared. The next year, like the Adventist William Miller (who had once convinced thousands to expect the Parousia by March 21, 1844, then April 18 of the same year), Whisenant just went back to the drawing board and revised his date till 1989, as he announced in *The Final Shout: Rapture Report 1989*. Theologically stubborn, Whisenant kept churning out the deadlines, and missing them, through 1992, 1995, and later years. Also in 1992, a Korean group calling itself "Mission for the Coming Days" predicted October 28, 1992, as the date for the Rapture. (I remember driving down Route 3 East in Clifton, New Jersey, one day and seeing one of their members hoisting a placard emblazoned with that date.) When the Rapture failed to materialize, at least some of the group members killed themselves, unable to face the shame and embarrassment. The year 1993 brought a flurry of predictions for the imminent beginning of the seven-year Tribulation, since that would mean the millennium would start right on schedule in 2000. Noncanonical books such as 2 Enoch and the Epistle of Barnabas teach the old millennial week theory: by the Bible's calendar, world history would last six thousand years, and the millennium would round out a cosmic week with a seventh "day" of Sabbath rest. But since this schema was not officially biblical, its failure seems not to have disturbed anyone too seriously. The Reverend John Hinkle, pastor of Christ Church in Los Angeles, predicted June 9, 1994, as the last day. Stan Johnson of the Prophecy Club calculated it would be September 12, 1997. Marilyn Agee, in her book *The End of the Age*, aimed for May 31, 1998. And there are more all the time.

THE END IS NEAR

I recall when I first read Ronald A. Knox's classic *Enthusiasm*. These words struck me:

> For that is the real character of the enthusiast; he expects more evident results from the grace of God than we others. He sees what effects religion can have, does sometimes have, in transforming a man's whole life and outlook; these exceptional cases (so we are content to think them) are for him the average standard of religious achievement. He will have no "almost-Christians," no weaker

brethren who plod and stumble, who (if the truth must be told) would like to have a foot in either world, whose ambition is to qualify, not to excel. He has before his eyes a picture of the early Church, visibly penetrated with supernatural influences; and nothing less will serve him as a model. Extenuate, accommodate, interpret, and he will part company with you.

Quoting a hundred texts—we also use them, but with more of embarrassment—he insists that the members of his society, saved members of a perishing world, should live a life of angelic purity, of apostolic simplicity; worldly amusements, the artifices of a polite society, are not for them.[4]

I remember thinking: "He's talking about the people who wrote the New Testament! No wonder biblicists, pietists, fanatics, and the twice-born feel so at home quoting it, believing it, obeying it literally!" The New Testament is not a book of laid-back religion. It is not a book for thoughtful intellectuals who see things in grays, not just black and white, because most often things are in fact gray. No wonder we have to engage in "hermeneutics" and demythologizing to make the scripture palatable, and not to our sinful preferences, but to our better judgment! At any rate, nowhere does the "enthusiastic," the fanatical character of the New Testament writers make itself clearer than in this matter of the end of the world. Our modern fundamentalist friends are more biblically faithful than they know, precisely because they think in the same irresponsible way the New Testament sectarians did, and as a result they wind up in the same rut, incorrigibly making the same mistakes. For it is no accident that our dispensationalists and premillenarians keep jumping the gun, keep setting dates and then setting new ones, having learned nothing. For they are following all too well in the dead-end footsteps of their models, the New Testament Christians. The ancient believers may not have talked about Russia and the Common Market, but they foolishly matched ancient scripture verses, "led" by the Holy Spirit to do so, with current events, and they misfired every time. Let us look at the most outstanding examples of New Testament writers making premature, unfulfilled predictions of the Parousia.

> But we would not have you ignorant, brethren, concerning those who are asleep, that you may not grieve as others do who have no hope. For since we believe that Jesus died and rose again, even so, through Jesus, God will bring with him those who have fallen asleep. For this we declare to you by the word of the Lord, that we who are alive, who are left until the coming of the Lord, shall not precede those who have fallen asleep. For the Lord himself will descend from heaven with a cry of command, with the archangel's call, and with the sound of the trumpet of God. And the dead in Christ will rise first; then we who are alive, who are left, shall be caught up together with them in the clouds to meet the Lord in the air; and so we shall always be with the Lord. (1 Thess. 4:13–17)

Surely here is someone who takes for granted that he and the bulk of his audience will survive to see the coming of Christ at the end of the age. R. A. Torrey claimed that the words implied no such thing but merely held open the possibility that the Parousia might occur in Paul's day. On the possibility that things should so transpire, Torrey said, Paul would naturally speak of the survivors as including himself.[5] But that seems arbitrary. If the writer did not expect that he and his readers would shortly see the End Time events, would not it have been entirely more natural to say, "Those who are alive and remain"?

> Indeed God deems it just to repay with affliction those who afflict you, and to grant rest with us to you who are afflicted, when the Lord Jesus is revealed from heaven with his mighty angels in flaming fire, inflicting vengeance upon those who do not know God and upon those who do not obey the gospel of our Lord Jesus. They shall suffer the punishment of eternal destruction and exclusion from the presence of the Lord and from the glory of his might, when he comes on that day to be glorified in his saints, and to be marveled at in all who have believed, because our testimony to you was believed. (2 Thess. 1:6–10)

These very readers, the same ones now undergoing persecution, will soon find welcome relief by the intervention of the returning Christ, who will, at the same time he rescues them, deal out vengeance to their erstwhile tormentors. This is the end of the age we are talking about and which the readers are flat-out told they will shortly see. There is no talk here about how, if the Thessalonians are lucky, they *may* experience miraculous intervention.

> Besides this, you know what hour it is, how it is full time now for you to wake from sleep. For salvation is nearer to us now than when we first believed; the night is far gone, the day is at hand. Let us then cast off the works of darkness and put on the armor of light. (Rom. 13:11–12)

There is no slippery and evasive talk here about how it *might* be time, at *any* time, for Christ to return so that one had better stay busy just in case. I admit that does seem to be the point of the parables in which we are told there is no way to know when the master will return. But that is hardly the point here: it is fully time! It can no longer be delayed! The dawning of the Parousia is "at hand." That does not mean it *might* be near. It does not say there is nothing we know of standing in the way, but then again it might take another thousand years, as apologists wish and vainly pretend that it says. It is such "eel-wriggling," as the Buddha called it, that makes us mistrust their sincerity.

> Let all men know your forbearance. The Lord is at hand. (Phil. 4:5)

Again, "at hand" has to mean it is very soon, not that it *might* be for all we know.

> The end of all things is at hand; therefore keep sane and sober for your prayers. (1 Pet. 4:7)

In other words, you don't want to be caught flat-footed. There is time enough, but *only* time enough, for you to make sure you are serious.

> You also be patient. Establish your hearts, for the coming of the Lord
> is at hand. Do not grumble, brethren, against one another, that you
> may not be judged; behold, the Judge is standing at the doors. (Jas.
> 5:8–9)

As if "at hand" were not clear enough, we learn here that the divine
Judge is just on the point of entering the courtroom, not that he is
poised and *waiting* there for an indefinite period, which would be an
altogether pointless metaphor—for what?

> Children, it is the last hour; and as you have heard that antichrist is
> coming, so now many antichrists have come; therefore we know that
> it is the last hour. (1 John 2:18)

What is there not to understand in the phrase "the last hour"? One apologist urges us to take the writer to mean "*a* last hour," which is about as
absurd as the recent movie title *Final Destination 2.*[6]

> Blessed is he who reads aloud the words of the prophecy, and blessed
> are those who hear, and who keep what is written therein; for the time
> is near. (Rev. 1:3)

One would hardly say "near" if one meant "indefinite." And if that is
what the writer meant, whence the note of eager anticipation?

> I am coming soon; hold fast what you have, so that no one may seize
> your crown. (Rev. 3:11)

Surely only a cruel and sadistic deity would encourage his worshipers
with words of endurance if he knew, as he must, that his servants must
endure for at least two more millennia. I think it is obvious from the
identification of the Beast of Revelation as Nero and/or Domitian that
John intended to warn his readers about impending events of their own
time, things they would live to see. If the Antichrist was going to come
only centuries or millennia later, why even write the book of Revela-

tion and pointedly mail it to seven contemporary churches, telling them what wisdom and endurance it will require if they are to weather the coming storm? The angel explicitly tells him not to seal up the book for the sake of future readers, since the time described therein is soon to come (22:10).

> And he said to me, "These words are trustworthy and true. And the Lord, the God of the spirits of the prophets, has sent his angel to show his servants what must soon take place. And behold, I am coming soon." Blessed is he who keeps the words of the prophecy of this book. And he said to me, "Do not seal up the words of the prophecy of this book, for the time is near. Behold, I am coming soon, bringing my recompense, to repay every one for what he has done." He who testifies to these things says, "Surely I am coming soon." Amen. Come, Lord Jesus! (Rev. 22:6–7, 10, 12, 20a)

> "And if the Bible was as old as it seemed, what did 'quickly' mean? It must not have meant soon, unless it was from the perspective of someone with a long view of history. Maybe Jesus meant that when he came, he would do it quickly." (*Left Behind*)[7]

Contra such apologetical gibberish, "soon" does not mean the same thing as "suddenly." The latter might open up some wiggle room, as if the Parousia would pour in like a flood once it began—whenever that might be. What we are seeing in all such pathetic and tortuous rationalizations is a phenomenon very like that whereby the early Islamic savants created a whole new grammar that would enable them to seem to solve problems in the text of the Koran where, on the ordinary rules of Arabic grammar, the text would make no sense.[8]

The passage from *Left Behind* also hints at the oldest trick in the book: the coming will be "soon" or "quick" from God's perspective, not ours, and he's got all the time in the universe. But what sort of a revelation is it that is couched in terms unintelligible to those for whose sake it is vouchsafed? Given God's infinite expanse of cosmic eons, what could "soon" possibly mean if it bears no relation to our own use of the word? After all, if God is talking to human beings, he has to use human terms if he wants to be understood. And if he really meant, "I am coming thousands of years in the future," why didn't he just say so?

> From the fig tree learn its lesson: as soon as its branch becomes tender and puts forth its leaves, you know that summer is near. So also, when you see these things taking place, you know that he is near, at the very gates. Truly, I say to you, this generation will not pass away before all these things take place. (Mark 13:28–30)

Here the usual out is to try to make the Greek word *genea* mean "race" or "nation," which it can depending on the context. But this isn't one of those times. What would be the sense of saying, "This race of people will not pass away before all these things transpire," if "these things" include the testing and salvation of this very race? Another favorite dodge is to pretend that "this generation" means not Jesus' contemporaries but rather whichever generation finds itself contemporary with these events, in whatever century, millennium, or geological epoch in which they might occur.[9] But that is useless tautology: "The generation that sees these things happen will live to see them happen." No, it must mean what it obviously means: the Parousia will bring history to a sudden end in the lifetime of Jesus' contemporaries. "This is the only interpretation which the words will bear; every other involves a wresting of language, and a violence to the understanding" (J. Stuart Russell).[10]

The characters in *Glorious Appearing* employ a similar evasive tactic: "We know that following the phenomena in the sky comes the sign of His coming, but nothing tells us whether that will be immediate. God has his own timetable."[11] Uh, that's what we *mean* by "sign." The thing signified is about to happen! Picture a war movie, "Okay, Bert, when I give you the sign, run like hell!" Does the speaker mean to intimate that his signal does not necessarily mean the time has come to flee? Likewise, when Jesus says you can take the events he describes as the sign of the arrival of the kingdom, can he really mean that it may not be near at all? "If the bugle gives an uncertain sound, who will know to prepare for battle?" (1 Cor. 14:8).

"For whoever is ashamed of me and of my words in this adulterous and sinful generation, of him will the Son of man also be ashamed, when he comes in the glory of his Father with the holy angels." And he said to them, "Truly, I say to you, there are some standing here who will not taste death before they see that the kingdom of God has come with power." (Mark 8:38–9:1; cf. Matthew 16:27–28; Luke 9:26–27)

This one can be understood as already backpedaling from the previous, premature promise. In that one, the whole generation was to witness the arrival of the kingdom of God, but in this verse, only "some" are to last that long. Eventually the guest list will shrink to one single disciple, in John 21:23, and once he is gone, the promise will, unfortunately, still be remembered—by the wrong people: "Where is the promise of his coming? For ever since the fathers fell asleep, all things have continued the way they were from the beginning of creation" (2 Peter 3:4).

Mark himself has retreated from this promise in what directly follows, for all Jesus' contemporaries are dead by the time he is writing. He might like to simply omit the troublesome promise, but as we have just seen, the skepticism of outsiders made that impossible. So the thing to do was to reinterpret the promise of Jesus as if it referred, not to the Parousia at the end of the age, but rather to some event that *did* happen in the lifetime of Jesus' contemporaries. But since he was stuck with a version of the saying according to which only *some* would see it, he had to restrict the number of witnesses on some other basis than the rest having died. Thus Mark has Jesus take with him only the inner circle of disciples to witness his Transfiguration, understood as a foretaste of his heavenly glory. The event, though quite dramatic in its own right, falls far short of the Parousia of the Son of Man, but it may be the best remaining option. It is pretty much the same strategy of satisfying the expectation that the return of Elijah would precede the advent of the Christ by having Elijah appear on the mountaintop, but only to a very small audience.

THE SECOND COMING OF THE REPRESSED

Why do fundamentalist readers completely ignore these time indications? Why, of course, because none of them came true. They cannot afford to admit that the Bible, or Jesus himself, could have been that wrong. Like cynical secularists, fundamentalists love to deride the poor Jehovah's Witnesses for their repeated false dates for the Second Coming. It is obvious to them that the Witness sect deserves no further consideration once one knows how they repeatedly shot their credibility. What kind of theological or spiritual guides could they be if in the one matter in which their claims may be falsified—they are? So how can fundamentalists not see that the New Testament writers made the same mistake? They cannot afford to see it. They have altogether too much invested in their beliefs. It is a prime case of cognitive dissonance.[12] They refuse to face a devastating truth because, no matter how guilty a conscience one may have, it is better than having to admit how wrong one was and to have to start over again.

In Freudian terms, one may say fundamentalists are *repressing* the trauma of the failure of the one testable Bible promise. But the repressed returns. Refused direct acknowledgment, it will make itself known in other, oblique ways, to try to get the attention of the one who has repressed the trauma and is consequently suffering for it in many ways, from general feelings of anxiety or guilt, to psychogenic physical complaints, to nightmares, or the recurrence of once-but-no-longer-appropriate behavior patterns. In terms of End Times expectation, the trauma was learning or suspecting that the Bible was wrong about the Second Coming and that, for example, the long-dead Domitian was *the* Antichrist. One might begin to heal if one allowed oneself to face the trauma and learn the lesson: such speculations are foolish, and maturity requires we plan our futures on the basis of our own opportunities and abilities, not by the dictates of some ancient book. But we fear we will not be up to that kind of challenge. So we continue in the infantile pattern of behavior. We keep trying to match the Bible with today's news because that will mean, like little kids, we need not take responsibility for a future that, like or not, we will continue to live in. Instead, we will try to find out who *else* might be the Antichrist, when *else* Christ might return and make things simple for us, fulfill our childish revenge fantasies. We repeat the behavioral loop of past generations of pietistic biblicists because we are afraid to face the prospect of personal and intellectual maturity, which is to say scientific modernity.

THE FINAL SOLUTION

Stephen King has a particularly nasty short story called "Survivor Type." In it, a surgeon finds himself like the man in a thousand cartoons, stranded alone on a desert island. There is precious little food, but he cannot allow himself to die of starvation; his instincts are too strong. So, to the reader's horror, he gradually, carefully amputates one part after another of his starving body to provide himself food. He regains some measure of stamina and vitality but at the cost of devouring his own flesh. And it is a doomed effort to begin with, for obvious reasons. I think of that story when I think of a fascinating old book by J. Stuart Russell, *The Parousia: A Study of the New Testament Doctrine of Our Lord's Second Coming* (1887). He would be, I am sure, quite surprised and gratified if he could know that a century later there would be a school of thought taking his work as their chief inspiration, namely "Preterism." The word means "Past-ism," and it implies that all the New Testament prophecies, including somehow even the Second Coming of Christ, have already been fulfilled in a literal manner, but we have hitherto misunderstood them. Now this approach has much in common with, and yet must be distinguished from, the critical approach to the book of Revelation, also called Preterism.

Precritical interpreters understood Revelation in either one of two ways. The futurist school understood the symbols of the book to predict events that lay in their own future, albeit no longer very far off. John was predicting the events of the End Time, and their fulfillment lay far in the future for him. Historicists, on the other hand, following the Protestant Reformers, understood the Revelation as an allegory of church history in the future subsequent to John. For them, for example, the Beast was the papacy. The False Prophet was Muhammad. Either school of interpretation could and did interpret the text as implying that the end was not far off in their own future. Preterism, on the other hand, was a critical approach precisely because it was predicated on the realization that the predictions of the book of Revelation might have been mistaken, just like the climaxes of virtually all other predictive apocalypses. Critics like R. H. Charles were enabled to look at the text with new eyes, alert to new possibilities. And suddenly it became clear, for instance, that 666 stood for Nero and denoted Domitian, both long dead and not likely to return.

Another major example would be that of the eastern kings across the Euphrates and the centaur locusts from the bottomless abyss.

And the fifth angel sounded forth, and I saw a star from the sky having descended to the earth, where it received the key to unlock the shaft of the Abyss. And he proceeded to throw wide the lid of the Abyss, and from the shaft poured a vast cloud like the smoke of a colossal furnace. The sun, and thus the air, was darkened by the exhalation of the shaft. And from the sooty mist emerged locusts to land upon the earth, and they were given the same power as earthly scorpions have. And they were cautioned not to harm the grass of the earth, nor any green plant nor any tree: nothing but those individuals lacking the ownership seal of God on their foreheads. And even these they were warned not to kill, but rather to torture for five months. And the torture they inflict is like that of a scorpion when it stings its victim. And in those days their victims will desperately seek death but not find it. They will covet death, only to have it elude their grasp. And these locusts might be compared to horses caparisoned for battle, on their heads something like crowns made of gold, with their faces resembling human faces. And they had hair like the hair of women, and their teeth were like the fangs of lions, and their thoraxes looked as if armored in iron breastplates, and the sound of their wings was like the sound of many horse-drawn chariots clattering to war. (Rev. 9:1–9)

And the sixth angel blew his trumpet, and I heard one voice originating from between the four horns of the golden altar that stands before God, telling the sixth angel, still holding his trumpet: "Release the four angels bound at the great River Euphrates!" And the four angels, long since prepared for this specific hour and day and month and year, were let loose to exterminate a third of humankind. And the count of the cavalry soldiers was two hundred million strong: I heard them count off. This is how I saw the horses in the vision, as well as those mounted upon them, wearing breastplates of fiery bronze, of jacinth, and brimstone, with the heads of the horses like lions' heads, and out of their mouths stream fire and smoke and sulfur. And from these three plagues, a third of humankind was killed, by the fire and the smoke and the sulfur streaming from their mouths. For the power of the horses lies in their mouths and in their tails. For their tails are like snakes, each having multiple heads, and with these they wreak havoc. (Rev. 9:13–19)

And the sixth emptied his bowl into the great river Euphrates, and suddenly the water had dried up! This was to prepare the way for the kings from the sunrise. (Rev. 16:12)

Lying thinly veiled beneath this description is a portrayal of the Parthian cavalry and chariots, feared enemies of Rome who, it was believed, would one day sweep across the Euphrates to conquer Rome. The women's hair represents the horsehair crests of the Parthian horsemen. They wear breastplates, as real soldiers did, and the noise of the massive insect wings like the clash of armor in battle—is just that! They come from across the Euphrates: from Parthia. The upshot is that John meant to predict the final invasion of the dreaded Parthians from the east to destroy Rome. Just as one need no longer trouble oneself to decode some international leader's name to get 666, so there is no point speculating as to whether the eastern hordes are communist Chinese or if the locusts are, as Hal Lindsey guessed, Soviet helicopter gunships. No, John had in mind contemporary players on the stage of ancient history, and since all this played out (whether accurately or consistently) in the past, over nineteen centuries ago, it is over and done. Except for the little detail that it is wrong. Parthia did not take Rome down. And Christ did not return. We seem to have a major decision to make: are we willing to trade faith in the accuracy of the Bible for a more plausible understanding of the Bible?

But the movement stemming from J. Stuart Russell's *Parousia* does not see itself faced with that choice. Like Russell, but unlike R. H. Charles, these Preterists believe they can have their Communion wafer and eat it, too. What if the eschatological predictions of the New Testament *all* had reference to contemporary events—and *were fulfilled*? What if they all referred to the fall of Jerusalem and with it the end of the sacrificial system and the dawn of a new covenant through Jesus Christ? "Sometimes the old, or Jewish, economy is spoken of as this aeon, the present aeon . . . ; and the Christian, or Gospel, dispensation as 'the coming aeon,' and 'the world to come' . . . (Ephes. 1. 21; Heb. ii.5). The close of the Jewish economy is called 'the end of the age....' Since, then the old economy was finally set aside and abrogated at the destruction of Jerusalem, we conclude that the new aeon . . . received its solemn and public inauguration at the same period, which coincides with the Parousia."[13] Suppose all the imagery of cosmic catastrophe (stars colliding with the earth, the sun going out, the sky snapping up like a window shade) was simply a collection of well-established metaphors drawn from Old Testament prophets who had described previous historical events in similar "world-shaking" hyperbole.[14] Well, it would mean that pesky critical scholars would not be able to say that Jesus and the New Testament writers were mistaken. It would save face. But the price would be high: there would be no more Christian eschatology, no reason to believe in a yet-future Second Coming of Christ. One would have, at one blow, exorcized apocalyptic from the New Testament like a foul-smelling demon. And that would not necessarily be bad. Christian theology could return itself to the earlier view of prophets like Isaiah and Jeremiah, innocent of the determinisms and dispensational timetables of Zoroastrianism. It would mean an open-ended model of a history that could end, if at all, with a whimper or a bang, or with the millennium, as we so decide. Perhaps not a bad trade at all.

But what of the return of Jesus, the resurrection of the dead, the translation of the living believers? One expects Russell at this point to start demythologizing and allegorizing, retreating into some kind of "realized eschatology." But he does not. He does the next best thing, suggesting that all these things did happen in connection with the fall of Jerusalem. They occurred literally and in 70 CE. Russell says that, not having been present, we cannot know whether the events were visible to the eye of flesh.[15] It would have been a "Secret Rapture" in the most literal sense possible. But did not Christians appeal to Zechariah 12:10, "every eye shall see him, every one who pierced him"? This thing would not be done in a corner! Or would it? John implies such a change in plans, a restriction of the Second Coming to a private event: "Lord, how is it that you will manifest yourself to us, and not to the world?" (John 14:22), just as Elijah's return was seen by a small few.

As for a contemporary resurrection of the dead, remember, Matthew portrays just such a thing in Matthew 27:51–53, as does Revelation 11:11–13, where the Two Martyrs, compared to Moses and Elijah but whom Russell identifies as Simon Peter and James the Just, are actually resurrected and elevated to heaven publicly, though by themselves. Russell notes that such an event may have escaped human, physical eyes in the very nature of things.[16] But the heart of the "End Time" resurrection for Russell is the Harrowing of Hell, the descent of Jesus to Hades to liberate the worthies of the Old Testament, barred from heaven until Jesus paid the price of admission by his precious blood.[17] Who saw this? Only angels, but it would seem to be enough to answer to Christian hopes of the resurrection.

But the Rapture of the living? Could that have happened? Darn right, says Russell.[18] Their vanishment was lost amid the general confusion of the destruction of Jerusalem. For Russell, it is implied, the patristic account of the Jerusalem church fleeing the doomed city to take refuge in Pella is a mundane, after-the-fact explanation by those who knew that a whole generation of Christians—Christ's contemporaries—was simply all gone. This would handily explain the dearth of information we possess about the immediate "postapostolic" genera-tion.[19] They were caught up from the earth! (In this manner Russell even seeks to explain why Mark ended so abruptly at 16:8, why Luke ended Acts before relating the death of Paul—they were raptured before they could finish!) Christianity had to start again. And that in turn might explain why the quality seems to have dropped so precipi-tously, as all Church historians, not to say latter-day sect founders, believe it did.

One thing is sure: Russell was the man Diogenes was looking for. His long, packed text contains a number of statements bracing in their honesty. He has no patience for the kind of exegetical evasions we have criticized: "This is not criticism, but mysticism. So artificial and intri-cate an explanation could never have occurred to the disciples, and it is surprising that it should have occurred to any sober interpreter of Scripture." "Language is incapable of conveying thought with accuracy if these words do not affirm that the return of our Saviour to His dis-ciples was to be speedy."[20] "This is a nonnatural method of interpreta-tion, which simply evacuates words of all meaning."[21] And, extravagant as his thesis seems, he has to resort quite seldom to the sort of text twisting he condemns in others. For instance, desirous of avoiding the implications of references to the end of "the world" because he wants to restrict the eschaton to Jerusalem and its environs, Russell adopts the old Calvinist dodge (embraced on behalf of the post-Calvin "limited atonement" doctrine that denies Christ died for everybody) whereby "the world" can mean something other than the whole world popula-tion. We feel a bit less uncomfortable when he contends that "All the tribes of the earth shall mourn" (Matt. 24:30) means only the tribes of "the land," that is, of Palestine.[22]

Yet even these embarrassments might have been obviated had Russell been able to avail himself of the Higher Criticism. In a later era, he might have adopted the solution of J. A. T. Robinson and H. B. Sharman, who thought the Synoptic Apocalypse originally *did* mean to predict only the fall of Jerusalem, with no worldwide, history-extinguishing repercussions, but that such wider horizons were added to the text later, albeit already before Mark. Frankly, it is amazing that Russell, taking it all at face value as transcripts of the words of Jesus, is able to make as persuasive a case as he does.

But I think the Preterist case contains a fatal flaw. How do Preterists know that the rhetoric of cosmic catastrophe is mere metaphor for events that will "rock your world"? Simply because they are able to catalog plenty of examples of such imagery embellishing ancient predictions of historical events including the defeat of Babylon.[23] Isaiah spoke of the stars falling, of the sky rolling up, and so on, when in fact all that happened was the defeat of Babylon (13:9–10, 13) or of Bozrah (34:5–6). Micah had the mountains melting like wax at the coming of God to judge Samaria (1:3–4). And if such language need not imply literal cosmic catastrophe in such cases, why take it literally in the New Testament apocalypses? But this is completely circular. What Preterists are doing in the case of Old Testament prophecy is drawing the same inference Russell did concerning the New Testament ones: from the evident fact that no such cosmic pyrotechnics occurred, they infer that none were ever *supposed* to; it was just figurative. (Again, we recognize Mark's apologetic sidestep: if in fact the end of all things did not transpire before some of the disciples died, what *other* event can we substitute for it that some *did* live to see? Ah! The Transfiguration!) Robert P. Carroll, dealing with Old Testament prophecy, sums it up well: "[T]he need to treat the language as symbolic only arises because of the failure of the predictions in the first place."[24]

It seems that what we are dealing with in the Old Testament is a series of delays and disappointed, or only partially fulfilled, promises. Perhaps Antiochus Epiphanes did perish, but the kingdom of God did not come. Maybe the empire of Babylon did fall, but the sky did not fall. Maybe the Persian Empire did become unstable, but that didn't issue in Zerubbabel becoming the new Messiah. The chest-thumping assurances of apologists like Tim LaHaye that Old Testament prophecy had proved 100 percent accurate are just empty utterances of those who have not read their Bible closely enough. There are many signs of frequent predictive failure throughout the Old Testament. The famous Deuteronomic command to stone prophets whose prognostications fail is itself ample proof of frequent prophetic failure, isn't it?

Or think of the prophetic declarations that inform their audiences that there will be little delay before so and so happens: "'Once again, in a little while, I will shake the heavens and the earth and the sea and the dry land; and I will shake all nations, so that the treasures of all nations shall come in, and I will fill this house with splendor,' says Yahve Sabaoth" (Haggai 2:6). We usually overlook the peculiar note of deferral "in a little while." The prophet Habakkuk is disarmingly blunt when he says: "For still the vision awaits its time; it hastens to the end— it will not lie. Should it seem slow, wait for it; it will surely come, it will not delay" (2:3). The key phrase is "for yet a very little while" or "for there is still a very brief period." Similar phrases occur elsewhere in Isaiah.[25] Carroll explains what is going on in such passages:

> The "not yet" of prophecy took the view that the event of expectation was about to happen, soon it would happen, it was imminent. All these terms can be seen as positive versions of the more negative notion of a delay [as, one might add, in 2 Peter 3:9, "The Lord is not slow about his promise as some count slowness, but is forbearing toward you, not wishing that any should perish, but that all should reach repentance."]. By interpreting various notes on imminence in the prophetic traditions as hints of deferment or delay it is possible to see in them responses to or awareness of dissonance caused by the non-appearance of expectation. The interpreters of the traditions [i.e., the "sons of the prophets" guilds, 2 Kings 2:15; 4:1, 42; 6:1–2] were compelled to emphasize the nearness of the event in order to encourage the community to be faithful and to reaffirm their faith in the reliability of the expectation. Each text should be seen as the answer to the question foremost in the consciousness of the prophetic groups: "when?" or "how long?"[26]

By their own accounts, the prophets had to deal with hecklers in their audiences. Jeremiah: "'Look, they say to me, 'Where is the thing

Yahve has promised? Let it come!'" (17:5). Ezekiel had to come up with a comeback to this taunt: "The days grow long, and every vision comes to nothing" (12:22). His rejoinder: "Thus says the Lord Yahve: 'None of my words will be delayed any longer, but the word which I speak will be performed'" (12:28). Jeremiah finds himself abashed by the failure of his prediction: "Ah, Lord Yahve, surely you have completely deceived this people and Jerusalem, saying, 'It shall be well with you;' whereas the sword has reached their very life.'" (4:10).

So, as Russell says, we do in fact see a consistent, long-enduring pattern throughout Old and New Testaments concerning prophecy, only it is not what he thinks it is. Instead of Jesus following in the footsteps of the prophets with their use of spectacular symbolism to describe historical developments, what we have is the New Testament writers continuing to do as their Old Testament predecessors did: banking on soon-coming events as heralding the end of the universe in fire and meteor storms. They were wrong and they kept being wrong. And that is why today's fundamentalists, following the same trajectory, keep striking out, too. Perhaps if they allowed themselves to understand that the biblical writers had so grossly and repeatedly erred, they would learn their lesson. But that they will not do, for fear of forfeiting scriptural authority. And this traumatic truth about the Bible they repress, but it is a burden their consciences bear with difficulty, so it manifests itself in neurotic, repeating symptoms, notably the incorrigible desire to calculate the end of a world they are not mature enough to deal with apart from magical fantasies. Like Stephen King's castaway, they are eating their fingers to fill their stomachs.

NOTES

1. H. Richard Niebuhr, *Christ and Culture*, chap. 6, "Christ the Transformer of Culture" (New York: Harper & Brothers, 1951), pp. 190–229.

2. Dwight Wilson, *Armageddon Now! The Premillenarian Response to Russia and Israel since 1917* (Grand Rapids, MI: Baker Book House, 1977), p. 216.

3. William M. Alnor, *Soothsayers of the Second Advent*, chap. 2, "88 Reasons Wasn't Enough" (Old Tappan, NJ: Fleming H. Revell, 1989), pp. 28–33.

4. Ronald A. Knox, *Enthusiasm: A Chapter in the History of Religion with Special Reference to the XVII and XVIII Centuries* (New York: Oxford University Press, 1950), p. 2.

5. R. A. Torrey, *Difficulties in the Bible: Alleged Errors and Contradictions* (Chicago: Moody Press, n.d.), pp. 118–19.

6. As my daughter Veronica pointed out.

7. Tim LaHaye and Jerry B. Jenkins, *Left Behind: A Novel of the Earth's Last Days* (Wheaton, IL: Tyndale House, 1995), p. 122.

8. Günter Lüling, "Preconditions for the Scholarly Criticism of the Koran and Islam, with Some Autobiographical Remarks," *Journal of Higher Criticism* 3, no. 1 (Spring 1996): 82.

9. Torrey, *Difficulties in the Bible*, p. 116: "And 'this generation' of verse 34 clearly refers, if taken in context, to the generation existing when these signs shall appear."

10. J. Stuart Russell, *The Parousia: A Study of the New Testament Doctrine of Our Lord's Second Coming* (London: T. Fisher Unwin, 1887; repr., Grand Rapids, MI: Baker Book House, 1983), p. 87.

11. LaHaye and Jenkins, *Glorious Appearing: The End of Days* (Wheaton, IL: Tyndale House, 2004), p. 139.

12. See Leon Festinger, *A Theory of Cognitive Dissonance* (Stanford, CA: Stanford University Press, 1962). The theory grew out of a participant-observation experiment chronicled and analyzed in Leon Festinger, Henry W. Riecken, and Stanley Schachter, *When Prophecy Fails: A Social and Psychological Study of a Modern Group that Predicted the Destruction of the World* (New York: Harper & Row, 1964). For some of the many subsequent studies exploring apocalyptic disappointments and cognitive dissonance, see Jon R. Stone, ed., *Expecting Armageddon: Essential Readings in Failed Prophecy* (New York: Routledge, 2000). A particularly poignant and revealing case is documented in C. LeRoy Anderson, *Joseph Morris and the Morrisites* (Logan: Utah State University Press, 1981).

13. Russell, *Parousia*, p. 242.

14. Ibid., e.g., p. 451.

15. Ibid., pp. 121–22, 168, 210, 513.

16. Ibid., p. 442.

17. Ibid., pp. 206–207.

18. Ibid., p. 211.

19. Ibid., p. iii.

20. Ibid., p. 135.

21. Ibid., p. 234.

22. Ibid., pp. 104–106.

23. Ibid., pp. 79–81, 350–54.

24. Robert P. Carroll, *When Prophecy Failed: Cognitive Dissonance in the Prophetic Traditions of the Old Testament* (New York: Seabury Press, 1979), p. 66.

25. Ibid., p. 169.

26. Ibid., p. 168.

Chapter Seven

EARLIER CHRISTIAN APOCALYPSE NOVELS

"But a week ago I would have told you that millions of people all over the world disappearing into thin air sounds like a B movie."

—*Left Behind*[1]

ESCHATOLOGY AS ENTERTAINMENT

Ever since Chicken Little started the trend, it hasn't taken much to get people going with cries of "The sky is falling!" The deciding factor seems to be more the psychological state of the doom criers than the apparent proximity of doom. For whatever reason, fundamentalist prophets of doom have been getting quite a hearing in the last few decades, if the sales of their books are any indication. For instance, Hal Lindsey's *The Late Great Planet Earth* has racked up printing after printing and was the secret best seller (ignored by the *New York Times* list) in the 1970s when it first appeared. Lindsey has followed up with a series of sequels including *The Terminal Generation*. Moral Majority guru Tim LaHaye published a new edition of his guide to the End Times, *The Beginning of the End*, and new titles such as *Apocalypse Next* keep rolling off the presses. These books try to match up Bible prophecies and current events (both usually ripped out of context) to show that our current troubles are leading fast and furiously to Armageddon. And the utility of this? To scare the reader into getting saved. After all, who wants to be left holding the bag when the Antichrist starts passing out the thumbscrews?

Popular fascination with Antichrist and Armageddon has proven a boon for science fiction/fantasy writers, too. Seeing the success of *The Omen* series (now up to three theatrical movies, five novelizations, a cable TV movie, a related TV miniseries, and a theatrical remake), other writers decided to try their luck and have given us books like Robert R. McCammon's debut novel *Baal* (1978) and mystery writer James Patterson's *Virgin* (1980, rewritten in 2001 as *Cradle and All*, adapted for the small screen in 1991 as *Child of Darkness, Child of Light*). But fundamentalists had long since beaten them to the punch. They had already unleashed a stream of end of the world novels, appropriating the future fiction genre for evangelistic purposes. It is interesting to compare the two groups of apocalyptic novels, secular and evangelistic, centering on their treatments of the star of the show, the Antichrist.

The blue-nosed ethics of fundamentalism are often simply the backwater survival of the cultural values of yesteryear. A fundamentalist leader of the nineteenth century once wrote: "A novel is nothing but a well told lie." Novel reading was condemned along with smoking, drinking, and card playing as "worldly pursuits."[2] This sounds shocking and ridiculous to us, but it used to be a common prejudice. Plato thought that fiction writers were liars, as did the authorities in Shakespeare's day. That's why he had to call his plays "The True History of . . ." even when they weren't.[3] Such distaste for the imagination hung on longer among fundamentalists than anywhere else. One suspects the prejudice has something to do with biblicists' inability to recognize fiction in the Bible. They view the Bible as either "hoax or history." It doesn't seem to occur to them that there is a third option. Implicitly they still equate fiction with "hoax."

Thus it is no surprise that the fundamentalist breakthrough into fiction was slow and a long time in coming. Usually their fiction has had to justify itself as moral catechism or as evangelistic propaganda.[4] Jerry B. Jenkins's *Left Behind* novels conspicuously partake of both, but his books, as witness their fantastic popularity, also attest to a more recent trend among evangelicals: the marketing of "safe" Christian versions of whatever the general "worldly" crowd is reading, watching, or listening to. The *Left Behind* books are the equivalent to the huge number of born-again romance novels or to Christian rock music. Middle-class fundamentalists can enjoy them with no qualms. This, for instance, is the only reason there is no profanity in any of Jenkins's books, even out of the mouths of the fiendish minions of the Antichrist! At most, we are told a villain curses, but not what, specifically, he may have said. When we do hear the bad guys erupt in direct speech, they say only "blamed," not "damned," "what the devil," not "what the hell." And the F-word, practically as common as "uh" in modern America, appears not once in nearly five thousand pages! (Not that I'm complaining; I'm pretty prudish about such matters myself.)

BEGINNING OF THE END

The End Times genre got off to a most opportune start with three works: Joseph Birkbeck Burroughs's *Titan, Son of Saturn: The Coming World Emperor: A Story of the Other Christ* in 1905 (revised in 1914), Robert Hugh Benson's *Lord of the World* (1907), and Sydney Watson's *In the Twinkling of an Eye* (1910) and *The Mark of the Beast* (1911). Indeed, one may safely say that Burroughs, Benson, and Watson set a high watermark for the genre that very few of their successors have yet managed to reach.

Burroughs, a medical doctor and pious fundamentalist, writes, essentially, an astonishing hybrid of Stephen King's *The Stand* and Charles Sheldon's speculative devotional classic *In His Steps.* Burroughs's *Titan, Son of Saturn* somehow manages to combine the moral and literary sensibility of Sheldon with a pervasive element of the truly weird. He seems to understand that the figure of the Antichrist demands treatment as a pulp figure, just as Cyril J. Barber, in his preface to Arthur W. Pink's monograph *The Antichrist*, compares the Antichrist, quite naturally, to Darth Vader.[5] We first find ourselves in the improbably named northwestern American town of Newmosoto (some sort of vowel-shift jumble for "Minnesota"?), a cameo of small-town Victorian values and wholesomeness. Shortly—*bam!*—the Rapture occurs. Then it's off to the Iraqi desert, where we see Satan strolling beside the ruins of Babylon. After a sad soliloquy on his unfair treatment at the hands of Jehovah (all he wanted to do, he and his angels, was to set up a separate heavenly court in a far-flung frontier of the endless universe), Satan whistles up mighty cyclones that he uses as precision tools to unearth the lost tomb of Antiochus IV Epiphanes, the villain of 1 and 2 Maccabees, the Seleucid tyrant whose desecration of the Jerusalem altar contributed so much to the Jewish and Christian lore of apocalypse with its governing assumption that history repeats itself. While most of our End Times novels take the feature of the Beast bouncing back from a fatal wound to denote a resurrection after he is already active in the Last Days—a pivotal event clinching his authority and power—Burroughs understands the prophecy to mean that the Beast is instead a figure of the past, raised from the dead by Satan. And if so, then pray tell who better than the Little Horn?

Satan descends flight after flight of long, unlit marble steps until he comes upon the mummy of Antiochus; he then restores the missing life force. As a cautionary note to Satan, the process does not work until a heavenly voice joins in: "Come forth!" This ought to have tipped the devil off that he is being used, ultimately, as a tool in a larger scheme. But it doesn't. Once Antiochus understands that he has not in fact escaped premature burial but has been dead fully two millennia, he begins to remember how Jesus, too, had "found the keys" and escaped from hell. Satan claims to be the titan Saturn, father of the Olympians, though cast down, and that Antiochus is a titan, too, Saturn's son. As the two trek through the desert, Satan repeats the three desert temptations he had once made to Jesus, only Antiochus is glad to yield to them. But, as he is the Antichrist instead of the Christ, he thus passes rather than fails the test. Burroughs implies that Jesus, too, would not simply have failed as the Christ but would have been recruited as the Antichrist, protégé of the devil, had he acquiesced.

Appearing among the Russian troops in the Caucasus, site of ancient Tubal and Meshech, Antiochus gains renown as both tactician and revolutionary, as he begins, like a second Simon Bolivar, to foment a chain reaction of socialist revolution that overspreads not only Russia but all of Western Europe, minus England. (Keep in mind that this is all written thirteen years before Lenin and the Bolsheviks took power.) One of the first things Antiochus does is to order the erection of a kind of "tent of meeting," a small stone structure, the Spartan contents of which are hidden from casual observation by a pair of inner and outer doors. Burroughs deftly uses a distancing device as he lets us eavesdrop on a couple of laborers who wonder why the inner sanctum holds a black obelisk and a *pair* of chairs, though no one but Antiochus ever goes in or out . . . ! Of course he is conjuring up Satan/Saturn for worship and periodic counsel. And in one of several striking theological reversals, there is a scene in which Antichrist, full of himself and proud of his many victories, meets a withering rebuke from his diabolical patron, who reminds him that in himself he has no strength. Every triumph he owes, not to the arm of flesh, but to the grace of Satan, through whom alone he makes war and achieves victory. There is the Deuteronomic theology, the Pauline piety, of the Bible, only now on display in the communion of the Antichrist with his Father Below. And on the very verge of a disastrous Armageddon, we are not much surprised to hear Antiochus cry out, "Why have you forsaken me?"

Burroughs's Antichrist is a man of many names and titles. As with Arthur Pink's multifaceted Antichristology, most of these epithets are by-products of taking various obscure Old Testament prophecies out of context and treating them as esoteric predictions of Antichrist. If Isaiah predicts the movements of the king of Assyria, who will wipe out the northern Kingdom of Israel, Pink, Burroughs, and company take it as susceptible of a double fulfillment in the case of the End Time Antichrist persecuting Jews in general. So the Antichrist picks up a new alias: "The Assyrian." But whence the name "Titan"? This he picks up from late second-century Bishop Irenaeus of Lyons: "For it has in it the predicted number, is ancient, and removed from ordinary use, for among kings we find none bearing the name Titan. Among many people it is a name accounted divine, and of one who pretends that he vindicates the oppressed. It is a name of royal dignity, and still further belongs to a tyrant. Inasmuch then as this name Titan has so much to recommend it, there is a strong degree of probability that he who is to come shall be called Titan" (*Against Heresies* 5:30).[6] But then he also has the risen Antiochus call himself Napoleon, Napoleon Titan. Why? First, there is an etymology that, though false, is nonetheless just too tempting. Burroughs has read somewhere that "Napoleon" goes back to the Greek "Apollyon," or the "Destroyer" (Rev. 9:11). Actually, while "Napoleon" is Greek, it means "one from Neapolis," or a new city. Nablus and Napoli are variants. But the name is nonetheless apt, since soon after Napoleon Bonaparte's death the rumor circulated (precisely as in the case of Nero) that the emperor was not dead but had escaped and would soon return. Some esoteric groups, especially in Poland, developed the belief in a second coming of Napoleon Bonaparte as a messianic redeemer![7]

The theology of *Titan, Son of Saturn* is remarkable in many ways. Like *Left Behind*, it fairly drips with devotional and revivalistic preachments, but somehow they do not seem so out of place. That is, I think, because this sort of maudlin piety was part and parcel of the larger Victorian sentimentality. By contrast, it will stick out like a sore thumb in Jerry Jenkins's macho, spy-novel-esque series. There it reminds one inevitably of the grotesque tearfulness of the "muscular Christianity" of the Promise Keepers movement. Their members sported bumper stickers reading "Real Men Love Jesus." Haven't you had the impulse to apply your Magic Marker and change it to "Real Sissies Love Jesus"? I know I have.

Again, like the *Left Behind* series, Burroughs treats us to a good bit of Jewish versus Christian scriptural debate over whether Jesus is the Messiah. Burroughs, though hopelessly mistaken, as are all Christian apologetics on the point, is much more sophisticated than Jenkins/LaHaye. Singularly refreshing in *Titan, Son of Saturn* is the ecumenicity of it. Jenkins seems inconsistent when it comes to whether Roman Catholics are "real Christians." He shows us his hero Buck Williams making a nuisance of himself, hectoring Catholic bishop Peter Mathews (soon to become Pope Peter II, Supreme Pontiff of the Enigma Babylon One World Faith) over the question of salvation by faith/grace versus good works. The bishop is a straw man Catholic drawn right out of Protestant polemical manuals. He maintains that faith alone is not enough, and that Protestants have twisted scripture on the point. Never mind that the official Roman Catholic position has always been that salvation comes through faith and grace, with works an inevitable outflow of a genuine operation of grace.[8] Then we remember that Jenkins long served as the editor of *Moody Monthly* where one expects little care to be taken in setting forth the subtleties of Roman Catholic theology. But then we find ourselves pleasantly surprised to learn that the pope himself was taken up in the Rapture, and that, later in the book, some of those who missed the boat discover the technique of personal salvation in some literature they discover in a Catholic church library! Jenkins is to be congratulated after all: he must be aware of the astonishing extent to which the Roman Catholic Church in America has been permeated with "personal saviorism" ever since the late 1960s when the Catholic Charismatic movement managed to inject Protestant revivalism into Catholic catechism.

But no such developments were on the horizon in 1904 when Burroughs was writing. Thus it is an even bolder step for him to align Catholics alongside Baptists and other Protestant stalwarts against the Beast. This was at a time when many, many Protestants still believed the Roman pope himself was the Antichrist. And though Burroughs is clear that Jews are gravely mistaken in rejecting Jesus as Messiah, he goes out of his way to make sure we know that devout Jews, suffering Antiochus's wrath as they did two millennia before, were received into the loving arms of God, with or without Jesus.[9] By contrast, Jenkins leaves us with the distasteful doctrine that Orthodox Jews willing to die for their faith and for the Torah are destined for eternal torture in hell anyway! God *becomes* Antiochus in Jenkins's scenario, sad to say. Jenkins is in one sense optimistic about Jewish salvation: he has millions of Jews converted to Christianity by the fraudulent apologetics of Tsion Ben-Judah. But, as Jews are quick to point out, buying a ticket to the Christian heaven by converting to Jesus is only another form of renouncing Judaism to save your skin.

Maybe the most interesting aspect of Burroughs's soteriology is his advocacy of the much-scorned "Partial Rapture" doctrine. Jenkins follows LaHaye's lead in presupposing the pretribulation Rapture doctrine (see chapter 5 in the present book): the trumpet sounds, and the real, true, genuine born-again Christians will vanish from the earth. Only unbelievers, apostates, and hypocrites are left, no matter their previous profession of faith. Some hold an ultrastrict version of the doctrine whereby no one has any chance of salvation henceforth. No one is saved during the ensuing Tribulation. (As I read it, this is the view taken in Joe Musser's 1970 novella *Behold a Pale Horse*.) But most pretribulationists seem to believe that people left behind can yet come to saving faith in Christ, though it will be too late to escape the horrors of the Antichrist and the Tribulation. It is these who must "endure to the end" in order to be saved. But the Partial Rapture doctrine supplies a kind of fundamentalist Protestant version of purgatory: only those born-again Christians will be caught up who are in close communion with their personal savior, who are led by the Spirit and have "a closer walk with Jesus." The controlling Gospel passage here is Matthew's parable of the wise and foolish virgins (Matthew 25:1–13). In it Jesus depicts faithful, vigilant disciples under the figure of five bridesmaids ready to be admitted to the reception, no matter how long the bridegroom may be delayed. They are ready, because they have brought extra oil for their lamps in case they run out during a chance delay. There are also five bridesmaids who do not plan ahead and are not prepared. The groom's party is long delayed, and the foolish maids' lamps have expired. They run to the village at the last minute to replenish their supply, but it is too late. The door is shut by the time they return, and no one will let them in to the wedding feast.

Unlike certain other parables, such as the great supper, the warning seems not to be to repent and be saved before the judgment comes, but rather for the repentant to remain vigilant and not be caught off guard. It is, in other words, an in-house warning. It does seem that whoever told this parable was thinking of Christians asleep at the switch, not fake Christians or hypocrites. The ensuing Tribulation functions as a furnace to smelt away the impurities of their faith, to get them ready, as they should have been when the Rapture came. Of course, nonbelievers may convert to Christ, too, but that is a different matter. In *Left Behind* we are shown many portraits of people who had been unbelievers of one kind or another before the Rapture and who convert in the wake of it. That is quite consistent with the pretribulation model. In *Titan, Son of Saturn*, we see that many or most true Christians were left behind and proceed to pull themselves together as quickly as they can, devoting themselves to prayer and evangelism, stoking their courage for eventual martyrdom. That, too, is consistent, consistent with the Partial Rapture doctrine. But then it seems to me that *Left Behind* wants to have it both ways. On the one hand, you can see, from a fundamentalist standpoint, how secularists like Buck Williams and rationalists like Dr. Chaim Rosenzweig would be left holding the bag after the Rapture. But on the other, we have cases like poor Reverend Bruce Barnes. He was no hypocrite, no fake, no secret unbeliever. Though an evangelical youth minister, he just somehow had not "really" received Christ into his heart. As Edmund Cohen perfectly describes it, poor Bruce was crossed off the guest list merely for vague "devotional shortcomings."[10] It is hard to see, even from the fundamentalist standpoint, in what sense Bruce was "not a Christian." His case much better fits the Partial Rapture scenario, as do the many, many others like his we meet in the pages of the *Left Behind* books.

Why is this important? Because it points up the hyperintrospective, super-subjective variety of pietism advocated by Jenkins and LaHaye: take it seriously, and you are forever tortured like the Puritans who could never be sure they were among the elect and feared that if their heartfelt piety were not sufficient evidence, then nothing was. Poor

Barnes! He knew beyond doubt that Jesus had died for his sins and that as long as he believed that, which he did, he would be saved. But he wasn't. What did he lack? It is hard to say. As Karl Barth knew, this kind of navel-gazing takes the focus off of Jesus Christ and places it squarely on the unstable conscience of the introspective believer.[11] It implies salvation by works: yes, sure, Jesus died for sins, we know that. But it all hinges on our subjective reception of it, and of that we can never be sure. So just who is the savior? Christ, who may be supposed to have done a good and thorough job of it? Or the believer, who is plainly doing a tremulous and inconsistent job of it?

I suspect it is more the narrative demands of the story that requires hapless characters like Rev. Bruce not to have been genuine Christians after all. The same thing happens in Watson's *In the Twinkling of an Eye* where the Secret Rapture leaves several people, who *thought* they were good fundamentalists, quite surprised. A daunted Salvation Army worker sobs: "The Army's methods fascinated me—the young officer who came to our town, was a very taking fellow. He talked to me in an after meeting, I wept with the many emotions that were at work within me; I went to the penitent form—and—afterwards joined the Salvation Army—but I know *now*, I was not really saved."[12] Likewise, a promising young Methodist pastor, left behind, confesses: "God help me! I know now that I have only been a *minister*, by training and by profession. I have never been a son of God by conversion, by the New Birth!"[13] If we read their plaints carefully we will see that there is no retrospective recognition of insincerity or hypocrisy. Rather, it is only *now*, in the cold light of the "morning after" of the missed Rapture, that they *infer* the falseness of their profession, and that, of course, from the simple fact of their having been left behind.

THE ANGELIC POPE

Robert Hugh Benson, brother to two other noted English writers (biographer and critic A. C. Benson and satirist and ghost story writer E. F.

Benson) and son of the archbishop of Canterbury, was a Church of England priest who subsequently converted to the Roman Catholic Church. He is known as one of the leading lights of the Catholic literary revival, along with G. K. Chesterton and Hilaire Belloc. His novel *Lord of the World* is written with a stylistic beauty that wears well even today, though we would not expect today's writers to employ it. Jerry Jenkins is surely wise to have written the *Left Behind* books in the brisk, action-oriented style of today's mystery and adventure novels. And he does what he does as well as Benson did. But there are heights, depths, and philosophical insights in Benson that Jenkins never approaches. Again, let me be careful here: there is no reason every novel has to be as excellent in every way as every other. Still, there are valuable points of comparison and evaluation.

Benson was strangely prescient in this novel of the future, set in the early twenty-first century but written in 1907. Where Jenkins's novels link characters via cell phones, Benson could imagine only improved telegraphs. But Benson did anticipate ultradestructive bombs nearly forty years in advance of the Manhattan Project. And before there were airplanes, he had ubiquitous air traffic aboard *volors*, flying vehicles whose wings beat the air.

The Antichrist, the eponymous Lord of the World, is a mysterious American politician and diplomat who manages to turn the world aside from an impending doomsday war between East and West. The East, by the way, is a vast empire controlled and motivated by religious zealotry not unlike the Islamo-Fascism of our own day, although Benson imagines it as a melding of pantheisms: Buddhism, Hinduism, and Sufism. The West, at least Europe, including Africa, never freed from colonialism in this scenario, is at least philosophically unified by allegiance to humanism and communism. All Christianity has either collapsed or been folded into Catholicism, theological liberalism having eroded Protestantism to a creedless vanishing point. And Catholicism is on the defensive. By an accord with the governments of Italy and Britain, Catholicism is largely restricted to the city of Rome (now an autonomous papal state retro-simulating the society and technology of the nineteenth century) and to Ireland, though there remain numerous individual Catholics elsewhere. One of these is vigorous young priest Percy Franklin. He will become the major Christian counterpoint to the rising Antichrist, not so much a Christ-analogue as an Anti-Antichrist (somewhat equivalent to Rabbi Tsion Ben-Judah in *Left Behind*).

The Antichrist in *Lord of the World* is not simply a demon or a monster in human form, not just Satan using the ideologies of the world cynically as tools of domination. The satirical genius of Benson is that Julian Felsenberg is only the individual face of humanism. His evil is the evil Benson perceives in humanism. And even here he does not so much caricature as take trends to extremes to which humanism's real-world advocates are sometimes in danger of taking it. This humanism is collectivistic: it merges the individual into the state and the species, with the result that there remain no individual rights. This humanism assumes the role of Mother Nature, embracing doctrines of social Darwinism and survival of the fittest. This humanism is self-glorifying to the point where it outlaws belief in a transcendent deity as treasonous and institutes a Masonic worship of humanity itself. The state facilitates suicide under the euphemism "euthanasia" and "helps along the very aged and the very sick" by the same means. This humanism is dehumanizing. And yet it is a faith nourishing, for the time being, the hungry souls of those whose conventional faith has been eroded through science and modernity but who still yearn to merge their petty individualities into some greater cause or reality.

One of the great strengths of Benson's *Lord of the World* is the depth of insight he conveys into the psychology of faith. He brings us inside the heads of characters so that we see Mabel (the wife of a British communist official) as a true believer in humanism. We understand how her faith is real to her and both comforts and inspires her. The same is true for Father Percy with his embattled, yet deeply rooted Catholicism. And when both characters endure crises of their very different faiths, it seems entirely real. The adoration the world's population feels for Felsenberg is compelling, too. Benson makes us feel his characters' quasi-religious awe at the fact that, with Felsenberg's advent, war and factional strife have ceased, that the superman for whom the world has pined has come and taken hold of history. He has midwifed the human race into a new evolutionary stage, even into a collective sanctification in which war will never be possible again. He is declared Messiah by some, the Son of Man by others, God incarnate by all, as he embodies the very essence of humanity. There is no God but Man, and Julian Felsenberg is his exemplar, finally emerged from the pool of human potential. Benson lets us see precious little of the man himself, making us view him as the figurehead of the adoring faith of the world. It is almost contagious. I know of no other Antichrist novel so effective in its portrayal of the power of the central antagonist, despite the use of so few strokes to paint him.

Benson is even more effective in conveying the psychology of faith than he desires or intends, at least as I read him. For he makes his hero Percy Franklin the best possible example of what Jacques Derrida calls the error of presence metaphysics: the fallacy that whatever appears before the mind's eye with sufficient clarity must be self-evidently true. Writing like a spiritual guide and adept (which he was), Benson discloses the steps by which deep contemplation seems to transport one to another dimension where the truths of faith shine forth as objective entities, the experience of which seems more real than the ephemeral phantoms of the physical senses. He does not suspect that, as Derrida argues, nothing is self-evident but only appears so because the subconscious has so cleverly hidden the otherwise-revealing seams and junctures, the concealed processes of composition and relation. There are footprints in what seems to be the field of virgin snow, but they have been cleverly effaced by those who made them. Benson joins his character Percy Franklin in believing that in "faith" one has available an alternative epistemology allowing one to believe by an act of will what reason cannot establish but what requires rational establishment.

No less clearly does Benson illustrate the dynamics of what Peter L. Berger and Thomas Luckmann call "plausibility structures."[14] Father Percy struggles with doubt as long as he lives in England, and he will struggle again at greater depth, but once he is called to Rome, he finds himself a fish back in water. His soul can breathe more freely. I know how he felt: while studying at secular Montclair State College, I grew to feel very isolated from the God whose message I strove to spread among the largely indifferent students. Doubts plagued me, though, and so, to compensate for them, I redoubled my evangelistic zeal. As soon as I arrived in Wheaton College ("the evangelical Harvard") for some summer courses, how the clouds did lift! Among the like-minded, the herd of kindred souls, my pesky doubts evaporated to a merely theoretical residue—until I got back to Montclair State in the fall! That's how it works. Implying nothing as to the inherent strength or weakness of our beliefs, we find them much more compelling when ensconced amid a social structure in which those beliefs are taken for granted. Benson depicts just these psychodynamics without, as far as I can tell, realizing it. Of course when things change for the worse, his Catholic hero does manage to endure to the end without any reed of worldly security, which is what makes him heroic.

Benson was a man of great faith. He conveys that faith powerfully, though I should say not convincingly to anyone not already with him. The reader is not likely to be convinced, as his characters are, that Roman Catholicism provides the only account of the human predicament or of human nature that makes adequate sense just because he says so. And yet it is very evident that he knows firsthand the experience of faith, even of mysticism, even to the extent that he can place himself inside the soul of others who share a faith inimical to his own. Such gifts are not requisite for writing a novel of the Antichrist, but it is worth noting them because of the great contrast with the ever-present (and ever-preachy) faith of the heroes in Jenkins's *Left Behind* epic. These authorial testimonies to the reader come across as dogmatic, pedantic, and flatter than a pancake. And why? Not because Jenkins is less familiar with fundamentalist piety than Benson was with Catholic devotional mysticism. Rather (forgive me for saying this), it is because the faith he conveys is itself shallow, pat, and unimaginative. Any evangelical (or ex-evangelical) reader will recognize the authenticity of the occasional prayers in Jenkins's narrative. They are the bland, insipid, "talk to the ceiling" prayers typical in these circles, including the famous "Lord, we just, we just, Lord" prayer. For instance:

> "'God,' Mac whispered, 'we're long past asking why things happen. We know we're on borrowed time and that we belong to you. We don't understand this. We don't like it. And it's hard for us to accept. We thank you that Annie didn't suffer,' and here his voice broke and became barely audible. 'We envy her because she's with you, but we miss her already, and a part of David that can never be replaced has been ripped away. We still trust you, still believe you, and want to serve you as long as you'll let us. We just ask that you'll come alongside David now, unlike you ever have before, and help him to heal, to carry on, to do your work.'"[15]

This kind of prayer makes one realize why liturgical churches use scripts for praying, poetical liturgy instead of banal religious chatter. It is just the same with vestments: priests wear gowns and stoles so that congregants are not distracted by the tasteless clothing styles of a preacher who may be too heavenly minded to be a good judge of fashion for the solemn occasion. (Of course, you might object that I ought to give Jenkins's characters a break: they are in a crisis and must speak out of their feelings. Maybe so, but if it was me, I'd whip out my Bible and pray some lament from Job or Psalms.)

TALKING TO THIN AIR

Shortly after these books were published, Sydney Watson penned a two-parter on the End Times: *In the Twinkling of an Eye* (1910) and *The Mark of the Beast* (1911). His young protagonist, Tom Hammond, is in many ways reminiscent of Jenkins's hero Buck Williams. Tom is an up-and-coming newspaper editor who gets drawn, partly through a romantic infatuation, into new preoccupations with both Jewry and the preaching of the End Times. He shortly discovers that almost everyone he runs into (thanks to authorial providence) is on fire with the expectation that Jesus will return soon, or if they are Jewish, that King Messiah will shortly appear. Soon his new Jewish friends wind up converting to Christ anyway, so the difference is moot. Not surprisingly, the eschatological itch rubs off on Tom, too, and he is commencing to utilize his best-selling newspaper as a bully pulpit for the End Times tidings, when the Rapture saves him the trouble and turns the job over to his unbelieving assistant editor.

Watson mentions in his introduction to *In the Twinkling of an Eye* how he got the idea of writing the book from reading an evangelistic leaflet called "Long Odds" (i.e., what are the chances the pesky fundamentalists are right?), depicting the sudden Rapture and its chaotic aftermath. Why not a book-length treatment? In his own book, he has a character read the full text of "Long Odds," which sets him thinking. What a clever use of a subtext! The reader beholds someone just like himself—reading an improbable cautionary tale about the Rapture. The poor fools in "Long Odds" never heeded Rapture preaching, and look what happened. But Tom Hammond read this story, and he converted, just in time! Reader, don't you want to be like him?

How strange and fascinating it is that Watson so accurately depicts both the disdain of outsiders toward the pretribulation zealotry and the spirit of the Rapture-fixated themselves. Though we are invited to identify with the saved Rapturists, we may find ourselves hard-pressed not to think they *do* look like fanatics! Every major character who becomes a convert to Rapture-Christianity seems much more human, vibrant, and personable *before* conversion. From the Jew Abraham Cohen, busy fashioning ornamentation for the Jerusalem temple soon to be rebuilt, to editor Hammond, to young Madge Finisterre, visiting London from Dutchess County, New York, another Holly Golightly— until the Holy Spirit drains the sparkle out of her! His preconverts are by no means sinners, much less unsympathetic, and when they get converted, the only difference it seems to make is an air of heavenly-minded distraction and an obsession with the Rapture. This is not moral repentance but only cult recruiting. I doubt Watson means to communicate that, but his portrayals of both pre- and postconversion personalities are so well drawn we cannot help getting that message.

Watson's skill is on display in a series of remarkable scenes in which some culminating plot thread is suddenly severed by the disappearance of one party in the Rapture! You know it's got to be coming sooner or later, and probably sooner, but when it does, one finds oneself surprised! It takes much more skill to pull this off, which is why most of these end of the world novels instead take off from the far side of the Rapture, explaining it and describing the drama of it only *after* it happens. The Rapture may be played as the premise of the story, the climax of the story, in a deus ex machina ending, or, as in *In the Twinkling of an Eye*, as almost an *anti*climax, prematurely cutting across the implicit plot logic prevailing hitherto. In the midst of life we are in . . . Rapture!

The Mark of the Beast starts well, with the meeting of two intriguing characters, a wealthy Jewish occultist, Judith Montmarte, and a British explorer of Tibet, Colonel Youlter. The bewitching beauty takes the opportunity afforded by a weekend soiree to which both have been invited to learn all she can from the old savant regarding Oriental mysticism. But their conversation turns instead to the ancient sexual congress between the errant sons of God and the objects of their blasphemous lust, the dawn-age daughters of men (Gen. 6:1–4), dalliances that issued in the birth of the *Nephilim*, diabolical giants. The doughty colonel opines that, given the present moral and spiritual decline of modern society, the outrages of the antediluvian world seem on the verge of repeating themselves, and he doubts not that there will even be a renewal of these unspeakable liaisons between demons and mortals. And this, it seems, is just what Judith, secretly crazed with hated of Jesus Christ and his religion, wants! How she would love to mate with whatever manner of fiendish sperm donor if she might give birth to the prophesied Antichrist! Shortly thereafter she disappears for a year, returning a proud mother. In all this, Sydney Watson acquits himself well as a classic writer of weird fiction, raising terrible hints, leaving his readers' worst imaginations to fill in the blanks he has drawn. And through the rest of the book he does not shrink from providing cameos of End Time horror when the narrative dictates.

But in *The Mark of the Beast*, Watson skimps a bit on the characterization. The characters, hardly filled out, are mainly just clones of characters raptured in the previous book, playing pretty much the same roles as their predecessors. The three we come to know best eventually receive martyrdom at the hands of the Beast that is so summary as to be anticlimactic. Oddly, a truly ghoulish martyrdom scene centers around a young Jerusalem couple whom we have scarcely met before they are foully done in. Lucien Apleon, the Antichrist himself, is introduced in a scene smacking nicely of old-time devil folklore (he appears before the desk of Hammond's successor at the *Courier* and subsequently disappears, as if into thin air, though we cannot be completely sure he did not simply arrive and depart silently). He stars in a couple of nicely dramatic scenes, but his final defeat happens offstage in a mere summary of what happens in the Great Tribulation after the events Watson has chosen to recount. It is a strange and arbitrary plot structure.

Like Arthur W. Pink after him, Watson has borrowed from Scottish dispensationalist divine G. Campbell Morgan the theory that the Antichrist is the very reincarnation of Judas Iscariot. But, having summarized exegetical arguments for this identification, he does nothing further with it. The notion of a returned Judas, eager to gain revenge upon Jesus, is a great idea: too bad it's wasted here.

On the other hand, one of the Antichrist's best scenes is a face-off with another false Christ, of whom Watson assures us there were many, and he has an interesting take on them. Watson has them emerge as outspoken foes of Antichrist, claiming to be Jesus and promising to save mankind from the present Tribulation! We usually think of the End Times Pseudo-Christs as obedient spin doctors for Satan, telling everybody that, despite the earthquakes and plagues, everything's copacetic. Watson allows fifteen minutes of fame to one of these bargain-basement Jesuses, the unfortunately christened "Conrad the Conqueror," who appears in London challenging Lucien Apleon, whom he correctly brands the Antichrist, claiming himself to be the returned Jesus Christ! Now, that's pretty ingenious! Poor Conrad promptly gets incinerated for his trouble. Let's face it, with a stage name like "Conrad the Conqueror," there's no way a guy's got what it takes to defeat the Beast.

It is interesting that Watson identifies the Two Witnesses of Revelation 13, not as Moses and Elijah, but as Enoch and Elijah. Given Revelation's ascription to one of the witnesses the Mosaic power to inflict Exodus-like plagues, one wonders that Watson would identify him otherwise. The overt Moses symbolism of the text, which Watson even admits he recognizes, has to give way in the last analysis to a bit of fundamentalist text harmonizing. Since Hebrews 9:27 ("it is appointed for men to die once, and after that comes judgment") lays down the rule that every person gets to die but a single time, then Watson has a hard time with the notion of Moses dying back in Deuteronomy but showing up again in the flesh in Revelation 13, only to die (and rise) again. Elijah didn't die the first time, he ascended to heaven instead, so it's all right for him to come back and die. But Moses, like a shortchanged cat, has already used up his allotment of lives. But there is another at home like Elijah, Enoch. He hadn't died either; now's his chance!

Er, why, then, the Moses imagery? John no doubt did intend Moses as Elijah's partner. According to ancient Jewish belief, Moses, too, evaded death and ascended to heaven. Some discerned this in the wording of Deuteronomy 34:6, which notes that no one knows where Moses was buried. Is that a coy way of saying that he has no known tomb, since he didn't need one? Philo and Josephus both depict Moses as ascending into heaven, not dying. That is no doubt what John the Revelator believed. And so did Mark, which is why he has Moses and Elijah appear from heaven to talk with Jesus on the Mount of Transfiguration.

In pairing Elijah with Enoch rather than with Moses, Watson is actually in good company. Any ancient Christian writer who mentions the martyrdom of the Two Witnesses names them Elijah and Enoch, not Elijah and Moses. If these writers were all dependent upon Revelation as their source, it is quite odd that none of them would have caught on that the plague-wielding prophet was supposed to be Moses. Thus Bousset inferred that Revelation is not the source of the mythemes and images it displays but merely one of many heirs of them. There must have been a common oral tradition about the End Times to which Revelation and subsequent apocalyptic writers all commonly and independently referred. Thus when the Revelator in chapter 11 makes the second prophet into a returned Moses, he is changing the venerable tradition of a return of Elijah and Enoch. He is the innovator, ringing a change on the received tradition. The other writers have not changed the tradition as John set it down. He was the maverick, not them. But Watson's reasoning may be quite apt. I would suggest that the ancients, who originated the Two Witnesses motif, employed the same logic, and thus the original story of the Two Witnesses did feature Enoch and Elijah. And remember, Enoch, in ancient Jewish belief, was said to have accumulated revelations during heavenly journeys and to have returned to share them with his family. Moses, too, had ascended to heaven (by way of Sinai) and there received laws and instructions to pass on to those waiting below, after which he, too, returned to heaven. So either would have been good choices for witnesses who are trying to convey to mortals the truths they had learned from God.

RAGNAROK RFD

Surprisingly, given his limited command of the English language (his native tongue, spoken with the eloquence of a Jethro Bodine), healer-evangelist Ernest Angley produced his own apocalyptic novel, *Raptured*, in 1950. Or perhaps he hired someone to do it. If the Galilean fisherman Simon Peter could not have written the Greek of 1 Peter, neither could the inarticulate Angley have written this book. The book is written with a childish simplicity, though whether the author cannot rise above such a level or whether he is condescending to his anticipated readership is impossible to tell. In any case, *Raptured* paints the apocalyptic scenario on a surprisingly small canvas. The Rapture and the horrors of the Tribulation are all played out on the stage of a small town called Alabesta in an unnamed state. Rare mentions of Hitler and of the radio are all that necessitate a historical setting a generation later than that of the novels we have considered already. The book takes for granted Protestant America. Everyone seems to be either an on-fire Christian, shouting in church three times a week, or a backslider, or someone fallen away. Even rare unbelievers have strayed from a good Christian upbringing. We find no Jews, atheists, or even Roman Catholics in the island universe of *Raptured.* Jews come in for mention briefly, but they are far off in Palestine, no more real than the Sunday school Jews of the Bible. This restriction of the scope of the action necessitates the shoehorning of cosmic events and the fulfillments of ancient prophecy into an altogether too restricted framework. We see two of the Horsemen of the Apocalypse (War and Famine) trotting down the streets of tiny Alabesta. Locals are recruited as thugs to enforce the decree that everyone shall take the mark. And when we finally get a look at the Beast, in his bejeweled linen turban and robe, he and his retinue are for some reason passing through the little town off the beaten track. It is all reminiscent of the peculiar microcosmic scale of soap operas in which the small town of Port Charles harbors the headquarters of national newsmagazines and television shows.

In contrast to later offerings in the genre, *Raptured* inhabits a curiously naive world that knows nothing of apologetics or epistemology. How does one know the Rapture doctrine is true? Because one first learned it as a child from devout mothers and grandmothers. What would move anyone to doubt and reject the doctrine? Nothing other than a desire to be thought smart and sophisticated. Higher education is the enemy; author and intended readers view it as mere brainwashing by unbelievers. Angley (or the Pseudo-Angley?) simply assumes that all true believers in Christ will believe in the pretribulation Rapture, as if it is the sum and substance of the Christian faith.

Another notable aspect of the book is that it sets forth unselfconsciously the deeply paranoid character of fundamentalist eschatology.

The whole world is wrong, while uneducated Holy Rollers are right. That is a delusion of grandeur. With it naturally follows a persecution complex: all the world hates true Christians and for no other reason than that they are Christians, and nothing else does the world hate but Christians.

As might be expected, there is virtually no attempt at characterization in this book. Every single character is someone who is chagrined to have just missed the Rapture, or else a fiend rejoicing to do the Antichrist's nefarious bidding. Nor is there any real attempt to narrate the wonders of Revelation in any convincing manner. Most of the plagues, divine visitations, and so on are simply stipulated, as is the final appearing of Jesus. And yet *Raptured* must be credited with one distinctive spin on a common theme, namely, the mark of the Beast. In other books, those who take the path of least resistance are generally just a bunch of unsympathetic sad sacks. It's too late for them, and now they're just screwed. Too bad. But in *Raptured*, to take the mark of the Beast is depicted as a kind of demonic conversion, virtually demon possession, with a concomitant change of the personality and character.

And the author lingers on this unique feature long enough for it to provide the one interesting subplot. Through most of the book we are acquainted with Jim, a man who has resisted the pious teachings of his silver-haired mother and, though of good character, he cares not for churchgoing and has deferred surrendering his life to Christ until some indefinite future. As if that were not enough to worry his mother, Jim marries an educated girl who ridicules Jim's mother's faith. She naturally functions as a drag away from Jim returning to Jesus. He is, of course, left behind in the Rapture, and he has his intellectual hussy of a wife to thank for that. The night of the Rapture, she becomes seriously ill. Jim goes out for a doctor, but already it has become impossible to gain any professional attention or conduct any commerce without the mark of the Beast. Jim knows that to take the mark will damn his soul, but so great is his sense of husbandly duty that he takes the mark. Little does he know that, just as he is taking it, back home his wife expires! But by this time, his eyes fairly glowing with hellfire, he is happily blaspheming God and worshiping the Beast!

PALESTINE AND PETRA

The very next year, an infinitely better Antichrist novel appeared, Carrie E. Gruhn's excellent *A Trumpet in Zion* (reprinted in 1969 as *The Lost City*). The focal character is a young woman, Tanya, who has somehow managed to escape immediately post-Nazi Germany, where she had narrowly avoided starvation in a concentration camp. Most of her relatives were not so lucky, but she is reunited with her mother on the boat ride to British Palestine, where, married to a pair of Jewish men, they are assigned to live and work on a remote kibbutz. Paul, Tanya's sight-unseen husband, is a selfless doctor whose skills and compassion smooth things over between their settlement and the nearby, otherwise hostile Bedouin village. An apparent love-triangle soon forms between the flirtatious Lilah, a hussylike career woman from America, Tanya, hardly more than an Old World child, and Paul. Her inferiority complex torments Tanya with fears that Paul must prefer the more worldly female to herself, especially since the two belong to an inner circle active in various secret diplomatic projects.

It soon develops that a world tired of conflict and poverty is willing to heed the proposals, designed by Paul and his secret cadre, to form a World Union to abolish war and to redistribute food resources as needed until all nations can get up to speed economically. The new world leader is named Prince Damon (uh-oh!), and he is a Jew. When Damon announces plans to have Jews rebuild the Jerusalem temple, many decide he is the Messiah. In the meantime, Paul has seen a missionary friend, a Christian named Dal, vanish into thin air while explaining the soon-coming Rapture! This is enough to convince him to embrace Jesus as Messiah, and author Gruhn lets loose with the proof from prophecy, as all these books seem to do sooner or later. Dal, it seems, had also instructed Paul as to the inevitability of the

Antichrist's rise, and Paul soon suspects that his colleague and now sovereign Damon may be the Antichrist instead of the Christ. These fears are realized on the very day the temple is dedicated. There stands Prince Damon, announcing to the pious crowds that sacrifice will henceforth be offered not to Jehovah, his sworn enemy, but to the Beast. Gruhn does not feel compelled to describe a literalist fulfillment of Revelation all the time, but sometimes she is so literal that (paradoxically) one cannot quite picture what she is describing. The Beast is a case in point. It appears to be some sort of disgusting creature of which no one has seen the like. Damon has him practically on a leash at his side. Some zealot from the crowd aims a rifle at the disgusting critter and seems to have killed it. But despite the huge loss of blood, the thing bounces back as pugnacious as ever. This is the Beast 666? Creepy but anticlimactic. Damon turns out to be the False Prophet, the Second Beast of Revelation, since he causes a statue of his infernal familiar to be built and orders everyone to pray to it.

This disaster is the signal for Paul to lead some of his followers on a hard journey across the desert to the ancient Nabatean Arab city of Petra, whose natural situation and intricate ground plan affords defensive shelter against all foes, ancient or modern. The expected plagues and earthquakes are proceeding apace, and Prince Damon uses his mark to control food rations, which he doles out according to the terms of the World Union. Paul leaves the impregnable fortress to do some evangelism among fellow Jews, and eventually Tanya is dismayed to find Lilah has returned, bearing two letters—or actually three. One is a letter to Tanya from her husband. The second is a letter from Paul to the leaders at Petra, directing them to obey Lilah as they would him, as she is a trusted colleague. The third is a page of a love letter from Paul to Lilah! By mistake, this last comes to Tanya's eyes, confirming her worst fears. But, putting her private concerns on the back burner, she intervenes on Lilah's behalf with the leaders and gets them to heed Paul's request. Only it turns out not to have been his request! We discover that Lilah bears the mark of the Beast and has become one of his chief lieutenants! She was acting with the hellish bitterness of the scorned woman, as Paul had in fact never yielded to her. She forged all the letters, including the illicit love letter. Her plans to open the fortress to the minions of the Antichrist fail, and Paul returns just in time to see the skies split and the Christ on horseback descending from the sky.

The characters are real, the plot is suspenseful, and the description of the Palestinian situation after the war is convincing. It is quite fascinating to see history take a major detour, as if it veered off the path into a speculative future—fifty-five years ago! The book should function as a cautionary tale concerning the dangers of predicting the End Time. That is, if any fundamentalists still read it. In terms of our survey of the progress of the genre, it is just worth noting that *A Trumpet in Zion/The Lost City* preceded *The Omen*'s too-obvious use of a name for the Antichrist that sounds like "demon." "Damon" is another version of Damian (English) or Damien (French) and comes from the Greek verb *damao.* It means "conqueror." "Demon," on the other hand, comes from the Greek *daimon,* referring to a spirit, ghost, or genie. *The Lost City* also prefigures the role of Petra as the Tribulation refuge for Christians and Christian Jews in the *Left Behind* and *Christ Clone* series. Gruhn is a bit more charitable than Jenkins, for her protagonists would allow even unconverted Jews to take up residence there, while Jenkins's allowed them only an evangelistic pitch and a ticket home.

DAYS OF FUTURE PAST

All these books are decidedly outdated. Yet they do not suffer the embarrassment the failed predictions of the Parousia do. They only attest in a creative fashion their authors' vigilant faith that it *might* happen at any time, hence possibly in their day. Each of these books makes a point similar to that of Sinclair Lewis's *It Can't Happen Here.* Lewis warned that Fascism is imaginable even here in America, the Land of the Free. These Christian authors are trying to show their complacent readers that "it *can* happen *now.*"

NOTES

1. Tim LaHaye and Jerry B. Jenkins, *Left Behind: A Novel of the Earth's Last Days* (Wheaton, IL: Tyndale House, 1995), p. 120.

2. John Charles Ryle, *Holiness: Its Nature, Hindrances, Difficulties, and Roots* (Greensboro, NC: Homiletic Press, 1956), p. 241: "But, alas, how often their goodness vanishes like the morning cloud, and like the dew that passes away! The boy becomes a young man, and cares for nothing but amusements, field sports, reveling and excess. The girl becomes a young woman, and cares for nothing but dress, gay company, novel-reading, and excitement. Where is the spirituality which once appeared to promise so fair? It is all gone: it is buried; it is overflowed by the love of the world. They walk in the steps of Lot's wife. *They look back.*" Bishop Ryle died in 1900.

3. See William Nelson, *Fact or Fiction? The Dilemma of the Renaissance Storyteller* (Cambridge, MA: Harvard University Press, 1973).

4. Sydney Watson, author of one of the earliest apocalyptic novels, knew he had to reckon with "the Christians . . . who will at first sight condemn the use of the fictional element, the dramatic colour in this book" (*In the Twinkling of an Eye* [Los Angeles: Bible Institute of Los Angeles, 1921; repr., Old Tappan, NJ: Fleming H. Revell Company, 1933], p. 6).

5. "As with Darth Vader of *Star Wars*, the powerful figure of this 'prince of darkness' attracts attention. He represents the 'dark side of the Force,' for he has perverted the power given him and, as the epitome of lawlessness (i.e., as the Man of Sin) now seeks to extend the sphere of his influence to every corner of the universe." Cyril J. Barber, foreword to Arthur W. Pink, *The Antichrist* (Bible Truth Depot, 1923; repr., Minneapolis: Klock & Klock, 1979), p. 5.

6. Quoted in Joseph Birkbeck Burroughs, *Titan, Son of Saturn: The Coming World Emperor. A Story of the Other Christ* (Oberlin: Emeth Publishers, 1914), p. 223.

7. James Webb, *The Occult Underground* (LaSalle, IL: Open Court, 1988), pp. 251–53.

8. Alan Schreck, *Catholic and Christian: An Explanation of Commonly Misunderstood Catholic Beliefs* (Ann Arbor, MI: Servant Books, 1984), p. 27: "Catholics understand that our 'good works' or 'merits' are really God's gifts or graces. And yet, the Bible states that God commands and expects his people to perse-

vere in 'good works,' just as he expects them to persevere in faith—not because it is our faith or works that save us but simply because this is the way that God has ordained for each person to cooperate with his plan of salvation and to accept this salvation. The Council of Trent clearly stated that of the two (faith and works), faith was the primary means of accepting salvation ('the beginning of human salvation' from our perspective)." David B. Currie, *Born Fundamentalist, Born Again Catholic* (San Francisco: Ignatius Press, 1996): "Evangelical and Catholic theologies both accept as the starting tenet of soteriology that we are saved by *grace*. God gives us his life as an act of generosity on his part. . . . We need to remind ourselves that on this point we are in total agreement. We are saved by grace. . . . The *Catechism of the Catholic Church* puts it this way: 'Since the initiative belongs to God in the order of grace, no one can merit the initial grace of forgiveness and justification' (CCC 2010)" (pp. 111–12). For a less conciliatory view, see Karl Keating, *Catholicism and Fundamentalism: The Attack on "Romanism" by "Bible Christians"* (San Francisco: Ignatius Press, 1988): "We indeed will be judged by what we do and not just by the one act of whether we accept Jesus as our personal Lord and Savior. Yet it is not to be thought that being do-gooders is sufficient. The Bible is quite clear that we are saved by faith. The Reformers were quite right in saying this, and to this extent they merely repeated the constant teaching of the Church. Where they erred was in saying that we are saved by faith alone" (pp. 174–75).

9. Burroughs, *Titan*, p. 193.

10. Edmund D. Cohen, "Review of the 'Left Behind' Tribulation Novels: *Turner Diaries* Lite," *Free Inquiry* 21, no. 2.

11. This is how Dietrich Bonhoeffer expressed the same concern: "Our task is simply to keep on following, looking only to our Leader who goes on before, taking no notice of ourselves or of what we are doing. We must be unaware of our own righteousness, and see it only insofar as we look unto Jesus; then it will seem not extraordinary, but quite ordinary and natural" (*The Cost of Discipleship*, trans. Reginald H. Fuller with Irmgard Booth [London: SCM Press, 1949; 2nd ed., 1959], p. 176).

12. Watson, *In the Twinkling of an Eye*, p. 234.

13. Ibid, p. 225.

14. Peter L. Berger and Thomas Luckmann, *The Social Construction of Reality: A Treatise in the Sociology of Knowledge* (Garden City, NY: Doubleday Anchor, 1967), especially pp. 154–160.

15. Tim LaHaye and Jerry B. Jenkins, *The Mark: The Beast Rules the World* (Wheaton, IL: Tyndale House, 2000), p. 126.

Chapter Eight

LATER CHRISTIAN APOCALYPSE NOVELS

*T*he Omen was published in 1976, and I think it makes sense to use that book as a convenient division point between earlier and later Christian Antichrist novels. The ones written and published in the wake of David Seltzer's *The Omen* are occasionally influenced by it in minor ways, but they also seem to share the greater sense of narrative verisimilitude as in *The Omen*. There is more of a feeling of reading a modern novel, less of enduring an elaborate evangelistic tract. *The Omen* is an early example of this more mature literary sophistication, but not the prototype of it, since some few of its Christian cousins preceded it by a few years. I begin this chapter with my own sentimental favorite among these post-1970 Antichrist novels: Salem Kirban's *666* (published in 1970, the same year as Lindsey's *Late Great Planet Earth*). His name may ring a bell even if you have not run across his books. Stephen King mentions him in his own near-apocalypse thriller *The Dead Zone*. Johnny Smith, King's clairvoyant protagonist, is rummaging through a pile of fringe leaflets and books left by his late mother, who had gone off the deep end during the five years he slept in a coma. "One of them, by a man named Salem Kirban, struck him as nearly pagan in its loving contemplation of a bloody apocalypse and the yawning barbeque pits of hell."[1] This description is not much exaggerated. Kirban's Antichrist is Brother Bartholomew, a holy man from Iraq who makes an international name for himself as a peacemaker and mediator. The constitutional ban on immigrants running for president notwithstanding, both parties nominate Bartholomew for president. But that is only the beginning; soon he is drafted as head of the new Federated States of Europe as well. After a cryogenic recovery from an attempt on his life, Brother Bartholomew goes insane, bringing the world, literally, to the edge of destruction. Despite several, well, gross stylistic flaws (like veering erratically from first- to third-person narration!), Kirban effectively paints Brother Bartholomew as a seductive Pseudo-Christ futilely trying to secure his grasp on a world rapidly collapsing upon itself. It may be a heap of ruins when the smoke clears, but he aims to call himself king of that particular hill.

One of Kirban's associates, Gary Cohen, tried his hand at a Rapture novel of his own, *Civilization's Last Hurrah* (1974), reissued some years later as *The Horsemen Are Coming*. In 1978 Frank Allnutt wrote *The Peacemaker*. In it, a thinly veiled Henry Kissinger turns out to be the Antichrist (though the picture of him on the cover actually depicts then-president of France Valerie Giscard-d'Estang!). It is an irony that the first reaction of apocalyptic-minded fundamentalists when they hear of a skilled negotiator and benefactor is to get suspicious! If the Antichrist is expected to bring a short-lived and illusory peace to the world before showing his true colors, fundamentalists have come to believe that effective peacemaking *is* the true color of the Beast. No wonder they feel more comfortable with "wars and rumors of wars." In his study of End Time expectation since the nineteenth century, *Armageddon Now*, Dwight Wilson is easily able to show that avid prophecy buffs cared not a whit for the injustice dealt out to Arab and Turkish populations as long as the eschatological scenario seemed to be chugging along on schedule. Hoping that Benito Mussolini might be the one who would revive the Roman Empire, one pious couple managed to meet with him and showed him from (their interpretation of) scripture how the Roman Empire must rise again for the Last Days. *Il Duce* was much intrigued![2]

Without exception, and without pretending otherwise, these novels are aimed at scaring readers into getting right with God ahead of the

Rapture. Invariably the protagonists have been warned by "saved" loved ones to repent before it's too late. The loved ones disappear into the sky, and the protagonist, reasoning that it's better late than never, prays to receive Christ as his or her personal savior, and swallows hard, because now he or she knows what lies ahead: the terrors of the End Time. The warning is clear, like in the old army VD reels: "Men, don't let *this* happen to *you!*" The books are given to real-life counterparts of these unsaved relatives and friends as an evangelistic tool. But surely the majority of their readers are already born-again Christians. Why are they reading them? Well, remember what Stephen King said about Salem Kirban relishing the barbeque pits of hell. It's chop-licking entertainment to see all those sinners get what's coming to them. Since true believers are sure nothing is going to happen to them, they can sit back and enjoy the bloodletting fun, just as they look forward to doing from a balcony seat in heaven once the Tribulation begins here below. The books dangle the apocalyptic horrors before the reader with a resounding note of "I told you so!" In Cohen's novel we see the Tribulation masses reduced to eating processed human flesh. A cover blurb promises "a couple of delightful evenings with the book." Oh, how the narrators relish the shock and confusion they describe stamped on the faces of glib unbelievers, too sophisticated to give a second thought to the End Time preaching of the "fanatics" and "Holy Rollers" who, having now been raptured, are proven to have been right all along! It is like the modern myth of the nerd gloating over the idiot jocks who used to kick sand in his face, because now he owns a computer software company and they are waiting tables.

THE BEGINNING OF THE BIRTH PANGS

Packing the punch of a *Twilight Zone* episode, Joe Musser's *Behold a Pale Horse* (1970; reprinted in 1982 as *The Coming World Earthquake*) is a grim and chilling cautionary tale warning the unsaved reader that, after the Rapture, there is no chance for salvation. The novella follows the budding romance of Gary Everest, a TV and radio reporter highly reminiscent of Jenkins's hero Buck Williams, and Diane Carms, daughter of a fundamentalist Bible professor, who meet in Israel just before the birth pangs of the Tribulation erupt. Arab-Israeli tensions are building, geopolitical balances are shifting with dizzying speed, and the United Nations has just taken major steps toward becoming a world government. With the passing of the pope, the world religions come together to elect one Biv Jabarkos as an ecumenical pope. When the "governor general" of the UN is assassinated, the delegates draft the new pope Christos II (*uh*-oh!) to fill that office, too, as he seems to be the only leader with sufficient wisdom to shepherd the world through current and impending crises. During an unprecedented world earthquake that kills millions and disrupts civilization, Professor Carms quietly vanishes in the hills on an archaeological dig.

During recovery efforts after the quake, people begin to notice that almost all those missing are babies and little children. No one knows why, except for the reader, for Professor Carms had previously tried to warn Gary and Diane about the End Times. It was a soft sell, and neither of the young people took it all that seriously, too busy with their budding romance, marriage, and new baby. Tragedy strikes as their infant son dies from a congenital ailment of some sort. So they can sympathize with all the families whose children have mysteriously vanished. But after the dust begins to settle, Diane starts to connect the dots and to wonder if the Rapture has taken place. Gary, too, has a nightmare that suggests the same, although it features potent imagery he does not understand. Finally, about to crack, in a scene recalling both *Psycho II* and Stephen King's *Pet Sematary*, Diane insists that their baby's coffin be jimmied open. It is as empty as the tomb of Jesus. And this serves as the terrible signal that the Rapture has behind left these casual unbelievers to face all hell, which is just about to break loose.

To his credit, Jerry Jenkins has a similar chilling scene in which his hero Rayford Steel confirms his suspicions that the Rapture has occurred and that his wife is gone with the wind. He reaches his empty house, calls out her name, searches room by room, and then enters the bedroom where he last saw her in the wee hours. Knowing yet fearing what he will find, he whips away the covers on her side of the bed and finds her emptied pajamas! The scene has the force of opening the casket in a vampire movie—well done!

By the way, Joe Musser can take credit for originating the urban legend so popular among fundamentalist conspiracy theorists that there exists a Common Market supercomputer in Belgium called the Beast, and that it can and does surveil, and will one day control, all humanity. One takes the mark of this Beast in the form of the Universal Product Code (or some such—there are variant versions). There is no such machine. It has fictional antecedents, like the movie *Colossus: The Forbin Project* (1970), but the Belgian Beast computer was Musser's brainchild. He cooked it up for use in *Behold a Pale Horse*, but then saved it for his screenplay for the 1973 David Wilkerson Associates movie *The Rapture*, one of the clumsy evangelistic Tribulation pseudo-documentaries popular in the 1970s. When the idea took on an afterlife as an urban legend, poor Musser tried to explode it, without much success. The idea had gotten out of control, just as the supercomputer itself did in the movie!

BALIZET AND BAPHOMET

Carol Balizet's entry in our genre is her excellent 1979 novel *The Seven Last Years*. This lady can write! We never for a moment get the impression that she is learning her craft *trying* to write. There is a completely unselfconscious competence that permeates the book. Balizet maintains a steady, measured pace that allows a surprising degree of characterization as well as a sense of several years' scope. Her depictions of the shabby world on the eve of the Tribulation and the pouncing dangers of the Tribulation trap the reader in a claustrophobic nightmare. Unlike several of the earlier Antichrist novelists, Balizet takes the trouble to imagine the logistics involved with a massive endeavor like dispensing the mark of the Beast to whole populations, as well as detecting those who refuse to receive it. Too many of these books give the matter little thought, as if it were a matter of administering a vaccine to a small town. But if we are to picture these things happening in the world we live in, we cannot assume bureaucratic inefficiency would miraculously disappear under Satan's regime. Otherwise it becomes an oversimple miracle play or Christmas pageant.

As we will see in Jenkins's case, it is hard to know how overtly to portray miracles in a novel that generally relies on naturalistic narration. Balizet realizes that to witness a suspension of natural law would allow no glibness. When one character sees his rescuer pass through a wall instead of the door, the poor fellow's teeth begin to chatter in terror. But later, when the same character, lacking any normal means to travel to Israel from America, closes his eyes and prays that God will teleport him there instantaneously, it works. Maybe God is capable of doing just anything. But who has ever seen such a thing? Here Balizet throws hard-won verisimilitude right out the window. But she is not as extravagant as Jerry Jenkins is, for example, when he has his Christian refugees walking around unharmed in the flames of an atomic bomb or watching enemy missiles pass harmlessly through their own airplane fuselage like phantoms. Even if you believe in such things, it is hard to make them believable to the reader. On the other hand, Balizet indulges in what I call "charismagic," the belief of Pentecostals that they can "take authority" over menacing animals and stupid criminals by using the name of Jesus as a magical incantation.[3] ("The Force has a strong influence on the weak-minded.")

Balizet is also one of the few who thinks to provide a glimpse of things as they appear from the Antichrist's viewpoint. Like Jenkins, she holds an "Adoptionist" Antichristology. Bishop Uriah Leonard is a grasping megalomaniac to begin with, wittingly in league with Satan, but after he is assassinated and comes back to life, he becomes a host body for Satan incarnate. On the eve of Armageddon, one of his lieutenants asks him, "Do you feel any fear? Any doubts?" The antipope replies, "I have spent too many years, too many centuries of effort to be stricken now with doubts. I must do what it is my nature to do."[4] And yet he insists that there is more to the story than the Bible lets on, that he may win in the end. It is only a terrible suspicion, nervously dismissed, when the False Prophet (this time, the Israeli prime minister) wonders if maybe he and the Antichrist have all along been saps and stooges, cluelessly acting roles assigned them by their Divine Enemy.

Balizet is a bit more cagey on the subject of the Two Witnesses of Revelation, chapter 11. They are a pair of preachers named Elias Johnson and Amos Mozell. Are they actually Elijah and Moses, returned from heaven? Or are they modern-day successors? We have to figure that one out ourselves.

Though the theology of *The Seven Last Years* is solidly fundamentalist (e.g., pretribulationist), Balizet is decidedly more merciful than some of her fellow writers. For instance, taking the mark of the Beast isn't necessarily the end of the story. Balizet has a few characters take it and repent later on. Her Jesus is a bit more forgiving. And when Jesus Christ appears at the close of the story and various characters behold the dawning light of his countenance, it is almost like seeing the Clear Light of the Adi-Buddha in the *Bardo Thödöl* (or *Tibetan Book of the Dead*): it seems to offer a final chance for reflection and repentance, even to draw some toward it despite themselves.

Let one scene in particular stand for the imaginative quality of *The Seven Last Years* as a whole. Bishop Leonard is meeting with his cabal of advisers, a ragtag group composed of Celeste (a Satanist channeler), Lawrence Royal (a Donald Trump clone), Francis Chapman (Royal's chief of staff), and Francis's homosexual lover, Douglas. In a well-handled prior segment, we have witnessed Douglas's gradual yielding to Francis, to his manipulations more than his seductions. We have seen him sell out one moral conviction after another. But of late he has begun to think twice about his position, and Bishop Leonard senses it. So he questions him, as Jesus did his disciples at Caesarea Philippi when Jesus asks who the crowds believe him to be, then who the disciples believe him to be. Douglas blurts out, "I say that you are the Antichrist, the son of Satan." And the pope collapses in hysterics.[5]

BETZER'S BEAST

Dan Betzer's *The Beast: A Novel of the Coming World Dictator* (1985) is almost a twin to Joe Musser's *Behold a Pale Horse*. Like Musser's, Betzer's book is a short novel focused on the trials and (great) tribulations of a newsman, in this case a network news exec, Clay Daniels. Important to the plot, once again, is his girlfriend, whom he gets pregnant and who loses the baby, this time in the Rapture. Just as Musser made sure we knew his likeable couple were nonetheless sinners (they drank wine and fornicated), so does Betzer remind us constantly that Clay and Marsha are living in sin, and that Clay smokes like a stack. What's funny about this is that both authors are tacitly admitting that their characters, though lacking the ticket to salvation, a "personal relationship with Christ," are basically decent, dedicated people. Uh, then, how come they are doomed to hell? Well, uh, you see, they smoked and drank. They had the membership badge of the worldly, not of the saints. In the same way, the Amish can tell you're a sinner if you wear buttons instead of hooks on your coat.

The Beast also covers roughly the same chunk of time as *Behold a Pale Horse*: a brief geopolitical run-up to the Rapture, the mysterious disappearance, followed by an outbreak of chaos, and the unveiling of a charismatic international figure ready to pick up the pieces. The horrors of the Tribulation are left to the imagination, but, again, the characters' worst fears are confirmed by a funeral miracle. In Musser's novel, it was the discovery of the baby's empty casket that confirms the Rapture has occurred, but in Betzer's, the Antichrist, European statesman Jacque Catroux, himself interrupts Clay's girlfriend's funeral and raises her from the dead! This seals Clay's and everyone else's loyalty to him as the book ends. Again, we have the impression that Betzer figures the welcome mat was taken to heaven with all the born-again Christians. No more chance to be saved.

Among the distinctive characteristics of Betzer's approach is his rejection of the common theme of the Antichrist deceiving his public. No, Betzer's Man of Sin harbors no antimessianic secret. He flatly declares his role as Lucifer's son and Christ, rightly confident that his miracles can win his subjects over fair and square. Another interesting variation on these themes is Lucifer's motivation. As in all these novels, Satan is hardly to be supposed ignorant of Bible prophecy. Surely he knows his Bible at least as well as the characters—fundamentalist hacks—who educate the readers. So why bother with the whole exercise in wasted effort? Well, talk about hubris! Betzer's Lucifer figures there must be a way he can beat the odds and win! He assigns his son to look into it and report to him. It all looks quite different from his standpoint: to him the Rapture denotes that Christ/God has given up and surrendered the field! This intriguing element, the idea that in the Bible we are getting not necessarily the inerrant truth but only one side's version of events, never becomes explicit in the novels by evangelical authors, and for obvious reasons. Above all else, they take as basic the infallibility of scripture; indeed the unfolding of the End Time events functions as a (wished-for) vindication of their belief in biblical authority. By contrast, in *Constantine* (a 2005 Antichrist movie) we learn that hell has a different version of the Bible, one with "deleted scenes" and "lost episodes," which presumably have things going the devil's way, particularly in the case of Mammon (*Constantine*'s version of the Antichrist).

It would be interesting to see what would have happened next with Clay Daniels, Jacque Catroux, and the rest (though, in broad terms, I guess we know, don't we?). But Betzer's book ends with the Beast's grand debut. It seems as if he expected to follow up *The Beast* with at least another volume, but as far as I can tell, he never did. Too bad. He is a talented writer.

Like the ancient apocalypses, these books, one suspects, serve another, perhaps hidden, purpose. They bolster fundamentalist readers' faith in the Second Coming of Christ by putting it in narrative, past-tense form. According to their faith and the preaching of their churches, all this should be happening very, very soon. Yet time passes, generations pass, and still it does not happen. No one acknowledges the disappointment. Instead they tacitly cushion it by reading these books that depict it happening in the readers' own day. Believers would like to see real narrative accounts of the Rapture, say, in *Newsweek*, but lacking this they must content themselves with make-believe, served up by these novels with their fictive depictions of baffled newsmen trying to explain all the crashes of cars left driverless and planes whose cockpits are suddenly vacant. Nor is it only novels. A growing series of pathetically amateurish movies tell and retell the same story. There are even gag newspapers featuring mock-up news and photos of the Rapture and the Tribulation. Just as John G. Gager suggested about 4 Ezra, 2 Baruch, 1 Enoch, and the rest, the point is to invoke the wished-for apocalypse and to provide the vicarious thrill of living through it.[6] It is End Times fantasy camp. It is a kind of theological pornography: vicarious make-believe designed to take the edge off otherwise desperate frustration.

SEND IN THE CHRISTS . . . THERE OUGHT TO BE CHRISTS . . . DON'T BOTHER—THEY'RE HERE

I don't think there can be much doubt that the best of the recent Christian Antichrist novels is James BeauSeigneur's *Christ Clone Trilogy*. BeauSeigneur is a far better messenger for not hammering it home. He is writing fiction that he knows will only make its proper impact on the reader if he first seduces the reader into a suspension of disbelief, as all literary creators do. He is not summoning you to jump ship and swim over to the world of evangelical Christian belief. Rather, he beguiles you into coming along for the ride in a series of novels that are inviting, even compelling, as purely imaginative adventure. And once you're in there, why, if you decide you want to stay, that's your business.

The Christ Clone Trilogy first circulated in 1988, 1997, and 2003 from a small publisher, proving such a cult favorite that it was taken over by Warner Books, updated a bit, and reissued in 2003–2004. Beau-Seigneur's boldness of imagination is indexed by his inclusion of an initial warning to fundamentalist readers not to jump to conclusions that he is indulging in heresy, but to hang on and see how things turn out, a warning to which he refers them again and again in footnotes throughout the book. Reading this, I was reminded of the unhappy experience of the Reverend Paul Leggett, a friend with whom I viewed the Francis Ford Coppola film *Bram Stoker's Dracula* when it premiered in 1992. A film purist, Paul was initially quite skeptical toward the movie and its departures from the source material, but soon he fell silent and was caught up in the magic of the film, a very fine version of the vampire classic. The next day he was interviewed on a local Christian radio station, responding to callers outraged that he could praise such a film! It was like being lowered into a tank of hungry piranha! BeauSeigneur clearly knew his audience well enough to know what to expect from them.

He is a wonderful storyteller, inspired, not hampered, by his theological convictions. Such a story as he tells requires massive amounts of both convincing scientific and geopolitical detail. (Luckily, Beau-Seigneur has plenty at his disposal, having been a professor of political science and served at the National Security Administration.) The only miss is, I think, a clever though grossly implausible gimmick for explaining how the Turin Shroud could be genuine yet be carbon-dated to the fourteenth century. It had lain hidden in the Ark of the Covenant for more than a millennium, and the atomic clock began ticking only once it was removed. This is because of some Von Däniken-like nonsense about the Ark of the Covenant being a space warp bigger inside than out and suspending the passage of time. But on the whole, Beau-Seigneur is a master of political machination and "hard science fiction." And the central scientific conceit of the trilogy is, obviously, that someone decides to clone whomever it was who left *living cells* on the Shroud of Turin, with the result that Christ ("Christopher Goodman") appears to be reborn into our history—with the awful suspicion that maybe he is instead the Antichrist (an idea also used to good advantage in Thomas L. Monteleone's novels *Blood of the Lamb* and *The Reckoning*, discussed in the next chapter).

All these novels sooner or later get to the Rapture, and so does *In His Image*, the first in the trilogy. But here BeauSeigneur is highly original. Instead of the raptured Christians vanishing into thin air, they just *drop dead* by the millions with no apparent cause. They have been "taken up" spiritually, not physically. And there is certainly more than enough wiggle room in the New Testament for this interpretation. After all, it never says precisely *how* the saints are to be caught up. It could as easily be chariot rides like Elijah's! And BeauSeigneur's method allows for a lot more ambiguity. The standard vanishing act would seem to make it a little too obvious that the fundies were right all along. Even if you say, "Well, yes, but people didn't catch on because of Satan 'clouding men's minds' like the Shadow," you're still sacrificing narrative verisimilitude. The more overt supernatural interventions you have, the less like familiar reality the narrative is going to seem.

Like *Left Behind*, *The Christ Clone Trilogy* sets forth a fundamentalist agenda, but with infinitely more finesse. When we meet "Messianic Jews," they are less like American "Jews for Jesus" (really just Jewish converts to Protestant Fundamentalism sporting yarmulkes for camouflage purposes) than like Lubavitcher zealots—only with Jesus as Messiah, not Rabbi Schneerson. The obligatory "Jesus fulfilled prophecy" rant, though based on no more sound a grasp of the ancient texts and their probable contexts, does not, at least at first, come across as obnoxious preaching, as if someone had inserted an evangelistic tract between the pages of the novel, which is the way it sounds in the *Left Behind* books. In one scene, a Hasidic rabbi on the verge of conversion reads a passage, not saying where it came from, to a stubborn Orthodox friend. The latter begins to fulminate that it sounds like some clumsy Christian pastiche of the Hebrew prophets, trying to make it look like Jesus' saving death was predicted in scripture. Then the rabbi tells him he has been reading from the book of Isaiah, chapter 53! It is *Jewish* scripture! Why has his friend never heard the passage read in synagogue? Because, er, uh, that text is always skipped lest hearers notice the "similarity" to the story of Jesus! The scene is brilliant. Too bad it is based on what amounts to an urban legend. The fact is that the Haftorah readings, that is, texts from outside the Torah, do not cover all the text of the prophets, but only passages selected for similarity of theme to the Torah readings, which are comprehensive. And the system dates back to the Seleucid period (more than a century before Jesus), when public reading from the Torah was forbidden, but not the reading of the prophets; hence, thematically linked prophetic texts were read instead. Isaiah 53 was one of many, many texts perforce left on the cutting room floor.

Rest assured, however, BeauSeigneur will eventually get around to the whole raft of "fulfilled prophecies," but as these coincide point for point with those given in the *Left Behind* books, I refer the reader to chapter 2, where I have already discussed the prophecies.

Even when the author has taken great pains, as BeauSeigneur has, to simulate the real world, the sudden impingement of the supernatural is always hard to credit. It must be handled very cleverly. And suddenly the two-thousand-year-old apostle John walks on stage! BeauSeigneur thinks of him along the lines of the Wandering Jew, just as Joseph Smith did. It seems that in John 21, though Jesus didn't say the Beloved Disciple would *never* die, he *did* mean to predict that John would linger in the world carrying on Christ's work until the Second Coming—at which time he would finally die *as one of the Two Witnesses of Revelation, chapter 11*. You can just hear the stiff-starched fundamentalist reader, with his inquisitor's microscope, beginning to bristle when BeauSeigneur has John admit he should have been a bit more clear with certain things in his Gospel! Of course, the whole idea that the fourth Gospel stems from John the son of Zebedee in the first place is an article of fundamentalist faith, not of critical scholarship. But what a disarming moment it is when, to answer a character's question, John the apostle and evangelist asks the man if he has never read Harnack, who already managed to figure out the answer! Imagine: John referring to Adolf von Harnack, one of the great New Testament critics of the nineteenth and twentieth centuries—it's worthy of Nikos Kazantzakis!

That little detail also shows that BeauSeigneur is not living in quite as small a theological bubble as Tim LaHaye, for when LaHaye and

Jenkins want to impress us with Tsion Ben-Judah's biblical erudition, they refer only to "commentaries." And we know which ones: all dispensationalist fundamentalists. There is no way he is reading R. H. Charles, no chance he is consulting Bruce J. Malina, Margaret Barker, or Elisabeth Schüssler Fiorenza. There is no use of scholarly monographs or learned journals. For LaHaye's type of Christianity is innocent of these things. They would complicate the picture too much. The diversity of perspectives such learning supplies would simply make it impossible to map out Tribulation timetables and such nonsense.

One oddity in the author's identification of John as one of the Two Witnesses is that it implicates John in the combustion deaths of Israeli police who try to interfere with his preaching. For a man who has had over two millennia to think about it, he doesn't seem to have learned the lesson Jesus tried to teach him in Luke 9:51–56, when James and John, stung at their rebuff by a Samaritan village, ask Jesus, "Don't you want us to call down fire from the sky to destroy them as Elijah did?" and Jesus replies, "You don't realize what Spirit you belong to! For the Son of man came not to destroy men's lives, but to save them!" Apparently, John is still quick to unholster a lightning bolt!

BeauSeigneur's second volume, *Birth of a New Age*, provides a spectacular and suitably gruesome account of the effects of asteroids striking the earth. It is all the more chilling for the simple, clinical prose with which the process is described. BeauSeigneur's refreshing wit is evident even here, as he has a young astronomer discover a trio of new asteroids, one of which will graze the earth with horrifying results, the second striking it with equal devastation, and the third pulverized by nukes but raining down arsenic into the water table. Not suspecting their danger, she dubs the three heavenly bodies Calvin, Hobbes, and Wormwood. The last represents Miss Wormwood, the schoolteacher from the *Calvin and Hobbes* cartoon strip. So, totally ignorant of the book of Revelation, the astronomer fulfills prophecy by naming the poisonous asteroid after a cartoon character!

The descending asteroids are shortly followed by a cloud of bird-sized insects, the anthropomorphic locusts from the Pit of Abaddon.

The *Left Behind* books also take these aspects of the Revelation literally, and this is a mistake. As Bruce J. Malina has made clear, the Revelation of John is overrun with ancient astrological imagery. Malina departs from traditional scholarly opinion by interpreting the book as a review, à la 1 Enoch, of the primordial history, not a preview of the end of history. If I read him right, he takes the descent of the "star" Wormwood to denote no natural disaster but rather to symbolize the descent to earth of the fallen sons of God (Gen. 6:1–4) to poison the human race with moral corruption. I cannot follow him in this, though it is an intriguing and worthy hypothesis. I believe Malina neglects the patent references to events anticipated in the time of the Revelator, so I would put his puzzle pieces together like this: though no star was anciently called "Wormwood" (literally, "Absinth"), the old astrologers did place poisonous plants such as wormwood under the influence of a particular constellation, Scorpio, which lay adjacent in the heavens to Sagittarius the archer and to the Centaur. All three of these zodiacal figures bore scorpion tails, and the last two were both depicted as Centaurs. I suspect that the plummeting to earth of Wormwood refers to Scorpio's "sinking" beneath the horizon with the turning of the great heavenly wheel. The man-faced, long-haired, armored, barb-tailed locusts are straight descriptions of Sagittarius and the Centaur in ancient iconography. And the dominance of Scorpio, Sagittarius, and the Centaur upon earthly events cleared the way for the Parthian cavalry (whom Revelation's locusts also resemble) to cross the Euphrates and to invade Rome. I think that is what the Revelator meant to predict.[7] So Beau-Seigneur might have saved himself the asteroids (though I'm glad he didn't) and especially the locust monsters that are something out of a Toho Studios movie.

However, when he shortly introduces, as he feels he must, an at least quasi-literal portrayal of the horsemen spewing across the Euphrates (Rev. 9:13–19), which I take to be synonymous with the locusts, BeauSeigneur shows he knows how to deliver the horror! In a rapid-fire succession of vignettes that would be in place in any lunatic horror movie, he has a horde of demons possess and destroy the entire populations of all Middle Eastern countries (except Israel), spurring their hapless hosts to unthinkable deeds of murder and mayhem—only BeauSeigneur is fully capable of thinking of them and of putting them on paper. Well, I guess he knew how C. S. Lewis felt after putting himself inside the head of Uncle Screwtape.[8] Maybe he felt he needed a shower afterward, but he didn't flinch when the narrative required him to play horror hardball.

Eventually, the Christ clone gets shot down, only to rise up again, securing an international following, as might be expected. During the time of his dormancy, he communes with God and discovers the true nature of his mission. Christopher does not like what he hears from Yahweh (as the book calls him), because he has earlier been taken under the wing of a retired diplomat named Robert Milner and his partner, Alice Bernley, who are insidious higher-ups in the worldwide New Age movement.[9] They have poisoned Christopher with the doctrines of their faith, aptly described by Brooks Alexander of the fundamentalist Spiritual Counterfeits Project as "cosmic humanism."[10] The Christ clone unleashes a torrent of New Age drivel, much of it a parody of Scientology, explaining that Yahweh, Lucifer, and himself are "Theatans" (to be pronounced just like L. Ron Hubbard's "Thetans"), highly evolved beings from another planet. As Christopher recounts all this hogwash to his old friend Decker Hawthorne (the hero of the story if there is one), Hawthorne finds himself stuck accepting it because he is in way too deep already to think of turning back (which is exactly the plight of the Scientologist believer at the late stage of initiation when he finally learns the same stuff). Into the cauldron of beliefs that Christopher proposes to preach goes everything from pyramids and crystals to Buddhism, ancient Gnosticism to positive thinking. The result is that Christopher has embraced the role of Antichrist in that he sets himself heroically against the biblical God, whom he characterizes as a murderous, megalomaniacal tyrant.

BeauSeigneur puts into Christopher's mouth a lengthy and detailed critique of the biblical Jehovah that is highly reminiscent both of modern atheist polemic and of ancient Marcionite and Gnostic Christianity. The reader has to wait for the third volume (*Acts of God*) to hear BeauSeigneur, through one of his characters, try to talk his way out of the grave he has dug. I think he gives the Antichrist the better argument. We are left wondering just why we ought to worship a God who will snuff us if we don't kowtow to him, who perpetrates genocide and the execution of heretics. We are left wondering why we ought to regard critical thinking, self-reliance, and infinite human potential as such blasphemies.

The author also unsheathes the dull and brittle sword of apologetics for the resurrection and against other religions. He wants to know, if Jesus' corpse were still on earth, why the Roman or Sanhedrin authorities did not make short work of Christian preaching by producing it. Of course, the book of Acts says Christians began to preach the resurrection only *seven weeks* after Jesus died, by which time, as Reimarus pointed out so long ago,[11] the body would have been hopelessly corrupt and unidentifiable. (Mishnaic law declares a corpse legally unidentifiable after the third day!) The stunning irony here is that BeauSeigneur in the very same chapter provides an explanation of the Rapture (hence of the resurrection) whereby the assumption of the immortal resurrection body entails sloughing off *and leaving behind* the old, fleshly body. In that case, Jesus' earthly body *would* have been available in the tomb for the curious to exhume.

BeauSeigneur demands to know how it could be that the very men who claimed to have interviewed the resurrected Jesus were later willing to die as martyrs to that conviction if they were liars and hoaxers. But we know virtually nothing about their deaths, only that James son of Zebedee was executed by order of Herod Agrippa I (Acts 12:1–2). Nor do we possess direct testimony from any of these men as to what they may or may not have experienced of a resurrected Christ, if anything. We have only the hearsay of the Gospel Easter narratives, which BeauSeigneur, an inerrantist evangelical, imagines to be of equal value.

For BeauSeigneur, Muhammad cannot have been a genuine prophet because, legend says, the mountain would not heed his call to come to him. Then one supposes Jesus is neither to be trusted as a spiritual expert, since no Christian has ever been able to cash in Jesus' reported promise that even one with a modicum of faith should be able to uproot mountains and send them flying (Mark 11:23). If Joseph Smith's claim to have found the golden plates of Moroni is suspect because there were but eleven witnesses, and they were either still doubtful or were Smith's cronies, what better evidence have we for the resurrection of Jesus, seeing that the Gospels know only of appearances to small groups of friends and followers, and that in locked rooms, never in public? All alike smack of imposture.

And since we cannot know whether the Buddha really attained Nirvana, BeauSeigneur scoffs, we are left to our own best judgment to evaluate his teachings on their own inherent merit. But that is just the way the Buddha himself is said to have put it: he simply invited people to try his method. It could never be a matter of "authorities" or miraculous proofs, for these have nothing to do with whether or not the method avails for the individual. It is a gross category confusion when BeauSeigneur's character declares, "We have, therefore, nothing on which to base our decision about the truth of any of these religions except what the founder of these religions said and whether the teaching seems to work in our own lives."[12] And what, pray tell, is the matter with *that?* Wasn't that good enough for Jesus? "He who has ears to hear, let him hear." Performing miracles can prove only that one can perform miracles, not that one's religious opinions are correct. At this point, we are intended to be smirking right along with the characters that are "in the know," but there is a narrative irony that BeauSeigneur doesn't mean to create: his heroes are cocksure in their ignorance, though, lucky for them, their author seems to share it and to have built his narrative world accordingly.

Throughout the trilogy, the author leaves the question wide open as to whether Christopher is more deceived than deceiving. Has he merely fallen in with the wrong bunch—those New Age nuts? Have they caused him to swerve off course to become the Antichrist despite himself? Christopher is frequently compared with the child prodigy

Jiddu Krishnamurti, initially touted by Theosophists as the Lord of the Age. Recruited in 1909 by Charles W. Leadbeater (who had a notorious fondness for young boys), Krishnamurti was heralded as the new Christ and the avatar of Maitreya Buddha and was trained for the position, to which, however, he never really warmed. Young Krishnamurti saw he was being manipulated and repudiated his sponsors' messianic ambitions for him in 1929.[13] We find ourselves wondering if BeauSeigneur is hinting that Christopher, too, will break with his mentors. But he doesn't. It develops that it is he who has been playing them and everyone else for fools. His humanitarian compassion is simply an act, a façade; he is bad to the bone. He didn't *go* bad; he was already there.

Certain features are bound to recur in these books given the common source material, for example, the eventual retreat to the lost sandstone city of Petra, which becomes the arena for Armageddon, where finally Jesus Christ rips the fabric of the dimensions to appear astride a white horse.[14] When Jesus finally appears, BeauSeigneur has the sense to let less stand for more. His Jesus kicks demonic butt, greets the resurrected faithful, and promises to sit down to answer questions later; meanwhile he has business to attend to. Unlike Jenkins's Jesus in *Glorious Appearing*, BeauSeigneur doesn't trivialize the Last Adam by making him into a devotional teddy bear. *The Christ Clone Trilogy*, despite its crude theology (to be expected in such projects), packs many a wallop and is filled with vibrant writing and plenty of surprises. BeauSeigneur even comes up with a way for the legions of those hoodwinked into taking the mark of the Beast to undo it! Here's hoping he is planning something for the far side of the millennium, when he still has the rebellion of Satan, Gog, and Magog to chronicle.

ANGELS ON THE GROUND

The first thing you notice about Paul Meier's 1993 Rapture novel *The Third Millennium* is that his Antichrist has a rather familiar name: *Damian* Gianardo. Well, why not? We have already seen how one apoc-

alypse tends to contribute a detail here or there that subsequent apocalypses will take up and make part of the tradition. As for the rest of
it, you know the drill. First we get the soap opera, which takes quite a
few pages, because modern readers expect a bit more naturalism in
narration. They want the characters to be more rounded. Suddenly the
Rapture occurs, and it is only the one character who is a backslidden
born-again Christian—whose father happens to be the leading dispensationalist preacher in Dallas—who is able to shed any light on the
matter. (Again, in this narcissistic narrative universe, someone we
would dismiss as a sectarian hack becomes an authority greater than
Kant or Einstein!) The US president takes advantage of the reduction
of the population and its damage to the economy; by freezing their
assets and threatening to nuke them, he bullies Japan, Britain, and Italy
into joining the United States, which will move its headquarters to
Rome and will be known henceforth as the New Roman Empire.
(That's why the president has an Italian name.) There is little attempt
at subtlety or political verisimilitude here. As in all these novels, it
almost appears that the very improbability of events reinforces their
divine ineluctability as parts of the fore-ordained juggernaut of
prophecy. But does that mean God devised and designed the rise of
the Beast, the False Prophet, the Harlot Babylon, and so on? That it
was *his* idea? Or are we not rather to imagine that John the Revelator
simply saw in advance the evil that men (and devils) do and forewarned us of it? In that case, wouldn't the events need to make sense
in and of themselves, with their own geopolitical and scientific logic?
They do in *The Christ Clone Trilogy*, less so here.

As usual, Jewish characters are moved by the conformity of these
events to Bible prophecy to reexamine the prophetic claims for Jesus of
Nazareth as the Jewish Messiah, and they are convinced, that is, converted. *The Third Millennium* is one of the clearest examples of two
trends that several of these novels feature. For one, there is a very
clever sleight-of-hand tactic to convince the reader of biblical inspiration and inerrancy. Again and again one reads of striking fulfillments of
ancient prophecy in modern events. As Angley put it in *Raptured*, "It was

so strange to sit there and listen to the rapture being talked about as something that had already taken place."[15] Yes, we are reading fiction, but the mere fact that all this vindication of the Bible is being presented in past tense has an impact. It fabricates the impression, as we, as obliging readers, temporarily suspend our disbelief, that we are marveling at spectacular biblical, prophetic fulfillments. The writer intends that we shall subconsciously carry this impression away with us when we close the book.

When the Christian backsliders and the not-quite-yet converted Jews are taken aback at these ineluctable fulfillments, we get the impression that a noose is tightening around them. The unbelievers are shown as running out of excuses not to believe. They are coming face to face with the truth they should have believed in all along. There are two levels of communication here, I think. For one, the daunting truth is coming to roost for the characters that the once-sunny, bright, and breezy world they thought they lived in is rapidly giving way to the predicted End Times scenario, so they'd best get serious with the Lord. Second, and this is the more serious subtext: the reader, if not already a born-again Christian, is being led to feel he has been roped and tied, that there is now no more escape, no more excuse, for not embracing the born-again worldview, not just about the Tribulation, but about everything else: devotionalism, anti-evolutionism, Nicene Christology, Trinitarianism, Reformation theology, believing all non-Christians are damned, going to church every week, thinking only so far lest one drift into heresy, and so on. But the evangelical writer does not realize that the one is a symbol for the other: for the rest of us, finding ourselves captive within the restraints of fundamentalism would be to wake up in the Great Tribulation. They don't notice it because they have long since given in to the Stockholm syndrome, identifying with the captor. "Crucifixion? Best thing the Romans ever did for us!"[16]

Meier's narrator is none other than the archangel Michael, and the narrative is a report he has filed with the heavenly bureaucracy, sort of an X-File, if the X is understood as a Greek letter *chi*. For one thing, I think he's got the wrong angel. Michael is the messianic warrior. Meier wants Gabriel, the angel who brings news from the divine throne to mortals including Daniel, Mary, and Muhammad. Meier's Michael falls somewhere between John Travolta's *Michael* and Clarence, Angel Second Class, in *It's a Wonderful Life*. He is a bit too free with the stupid joke or wry observation, including the idiotic bumper sticker motto "My Boss Is a Jewish Carpenter." But his appearances like clockwork on Jewish holidays are a handy way of punctuating the narrative.

The Third Millennium also commits the sin, to my mind, that is so prevalent in these Rapture novels. It confuses the revelation of events in the book of Revelation with the events themselves. For instance, Michael tells one character that soon Jesus will be breaking the fourth seal, and that so-and-so will ensue on earth. But wait a minute: the book of Revelation depicts the Lamb breaking the seals as contemporaneous with John. They are moments in his vision, and symbolic ones at that. The Lamb receives the seven-sealed scroll, which unfurls gradually throughout the book, like a great tapestry showing scene after scene of the future, like Nephren-Ka's wall mural depicting all future ages in advance in Robert Bloch's "Fane of the Black Pharaoh;" the priests rolled back its covering a foot or so a day to reveal what had been predicted long ago of the present. The Revelation of John does not predict that Jesus is someday going to break a seal with this and that result. No, it records John's vision in which the breaking of the seals signals new visions, new glimpses of the future and what is to happen. To point this out may seem like nit-picking, but I think it is symptomatic of the way fundamentalists read the Bible: it is almost as if they hate metaphor and figure. If they should admit its presence even in the book of Revelation, then maybe the door would be open for beginning to take parts of the Gospels as symbolic (as Origen did).

I have already dismissed the characters in *The Third Millennium* as the typical narrative manikins necessary to telling a story at all. That's all they are good for, and there is no way to care about them or to identify with them. But on the other hand, when Meier steps across the line to characterize larger-than-life beings, at least in the case of the Two Witnesses, Moses and Elijah, he pulls it off better than any of our other authors. He has the pair of ancient prophets descend from the stormy sky before rolling TV cameras. They appear on screen more like photographic negatives, a very nice touch denoting their supernatural otherness. And Meier is not afraid to let them speak with an authoritative tone bordering on arrogance. Moses is properly Hestonian and imposing, his historic importance converted to a mighty frame and stentorian voice.

Another seemingly minor aspect of *The Third Millennium* that is nonetheless revealing is the blunt characterizing of God's favorites, not with biblical euphemisms like "the saints" or "believers," but simply as "evangelical Christians."[17] At least the cards are on the table here. Our sect is going to heaven; yours is going to hell.

To end our reflections on Meier's enjoyable *The Third Millennium* where we began them, with the Antichrist, his treatment of this character is virtually unique. He never tells us straight out that Damian Gianardo knows he is in league with Satan. Of course, he must be, but that is evident to us only because, thanks to the constant reassurances of the narrator, we know the story is taking place within the fundamentalist framework. But it is not at all clear that Damian knows that. To the end he seems mostly a brilliant, albeit ruthless leader who finally dares way too much and loses control of the mess he has made of the world. His lieutenants come less to worship him than to snicker at his megalomania behind his back. He is like old, grasping Mr. Potter in *It's a Wonderful Life.* So perhaps it is fitting that, as with Mr. Potter, we do not see Damian receive his comeuppance. Presumably Jesus grabs him with the vaudeville hook and pitches him into the Lake of Brimstone as in all the other Rapture novels, but the event is not narrated. Maybe Michael ran out of parchment.

THE 666 CLUB

The 1995 novel *The End of the Age* bears the name of Pat Robertson as its author, but remember what I said in chapter 1 about the use of pseudonyms in apocalypses. Like most other books bearing Robertson's name, this one was surely penned by an unnamed ghost writer. Be that as it may, *The End of the Age* certainly represents the Pat Robertson variety of American evangelical Christianity. The cast of heroic Christians (clearly meant to be the store window display models) includes a couple of nuke-wielding generals operating out of clandestine military bases in New Mexico; a converted advertising exec, now putting his sleazy skills to work for Christ; a Bible-quoting NBA player; and (not surprisingly) an idealized version of Pat Robertson himself: a former televangelist and Christian broadcaster now turned "prophet"[18] and survivalist. He has an athlete's muscular body even into his sixties: "Al could see a man with his shirt off pounding tent pegs into the ground with an eight-pound hammer. *That must be Pastor Jack*, Al thought."[19] Here one recalls Robertson's dubious claims in 2006 to have leg-pressed two thousand pounds. And then Pastor Jack is served by one Vince D'Agostino, former chief of staff for a disgraced president of the United States. Vince is now working for Pastor Jack in the same capacity, reinforcing Robertson's one-time presidential delusions. And his survivalist retreat includes a super-high-tech satellite broadcasting array. Remind you of anyone?

The novel envisions the aftermath of a large asteroid smacking into the earth. The disaster ushers in the End Times, the descent of the space-stone fulfilling the prophecy of Wormwood's meteoric fall (Rev. 8:10–11). Like *The Christ Clone Trilogy*, *The End of the Age* spends enough time and detail on the science of the disaster and its political-economic ramifications to make it seem real to the reader, something the author cannot seem to do later on, at the climax, when he merely notes in sparse prose that God has dispatched supernatural entities to win the final battle: "The archangel Michael had been sent by Almighty God with the largest contingent of angelic powers ever known in the history of the world."[20] (Would someone please check that statistic?) "Soon, Michael had cleared every satanic alien from the skies."[21] This is actually *less* narrative detail than the book of Revelation offers!

We expect to see daring exploits of what another writer might call the "Tribulation Force," but in fact we see only one: our born-again ad executive motorcycles from Albuquerque to occupied Dallas in disguise to pick up some supplies and meets a feisty Christian operative who comes to his aid, kills one of Antichrist's cops on the beat, and turns out to be the long-lost daughter of Pastor Jack. By far most of the book is exposition. This is divided between the perhaps too fulsome data stream about the natural disasters and their effects on the one hand and pedantic exposition of Revelation on the other. In these long passages, couched as scenes of informal Bible study for the benefit of new converts, the dialogue is as palpably phony as the "conversations" one sees on a late-night infomercial before one changes the channel.

The theology of *The End of the Age* is predictably annoying in some places, surprisingly different in others. It is ironic that Pastor Jack understands quite well that ancient peoples supposed that natural forces were controlled by fearsome spirits who had to be mollified by sacrifice and worship: "In ancient days," wrote Pastor Jack, "primitive tribes felt that volcanoes were caused by angry spirits. In order to appease these spirits, they devised elaborate rituals and offered sacrifices."[22] But has Pastor Jack, that is, Pat Robertson, gotten any further in his thinking? Apparently not, for a mere five pages later we read Jack's musings on the horrific fusillade of earthquakes, volcanoes, and tsunamis erupting all around his sheltered retreat: "Redemption will come, indeed, . . . and soon. But not until this planet, which has at long last tasted the very wrath of God, first tastes the wrath of Satan."[23] What's the difference here from the "primitive tribal" view? And the envisioned ritual that would turn aside the supernatural suffering? You guessed it: receiving Jesus Christ as one's personal savior: "Her husband was among the unaffected, and he tried to persuade her that her torment would cease if only she would surrender her life to Jesus Christ."[24] In Moses' day, looking at the bronze serpent did the trick (Num. 21:6–9), but times have changed. So religion has become a protection racket.

Thankfully, Jews come off pretty well in this book, mustering the backbone to denounce the Antichrist and his messianic pretensions.

Nor is anything said about their having to become Protestant funda-mentalists ("born-again Christians") in order to be saved. Perhaps this is because they are on the verge of the next dispensation, the Millen-nial Kingdom, at which time Jews, Jesus-believers or not, will enter upon their own theocratic destiny assigned by God. Or so say dispen-sationalists, and Pat Robertson, being a Southern Baptist, is not likely to be completely free of their influence. On the other hand, and this is astonishing, *The End of the Age* repudiates the dispensationalists' pret-ribulation Rapture doctrine. "How come God doesn't get you Chris-tians out of all this? If you guys are so special and if your God has all this stuff worked out, then why are you all still here, anyway?"[25] The answer, a good one that somehow seems to escape the pretribulationists with their plans to munch popcorn on the sidelines of Armageddon, is that Christians have always been called on to suffer in witness to their faith, and that nothing makes it any different now. "Of course, I'm excited, Carl. What I've been waiting for all my life as a Christian is about to happen. But before it does, all of us are going to have the seven toughest years of our lives to get through. And, then Jesus will come for us."[26] As it turns out, though, the born-again squad has a pretty cushy time of it in their mountain retreat.

Muslims are mentioned briefly, with a tip of the burnoose to them because they will not bow the knee to the Antichrist. Hindus are not so lucky, not being "People of the Book," not part of the biblical tradition. Shiva, who is simply God to millions of Hindus with a sophisticated theology, is repeatedly equated with Satan in this book. An ugly piece of theological slander. Theological liberals are caricatured, too: "The leading professor of Christian apologetics at the University of Chicago summed up the feeling of his colleagues, saying, 'I can say without hes-itation that Mark Beaulieu embodies all that we have hoped for in the Messiah."[27] There is no such department at the University of Chicago Divinity School, and if there were, its ultraliberal faculty would no more entertain the notion of a single modern individual as the Messiah of God than Pat Robertson would—unless he had himself in mind for the job.

There are other odd confusions about non-Christian religions. "She told me that observant Jews were constantly speaking as if the Messiah could return any day."[28]

Return? For Jews, the Messiah has not yet come the first time. And then we read of the president of Baghdad, Ibrahim bin-Ishmael, "who claimed to be a descendant of the first Ishmael, the son of Abraham by the servant girl, Hagar. The first Ishmael was thought to be the progenitor of all the Arab people. This unusual leader was an Arab mystic who was persuaded that the heritage he had received from his family—the family of Ishmael—was superior to that of the camel driver Mohammed. Thus, he spent many hours in solitary prayer vigils, seeking supernatural revelations that would equip him to offer new religious truths to his people."[29] The only one of these truths we see revealed is his sudden revelation that President Mark Beaulieu is the Messiah.

Someone seems to have confused Ishmael the son of Abraham with Isma'il (Arabic for Ishmael), the son of the sixth Shiite imam, Jaffar es-Sadik (died 765 CE). Isma'il was in line to become the seven imam following the death of his father, but he died young (in 755 CE), while his father lived. So a succession schism arose, one faction promoting the imamate of Isma'il's younger brother Musa al-Kazim (died 799 CE), the other plumping for Muhammad ibn-Isma'il, Jaffar's grandson, the son of Isma'il. The first group (now called the Twelvers) traced their imams on through the twelfth, Muhammad al-Mahdi. He disappeared without a successor in 939 CE, when it was believed that God hid him somewhere on earth in protection from his enemies, until the day when he should return as the Mahdi, the Rightly Guided One, along with Jesus, to destroy Dejjat, the Antichrist. The latter group (the Seveners, or Isma'ilis) traces its succession of imams into the present day. The Isma'ilis went on to become a radical Gnostic sect. But all Shiites believe that the hadith (traditions) stemming from the circle of the Prophet Muhammad's immediate family (the "Pillars") supercede those of his Companions (early disciples). This sets them apart from the Sunni majority.

The author of *The End of the Age* seems to want to depict Ibrahim bin-Ishamel as some kind of Isma'ili Shiite mystagogue like, for example, Hamsa ibn-Ali ibn-Ahmad, a tenth-century Isma'ili sage who proclaimed the Fatimid caliph Tariqu al Hakim to be Allah incarnate. But since the Iraqi president claims descent from the ancient patriarch Ishmael, who, as the very same sentence states, was the father of *all Arabs anyway*, it is a little hard to see what privilege he is claiming.

As already noted, *The End of the Age* is atypical for Christian apocalyptic novels in embracing posttribulationism. But it goes further than that. The book is also amillennialist in orientation, meaning that, for all the slavish literalism with which the Revelation of John is taken, the book rejects the idea of a messianic interregnum between the Parousia and the dawn of eternity, the kingdom of God proper. When the angels clean the prophetic clock of the Antichrist, they dump both him and his patron Satan into the Lake of Fire. Revelation 19:20 has the Beast and his False Prophet thrown into the Lake of Fire, but not Satan. He is interred in a holding cell for the duration of the millennium, to emerge thereafter for one last hurrah (Rev. 20:1–3). Not in this book, though.

Of one character, about to pray the magic prayer, which, like Billy Batson's uttering "Shazam!" will transform him into one of the saved, we read that "He was about to meet the same Jesus Christ who had spelled out all these truths so many years ago."[30] Uh, *how?* The author intends that, right there on earth, sitting on the couch, the character will initiate a "personal relationship with Jesus Christ," basically a devotional mind game of "imaginary playmates." But can he expect to meet *the real thing?* Jesus Christ himself, returned from heaven after two thousand years? Astonishingly, he does not. The novel stops short of the Parousia itself. Jesus doesn't show up and start shaking hands. That is probably a good idea, since, as the attempts of some of the other authors in this genre demonstrate, it is very hard to pull off such a climax effectively.

But I wonder if, just possibly, the door is left ajar here for another reading. Earlier on, we have been told that Jesus never anticipated a worldly kingdom to overthrow Roman rule. "He spoke to them about a spiritual kingdom composed of people who voluntarily made Him King of their lives."[31] Is it possible that Robertson's writer has demythologized the Second Coming of Jesus? Or are we to understand that Pastor Jack, the intranarrative counterpart to Pat Robertson, has taken the place of Jesus as the Vicar of Christ on earth? We are left with Pastor Jack as the triumphant Christian sage in his mountain kingdom. In reality, most of us probably find it a lot easier to imagine a President Pat Robertson as a sinister Antichrist character who would use slogans of Christianity and American patriotism as banners behind which to hide a Taliban-like reign of holy terror. Let's hope that one remains firmly in the realm of fiction.

The End of the Age, like most of these books, tries to build up the faith of its sectarian readers by showing how their beliefs would not look so nutty after all if translated into real-world events. (That is why it is so disappointing when they suddenly give up and say, "Okay, at this point a bunch of angels intervened, and the good guys won.") And though we must be willing to engage in the "willing suspension of disbelief for the moment"[32] while reading if we are to appreciate these novels *as fictions*, it is hard to do unless one is already a fundamentalist, used to much different standards of verisimilitude, for fundamentalists have long been working hard to believe they are living in the myth-world of the Bible. For the rest of us, despite all the familiarizing, naturalizing references to basketball players and the Joint Chiefs of Staff, we are reading a book that might as well be trying to depict the eschatological vindication of the John Prum Cargo Cult in the New Hebrides.

THE END OF PAGES

One of the hilarious ironies about apocalyptic novels and treatises is that they regularly need updating! The End turns out not to have been quite so near as initially envisioned. David Dolan's *The End of Days* partakes of that irony, having first appeared in 1995, the same year as Robertson's *The End of the Age*, but before it could be rereleased (in 2003) Dolan was obliged to update the action to take account of world developments since the first edition.

More than any other Christian novel of the Last Times, this one focuses on the Two Witnesses of Revelation, chapter 11. (They are perhaps nearly as important in *The Christ Clone Trilogy*, but then that is a longer work with much more going on.) Dolan agrees with Beau-Seigneur, however, in identifying one of the two prophets as John, son of Zebedee, one of Jesus' disciples. The exegetical rationale is pretty much the same: as Joseph Smith also posited, Jesus was after all telling Peter in John 21:22 that John (assuming he was the "Beloved Disciple") would remain alive on earth until the Eschaton. His partner turns out to be Nathanael, another Johannine character, a disciple who does not even appear in the Synoptic Gospels. How does Dolan figure him for the other witness? He is thinking of John 1:51 ("You will see heaven opened, and the angels of God ascending and descending upon the Son of Man."). Though most take the verse to be comparing Jesus with Jacob's ladder in Genesis 28:12 ("And he dreamed that there was a ladder set up on the earth, and the top of it reached to heaven; and behold, the angels of God were ascending and descending on it!"), making Jesus the *Axis Mundi*, the central channel of communication between heaven and earth, it is certainly possible to read John 1:51 as a promise that Nathanael will witness the coming of the Son of Man with his apocalyptic angels. But the passage says nothing about abiding, still alive, to see that sight as in Mark 9:1 ("There are some standing here who will not taste death before they see the kingdom of God come with power."). Nor does it specify that Nathanael will see any of this on the Day of Judgment. Maybe it means that, like John in the Acts of John, Nathanael will see angels visiting Jesus during Jesus' earthly lifetime. But who's criticizing? It's fiction, for Pete's sake! Let a hundred flowers bloom!

Dolan expands the role of the Two Witnesses by not restricting their ministry to Jerusalem, as Revelation 11 might seem to suggest. Yes, it depicts them there, but it also says the whole world rejoices when death silences the Two Witnesses and puts a stop to their plagues, and Dolan must infer from this that the world got a close look at them. So in his novel, John and Nate take a world tour, miraculously teleporting from one continent to another in the manner of Philip the Evangelist in Acts 8:39–40, where the Spirit is said to have "rapt up" or "raptured" Philip at the end of one evangelistic engagement to take him to his next assignment. And, interestingly, this is the only form in which the Rapture occurs in *The End of Days.* In the introduction, Dolan says the whole matter is too contentious theologically, so he is leaving it out! Of course, that means the book is implicitly posttribulationist, in that it depicts the deliverance of living saints coincident with the final coming of Christ, and none of the business about a mysterious vanishing of millions, the very premise of nearly all the other books in this genre.

Another clever touch comes when Dolan has his Antichrist denounce the Two Witnesses as the Antichrist and his False Prophet![33] Though a throw-away item, the accusation is significant, recalling Rene Girard's discussion of Sophocles' *Oedipus Rex*, in which a plague ravages Thebes and all seek a scapegoat to blame and to banish, as they suppose, along with the plague. Though the role of scapegoat eventually settles upon Oedipus himself, Girard contends, it might have floated in a different direction and settled on the shoulders of some other candidate, hinting that such a choice is never inevitable and never required by the facts.[34] It will inevitably be arbitrary because it is artificial and superstitious. And in the history of apocalyptic expectation, it has become very clear that the musical chairs game of who gets identified as the Christ, the Antichrist, and the Two Witnesses is in the eye of the beholder. It is a matter of politics, even if theological politics.

It is unwittingly revealing that the apostle John, ostensibly one of the writers of scripture, is himself depicted as dependant upon scripture. He is able to correct the characters' previous interpretations of this verse or that sign (which is an amusing way for Dolan to pull rank over the reader's opinions!), but basically John is shown as standing on the same side of scripture as we are: the receiving end. Here is someone who was privy to the very teaching of Jesus Christ for years, and he is in the same miserable position, essentially, as we mere Johnny-come–latelys who have to make what dim sense we can of fragmentary texts. This betrays the fundamentalist belief that the Bible was virtually dictated to passive individuals via automatic writing, in which case God might as easily have used Herod Antipas as John the Beloved Disciple for the job. Further, it reflects the fundamentalist idolatry of the Bible. The Bible is the God of fundamentalism and the Christ of fundamentalism. John is the disciple, not of Jesus, but of the Bible.

And, speaking of God and Christ, it ought to be observed that, from the standpoint of traditional orthodoxy, *The End of Days* veers into error and heresy. "What if this 'Son of Man' is also the Son of God—of the same substance and nature as the Father? This is exactly what Yeshua [Jesus] claimed to be."[35] But Jesus is never depicted anywhere in any Gospel as making such a claim. If he had, the Council of Nicea would never have been necessary. Again, fundamentalists simply equate their beliefs with the teaching of the Bible. "The New Testament teaches that the one eternal God is manifested in three forms: the invisible Father, the visible Son, and the Holy Spirit."[36] Well, that is one way of putting together and synthesizing the various New Testament statements on Father, Son, and Spirit, but the point is: all such constructs postdate the New Testament. That is no shame unless one is a biblicist who fears to hold any opinion not explicitly taught in the Bible, in which case either one must hold very few theological opinions, or one must read them into the Bible. And Dolan is doing the latter here.

But what is heretical about it? If it matters, what he comes up with is not Orthodox Trinitarianism but rather Modalism: there are not three divine persons sharing one divine essence but rather only one divine person manifesting himself in different ways appropriate to different occasions.

Dolan's Antichrist is Prince Andre of Spain. I imagine he has been inspired by the brief 1970s fundamentalist flirtation with Spanish king Juan Carlos as a candidate for Antichrist. His name (Greek for "man") hints that he will exalt humanity against God. Andre happens to get assassinated right on camera and then rises from the dead, also on camera for the world to see. This miracle seems to be the sole reason for his meteoric rise to the post of emperor of all Europe, then of America and Israel, too. This would never happen. First, Prince Andre is stabbed in the head, awakens, and pulls the knife out—something one might easily fake with simple stage props. But even if proven genuine, what about such a freak of nature would lead the nations to yield up their sovereignty to him? How would a resurrection qualify a man to rule? Would you vote for Dennis Kucinich just because you saw him rise from the dead? Dolan has the Antichrist's subjects eventually rise up against him, but he does not persuade us (me, anyway) that any of them would ever have accepted his political and religious outrages for a minute. This Antichrist is simply a piece of furniture: he is scheduled as part of the eschatological scenario, so there he is, like Santa in the Macy's parade.

We have seen in some of the other End Times novels how difficult it can be to present otherworldly spectacles and miracles in a plausible way consistent with modern, naturalistic ("realistic") narration. Dolan often fails to carry it off, in my opinion.

> Eli discovered a delightful surprise one morning as he shared his faith with a visiting tourist. "Guess what, Moshe. I just shared the gospel with an Italian woman—in perfect Italian!" he announced in awe. "I didn't even realize I was speaking her language until she told me she was from Naples! And I've never even been to Italy!"
>
> "I spoke fluent Japanese only yesterday," replied Moshe with just a touch of pride.
>
> "We seem to have received the gift of tongues in the same way the first believers did on Shavuot [Pentecost] here in Jerusalem, and we didn't even know it!"[37]

Isn't that just neato! It is all taken in stride, as if we are reading a fairy tale. The use of modern idiom comes across as similarly ridiculous, as when Dolan refers to those whom Revelation 14:4 calls "those who have not defiled themselves with women, for they are virgins" as "the 144,000 single men"![38] But surely the greatest of these modern-izing absurdities is Dolan's naive assumption that the ancient apostles of Jesus were no different from modern-day evangelical Christians. "Yochanon [John] resumed his exhortations from the Word of God. After quoting Isaiah and Yeshua, he finished with a call for repentance and offered to pray for anyone wishing to receive the Lord into their lives."[39] To anyone with a rudimentary sense of historical perspective, this is just comical. And it also betrays the arrogance of evangelical Christians to whom it never so much as occurs that their faith is in any respect different from the primitive faith of the apostles two millennia ago. In sum, evangelicals envision neither a genuine past nor a genuine future. Looking backward, they behold only a projection of their own post-Victorian piety. Looking forward, all they see is a set of events on an End Times chart. And there in the middle they rest, snugly and smugly, like a bug in a rug.

CASTING THE ANTICHRIST

How do the various novelists treat the Antichrist? Who is he? How does he rise to power? Watson's Antichrist (in *The Mark of the Beast*) is one Lucien Apleon (from Apollyon, "the Destroyer" in Revelation 9:11). He is a charismatic international figure who, having established a wide social and artistic reputation, is said simply to have been "made" head of "the Revived Roman Empire." Not much attempt at political verisimilitude here! In Angley's *Raptured*, even his own followers refer to their man simply as "the Beast," as if the book of Revelation were a blow-by-blow description of events, not a symbolic cipher for them. No loss, though; the Beast appears only once in the book. Allnutt's pseudo-Kissinger (Alfred K. Kiefer) starts out as the US secretary of state, but he rises to the presidency by systematically plotting the elim-ination of everyone above him. Cohen's Beast is named Baruch Mindor. "Mindor" is "Nimrod" scrambled, and Nimrod, in popular biblical lore, is the builder of the Tower of Babel who attempted to scale the ramparts of heaven like a flesh-and-blood Lucifer. Mindor is the premier of a united communist Western Europe, who quickly rises to the post of secretary general of the United Nations and consolidates it into a world government, just as Nicolae Carpathia does in the *Left Behind* books. It would be quite surprising to learn that Jerry Jenkins had ever even heard of Cohen's *The Horsemen Are Coming.* The scenario is a natural one, and no doubt both authors (not to mention Joe Musser, James BeauSeigneur, and others) cooked it up independently.

Cohen is unable to make Baruch Mindor more than a cardboard-cutout bureaucrat, unlike the colorful Antichrist of *Left Behind*. Betzer's Antichrist is more of a "round" character. That is, he is three-dimensional, not a mere narrative function given a name and a face. We are able to get inside his head, and we find he is literally the son of Lucifer and something of a reincarnation of Adolf Hitler besides! Betzer utilizes the modern myth of Hitler as an occultist as well as pulling in the Nietzschean notion of the Antichrist as a Superman who would bring in a new era of mankind. Physically, this Antichrist is described very much like Jerry Jenkins's Antichrist, Nicolae Carpathia, even down to the wardrobe. (Jenkins tells us to picture Carpathia as a young Robert Redford, but I cannot help thinking of Rutger Hauer.) Anyway, Betzer's Beast is Jacque Catroux, president of a United Europe. He has inherited certain charismatic gifts from his yet-unknown father, including flashes of prophecy, but it is not until a climactic vision of Lucifer (who confesses himself "well pleased" with his son) that he truly understands his identity, role, and powers. As of that moment, Jacque appears possessed by his father, much as Nicolae becomes Satan's channeler following his resurrection. Jacque does not die and rise, as the Antichrist is supposed to do, at least not during this book's narrative; one supposes that detail was satisfied by the fact that Lucifer has somehow transplanted the eyes and heart of Hitler into this new son, born in the very moment of Hitler's suicide.

Pat Robertson's Antichrist (in *The End of the Age*) is president of the United States and soon rises to the leadership of a worldwide Union for Peace in the wake of a devastating asteroid collision that has embroiled the world in economic as well as physical chaos. He is "Mark [i.e., of the Beast] Beaulieu," a name without much of a ring to it, but which is supposed to suggest a (false) Utopia, since, famously, Thomas More's allegorical realm of Utopia meant at once "good place" (*eu-topos* in Greek) and "no place" (*ou-topos*). "Beaulieu" is French for "good place." Balizet's Antichrist is Bishop Uriah Leonard, leader (like Damien Thorn in *The Final Conflict*, the third *Omen* movie) of a worldwide famine relief organization. When the American government collapses in the wake of a superdestructive earthquake, the good bishop is left as the only force capable of bringing order out of the chaos. Soon the papacy falls vacant, and Bishop Leonard is tapped for that job, too. As Pope Sixtus the Sixth (hint, hint), he becomes de facto ruler over Western Europe. James BeauSeigneur's Antichrist, Christopher Goodman, knows he must wind up in hell's torments, but he is eager to play the role assigned him, knowing that he will gain some comedy relief amid the torment by gloating over the poor fools whom he has seduced into sharing the Inferno with him. One of the brightest spots in these novels is the satire provided by their depictions of the Antichrist. He has been effectively used to poke serious fun at secular and religious bureaucrats, at the totalitarian abuses of humanist and atheist doctrines, and at dangerous modern trends toward Big Brother surveillance and conformity. And the effectiveness of these parodies seems not to be affected one way or another if the Antichrist is the campiest kind of pulp villain or a chillingly realistic sketch of a would-be tyrant.

NOTES

1. Stephen King, *The Dead Zone* (New York: New American Library, 1980), p. 124.

2. Dwight Wilson, *Armageddon Now! The Premillenarian Response to Russia and Israel since 1917* (Grand Rapids, MI: Baker Book House, 1977), p. 120.

3. Carol Balizet, *The Seven Last Years* (Grand Rapids, MI: Chosen Books/Bake Book House, 1979), p. 261.

4. Ibid., p. 359.

5. Ibid., p. 200.

6. John G. Gager, *Kingdom and Community: The Social World of Early Christianity*, Prentice-Hall Studies in Religion Series (Englewood Cliffs, NJ: Prentice-Hall, 1975), pp. 50–51, 55.

7. Bruce J. Malina, *On the Genre and Message of Revelation: Star Visions and Sky Journeys* (Peabody, MA: Hendrickson Publishers, 1995), pp. 139–49.

8. C. S. Lewis, *The Screwtape Letters* (New York: Macmillan, 1970), p. xiv: "But though it was easy to twist one's mind into the diabolical attitude, it was not fun, or not for long. The strain produced a sort of spiritual cramp. . . . It almost smothered me before I was done."

9. Alice Bernley is named after Theosophist medium Alice Bailey. Bailey claimed to be channeling "the Tibetan," whom she also called Djwhal Khul, while "Alice Bernley had a spirit guide whom she called Master Djwlij Kajm or sometimes 'the Tibetan.'" James BeauSeigneur, *Birth of an Age: The Christ Clone Trilogy, Book Two* (New York: Warner Books, 2004), p. 32.

10. One is reminded here of Robert Hugh Benson's depiction of humanism as the Antichrist's doctrine in *Lord of the World*. One of BeauSeigneur's minor characters, Joel Felsberg, even has a name reminiscent of Benson's Antichrist, Julian Felsenberg.

11. Hermann Samuel Reimarus, *Reimarus: Fragments*, ed. Charles H. Talbert, trans. Ralph S. Fraser, Lives of Jesus series (Philadelphia: Fortress Press, 1970), pp. 250–51.

12. James BeauSeigneur, *Acts of God: The Christ Clone Trilogy, Book Three* (New York: Warner Books, 2004), p. 153.

13. J. Stillson Judah, *The History and Philosophy of the Metaphysical Movements in America* (Philadelphia: Westminster Press, 1967), p. 102; Joscelyn Godwin, *The Theosophical Enlightenment* (Albany: State University of New York Press, 1994), pp. 366–67; Peter Washington, *Madame Blavatsky's Baboon: A History of the Mystics, Mediums, and Misfits Who Brought Spiritualism to America* (New York: Schocken Books, 1995), pp. 128–38.

14. BeauSeigneur intimates that it isn't really a horse, but that a horse is as close as he can compare it to. Nice touch. Me, I would have had Jesus ride Pegasus. Wouldn't that have been great?

15. Ernest W. Angley, *Raptured: A Novel on the Second Coming of the Lord* (Old Tappan, NJ: Fleming H. Revell Company, 1950), p. 97.

16. Graham Chapman, John Cleese, Terry Gilliam, Eric Idle, Terry

Jones, and Michael Palin, *Monty Python's The Life of Brian (of Nazareth)*, (New York: Ace Books, 1979), pp. 62–63.

17. Likewise in David Dolan, *The End of Days* (Springfield, MO: 21st Century Press, 2003), p. 280: "those born-again, fundamentalist Christians."

18. Pat Robertson, *The End of the Age* (Dallas: Word Publishing, 1996), p. 364.

19. Ibid., p. 366.

20. Ibid., p. 396.

21. Ibid.

22. Ibid., p. 260.

23. Ibid., p. 265.

24. Ibid., p. 302.

25. Ibid., pp. 71–72.

26. Ibid., p. 208.

27. Ibid., p. 316.

28. Ibid., p. 308.

29. Ibid., p. 305.

30. Ibid., p. 209.

31. Ibid., p. 191. Indeed? Where in any Gospel does Jesus ever say anything of the kind? Granted, in John 18:36 Jesus repudiates any worldly politics, but a kingdom of hearts ruled by him? As usual, the pietistic sloganeering of fundamentalism is simply equated with "scripture."

32. Samuel Taylor Coleridge, *Biographia Literaria*, chap. 14 (1817).

33. Dolan, *End of Days*, p. 148.

34. Rene Girard, *Violence and the Sacred*, trans. Patrick Gregory (Baltimore: Johns Hopkins University Press, 1977), p. 78: "The attribution of guilt that henceforth passes for 'true' differs in no way from those attributions that will henceforth be regarded as 'false'. . . . A particular version of events succeeds in imposing itself; it loses its polemical nature in becoming the acknowledged basis of the myth, in becoming the myth itself." P. 70: "And in asserting that there is no difference between the antagonists in a tragedy, we are saying that ultimately there is no difference between the 'true' and the 'false' prophet."

35. Dolan, *The End of Days*, p. 80.

36. Ibid., pp. 80–81.

37. Ibid., pp. 172–73.

38. Ibid., p. 157.

39. Ibid., p. 132.

Chapter Nine

MAINSTREAM APOCALYPSE NOVELS

"Is it tomorrow? Or just the end of time?"

—Jimi Hendrix

MY HEART, ANTICHRIST'S HOME

Those Antichrist novels originating in secular publishing take a very different approach from the ones reviewed in the previous chapters. Nevertheless, there is a surprising link between the two groups of books. *The Omen*, the first of the secular novels and movies and played just for spooky entertainment, originated from an idea of evangelical author Robert Boyd Munger.[1] He wanted the film to serve as a warning to the moviegoing public about the very real (to him) threat of the coming Antichrist. The producers even took on Hal Lindsey as a consultant, but he dropped out when he saw the project going off in what he deemed unscriptural directions. Some isolated bits of the evangelical motive remain, however, as when Father Brennan urges Ambassador Thorn, unwitting abettor of the Beast, to "receive Christ as your savior." The fundamentalist edge is at once blunted, however, when the wild-eyed priest explains that Thorn must receive Christ daily and sacramentally in the Eucharistic host.

Movies about the Antichrist invite the same flack as movies about

Jesus Christ. Like "purist" fans of Tolkien who boycotted Peter Jackson's film trilogy *The Lord of the Rings*, fundamentalists will take indignant exception to any perceived departure from scriptural authenticity. Yet it is precisely the creative flexibility (not surprisingly) that enables the secular creators to make more effective books and movies, whether of Christ or Antichrist. The fundamentalist End Times novels and movies are essentially exercises in translating theology directly to film or the fictional page, and the transition is not an easy one. These writers feel they must squeeze in every jot and tittle, every signpost on the foldout dispensational chart, but there are far too many of them for that. Witness the redundancy of several distinct "Final Judgments" in Jenkins's *The Glorious Appearing*. His guru Tim LaHaye must have insisted on preserving all the hairsplitting exegetical distinctions drawn by his fellow dispensationalist theologians. Because the Judgment is depicted in slightly different ways by different New Testament writers, with various emphases that cannot always be harmonized, LaHaye has poor Jenkins schedule a Judgment of the Nations, a Great White Throne Judgment, Judgment of the Beast and the False Prophet, and so on. That's some busy docket! In the hands of less capable writers than Jenkins, such cataloging results in a stiff and contrived collection of catastrophes and monsters that leaves little room for plot development or characterization. One way Jenkins avoids that pitfall, obviously, is the epic scale of his work. There is plenty of time to work everything in.

Not bound by the straitjacket of orthodoxy, the secular writers can pick and choose from the Bible (and the Antichrist tradition) those elements most conducive to a good yarn. Their aim is to entertain, not to evangelize. The born-again writers were trying to scare you out of hell; these authors are only trying to scare the hell out of you.

ESCHATOLOGICAL ERRORS AND EXTRAS

Besides their creative flexibility, the secular Antichrist novels sometimes contain a bit of outright fudging, as when *The Omen* attributes to the book of Revelation this bad poem:

> When the Jews return to Zion,
> And a comet fills [movie: "rips"] the sky,
> And the Holy Roman Empire rises,
> Then you and I must die.
> From the eternal sea he rises,
> Creating armies on either shore,
> Turning man against his brother,
> Till man shall be no more.

The book also attributes texts from the book of Daniel to Revelation, and passages from Revelation to the Psalms! In *The Final Conflict*, Damien Thorn quotes another phony prophecy from something he calls "the Book of Hebron, one of the more obscure backwaters of the Septuagint Bible," implying it might be something like 4 Ezra or 4 Maccabees, copied and collected along with the "deuterocanonical" writings like Sirach, 1 and 2 Maccabees, Tobit, Judith, 3 Ezra, the Prayer of Manasseh, Bel and the Dragon, Susanna, the Song of the Three Young Men, and so on, without being, like them, considered part of the Catholic canon. Damien's assistant is puzzled: "I never heard of the Book of Hebron." Well, neither did anybody else. It doesn't exist. But, assuming it did, this is what it would say:

> It shall come to pass that in the end of days the Beast shall reign one hundred score and thirty days and nights. And the faithful shall cry unto the Lord, "Wherefore art thou in the day of evil?" And the Lord shall hear their prayers. And out of the Angel Isle he shall bring forth the Deliverer, the holy Lamb of God who shall do battle with the Beast and shall destroy him.

Worse yet, having located the text in the Septuagint, that is, the Greek translation of the Hebrew Old Testament, Damien goes on to quote "the original Latin"! Yikes. And even if a Septuagint book could be in Latin, the words *ex insular angelorum*—"the island of angels"— have nothing to do with the *Angles*, that is, the ancestors of the English! And *wherefore* means "why," not "where." The author was as clueless about Elizabethan English as grade-school kids who think Juliet is asking Romeo where he is hiding.

The Abomination by Gordon McGill, the fifth *Omen* novel, adds another bogus quote to the book of Revelation:

> The people who have made war,
> Their flesh will fall in rottenness,
> Their eyes will rot in their sockets,
> Their tongues will rot in their mouths.

Of course, these sins of ignorance are nothing compared to a gaffe made in *Constantine*, where, as he explains the differences between the devil's version of the Bible (what an idea!) and the conventional canon, John Constantine comments that 1 Corinthians has only sixteen "acts," while the Hell Bible (called *The Book of Ethenius* in the movie novelization) has a seventeenth. Of course, he means "chapters." Some idiot must have looked at a Bible reference and thought citations like "16:3" denoted act and scene notations, as in a stage play.

But enough quibbling. On to the really interesting stuff! In *The Omen*, Damien is born of a jackal, a blasphemous mockery, one supposes, of the virgin birth of Jesus Christ. The Bible says nothing of this, though one recurring note in medieval speculation was that the Antichrist would be born of a harlot through the power of Satan. In *The Omen*, the Antichrist is a real son of a bitch. Maybe that's the gag.

The Omen also tweaks the tradition by making the mark of the Beast a kind of witch's mark detectable on the body of the Antichrist himself, whereas the Bible envisions Satan's hapless subjects having to receive a tattoo or a brand on forehead or hand. The mark, Revelation says, would contain the tip-off to the Beast's mortal identity, though: the number equivalent would work out to 666. In other words, it would refer to a famous name that readers would already know. They ought to be able to make the connection. But *you* would bear it, not *he*. Why this change? For one simple reason: the action of all three *Omen* movies takes place before the Tribulation begins. We never quite get to the reign of Antichrist or the Battle of Armageddon. Thus there is no occasion in the plot for anyone to take the mark of the Beast. So if that feature is going to enter into the tale at all, it's going to have to be the Beast's own mark.

But Jerry Jenkins makes even more of a mess of the mark of the Beast. While he makes effective and extensive use of the theme insofar as it entails the martyrdom of anyone who will not take the mark, he is less than clear, of all things, about the number 666. His Antichrist, Nicolae Carpathia, favors the number 216, which, the reader may or may not know (I didn't know until someone pointed it out to stupid old me), is 6 times 6 times 6, or 6 cubed. (That's okay; math class was the Great Tribulation to me!) The mark taken by the populace varies with their country of origin and includes the insertion of a satellite location chip. Plus there are various designs to choose from, like a personalized license plate.

Surely the silliest aspect of medieval Antichrist speculation concerns this business of identifying marks for the Beast. Medieval writers just could not resist making a cartoon caricature of him. Reasoning that he must be as monstrous in external appearance as in internal character, they warned that the Antichrist would have one dead eye and a useless arm, plus—rooster feet! Yeah, you're really going to have to be on your guard to avoid getting tricked by *this* guy! Well, compared to this, Damien's scalp scar of three sixes is pretty modest.

And if Carpathia is not literally the son of a jackal like Damien Thorn, he does have an analogue to the nefarious nanny Mrs. Baylock in *The Omen* (played to absolute perfection by Mia Farrow in the 2006 remake). Carpathia's honorary "aunt" who raised him maintains a government perch from which to advise him. She is something of a "bitch" herself. Her name is "Viv Ivins." Are we to think of the late, fanatical anti-Bush journalist Molly Ivins? I bet we are. But the important thing about her is that her name is made up of three Roman numeral sixes. "Vi, vi, vi-ns," or "666-ns." The Antichrist legend supports the presence of such characters in the books, because the ancients imagined the Beast as both intelligent and malevolent beyond his years, as well as educated and trained by a coterie of witches and sorcerers, analogous to Viv Ivins, Mrs. Baylock, and Sergeant Neff, Damien's military school instructor in *Damien: Omen II*.[2]

Regarding the apocalyptic predictions contained in the above-quoted pseudo-Revelation poem that set the stage for Damien's appearing, the Antichrist tradition does posit a renewed Roman Empire and the regathering of Israel. À la Hal Lindsey, *The Omen* understands the European Common Market (precursor to today's European Economic Community) as the Revived Roman Empire, or at least close enough. The mention of a comet might refer to the plummeting to the earth of the "star" Wormwood in Revelation 8:10–11. Or it may have something to do with the "great light" mentioned in the Fatima prophecies. In *The Omen*, its primary purpose is to signal Damien's birth, just as the Bethlehem star heralded that of Jesus. In *The Final Conflict*, this comet has become "the Trinity Alignment," the conjunction of three stars. In a gross insult to the audience's intelligence, the film has the eager astronomers actually witness the hurtling together of three stars in the heavens, as if such movements did not actually take eons of time.

PULP DOGMATICS

This all brings us to one of the most fascinating aspects of the whole matter. Books like the *Omen* series, Robert R. McCammon's *Baal* (1978), and James Patterson's *Virgin* (1980) make use of various features of the Antichrist legend, and their purpose is just to spin a scary yarn. But it is striking how well they manage to accentuate certain theological points better than the admittedly religious novels do. If one looks carefully, each of these books has a distinct theological structure.

McCammon's *Baal* rehearses the stock Satanic conception and *Wunderkind* themes, and, as in *The Final Conflict*, the Antichrist is portrayed as a perverted nihilist. Baal tells off a Catholic priest: "Your god is one of white-steepled churches. That's all; beyond the church doors He has no strength. Mine is the god of the alleys, the whorehouse, the world. Mine is the true king." The new element in *Baal* is that the Antichrist is set in an Islamic context. Muslims, too, are great believers in the Antichrist, whom they call "Dejjal" or "Dejjat." Instead of posing as the returned Christ (whom Muslims also expect), Baal masquerades as "the Living Muhammad," which is presumably supposed to be the same thing as the Mahdi ("Rightly Guided One"), the eagerly awaited Hidden Imam, descended from Muhammad through his cousin and adopted son Ali. All Shiites and some Sunnis believe this Hidden Imam will return with Jesus to destroy the Antichrist.

Baal highlights still another neglected aspect of the apocalyptic tradition, namely, the doctrine of the two ages. How do we explain the fact of suffering and evil in a world ostensibly created and run by a good deity? Apocalyptic thinkers believed that God was, for whatever reason (perhaps the sin of humankind), allowing Satan to rule the present age as he pleased. But things would not continue so forever. One day soon God would intervene and put things back on track. Then he would initiate a new age, a millennium of peace and renewal. In some versions, God would simply defeat Satan by an act of divine sovereignty. In other versions, it would be a proxy war, God's representative, the Messiah, pitted against Satan's agent, the Antichrist. Given which side is almighty, and which isn't, the outcome is a foregone conclusion. *Baal* sets forth a pre-Jewish scenario in which God and Satan are coequal powers locked in an eternal balance of good and evil. The danger posed by the Antichrist in this book is that he will permanently upset the balance.

Virgin is by and large a reworking of familiar themes in *The Omen* and *Baal*. This is no criticism: it comes with the territory. Both Christ and Antichrist are born, and the agents of each attempt to kill the other.

The new thing this time is that the rebirth/return of Christ is neither a mission of judgment nor one of millennial salvation. Rather, it signals a second chance offered to humanity. A chance to reboot Christianity, to go back to square one and make a better go of it this time. Christ will appear again as a humble teacher and healer, preaching a gospel of peace and forgiveness again. This time maybe we'll listen. Needless to say, this version can claim no scriptural support nor any from the wider apocalyptic tradition. And yet it would seem to be the most Christian of all, for who can picture the Buddha-like Jesus Christ of the Gospels presiding over Salem Kirban's "yawning barbeque pits of hell"?

Patterson's book also departs from the more common fundamentalist framework by taking its departure from the Catholic cult of Our Lady of Fatima. There the Virgin Mary is expected to appear to tread Satan underfoot at the end of the age. In *Virgin*, the pope finally reveals the long-sealed third prophecy of Fatima. There is such an oracle; Patterson didn't make it up. And it reveals that in the Last Days, now upon us, there will be a pair of virgin births, one of the Christ reincarnated, the other of his evil twin, the Antichrist. The trick is to determine which is which. As in *The Stand* (see below) the fate of humanity lies in the hands of human beings. God is involved, but he is conducting an experiment, putting his creatures to the test. They can avert their doom and the doom of the world if they prove themselves sufficiently clever and courageous. In Patterson's narrative, one twist follows the last until we learn there are actually *three* miracle births: two Antichrists and a female Messiah! (Kind of a theological version of the old Tony Curtis/Debbie Reynolds flick *Goodbye Charlie.*)

Virgin might be said to partake of the themes of Ira Levin's novel and film *Rosemary's Baby* in that the action centers on intrigues surrounding the impregnation of an innocent young woman with the spawn of Satan (*not* portrayed by Anton Szandor LaVey, despite the prevalent rumor). In neither work do we see the devil child grow up. He is only the Antichrist-elect. Because *The Omen* concludes with Damien still a toddler, that film was often compared to *Rosemary's Baby*. Well, Levin told the rest of the story in a very underrated sequel, published just before the new millennium: *Son of Rosemary*. The baby from the first book, Andy, is grown up and has won worldwide fame as a kind of Rick Warren crossed with Anthony Robbins and is an international mediator to boot. He greets his mother, who has just emerged from a coma the Satanist cadre placed her in shortly after the child's birth. She had sought to take the boy and give them the slip. But now those who sought her life are dead and their spell is broken. The universally beloved Andy has managed to conjure peace among the world's religions by getting them all to sign on for a millennium's eve candle-lighting ceremony. Simultaneously, the whole human race is going to light up the world with candles of hope for the future. Only the holdout atheists and Ayn Rand sect are unwilling, but finally even they agree to be good sports. Through all of this, Rosemary sees more and more definite signs that her son is not the benevolent fellow she and everyone would like to think he is. Maybe his father's side is more dominant than she thought. We witness one barely plausible lie after another, until Rosemary, too eager to "believe all things," is helpless to do anything to avert disaster. You see, the candles are all poisonous, ready to release a deadly gas! It is Satan's plan to rid himself of the whole stinking human race in one fell swoop. *Son of Rosemary* is a worthy sequel, a fascinating story, and should really have been made into a film starring the still-beautiful Mia Farrow. Well, at least we got to see her again in the 2006 *Omen* remake.

LIFE AND TIMES OF DAMIEN THORN

The Omen (book and film, 1976) has its own distinctive and effective theology: it portrays the coming of Antichrist as an inexorable doom, the fated scourge of humanity. Unlike the modern fundamentalist cheerleading for Armageddon (cf. Larry Norman's jaunty Calypso song "Keep Your Eyes on Palestine," which gleefully anticipates the end of the world in bloodshed and atomic fury), much of historic Christian belief has dreaded the end. After all, they used to call it Doomsday. It was a sword of Damocles suspended above a sinful world ripe for judgment. And the judge was to be the no-longer merciful Jesus Christ, avenger of his own blood (Heb. 9:28). In *The Omen*, the notion of a Second Coming of Christ is pretty much superfluous. The task is simply to avert the coming of Antichrist, at least for the present. Whenever he does come, he will do his foreordained duty as executioner of humankind, "turning man against his brother, till man shall be no more." The only chance to avert this doom is to slay the infant Antichrist, as Abraham slew (or nearly slew) Isaac, before it *is* too late. And it is too late. A sense of fatalistic foreboding gathers as the story builds and attempt after attempt to stop the child fails. The countdown is under way, and no one can stop it.

The book and movie versions of *Damien: Omen II* (1978) are mere filler, connecting the dots of how the young Beastling ascends to a position of power to make his play for eschatological world dominion. *The Omen* had already pushed to the limit the gimmick of Damien's enemies getting eliminated by a series of fantastic accidents and coincidences by Satan's watchful providence. But these invisibly engineered deaths become cartoonish in *Omen II*. The sequel does share the original's theological premise, but something altogether new occurs in the third installment, *The Final Conflict* (1980). This one reverses the whole premise of *The Omen*. Now another dangerous birth is impending: it is the birth (reincarnation) of baby Jesus, and it is going to be very dangerous to his opposite number, Damien Thorn. Every day the holy child lives, more power drains from the Antichrist, now an adult and head of a worldwide disaster relief organization. This time it is Damien himself who must frantically search out the child before it is too late. He gleefully embraces the role of Herod the Great, systematically eliminating every baby boy born in Britain (where the Book of Hebron predicted he would appear) at the time of the Trinity Alignment. If he fails, Satan forbid, the world will be forced to "endure a second ordeal of Jesus Christ," the dawn of the millennium. Despite the great number of New Testament texts that explicitly predict the heavenly descent of Jesus as an adult (e.g., leading a mounted cavalry from the skies), there is a single precedent in the book of Revelation for

The Final Conflict's version. Revelation 12:1–6 speaks of the birth of a man-child who is to rule the earth with an iron scepter.

The scene derives ultimately from Hesiod's myth of the birth of Zeus from Cronos and Rhea.[3] Disturbed by prophecies that one of his sons should overthrow him as he had overthrown his father, Uranos, Cronos made a practice of devouring each son as soon as he emerged from Rhea's womb. Pretty sick of this, Rhea conspired with her mother, Gaia. Next time Rhea was to bear a son, Gaia would quickly hide the newborn and give Kronos a stone wrapped in swaddling. This she did, and as Cronos wondered why this one was so crunchy, Gaia spirited baby Zeus away to an Aegean island to be reared in safety and secrecy. In Revelation, the divine woman clothed with the sun and crowned with stars gives birth to the Messiah in full view of a hungry Satan/dragon. Given eagles' wings, she flies off to the desert where she rears the baby Messiah in safety. When was this supposed to have happened? Hard to say. But there is certainly room for assuming it lies yet in the future, in which case it would be a rare prediction of a rebirth of Jesus Christ, as *The Final Conflict* posits.

But does the film not reverse its own expectation and have Jesus Christ return as an adult after all? Yes, but it is apparent that someone prevailed on the screenwriter to alter the planned ending, which however survives in Gordon McGill's novelization (1980). There, Jesus is actually reborn in Britain. The reason Damien and his minions could not find him is that he was born to Gypsies in the countryside, and the birth went officially unregistered. This, in case you were curious, is how there can be two more *Omen* novels set in the same old sinful world, replete with satanic cultists. The Christ has yet some thirty years to grow to maturity before the world will begin to change. By contrast, the fourth movie, *The Awakening* (1991; written by Harvey Bernhard and Brian McTaggert and made for cable TV), just ignores the ending of *The Final Conflict*. It simply forgets that Jesus returned to the earth to put a stop to evil. Maybe he was asking for too much money to appear in the sequel, and they just dropped his character.

Gordon McGill's *Omen* sequels, his novels *Armageddon 2000* (1983) and *Abomination* (1985)—never made into movies—center on the posthumous son of Damien Thorn, who had been assassinated at the conclusion of *The Final Conflict*. In that film/book, he had sodomized the heroine, Kate Reynolds, during a one-night stand. Now we find she was blasphemously *impregnated* by the act. She bears a tumorlike fetus, whose successful delivery kills her in the process, as it emerges through the anus. This unwholesome fruit grows to young manhood with a hellish ferocity far surpassing that of Damien Thorn. Whereas his father sought universal domination, as the viceroy of the Kingdom of Satan on earth, the son thirsts for chaos and destruction pure and simple. Such an agenda is too much even for satanic cultists, and this proves the downfall of the junior Antichrist. Exactly the same motif occurs again in the 2005 film *Constantine*, in which the demon Mammon, son of Satan, seeks admittance to the earthly plane, eager to rend and destroy. Satan does not relish the prospect, viewing Mammon's ambition like that of Absalom usurping his father David's throne. So he appears just in time to cast his squirming son back down to hell.[4]

THE STAND

There were many Antichrist novels that followed *The Omen*, and I will be discussing most of them. But the greatest of these is surely Stephen King's apocalyptic blockbuster *The Stand* (1978; revised, restored, expanded, 1991). King's eschatological epic is the best example of a novelistic, selective adaptation of scripture, especially Revelation. In the *Left Behind* books, one feels that Jenkins is afraid to take the book of Revelation symbolically, hagridden by the fundamentalist fixation with literalism. But if you can't take the cipher language of Revelation figuratively, you just don't know what a figure *is*. This is a weakness of the series I will discuss a bit more in a later chapter. But King's book, I think, is much more effective for its depiction of characters as real people trying to make sense of the Revelation. A terrible plague, the "Superflu," has devastated the population, leaving a pitiful remnant who divide up depending on whether they are receiving dreams of the Dark Man, Randall Flagg, or of the Christlike Mother Abigail, an elderly church lady who functions as a new Moses (like Jenkins's Chaim Rosenzweig). They come from all over the country to congregate in two settlements on opposite sides of the Rockies. It seems clear enough that the End Times have arrived, but precisely because the old predictions of it required wisdom on the part of the saints (Rev. 13:18), the good guys are left scratching their heads. It is not obvious what to do in any particular case, since the Revelation was a set of symbols hinting at events, not a clairvoyant description of those events, as in *Left Behind*. This gives King's opus much more of a sense of unfolding mystery as well as narrative tension.

I do not mean to charge Jerry Jenkins with bad writing, for he is obviously quite a good writer. No, it is a matter of a choice between two basic types of narrative. In Tzvetan Todorov's terms, the *Left Behind* books form a "ritual narrative."[5] Their approach is almost liturgical, a series of vignettes reinforcing by repetition the lesson taught by the story. Todorov explains it with reference to the medieval *Quest of the Holy Grail*, where from page one we are left in no doubt that Galahad will succeed in his quest for the Grail. We are not reading to find out if he succeeds. No, the episodes of the narrative are meant to illustrate the spiritual quest, a quest we know, as good Christians, will be successful so long as we do not turn tail and backslide.[6] In the same way, the Gospels do not generate anxious anticipation over whether Jesus will escape his enemies and cheat death. On the contrary, the reader knows going in what is to happen at the end. And if he should be in any danger of forgetting, there are constant reminders that the Son of Man will be delivered into the hands of men, and they will mock him and spit on him and crucify him, and on the third day he will rise again. All along the way, what we have are exhortations to follow in the hero's footsteps and to believe in the savior thus sacrificed for our sake. That is precisely the approach of the *Left Behind* books. They are continually preaching to anyone who is delaying his or her decision for Christ. Again and again such a reader is shown the ostensible danger in such a delay.

Stephen King's approach is different and more amenable to modern literary tastes: we don't really know what's going to happen. The righteous had better stay on their toes and do their best, or for all they know the Antichrist may very well win. Just as genuine uncertainty about future victory in a war lends urgency to those involved in it, so does the openness of the unknown ending lend heightened narrative tension to *The Stand*. That said, however, the Christian reader of King's book will at once recognize a genuine sensitivity to evangelical pietism. Mother Abigail, though she is a pillar of strength to her timid and confused flock, is hair-trigger sensitive to the inner struggle of the spirit surrendered to God against the temptation of "pride." This is pride understood in the specific pietist sense: the reliance on one's natural strengths instead of moment-by-moment waiting upon the Lord for his leading and empowerment. Finally her introspection forces her into the wilderness for a prayer retreat from which she feebly returns, centenarian frame shaken and more fragile than ever. Like Jesus at the Last Supper in John's Gospel, she bequeaths her wisdom and strength to her people, then expires. Feeling orphaned by the providence of God, Mother Abigail's people have to carry on as best they can, heir to greater strength than they realize. Frankly, King teaches the lesson of self-abnegating piety, receiving Christ's power in weakness, more effectively than Jenkins. The force of Mother Abigail's example speaks much more convincingly than the stifling, in-your-face didacticism of Tsion Ben-Judah and his brethren.

PAPAL PERDITION

John Zodrow's *In the Name of the Father* (a 1980 novel proudly billed as "A Chilling Novel of Occult Terror") appears to be a vast and elaborate burlesque on liberation theology as promoted in far-left Roman Catholic circles. In 1948 Cardinal Livingston Stamp rescues an orphaned white boy named Peter from the bowels of a cave in China. A local priest warns that a demon called Baz dwells in the cave, and we are given to believe he may be the same entity as an "imaginary" play-mate called Starbright, who keeps the boy company. This entity is located in an ugly talisman featuring a smirking head that partakes of the likenesses of a frog and a dragon. As the years go by, certain "coincidences" begin to suggest that the pendant is indeed a magical artifact capable of granting certain of Peter's less charitable wishes. Eventually the cardinal adopts the boy as his son. Peter sees that his new father would love it if he followed in his priestly footsteps and so enters upon seminary studies. A zealous student with an ascetical bent, he succeeds very well indeed. Parted from his beloved talisman for some years, Peter grows to maturity and serves an obscure Southern Californian town as a worker priest, shunning any thought of fame or a career like his father's in church politics. His only regret is that, amid a terrible drought, he cannot manage to persuade God to save his parishioners' farms by unleashing the rains.

But then one day his father sends him a package containing his old charm and a letter telling him he is to be promoted to monsignor—bad news, since he relishes his present position of anonymous laborer. Things take a sudden turn, superficially for the better. At his birthday party, a troubled young woman accuses him of raping her (she is actually seeking revenge for him refusing her naked advances), but she is suddenly killed by a freak accident. Peter believes a suspicious trio of unusually precocious schoolgirls have caused her death. Peter passes from disturbing half-remembered dreams to waking nightmares when he discovers that the three girls, who seem to be protecting him, are damned souls sent up from hell. With their help he becomes able to discover underground water sources and saves his town. His father, the cardinal, eager for a bright future for the boy as an agent for church reform, drafts Peter into service, and soon Peter is jetting about the world relieving famine and drought. Peter begins to suspect that his father has somehow cut a deal with the powers of darkness to further, if not his own frustrated ambitions, those he projects onto his adopted son. Hating the limelight, Peter is nonetheless maneuvered into being consecrated a bishop, but, after a "near" death experience, he emerges energized and newly dedicated to church reform. However, Peter is liberally inclined, not what his traditionalist father had in mind. One by one, obstacles in his path are supernaturally removed. More of his old friends are revealed as agents of Satan, and finally he tries to put a stop to the chaos. He manages to prevent the worst effects of a plane crash his infernal benefactors had engineered that would have eliminated various churchly opponents, though his father is severely injured in the violence.

After things settle somewhat, Peter agrees to go with his father and one of his acquaintances, a scholarly exorcist, to seek psychological counseling. But in the end they agree his problem was really just the repercussions of repressed childhood trauma following his parents' death in a plane crash in China. Living in a dank cave, after all, can't be very good for your emotional well-being. With new hope, Peter retires to the prayerful seclusion of a monastery atop Mount Athos for some years—until the death of Albino Luciani, Pope John Paul I. Peter has been made a cardinal in absentia, and now he is summoned, not only to the College of Cardinals for the new papal election, but to begin a term of service in Rome as the assistant to an old friend, an African cardinal who represents the third world interests in whose name Peter had once thought to revolutionize the church. As the convocation begins, old Livingston Stamp comes to the terrible realization that his adopted son is destined to become the prophesied Antichrist (or, as he is more often called in this book, the antipope). He hopes to gun Peter down before it is too late, but his attempt fails, and Peter is elevated to the papacy by acclamation after Pentecost-style flames appear above his head— thanks to the trio of evil ghost-girls, this time dressed as nuns. Peter will get to work ruining the Catholic Church by getting it involved up to its eyeballs in worldly politics, subsidizing third world revolutions, bringing democracy to the Church, and other disastrously liberal projects, all the work of a snickering Satan. The book ends with the announcement of Peter's acclamation as Pope Peter II. The exorcist who had earlier examined him hears the news and realizes his mistake. Then he stalks offstage, galvanized into some course of action that author Zodrow declines to reveal to us. This suggests he might once have intended a sequel but never wrote one.

Like his fellow Catholic Robert Hugh Benson, Zodrow does nothing with the Rapture, which is not a major point in Roman Catholic eschatology. Like *Behold a Pale Horse* and *The Beast* (discussed in chapter 18), *In the Name of the Father* focuses on the process by which the world gets to the brink of the Tribulation, with the rise of Antichrist, without taking us on a tour of the Tribulation itself. After all, we know it's going to be just a series of cataclysms anyway, right? Where's the suspense in that? By contrast, what led to such a mess? How did we get from here to there?

RAPTURE AND TORTURE

Though originating as a screenplay and never even novelized, the 1992 film *The Rapture* (written and directed by Michael Tolkin, starring Mimi Rogers and David Duchovny) demands mention here. Here is an apocalypse without an Antichrist. But that's okay: the spectacle of fundamentalist belief in the Rapture is terrifying enough. In some ways a cross between *Looking for Mister Goodbar* and *Videodrome*, *The Rapture* is a roller-coaster ride through the extremes, past the margins of life, both Sadean and saintly. Though eventually surreal, its most shocking moments are those most closely modeling the evening news on the one hand and the book of Genesis on the other. One TV reviewer scoffed at the film, thinking it a big-budget preachment on behalf of fundamentalism. But believe me, no fundamentalist would ever make a film like this. Pat Robertson's studios would never turn out a movie with so much as a single line like this film's "But who's going to forgive God?"

Indeed, it is tempting to view *The Rapture* against the backdrop of several awfully crude fundie flicks from the 1970s in which the End Times events as fantasized by Hal Lindsey take place before your eyes. To the outsider, these films, with their "Too bad you'll be going to hell" attitude, present a bizarre spectacle of a religion that attributes worse moral standards to God than to the hapless sinners he is imagined consigning to hell. It seems to me that Tolkin has tried to lay bare this moral paradox. He employs the same device used by Stephen King in *The Stand*: what if it turned out that the fanatics were right? It might reveal some implications of which the fanatics themselves had remained oblivious. Tolkin demonstrates that *even if true on its own terms*, the apocalyptic worldview of fundamentalism makes the universe into a madhouse of torture and masochism, where the secret to salvation is to love the deity precisely for tormenting you.

The main character, Sharon, turns from a life of kinky sexual adventuring to believing in Jesus. Disgusted with the meaningless of her endless, degrading liaisons, she starts to take seriously the witnessing of office mates and door-to-door evangelists. On the brink of suicide, she turns to God instead, and successfully turns over a new leaf—to the great consternation of her old sinful buddies. But time goes by, and we see that Sharon has not only stuck to her resolve but that she has managed to convert one of her old boyfriends, who is now an office executive and father of Sharon's daughter. They attend church and listen to the prophecies of a boy oracle who predicts the Rapture is at hand. Sharon's husband is gunned down by an alcoholic he'd fired, but Sharon takes it in stride, eerily serene in her faith. But she and her daughter miss the husband and father and decide to go out to the wilderness (a local campsite) to await the Rapture, when they hope to see him again. Weeks pass, and finally the increasingly desperate Sharon yields to her daughter's chilling request to "just go to heaven now" by suicide. Sharon shoots and buries her daughter, then chickens out of shooting herself. In jail she bemoans her religious delusions but almost immediately she hears the angel's trumpet! The Rapture comes! She had given up only hours too soon. Her daughter, now an angel, visits her to tell her it is not too late for her, if she will just tell God she loves him. But she refuses. How can she love a God who allowed her to do what she did?

Sharon has undergone a dramatic conversion, but the contrast is only apparent. She has simply moved from one point along the spectrum of shadow-world decadence to another. In both phases of her chaotic existence she experiences the strange joy that is but the epiphenomenon of something essentially terrible.

The Rapture is not a movie about religious extremism as opposed to religious normalcy. Nor does it seem to paint all religious people as fanatics. Rather, as I see it, the point is to ask whether the extremes of religion and its choice of arbitrary revelation over sweet reason are not the reductio ad absurdum of religion per se: is it only here, in Jonestown, that the real terror implicit in all religion is clearly seen because it is no longer obfuscated by the cowardly refusal to follow through on one's rightful convictions? The final point of the film seems clear to me: we hear again the disillusioned voice of Ivan Karamazov. If there really is a heaven, but the price of admission is to excuse the guilt of a God who allows innocent children to suffer, then the conscientious person has no choice but to hand back the ticket.

THE LAST TEMPTATION OF ANTICHRIST

Thomas F. Monteleone's *The Blood of the Lamb* (1992) and *The Reckoning* (1999) form an eschatological epic for the eve of the new millennium. These books are page-turning thrillers, grafting the theology and supernaturalism onto what seem in style and mood more of an espionage mystery novel. And it is an excellent fit! Monteleone is a master of both pace and detail, of color and characterization. Like Stephen King, he has a great talent for putting into words sensations the reader knows well but has likely never heard expressed. Nor is Monteleone ignorant of religion and theology, having received a Jesuit education. In fact, one wonders if the author has smuggled himself into the book as the Jesuit Dan Ellington, a Fordham University professor of English and the main character's best friend (not a lucky position to be in, as it will turn out!).

The Blood of the Lamb shares a common premise with *In the Name of the Father*, in that the hero(?) is a young man of mysterious origins who is raised within the Roman Catholic system and follows the seemingly inevitable path to the priesthood. Along the way each proves himself as both a compelling and attractive parish priest in inconspicuous surroundings—and a wielder of inexplicable powers. Only there is a dark shadow to it, a hint of things to come, as people mysteriously perish in the wake of these miracles. Both come to repudiate the yoke of the church, as well as their parentlike patrons within the church hierarchy. And both wind up becoming Pope Peter II! *In the Name of the Father* sets up the nightmare scenario feared by Catholic conservatives: John XXIII had opened Pandora's box, and sooner or later the nastiest of the demons he let loose are coming home to roost in Rome with the Antichrist assuming the throne of Peter. But whereas *In the Name of the Father* leaves us in suspense, seeming (as I suggested above) to hint at a sequel that never came to pass, *The Blood of the Lamb* does continue in a second volume. Finally, like Zodrow's *In the Name of the Father*, Monteleone's books show us a very liberal, progressive pope whose radical reforms (clergy marriage, liberation theology, pro-abortion and contraception, pro-fornication) are the devil's work. Ouch.

I do not mean to suggest Monteleone, a very creative fellow, borrowed (much less "plagiarized") material from Zodrow, the author of *In the Name of the Father*. He might have read Zodrow's book and thought, "Hey, I bet I could do some interesting things with some of those elements." And I wouldn't blame him if he did. But there is no real reason to think Monteleone took the trouble to read every previous book in the same genre. Some of the ideas both authors use are pretty predictable, almost inevitable, once one starts contemplating setting an Antichrist novel amid the intrigues of the Catholic Church. Monteleone also shares a huge plot element with James BeauSeigneur, author of *The Christ Clone Trilogy* (discussed in the previous chapter): The Antichrist is the Christ cloned from blood off the Shroud of Turin. In Monteleone's version, the bloody image of Christ was preserved on a genuine shroud, but it had become so fragile and threadbare over the centuries that its guardians managed to employ arcane scientific methods no longer understood to transfer the image, that is, the original chemical deposit, onto a new piece of cloth. This happened back in the fourteenth century, which thus turns out to be the carbon-datable age of the shroud, but not of the blood. So did Monteleone clone BeauSeigneur? Again, I see no reason to think so. Cloning off the shroud blood is a fairly obvious idea. John Coyne used it, too, though without reference to the Antichrist, in a horror novel called *The Shroud* (1983).

Peter Carenza is a handsome parish priest who loves his work and his people and has no ambitions beyond these. But one day he confronts a mugger and, without trying to, blasts the youth with blue lightning from his hands. This strange event is just the sign a certain clique in Rome has been awaiting for thirty years—ever since they arranged for the cloning of a new Christ from the shroud blood. They summon Peter to Rome and fill him in on the story of his genesis. He cannot accept it nor their manifest plans to confine and manipulate him, so he escapes, returning to New York. With the aid of his friend Dan (whom he has virtually resurrected after the man's severe torture by a Vatican agent) and Marion, a local (and beautiful) reporter, Peter heads off across America, trying to keep a low profile but stopping along the way to do good deeds only he can do. He decides that fame will protect him from the long arm of the Vatican better than attempted invisibility, and he is right. Peter gains almost messianic acclamation among the people. But as his powers grow, so does his confusion about his nature and destiny. He begins an affair with Marion and eventually, out of jealousy, kills Dan by telekinetically inducing a heart attack. More and more he spins into megalomania, alienating Marion and losing his former Christlikeness. The fascinating core of this book (and its sequel) is this strange turmoil and compromise within Peter. One suspects he will, by the end, turn back to the light, like Darth Vader in *Return of the Jedi*. The book might justly be subtitled "The Last Temptation of the Antichrist." Just as Nikos Kazantzakis adopted the figure of Jesus Christ, divine and human, to illustrate the struggle every human being faces between the divine and the devilish within him, so does *The Blood of the Lamb* explore the temptation of power, and of the danger Carl Jung warned of, possession by the archetype, psychic inflation.[7]

In terms of traditional Christology, what Monteleone has done is to depict (albeit from a refreshingly different perspective) the doctrine of the "enhypostatic humanity" of Christ. This fine-tuning of Christological doctrine by Leontius of Byzantium (died 543) presupposed that Jesus Christ possessed dual and complete divine and human natures. But Leontius sought to place a thumb on the divine side of the balance, saying that, while Christ was one person possessing both divine and human natures, the one person was ultimately divine, not human. His personhood was divine or came from the divine side. Though Jesus of Nazareth possessed the complete equipment of a human being (body, soul, and spirit), there would have been no Jesus of Nazareth except for the planned incarnation. (One might compare the case to a couple deciding to have a child so that child can become an organ donor for a sick sibling.) He attained personhood only in union with the divine person via the Incarnation. Nestorian, Ebionite, and other "heretical" views pictured a person, Jesus of Nazareth, who would have existed anyway. He was righteous and a fit host for the Incarnation. But if you took this approach, it seemed to make Jesus into a prophet or channeler for an alien, divine presence but not to identify him with it. So for Leontius, the humanity, though genuine, came to be understood as a function of the Incarnation.

In Monteleone's two books, the cloning of Christ turns out to be a fatal error for this very reason: the entity Peter Carenza would not have existed but for the hubris of Vatican conspirators who sought to save the world by cloning Jesus Christ. Unlike the original, Peter's personal core did not derive from God—since God hadn't sent him. It was humanity's bright idea, not the will of the Father. So this new cloned Christ had a vacuum at his personal center that Satan lost no time filling. We see all this in the recurring observations during which Peter ponders his nature and destiny, never really figuring it out till he passively recognizes that it was a done deal even without him signing on the dotted line.

We have seen that Robert R. McCammon's *Baal* plays off of Manichean dualistic themes according to which there is a genuine and open-ended conflict between good and evil, evenly matched, each with its own integrity of sorts. Well, Monteleone brings the same theme up in one of Peter's last pauses for introspection: he decides that his final tilt to the dark side is not so bad, in fact not "bad" at all. The assigning of the value labels "good" and "bad" are arbitrary if all you really have in the last analysis are A and not-A. You need both positive and negative. In the big picture, each role must be taken. C. S. Lewis, in what I regard as one of the most insightful passages in his *Mere Christianity*, discusses the same thing, explaining why Christianity differs from Zoroastrianism, another ancient dualism that grants priority neither to Ahura Mazda (God) or Ahriman (the devil). Lewis explains the weakness of dualism against Platonism, which the Jewish and Christians traditions have in common. If the sides are equally matched and independent of each other, why is either actually good or bad? Why not just "the home team" and "the visiting team"? The one I happen to like versus the other one, which you may like with as much or as little justification? But Platonism holds the privation theory: the "bad" is really bad in that it is something, once good in its pure state, that has gone wrong, like rotten fruit or spoiled meat. Hence the Christian doctrine that the devil was good (an angel) who went bad.[8]

Monteleone's books, like many others in the Antichrist genre, depict a wide range of religious types. It becomes clear that he views real holiness as feasible only in the case of pious individuals, not institutions. Peter's slide toward the devil is only hastened once his initial itinerant ministry (like that of the Gospel Jesus) consolidates into a bureaucratic institution (like the Catholic Church). And he is in Satan's vest pocket by the time he becomes pope. Peter's mother, a psychically gifted nun named Etienne, is the model of piety as well as a worthy sequel to Mary the mother of Jesus as a coredemptrix. But she, too, breaks with the Church. And when Pope Pete becomes desperate to track down and destroy a predestined heptad of holy heroes of faith who stand in the way of his End Times schemes, they are a motley crew: a Hindu housewife, a Chinese youth who can predict earthquakes, a Mormon package delivery driver, a Jewish accountant, a Catholic stigmatist, a clairvoyant Baptist church organist, and an Argentine Catholic construction worker. It matters not at all which faith, if any, they belong to. By contrast, builders and functionaries of institutions are treated pretty grimly by Monteleone. Fundamentalist televangelists are drawn as hilarious caricatures, while Roman Catholic bureaucrats are shown as little better than cronies of the mob or the KGB.

DEMOGORGON

In horror novelist Brian Lumley's Antichrist novel *Demogorgon* (1987), we meet a wonderfully dreadful bit of medieval folklore. Lumley has borrowed his Demogorgon from Milton's *Paradise Lost*:

> When straight behold the throne
> Of Chaos, and his dark pavilion spread
> Wide on the wasteful deep; with him enthroned
> Sat sable-vested Night, eldest of things
> The consort of his reign; and by them stood
> Orcus and Hades, and the dreaded name of Demogorgon.

Why should this long name engender dread, besides its shivery sound? Medieval lore had it that anyone daring to utter this name aloud would undo creation itself! It is hard to account for the persistence of a legend with a premise so easily exploded, but there it is. We can detect within it the germ of an earlier belief, the Gnostic doctrine of the *Demiourgos*, Demiurge, or "carpenter," a divine being subordinate to God or the gods who had created the material world. (This explanation for evil and imperfection finds counterparts in some of Gary Larson's cartoons on the same theme, such as a bearded and robed Creator cussing as he accidentally spills a beaker labeled "Human Beings" into the mixing bowl of creation.) Here was an anticreation myth told and retold by super-spiritual types who regarded themselves as too good for this world and who could not wait to flee it upon death, to return to a heavenly world of light from which they believed they had first emerged. "Demiourgos" became "Demogorgon," the name of an evil creator, which then became the formula by which creation might be undone. Lumley departs from the strict outline of these myths, picking and choosing as many of the ancient mythmakers must have done. He makes Demogorgon the son of Satan and the father of the Antichrist.

The action in *Demogorgon* does not unfold onto a suitably cosmic stage, as it at least begins to do in the *Left Behind* series. Lumley's *Demogorgon*, like *The Omen* series, *In the Name of the Father*, *Behold a Pale Horse*, and *The Beast*, contracts the action into a more manageable compass. Lumley quietly navigates this change by altering the Antichrist's mission; he is no longer the executor of the End, the provocateur of Armageddon, so Lumley need not trouble himself to describe such scenes. Instead, the Antichrist here is something analogous to the Wandering Jew. He is a continuing presence in the world, sowing havoc at every opportunity, something like Lucifer in the Rolling Stones' "Sympathy for the Devil." His birthplace is in Galilee, but not in Nazareth. He hails from Chorazin, traditionally the birthplace of the Antichrist. The tradition would seem to have grown from Jesus' denunciation of the village for giving him the cold shoulder in Matthew 11:21–22: "Woe to you, Chorazin! Woe to you, Bethsaida! For if the miracles done in you had been performed in Tyre and Sidon, they would have repented long ago in sackcloth and ashes! But I tell you, it will go easier on Judgment Day for Tyre and Sidon than for you!" Chorazin, accordingly, was the site to which Count Magnus journeyed on the Black Pilgrimage in M. R. James's "Count Magnus."

Lumley's story opens on the terrible night of Antichrist's latest, phoenixlike rebirth (1936). Under the name "George Guigos," he returns to Chorazin, bringing three hired assistants who have no idea what his real plans are. One of them, the twenty-two-year-old Demetrios Kastrouni, leaves the others to reconnoiter the area, while the others, older and more heavily muscled, commence digging, opening the way to a subterranean chapel of horrors. (The name "Guigos" is no doubt a reference to Ezekiel chapters 38–39, which gave rise to the legend of Gog and Magog, monsters and/or nations that reappear in the book of Revelation.) The poor flunkies think they are excavating buried treasure of which they will receive shares. When they penetrate the chamber, they behold a strange, antique mechanism. A great stone lever, at first barely moveable, ratchets up a huge stone tablet on which are inscribed diabolical commandments, each of which, appearing one by one with each new wrench of the lever, seems somehow to rejuvenate the tottering Guigos, as well as to release into the confined space one of the plagues of the Exodus. Guigos's stooges, gagging on flies and gnats, rebel, but their greed keeps them at it as Guigos assures them they are only hallucinating. But Guigos grows worried over the absence of young Demetrios, for his plan is to absorb all three men to restore his youth, vitality, and virility. He must have them in place by the stroke of midnight. Demetrios does show up in time, but once he sees the chaos unfolding, he decides this is no place for him and flees, leaving Guigos a man short. To make up the difference, Guigos instead absorbs their pack mule, giving his resultant new body the look of a satyr! Twenty-one years later, while both hunting Guigos and being hunted by him, Demetrios visits his old family home. As a favor to his father, he drives out to a villa his dad rents out to tourists. Sneaking around, he discovers it is occupied by the hideously malformed Guigos, now bearing another name. The villain is about to rape three captive women in order to produce three healthy bodies for him to absorb next time around. Demetrios tries and fails to kill his old foe. A fire in the building saves him, and he goes underground.

The story jumps to England in 1983, centering now on one Charlie Trace, a skilled burglar. We meet him as he is busy heisting jewelry from a gangland boss. He presents some of the ill-gotten gains to his voluptuous girlfriend Jilly. His life of risky roguishness is soon but a memory as he becomes enmeshed in something infinitely more adventurous, not to mention bizarre. He receives a visitor named Demetrios Kastrouni, known to us but not to Charlie. He informs Charlie, who had known precious little of his institutionalized mother and nothing of his absent father, that he is in fact the son of the Antichrist Guigos! Though

Demetrios manages to leave him a satchel full of information, Charlie refuses to credit the wild tale (even though Guigos's satyr hooves might indeed explain his own clubfoot deformity!) and kicks him out. But Demetrios is immediately killed in a freak accident reminiscent of *The Omen*, and this causes Charlie to reconsider the whole matter. Breaking up with Jilly, he books a flight for Greece to follow the trail. On the Greek Isle of Karpathos (shades of Nicolae Carpathia!), Charlie decides to visit a near-inaccessible mountaintop monastery, to seek more information from an old hermit, Saul Gokowski. On the last leg of his journey there, he encounters three fellow tourists, a seemingly gay couple, and a voluptuous woman named Amira Halberstein. He is soon in bed with her. As Charlie motorcycles his way up the mountain, he notices one of the men trying to beat him there. After an exciting chase, Charlie accidentally kills his rival, as it turns out, saving the life of Gokowski, the man's intended target. From what the hermit tells him, Charlie is convinced Demetrios was right. Years before, Charlie now learns, the old recluse worked on an archaeological dig, along with Guigos and Amira Halberstein's father, at none other than Chorazin! An angel visited Gokowski in a dream and warned him off the project. Eventually comparing notes with Demetrios, Gorkowski sought the destruction of the hidden stone tables, the source of Guigos's power. But the mission failed.

Surprisingly, Charlie, already believing the worst about himself, discovers that, though Guigos's offspring, he must not be the Antichrist after all. Reminiscent of the Whateley twins in H. P. Lovecraft's "The Dunwich Horror," it seems Charlie had a stillborn half-brother who was massively deformed and was the proper reincarnation of his father. But his role in the adventure is hardly over. He returns to Amira and confronts her with what he knows. She, however, drugs and abducts him with the help of her surviving compatriot in Guigos's employ. After he returns to lucidity, Amira claims to have conspired against him only under duress; her father is in the Beast's power. At length they arrive in Palestine, where they are to meet with Guigos and his other sons (offspring of Guigos and those three women he raped). The Israeli military have in the meantime been brought up to speed, and they hit Guigos's compound with everything they've got. But he withstands their best efforts. In a final showdown at the Chorazin cave, where Guigos hopes to absorb his sons and rejuvenate himself, Demetrios Kastrouni, thought dead, joins Charlie, Gokowski, and Amira. He and Charlie together manage to destroy the tablets, but not before Guigos sets the process in motion. But this time it's a bigger foul-up than before, since the only available third body is that of a pig! Guigos emerges from the transformation with a pig head (and, apparently, its measly brain). He imitates the Legion of demons inside the Gerasene swine (Mark 5:1–20) and plunges to his death in the Sea of Galilee.

Returning home, poor Charlie is still not in the clear, for he has to deal with the wrath of the gangster he robbed! Abetted by the hellish fury of the jilted Jilly, the mob boss tracks down Charlie and has his thugs work him over pretty thoroughly. Promising him more beatings to follow, the henchmen start to leave when Charlie senses the urgings of an inner voice telling him it is time for revenge. His eyes glow sulfur yellow as his hand beckons the roiling clouds above, and he invokes the power of Demogorgon to slay his enemies. What do you know? It seems he *was* the designated son and heir of the Antichrist after all! Lumley first planned to write a sequel in which, one suspects, Charlie Trace would have wielded his powers on a much wider scale and to more universal ends. But Lumley was dissatisfied with what he wrote of it and decided to shelve the thing permanently.

THE DESOLATION OF ABOMINATIONS

Is there any larger meaning to the phenomena of secular Antichrist novels? I have tried to show how a number of them do presuppose interesting theological schemas, but I am far from suggesting their authors are trying to teach us anything or that there is any lesson to be learned from what are obviously intended as entertainments pure and simple. And yet there is a larger message. The fact that what was deadly serious business for the authors of our Christian apocalypse novels has become merely fodder for entertainment signifies that what once happened to the myths of the Greeks is happening to the myths of Christianity. No longer believed literally (at least by a growing, leading segment of the culture), these stories and symbols have escaped the iron control of dogma and continue to function, better than ever, simply *as* fiction to spur the imagination. Did the Greek gods perish in dishonor once the great playwrights of ancient Greece began using them as characters in secular dramas like *Oedipus*, *The Birds*, and so on? Hardly. One might even say they had ascended to greater dignity as incarnations of the human truths so expressed. And while *The Omen* and *The Stand* do not possess quite such gravity, they do represent a new lease on life for myths otherwise doomed to oblivion in a scientific age.

NOTES

1. David Seltzer wrote both the screenplay and the novelization of *The Omen*. Some differences between the two suggest that Seltzer novelized an earlier version of the script than that which finally appeared on screen.

2. Sergeant Neff was played by Lance Henricksen, who went on to star in his own three-season television apocalypse, *Millennium*. He met the Antichrist there, too, albeit briefly, in the episode "Maranatha" (May 9, 1997).

3. For the text of Hesiod, see chapter 5.

4. Fans of *Buffy the Vampire Slayer* will recall the same theme in the second season's finale. There the vampires Drusilla and Angelus are all set to summon a demon who will suck the earth down the cosmic toilet into hell, but their confederate Spike, himself a thoroughly rotten vampire punk, decides he would much rather have the world continue as a theater for his mischievous predations, so he turns coat and helps Buffy defeat the apocalyptic scheme.

5. Tzvetan Todorov, "The Quest of Narrative," in Todorov, *The Poetics of Prose*, chap. 9, trans. Richard Howard (Ithaca, NY: Cornell University Press, 1977), pp. 120–42.

6. Like brave Sir Robin in the Monty Python version.

7. Stephan A. Hoeller, *The Gnostic Jung and the Seven Sermons to the Dead*

(Wheaton, IL: Theosophical Publishing House, 1982), pp. 126–27: "The ghastly apparition of spiritual pride soon rears its swollen head, and, instead of utilizing the power of the archetypes, individuals come to imagine that they have become a divine archetype themselves. Psychic inflation where persons imagine themselves godlike—rooted as they usually are in feelings of deep inferiority—makes a travesty of the individuation process and reduces the power of the gods to the level of the psychic caperings of fools and madmen."

8. C. S. Lewis, *Mere Christianity* (New York: Macmillan, 1952), pp. 48–50.

Chapter Ten

LaHaye's *BEHIND*

"The entire narrative has the effect of being the illustration of an idea; and thus the fantastic receives a fatal blow."

—Tzvetan Todorov, *The Fantastic*[1]

"The main characters in Left Behind *are curiously self-involved, even narcissistic.* Left Behind's *purpose in the fundamentalist church scheme of things is devotional. It is a sugar-coated fear manipulation. To the fear of going to burn in eternal fire if one's devotional life is not right is added the more easily imaginable fear of being left behind to suffer through the Tribulation—and perhaps not make the cut even then."*

—Edmund D. Cohen[2]

THE JENKINS APOCALYPSE

The great Christian apocalypse of our day is, of course, the *Left Behind* epic by Tim LaHaye and Jerry B. Jenkins. In what follows, I will treat Jenkins as the author when I am dealing with literary aspects of the books and LaHaye as the author when treating the theology expressed in the books. This seems to me a realistic and equitable distribution of credit (and blame) given the fact that it was Jenkins who actually set pen to paper (or finger to computer) and wrote the thing. LaHaye seems to have hatched the idea for the books, but he is more the silent partner, the theological muse.

NARRATIVE CRITICISM

Jenkins seems to have realized rather fully the extent of the challenge that he faced in writing this work: "Nothing could have been scripted like this, Buck thought, blinking slowly. If somebody tried to sell a screenplay about millions of people disappearing, leaving everything but their bodies behind, it would be laughed off."[3] Do we feel like laughing off the results? In this chapter, let me warn you right up front, I am going to take Jenkins quite seriously as a very capable author. But I am also going to confess that, given the inherent outrageousness of Tim LaHaye's sectarian theology, there is virtually no way to suppress a few giggles now and then. Some things so assault common sense and moral judgment that no author can lend them verisimilitude. On the other hand, verisimilitude is the degree to which the narrative conforms to the readers' set of assumptions and expectations, so it is likely, especially given the sales figures for the books, that fundamentalist readers do find the books completely plausible. The *Left Behind* series is strictly "in-house" literature, just like the ancient apocalypses themselves, when they warn how only the one with wisdom (as the sect defines it) can penetrate the revelations offered. It is not every author who can dismiss readers' failure to appreciate the book as being due to the lack of the Holy Spirit!

And yet, maybe that is not good enough, for just as Jürgen Moltmann once said, given the public character of the claim that Jesus Christ is Lord *of the world, not just of the Church*, must not Christians be able to articulate what that Lordship means in secular, including political, terms?[4] Otherwise his Lordship does not extend beyond the walls of the Church and that for only an hour or two each week. In the same way, isn't Jenkins obliged to satisfy the rest of us? If we are even to be sobered enough to take his eschatological warnings seriously, mustn't they connect with reality for us? If they are wholly implausible, then Jenkins and his buddies are just talking to themselves. Let's see how he scores.

I find the terms of the great structuralist critic Tzvetan Todorov very helpful for understanding, not just critiquing, Jenkins's books. In *The Fantastic*, Todorov outlines a set of categories for novels that appear to involve the supernatural.[5] Jenkins has written what Todorov calls a tale of "the Marvelous." We are not kept guessing. Supernaturalism is built into the ground rules, as in *The Lord of the Rings* or *The Chronicles of Narnia.* There is no attempt to create a sense of mystery and awe by raising the possibility of the supernatural and then leaving us tantalized in breathless suspense, as in what Todorov calls the tale of "the Fantastic" proper. Nor does Jenkins make any attempt to resolve a long-lingering tension, finally, in favor of a naturalistic but astonishing climax. This would have made it one of Todorov's tales of "the Uncanny."[6] (Perhaps Todorov needs a fourth category, one in which the tension is finally resolved into supernaturalism, instead of the miraculous being taken for granted from the start. We might call this a tale of the Revelatory. But Jenkins has not written one of those either.)

So there is no tension in the *Left Behind* series as to whether the predictions of the Bible are going to prove to be true after all: we know that going in, and characters who are unbelievers are pretty much ridiculed throughout. But what is a novel without suspense of some kind? The answer is that there is more than one kind of suspense. If we are told at the start that some strange event is to transpire, we are still left to wonder how on earth it will or can happen. For example, in the Gospels, when Jesus promises Peter that he will wind up denying him in just a few hours, despite his grand protestations of undying loyalty, the reader joins Peter in incredulity. After all, Jesus must be right. There is no way the story is going to allow him to be proved wrong. But how can we envision a zealot like Peter so utterly and thoroughly turning coat on his master? Especially since Jesus' prediction acts as a warning. Peter is now forewarned! Yet he will *still* deny Jesus! It is just like *Oedipus,* where the very efforts of the hero to avoid his prophesied doom are what set those terrible events in motion! And the reader watches in amazement as the pieces do indeed fall into place with an inexorable logic we could not have foreseen. This is what Jenkins does. How well?

The reader can see the various End Times items falling into place, the narrative being merely the medium for this to happen. This seems artificial, especially when Tsion Ben-Judah checks them off the list of vials and bowls and trumpet judgments, one by one, as if he's following the schedule of songs to be performed at a concert. Yet this notion of inevitable prophetic fulfillment may also function as a *subtext* conveying verisimilitude: events in the narrative have been undergirded with a sounding board against which they will strike as all the more realistic. That sounding board is scripture. The narrative simulates the ongoing process of historical events it describes, a progress that will serve in precisely the same way to bring the foreordained events to pass as with an apparently intrinsic, self-motivated quality, though behind the scenes (as the prophetic proof texts reveal) it *must* happen. Either way the whole thing is a charade—and must be! The angel empties out the bowl above, and the pestilence begins below. That's the way apocalypses work: the seer pulls back the veil (which is exactly what "*re-vel*-ation" means) to let us behold the hidden, inner workings of the historical process, and how/why it must shortly hurtle to an abrupt conclusion.

One more brief, nonbiblical illustration of a subtext meets us in the first volume of Jenkins's epic. The story of the lone pilot making warnings about equipment failure unheeded until it was too late functions as a subtextual anticipation, almost a verification, of the Cassandra-like Rapture warnings of the now-vanished Christians.[7]

And yet Jenkins is cheated out of some prime suspense opportunities by the fundamentalist theology he and LaHaye share. Nothing is at stake. Characters fear and mourn death, but they know it is just a temporary absence. The dead will return like the abductees at the end of *Close Encounters*. What's the big deal? Such confidence may be quite useful for comforting the bereaved at a funeral, but it ill serves novels of war, intrigue, and adventure, which *Left Behind* tries to be. Worse still is the utter evacuation of the mark of the Beast as a crisis test of faith. With the alternative being starvation and persecution, who will dare reject the mark? This should have been the great bellwether, the watershed, of character development in the books. Like the words of Jesus in the Gospel of John, the introduction of the mark 666 should have been a sword separating the sheep from the goats even before the official judgment. It should have functioned like *Krystalnacht* in Nazi Germany, a clear signal to choose either costly obedience (as Corrie ten Boom and her family chose) or the loss of one's life in the very attempt to save it (as the passive German neighbors of Jews did when they looked the other way). This is the game ball, and Jenkins and LaHaye fumble it. The born-again Christians in the book are not urged to shun the mark of the Beast but rather are assured in advance that there is no danger they will take it!

> If you are already a believer, you will not be able to turn your back on Christ, praise God. (*The Mark*)[8]

> God miraculously overcomes our evil, sinful flesh and gives us the grace and courage to make the right decision in spite of ourselves. My interpretation of this is that we will be *unable* to deny Jesus, *unable* to even choose the mark that would temporarily save our lives. (*The Mark*)[9]

LaHaye's "eternal security" theology ("If you have already trusted Christ for your salvation, you have the mark of the seal of God on your forehead, visible only to other believers. Fortunately, this decision, mark, seal is also irrevocable, so you never need fear losing your standing with him" [*Assassins*])[10] ruins the "trial/test" character of the mark. It is a foregone conclusion. But if this is so, why are the saints warned not to take the mark in Revelation 14:12?

The characters in these books serially occupy a few basic functional roles: the hero who infiltrates Antichrist's computers (first David, then Chang), pregnant heroine (Hattie, Chloe), friend on the verge of conversion but holding out (Chaim, Hattie), second-string believer pilot, who dies and is replaced by another (Mack, Abdullah, George, Lionel, Ree Woo, Kenny), two-fisted nurse (Leah, Hannah), can-do guy/procurer (Zeke, Laslos, Albie), surprise sympathizer in high places (Steve, Leah, etc.). Similarly, there seems to be a limited number of subplots that Jenkins replays over and over again. Someone is always getting captured and needs agents of the "Tribulation Force" to bail him or her out, an act that is often wrought thanks to the nick-of-time revelation of a secret fellow-believer well-met. These are hackneyed "recognition" scenes of the kind that already seemed overworked when Charles Dickens relied so heavily upon them. In short, it is as if Jenkins had a much simpler story to tell, but he found himself under constraint to spread it out into a series of twelve massive books, each around four hundred pages. Thus he had to start duplicating plots and cloning characters, repeating them again and again with cosmetic variations.

And, speaking of the Tribulation Force, Jenkins introduces the team name much too early, in the early months of the Tribulation, when it sounds like a flattering designation self-bestowed by a handful of pietists getting together to study the Bible and pray, the core group of a local church. Eventually you know Jenkins is going to make them into his born-again special forces commando team, but before it gets to that point, the name just invites mockery. In fact, once he does justify the term by giving them guns and guts, Jenkins invites chuckles again by shortening the name to the "Trib Force." This is unfortunate and reflects the diminutive nicknames given by fundamentalists to their own eschatological doctrines ("Pre-Trib Rapture," "Post-Tribbers"), a development that itself reflects how their theological debates have deteriorated into a parlor game.

One may also feel that these books rely a bit too heavily on the old *Hogan's Heroes* gimmick: the good guys manage too often and too easily to outwit the enemy, get inside their networks, hijack and destroy their equipment, and so on. It is an interesting judgment call to cast the Antichrist and his nefarious henchmen as bumbling incompetents. The Beast as Colonel Klink, Satan as General Burkhalter, the False Prophet as Sergeant Schultz. Of Satan, Paul wrote, "We are not ignorant of his devices." But Satan appears to be totally oblivious of ours. I suppose Jenkins is taking the same approach C. S. Lewis did in *The Screwtape Letters*. To quote Martin Luther, as Lewis did: "The devil, proud spirit, cannot endure to be mocked."

It is odd that in all twelve volumes no one curses. Even the unsaved say "blamed," "What the devil?" and so on. Jenkins, writing for a prickly, pious audience, is not at liberty to make the sinners sound very sinful. Pious eyes must be protected from that, as when Holden Caulfield felt compelled to erase the F-word from a school boys' room stall lest some little kid see it. Similarly, the heroes are interesting only once they step out of "sanctified" character to do and say things they sooner or later repent of, like Rayford's obsession with assassinating Carpathia. Later, he repents and returns to a proper "spiritual" state of pure passivity, awaiting the Lord's leading. David is most interesting when he feels free to let the sarcasm fly. But rest assured, he repents of it and returns to sanctified dullness. The default norm is eggshell-walking, white-bread blandness. Non-Christian characters are the "reality relief" figures. "Clearly this was not a church-going boy. He is so delightful, so bright!" (*The Mark*).[11] Hey, you said it; I didn't.

ANTICHRIST SUPERSTAR

The Jenkins Antichrist is a charismatic political leader from obscure Rumania. After a knock-'em-dead speech at the United Nations, the delegates draft him by acclamation to be the secretary general of the body, which he promptly refashions into a one-world government, the Global Community. I personally wouldn't have minded the irony of the UN, left-leaning but impotent, becoming, for fictional purposes, the "fearful master" of 1950s and 1960s right-wing paranoids, just like the 1987 TV miniseries *Amerika*, in which black helicopter gunships bearing the UN logo opened fire on the innocent. But UN members got their bustles in a tizzy over that one, and when the paperback novelization of *Amerika* came out, they called them something else. Maybe Jenkins didn't want to have to deal with the same thinness of skin.

The Antichrist's name, "Nicolae Carpathia," suggests Dracula, with his castle in the Carpathian range of Transylvania, once part of Hungary, but within Rumania's borders today. "Dracula," in turn, means "Son of the Dragon," not a bad name for the Beast. His full name is "Nicolae Jetty Carpathia," which we need to know if we are to reckon the number of his name. Jenkins poses a riddle for us readers and never solves it for us. Carpathia does seem to have a favorite number (with which he christens his private airplane, etc.), but it is 216. Surely we would expect 666! What happened? Well, "it turns out that the letters in 'Nicolae Jetty Carpathia' add to 216 in a system where the letter 'a' is assigned a value of one, 'b' is two, and so on to 'z' as 26." And then 216 is also the sum of six cubed, or, $6 \times 6 \times 6 = 216$.[12] That's appropriate: unraveling the number and name is supposed to require wisdom (Rev. 13:18), and Jenkins makes you work for it.

If there is a theological discipline of Christology, why not have one of *Anti*christology? The categories theologians have used to understand the Christ might help us understand the Antichrist, too. As nearly as I can tell, Jenkins depicts something of an adoptionist conception, whereby (as some early Christians believed about Jesus) Nicolae is a man who dies and rises again, but once he does he is filled with his god, who in this case turns out to be Satan. Once energized, or possessed, by his dark master, Nicolae doesn't seem that much different, since he was already a wily warmonger and a greedy tyrant before his assassination. But he does begin to manifest miraculous powers. In one revealing scene, Satan temporarily exits the form of the resurrected Nicolae, leaving him a blue-skinned half cadaver. It is as if Satan had entered Carpathia's corpse, lending it a false semblance of life, like a zombie. I do not mean to be flippant, but one wonders: should we assume a Nicene dual-nature Antichristology? Were there two natures but one person? I think not, because that would imply an impersonal human host, created expressly as a vehicle for the inhabitation of Satan, whereas we have already seen Nicolae as a self-willed rascal under his own steam. I am thinking Nestorianism, for it appears that Satan and Nicolae are separate persons, which leaves the human side dormant. After all, both are eventually to be consigned to the Lake of Fire, which implies two evil entities, both culpable.

MYSTERY BABYLON

Carl Jung once theorized that the Christian Trinity tends implicitly toward being a Quaternity: the feminine side of humanity seeks expression, too, with the ancient result that Mary the mother of Jesus was exalted, virtually and unofficially, to the Godhead, cocreatrix and coredemptrix.[13] The book of Revelation seems to partake of the same impulse, for if it depicts a demonic counter-Trinity (the dragon, the sea beast, and the land beast, or Satan, Antichrist, and the False Prophet), it also seems to give us a fourth: the Great Harlot Babylon. "And upon her forehead a name was written, Mystery Babylon the Great, the mother of harlots and abomination of the earth" (Rev. 17:5). It appears that the "mystery" element was supposed to signal the allegorical or cipher character of "Babylon," referring apparently to Rome, seat of the Roman Empire, the enemy of the persecuted saints in John's Apocalypse. But in the *Left Behind* books, "Mystery Babylon" has come to stand for an ecumenical superchurch representing all religions except born-again Christians (plus Orthodox Jews and traditionalist Muslims, who are headed for hell anyway). That seems quite a leap! Where does Jenkins come by this identification?

I think he has retained an unassimilated fragment of an older approach to Revelation that he otherwise does not accept; the Reformers took the historicist approach to Revelation (see chapter 6), whereby Revelation was read as a summary, in advance, of the history of Christendom. The Beast was the papacy and the Great Harlot Babylon was the Roman Catholic Church. It seems Protestant fundamentalists liked the sound of that, even those who rejected historicism for premillenarianism, which made the whole book into predictive prophecy of the End Times. Then, in the wake of the Protestant Ecumenical Movement and the Federal, National, and World Councils of Churches (of which, I suspect, most fundamentalists do not know that the Catholic Church is not a member), this changed. Babylon came to stand in their minds for a one-world religion embodying the worst (as they saw it) of ecumenical syncretism and theological liberalism. That is the way of it in the *Left Behind* books: a false religion used by the Antichrist only as long as he needs it to promote his schemes, then it is disposed of. Jenkins portrays the head of this false church as one Peter Mathews, formerly the Roman Catholic pope, on whom the papal miter devolved when the previous pope disappeared in the Rapture (itself a remarkable ecumenical gesture on behalf of Jenkins and LaHaye!).

We are asked to imagine that the various religions, presumably no more bereft of the Holy Spirit than they were before the Rapture, are somehow newly willing to set aside their differences and merge. Impossible. Worse yet for a novel: implausible. All this reflects the ridiculous fundamentalist view that all "other religions" are the same, since they're all *not Christian fundamentalism*. As if the chief tenet of Vajrayana Buddhism, Shiite Islam, Hasidic Judaism, and Vedanta Hinduism were rejecting Jesus Christ as one's personal savior, never mind what each positively believes. Born-again Christians have no time for niceties like that. But it must be admitted, whatever one's theological position, Pope Peter II and his church are right on target as a send-up of politically correct liberal Protestantism, especially Unitarian-Universalism, in its attempt to incorporate elements of paganism and American Indian religion.

But the name! Jenkins has them call it "Enigma Babylon One World Faith"! I won't deny that it has occurred to me to make up a lapel button with this name on it just to throw a scare into fundamentalists, but Jenkins really should have given it a bit more thought. I mean, isn't the Antichrist's creative team going to come up with something that covers its tracks a bit more? You're really going to pick a name that has conspicuous reference to just one thing—the book of Revelation's Great Harlot? It is as if Carpathia had chosen to call himself "The Beast" instead of "Supreme Potentate." More than likely, Jenkins got the name from the title of an old, rabidly anti-Catholic book, Ralph Woodrow's *Babylon Mystery Religion* (1966).

Jenkins raises the specter of the Holocaust, entitling Carpathia to the same degree of loathing as Hitler. And yet Carpathia's war on Jews seems underplayed. Jenkins does not know what to do with it. He cannot focus on courageous Jewish martyrs—because he believes they must end up in hell (out of the human frying pan and into the divine fire!) and naturally doesn't want to have to say so. He doesn't want to say flat out that Jews were surrendered to the ovens of Carpathia because they had not "received Jesus Christ"—much less that they awoke in hell for the same reason a few minutes later! It seems doubly strange that Jenkins takes the trouble to depict Muslims and Orthodox Jews as resisting the mark of Carpathia and repudiating his lordship—only to be damned in the end unless they repudiate their ancestral religions so they can accept Jesus as their personal savior! Why would they resist apostasy from their cherished faiths at Nicolae's urging, only to turn around and do the same thing in the name of Jesus?

Carpathia sums up the platform of ecumenical pluralism upon which his one-world faith rests: "Religions that saw themselves as the only true way to spirituality now accept and tolerate other religions that see themselves the same way. It is an enigma that has proven to somehow work, as each belief system can be true for its adherents. Your way may be the only way for you, and my way the only way for me" (*Apollyon*).[14] And that is wrong because . . . ? Of course, this will not do for Jenkins and LaHaye because it would seem to mitigate the universal need for faith in the atonement of Christ. And we can't have that! But why be so hagridden by logical implications only at this one point? I have never been able to understand how fundamentalists can be so willing to throw up their hands, piously yielding to the "antinomy" of the Trinity, whereby God may be both one and three at the same time, and reject out of hand the possibility that the various religions may all somehow be as true as they need to be to save their adherents. Their patience with the conundrum of the Trinity is predicated on the valid insight that the Divine Truth must far transcend the human ability to understand it. Why, then, must things be so cut-and-dried when it comes to the "apparent contradictions" between the world religions?

I love the ancient Buddhist parable of the blind men and the elephant in which half a dozen old men, blind from birth, agree to journey to a zoo, where they hope to form their own impressions of the famous pachyderm they have heard of all their lives. Circling the great animal, they converge on it, gingerly feeling before them. Grasping the tusk, the first declares the elephant to be like a spear. The second, taking hold of the ear, says that, no, the elephant is like a fan. The third, fingering the coiling trunk, decides the elephant is like a snake. The fourth, leaning against the broad side of the beast, attests that the elephant is like a wall. The fifth places his spindly arms around the mighty leg and announces that the elephant is like a tree trunk. The sixth, chancing to take the tail in his fingers, says the elephant is like a rope. All are partially right, right in describing their experience of the elephant, but all are equally wrong precisely insofar as they refuse to admit there could be any more to the object of their common perception than each has individually perceived.

Though it seems to have originated among Buddhists, the parable was embraced by Jainists and Sufis as well, quite appropriately, it seems to me. These faiths were humble enough not to suppose they had everything figured out. But the same cannot be said of LaHaye. Why is this a lie of the devil? "Well, Mr. Liberal Theologian, the joke's on you! You can make it sound pretty smooth, but—*gotcha!* That's the Antichrist's party line, and you've fallen for it!" Uh, wait a minute! Have we forgotten this is just a novel? Just a piece of fiction? It begs the question simply to assume that the doctrine of pluralism is just the kind of theology the devil would hold.[15]

The same sort of knee-jerk closed-mindedness is displayed, without a hint of explanation, on the matter of parapsychology: "As a believer, Buck was certain that clairvoyance was hogwash" (*The Indwelling*).[16] Huh? How does *that* follow? You mean, because Buck is a "believer," he has now become *more skeptical?* No, rather it is pure brand loyalty: fundamentalists usually regard any sort of psychic phenomena as "Brand X spiritual gifts." There are exceptions, though: Watchman Nee and John Warwick Montgomery both realized that, if there should turn out to be convincing evidence of things like mind-reading or clairvoyance, it need only be what parapsychologists posit anyway: rare talents latent in the human brain that are seldom activated. There need be nothing either spurious or satanic about them.[17]

THE TWO WITNESSES

Revelation, chapter 11, has two prophets condemn the Beast and preach the coming of the kingdom of God. They arouse the ire of the Beast who, however, cannot do anything at first to silence them. Finally, when the assigned term of their preaching is done, they succumb to mob violence but rise from the dead three days later and ascend to heaven. The powers ascribed to the unnamed men of God clearly imply they are supposed to be Moses and Elijah, one able to smite the land with Exodus-style plagues, the other able to summon drought and call fire down from the sky. Of course, the two men appear in the *Left Behind* books. When they do, and we hear them preaching not only Christianity but evangelical revivalism, it's like something out of the Book of Mormon: the very notion of making Moses and the prophet Elijah evangelical Christians is such a parody as to discredit the whole thing right off.[18] "The night before he had not been able to get close to Eli and Moishe, though he thrilled to see people coming out of the crowd and kneeling by the fence to receive Christ" (*Assassins*).[19] And when, at the end, Jesus returns, and Moses attends a convocation of Old Testament saints, receiving a gold watch from Jesus, there is no hint that we have seen him before, preaching with "Eli." It is as if Jenkins himself cannot really, deep down, buy the notion that Moses would be caught dead preaching evangelical fundamentalism.

A similar scene in which the eschatological epic of the Bible is trivialized and made a joke occurs on the eve of Armageddon itself, when Tsion Ben-Judah and the gang set up a 700 Club with phone/Web

banks of call-in counselors.[20] "During the broadcast, Chang had superimposed on the screen a Web site where those who were making deci-
sions to receive Christ could let Dr. Rosenzweig know at Petra" (*Glorious
Appearing*).[21] What is so comical here is the casting of suburban fundamentalism as the Force of Light in the cosmic struggle! Like substi-
tuting the Knights of Columbus for the Knights of the Round Table in
the Grail saga.

BORN-AGAIN PIETISTS ONLY!

You know those novelty maps showing the USA from the parochial
standpoint of New Yorkers or Bostonians, and so on? That's what this
book is like: taking the pious microcosm of fundamentalist faith as central and redrawing the whole map of reality from there outward. The
result is a grossly disproportionate spectacle in which world destiny
hinges on cultic exegesis and a narrow pietist idiom composed arbitrarily of random elements. Deconstruct this all-important "faith in
Jesus Christ" and what have you got?

Okay, number one, Christ died to pay the debt of sin for a
humanity estranged from God. Does it follow that, number two, one
must *believe* in this in order for it to work for him? One need not believe
in Adam's fall to suffer the effect of it. When you make belief in such
articles of faith the criterion of salvation, are you not reverting to
works? And speaking of that, it is far from clear that the New Testament even teaches the Lutheran Gospel dialectic. *Or* that such a
Gospel, if true, is compatible with number three, introspective piety,
which seems to turn the focus away from Christ to the struggling
believer. Finally, Rayford explains what was lacking in his pre-Rapture
life: sentimental treacle and the willingness to make an obnoxious jerk
of oneself preaching to one's acquaintances. He just didn't want to
become a fundamentalist. And he was screwed, because only members
of that sect will be saved. Going to a staid church instead of an amen-
shouting one is enough, apparently, to land you in hell.[22]

The series is heavily invested in pietistic subjectivism. But what sort of introspection could have revealed the specific falseness of their faith to Rev. Barnes and the rest of those who had supposed themselves to be Christians but found themselves holding the bag after the Rapture? What possible indications had they had—and missed!—of their "false" status? A bit of pride here? A modicum of doubt there?[23] Rayford's "own pride and laziness had cost him his wife and son at the Rapture" (*Glorious Appearing*).[24] Let me get this straight: because Rayford was self-accepting, figuring he was "good enough," this slight moral obnoxiousness is enough to make him miss the Rapture and (if not repented of) be tormented eternally in hell? And what, pray tell, is the difference, really, between his mediocrity and the chastened self-forgiveness he urges upon the suicidal Hattie? Did he or did anyone ever think they were "earning salvation"? Or is that the same thing as merely believing one will be held responsible for one's actions? (Paul still expects that— 2 Corinthians 5:10, "For we must all appear before the judgment seat of Christ; that every one may receive good or bad according to what he has done in the body.") Is this merest shade of a nuance enough for a criterion for salvation or damnation? Only fanatics think so. By contrast, Paul Tillich says: "From the point of view of human nature, the doctrine of a twofold eternal destiny contradicts the fact that no human being is unambiguously on one or the other side of divine judgment.... If the saint receives forgiveness, his reception of it remains ambiguous. If the sinner rejects forgiveness, his rejection of it remains ambiguous."[25] The pre-Rapture Reverend Bruce Barnes would be a prime example of the first, and the Orthodox Jews who refuse to convert to Christianity a great example of the second.

As if aware of the danger to his oversimple position, LaHaye, like all his born-again brethren, strives to stomp on human nature and vilify it. No one is any good. If there were any good in human nature, even if not all good, Tillich might have a point. But fundamentalism exists to stem ambiguity. No one would be a fundamentalist if he were willing to brook ambiguity. If human beings do not merely face a lifelong process of moral maturity, if instead they must jump from one shore, of wickedness, to the other, a shore of sanctified redemption, then we need the cross and the grace of Christ. And since that's what LaHaye wants us to need, then he and Jenkins pour it on pretty thick: "Were people insane? No, she decided, they were self-possessed, narcissistic, vain, proud. In a word, *evil*" (*Glorious Appearing*).[26] That's pretty cold.

> "They shouldn't love me," [Hattie] said, just above a whisper.
>
> "Of course they shouldn't. You know yourself. You know your selfishness, your sin. God should not love us either, and yet he does. And it is only because of him that we can love each other. There is no human explanation for it." (*The Mark*)[27]

> "Thanks, Tsion. God's been more patient with me than I deserve."
>
> "Isn't that true with all of us?" (*The Mark*)[28]

> "But what about you, Chang? Do you know who you are and who you're not? Do you understand the depth of your own depravity and realize that God saved you while you were dead in your sins?" (*The Mark*)[29]

> Are we to fall upon one or two unhappy people in their weakest moment and force upon them a sort of religious coercion? (Dietrich Bonhoeffer)[30]

Bonhoeffer had LaHaye pegged.

But if subjective pietism is not the real crux of this all-important Gospel, if it is instead belief in the plan of salvation, how are we not dealing with "salvation by (cognitive) works" and Gnosticism (salvation by special knowledge)? Fundamentalists hotly deny it, but *isn't* it finally a matter of believers in the right religion being saved and everyone else being disqualified?

It is clear that, for the Christianity on display in *Left Behind*, salvation is a matter of a particular ritual, almost a magical formula one must repeat. It is a definite technique, a method one must follow: "But from literature they found in the library, they learned how to trust

Christ personally" (*The Remnant*).[31] Like there's some trick to it. And there is, an esoteric technique. You'd better learn "everything you need to know about how to receive Christ" (*Armageddon*).[32] Chloe bids a woman, headed for the guillotine, to "ask him to save you by the blood of Christ" (*Armageddon*).[33] Didn't he already? And why on earth was Tsion Ben-Judah left behind to face the Tribulation? True, "he had come to the conclusion that Jesus of Nazareth fulfilled every qualification of the Messiah prophesied in the Old Testament. But he did not receive Christ as his own savior until the Rapture convinced him" (*Soul Harvest*).[34] Huh? The guy had turned from Jewish belief to Christian, and yet he had not "received Christ," as if that gimmick, that method, that mantra, were all-important. And to fundamentalists, it is. None of this is unique to LaHaye and Jenkins; we find another revealing example in Angley's *Raptured*, in which a young woman has courageously refused the mark of the Beast and is headed for the guillotine for it. But she's not out of the woods yet: "She was trembling all over. How sad to die without hope and without God. Mary was aware of the fact if she gave her life it would not save her. She must have a 'born-again' experience through the blood of the Son of God."[35] She believes in Christ as the only savior, but that counts for Jack Squat unless she has the magic "experience."

It is amazing how the work of salvation is placed in our own hands. Christ is like a chemist who has worked up a miracle cure, but it is up to drug companies, physicians, and so on, to dispense it if anybody is to be cured. Is that all Christ is according to Christian theology? Isn't he the savior, or does he merely *provide for* salvation? Is everything still up to us? Does salvation hinge on the micromotions of introspection? The neuroses of the tarrying bench?

Strikingly, it is only after the Glorious Appearing that all the talk about a "personal relationship" with Christ is justified: a telepathic communication, two-way prayer. It seems not to occur to Jenkins what a long shadow this casts back over the traditional evangelical claims to have a personal relationship with Christ, language that properly suggests a give-and-take between real interlocutors. But no one ever experiences that, only projection, make-believe, and chats with one's conscience doubling as an imaginary friend.

> Rayford closed the shades and lay on his back, pulling a single blanket over himself. . . . He began thanking God for the events he had witnessed, beginning with his own healing, but before he could even mention them, Jesus said, "I know, Rayford. I know. I am right here, and I will always be right here. I will never leave you or forsake you..."
> "Thank you, Lord."
> And believing Jesus was there, Rayford drifted off into the sleep of the redeemed. (*Glorious Appearing*)[36]

It is as much as to admit, "Hey, now we *really* have a personal relationship with Jesus! No more pretending!"

"Receiving Christ" is not a ritual of humility (it is often contrasted with "pride" as a Rapture-forfeiting alternative) but rather of *humiliation*.[37] But isn't "pride" or "self-righteousness" pretty much merely an annoying peccadillo? Why make it worthy of eternal damnation, unless, as Whitehead said,[38] God is a megalomaniac who "cannot share his glory with another"?[39]

INTELLECTUAL PRIDE

The *Left Behind* books reek of the *ressentiment*, the cowardly revenge fantasy, of the anti-intellectual who would love nothing more than to see the tables turned: to have the intellectuals who look down on him for his simple beliefs proved wrong. He awaits a day when God will make foolish the wisdom of this world (1 Cor. 1:20). On that day a degree from LaHaye's Christian Heritage College will be worth more than a degree from Harvard. In this way the early Christians reassured themselves that the intellectuals were really the stupid ones (1 Cor. 1:26–31; Matt. 11:25–26). In *Left Behind* and its sequels, intellectualism is a mortal sin. One misses the Rapture, one forfeits salvation, as long as one thinks too much instead of simply taking on faith the preaching of fundamentalists. What a damning admission! Their beliefs will not survive critical scrutiny, and then so much the worse for critical thinking! Listen to Rayford Steele trying to persuade his daughter just after the Rapture:

> "But you still don't buy it?"
> "I want to, Dad. I really do. But I have to be intellectually honest with myself."
> It was all Rayford could do to stay calm. Had he been this pseudo-sophisticated at that age? Of course he had. He had run everything through that maddening intellectual grid—until recently, when the supernatural came crashing through his academic pretense. (*Left Behind*)[40]

This is like the "told ya so" triumphalism, at the expense of the scientific rationalist, that we find in vampire movies. Only who is the joke on here? In fact the Rapture has not occurred. Later, the newly repentant Chaim confesses:

> "But I was so proud! So skeptical! Tsion and Cameron and Chloe and you and everyone who cared about me warned me, tried to persuade me. But oh, no, I was too intellectual. I knew better!" (*The Mark*)[41]

> "All I can say is that the enemy has a stronghold over the mind until one surrenders it to God. I was a pragmatist, proud, a journalist. I wanted control over my own destiny. Things had to be proved to me." (*Remnant*)[42]

> "That's not emotional; that's analytical. I'm more like you than like Mom, remember?"
> "Don't I know it. And because we are the way we are, we're still here." (*Tribulation Force*)[43]

In all this sorry self-abnegation we cannot miss a defensive pride in stupidity, a glorying in credulity, a Christian equivalent to the tragic confusion of African-American youth who regard academic success as "acting white." Did you know that *cretin* comes from the French word for "Christian"? Please understand, I am by no means making such an equation and never would. I am just bemoaning the fact that Christians like LaHaye have invited it. What they call repentance from the "sin" of "intellectual pride" is what the rest of us call a sacrifice of the intellect. "The command to sacrifice one's intellect is more demonic than divine. For man ceases to be man if he ceases to be an intellect" (Tillich).[44] Indeed, I would go so far as to suggest that the born-again attempt to get you to throw out whatever self-concept you already possess and to replace it with "Born-Again Christian" is a blatant case of what Jacques Derrida called "the dangerous supplement," the clever switcheroo whereby someone proposes to add something to a thing in order to supplement it and winds up supplanting it with something else instead. In this case, evangelists urge you to put away the sinful you and to be born again as the Christian you, the "real" you, as God designed you to be. But instead they have persuaded you to adopt the mask of false consciousness. Henceforth you seek to accommodate the programming you have received. Depending on how great your ego-strength may be, your true self may finally rebel against the false, imposed self-construct and cast it off again.

APOLOGETICS: WALKING BY FAITH AND PRETENDING IT IS SIGHT

The clearest display of the fundamentalist *ressentiment* against the intellectuals who reject their faith is the enterprise of Christian apologetics, the defense of the faith by means of any trick in the book, anything the traffic will bear. There is no argument so vapid, so obviously spurious, that apologists will not pick it out of the trash, dust it off, and use it to try to convince some novice of the truth of their faith. (Again, I do not say the Christian faith cannot be or never is served by better thinking than what I describe. I just wish Christians would stick to such higher standards.)

We have already seen the utter vacuity of proof texting the Old

Testament to make Jesus look like the predicted Messiah. What is the real basis for such messianic convictions? "Jesus is the Messiah. I know. He saved me" (*Apollyon*).[45] Yeah, that proves it, all right. And it provides crucial insight into the apologists' mindset. Why are they stubborn, invulnerable to criticism? Because of the stakes. A genuine scholar or scientist is grateful to be set straight; he has been set back on the right path of inquiry if someone shows him he's wrong. But for the believer, what is at stake is his membership in a cozy, mutually reassuring religious fellowship. That is what is hanging in the balance if he should reconsider any one of his arguments. No wonder he won't.

It comes as no surprise to learn that Ben-Judah is also an adherent of the quack science of Flood Geology: "This flood had a catastrophic effect on the world and still boggles the minds of scientists who find fish bones at altitudes as high as fifteen thousand feet" (*Remnant*).[46] Evolution is proved to be Satan's creation myth, as fundamentalists like LaHaye always say it is. Now we have it from the mouth of Satan himself! "I evolved out of the primordial ooze and water" (*Armageddon*).[47] Too bad Satan doesn't understand the theory of evolution any better than LaHaye does.

Ben-Judah stoops to the infamous "Trilemma" argument: given his claims to be God, Jesus cannot have been merely a moral teacher. Instead, he must have been God incarnate as he claimed, or a madman, or a deceiver. The fact that the venerable C. S. Lewis, too, employed this argument does not prevent it from being utterly spurious.[48] For one thing, it is a matter of considerable critical and exegetical dispute as to whether the historical Jesus ever made such claims. And as long as that debate is open, one cannot simply appeal to the statements of John's Gospel as the authentic claims of Jesus. You had better win that one first. Second, the argument is an example of the bifurcation fallacy: oversimplifying the options. Jesus might be, for an example, like Kris Kringle in *Miracle on 34th Street*, an otherwise normal man with "a delusion for good." And third, the argument commits the Apollinarian heresy: it presupposes that a divine Jesus must not have had a genuinely human mind, since it assumes that no true human mind could sanely hold a belief in its own divinity. If that were so, it would make no difference whether the belief were true or false! Even if Jesus were divine, it would explode his sanity to believe it![49]

It is striking that the books (especially *The Indwelling*) set up the resurrection of Antichrist Carpathia in the very terms evangelical apologists wish they had and claim to have for Jesus: his resurrection was seen by many witnesses, including hostile ones, and is even recorded on tape! And yet there is the realization that there will always be "skeptics" holding out. The attested resurrection is offered as confirmation by the Risen One of his own deity. Should not Rayford, David, and the others, if they were raised on evangelical apologetics, convert to belief in Carpathianism? And if they shouldn't, why should skeptics not reject belief in Jesus, for whom the same sort of claims, though much weaker, are made? "It was one thing to read the myths of and legends and perhaps eyewitness accounts of a resurrection centuries ago. But to have seen with one's own eyes a man come back from obvious death . . . well, there was a religion for today" (*The Mark*).[50] LaHaye and Jenkins, it seems to me, have succeeded in a goal they did not have in mind: satirizing Christian apologetics.

LITERAL INTERPRETATION, SO TO SPEAK

James Barr showed how fundamentalist claims to "take the Bible literally" must not be taken seriously. Barr showed how their real policy is to interpret the text any which way they have to in order not to have to admit it is in error.[51] The *Left Behind* books certainly perpetuate this "piecemeal literalism." Rev. Bruce scoffs at nonliteralists who were left holding the hermeneutical bag when the Rapture proved them wrong: "But those who had relegated this kind of teaching to the literalists, the fundamentalists, the closed-minded evangelicals, had been left behind. All of a sudden it was all right to take scripture at its word!" (*Tribulation Force*).[52] Yet he himself soon after admits that the four horsemen must be "imagery," not descriptions of actual individuals: "'Let me clarify,' Bruce was saying, 'that I don't believe it is God's intent to convey individual personality through the imagery of these horsemen, but rather world conditions'" (*Tribulation Force*).[53]

The locusts in *Apollyon* are hilarious: big bugs with wings and human heads.[54] Their chanting is inevitably reminiscent of the ending of *The Fly*.[55] And why would God send such improbable beasties? How can the authors not see that if anything in Revelation is a symbol, this is! (It stands, as we have seen, for the anticipated Parthian invaders.) If there are literally going to be such chimeras, why not have the Beast be a literal dragon like Ghidrah? Rayford tells his fellow pilots that "we are the wings of the eagle" mentioned in Revelation 12:14, to carry the people to safety in the desert.[56] But "God would provide manna and water and clothes that would not wear out."[57] Why is one figurative, the other literal? And where do they get the notion that Exodus conditions (Deut. 8:4: "Your clothing did not wear out upon you, and your foot did not swell, these forty years") would obtain during the Tribulation? The answer is surprising: it is pure subjectivity. Tsion Ben-Judah admits: "He simply impressed upon me to take the words as literally as I took any others from the Bible, unless the context and the wording itself indicated otherwise" (*The Mark*).[58] Existential subjectivity is the basis of biblical authority.

And yet Ben-Judah (LaHaye) is anything but literal, as is evident from his ridiculous application of texts, taken out of context, to refer to the Antichrist. They are just as arbitrary as those proof texts of Jesus. "When he read that 'He who kills with the sword must be killed with the sword,' and knew that even Tsion believed this was a reference to Antichrist, Rayford shuddered" (*Assassins*).[59]

Huh? "In all God's dealings with mankind, this is the shortest period on record, and yet more scripture is devoted to it than any other period except the life of Christ" (*The Mark*).[60] He may well have derived this wild estimate from Arthur W. Pink's exegetical fantasies, because Pink saw the Antichrist behind every corner of every Old Testament book.

If Pastor Jack in *The End of the Age* was an intranarrative version of Pat Robertson, it is doubly clear that Ben-Judah is an idealized Tim

LaHaye, as he sees himself dispensing "Bible scholarship" to the waiting millions—through these books! LaHaye would be quite important, too, if the universe were someday to transform itself into the likeness of his delusions. Only it would be good if he could refrain from simply identifying his doctrines with the teaching of the Bible, sometimes without even a single proof text, in or out of context, as when he says that Buck, Chloe, Rayford, and the rest are "what the Bible calls 'tribulation saints.'"[61] Where does that phrase occur in scripture? It reminds me of the old joke that the red-letter edition of the *Scofield Reference Bible* has Scofield's notes printed in red.

There is, however, a form of literalism on display throughout the novels. The book of Revelation changes from a set of symbols referring to some object (the future crisis) and instead becomes an object in its own right to which history must conform in detail: an "End Times Road Map."

THEODICY AND THE IDIOCY

It is surprising that various characters in the *Left Behind* books confess their surprise, even dismay, that God deals with the human race in such a drastic manner. But it's not as if LaHaye and Jenkins plan to supply any satisfactory answers or that there are any to supply. Such soul-searchings on the part of the characters are merely strategic attempts to anticipate the reader's indignation—and to defuse it. LaHaye and Jenkins, through these characters who "dare" to question, pretend to identify with the reader, but it is just an attempt to dispense with the questions, as if they are saying, "Yeah, I know what you mean. But then what can you do?" But the characters in the book are faced with the Tribulation plagues as a fait accompli. You and I are not. And we still have the option of saying that it *does* matter if a theology has a gross contradiction running down the middle of it like the San Andreas Fault. We are fully entitled to reject such an incoherent God-concept as LaHaye and Jenkins offer us.

Yea, it is yet another attempt to reach you by a loving God who has run out of patience. (*Assassins*)[62]

The downside of the judgments that finally catch some people's attention is that thousands also die from them. (*Apollyon*)[63]

You see, Cameron, these are the things I don't understand. If God is personal like you say, cares about his children and is all powerful, is there not a better way? Why the judgments, the plagues, the destruction, the death? Tsion says we had our chance. So now there is no more Mr. Nice Guy? There is a cruelty about it all that hides the love I am supposed to see. (*Assassins*)[64]

He couldn't make it compute with the God he knew, the loving and merciful one who seemed to look for ways to welcome everyone into heaven, not keep them out. (*Armageddon*—Rayford, pondering terrible plague suffering by people with whom God had run out of patience)[65]

Some have legitimately questioned how a loving and merciful God could shower the earth with such horrible plagues and judgments. (*Armageddon*)[66]

But finally, LaHaye does toss us a sop: "Yet I ask you, what else could he have done after so many millennia to shake men and women from their false sense of security and get them to look to him for mercy and forgiveness?" (*Armageddon*).[67] Where is all this headed? Ultimately, here: "Well, too bad, but at least *my* butt's not fricasseeing in hell." But that's the wrong conclusion. In Dostoyevsky's *The Brothers Karamazov*, the saintly Alyosha asks his worldly brother Ivan why he will not return to Mother Church. Ivan says he cannot, because then he would have to excuse God's behavior, for example, allowing the innocent suffering of children. If one were to be satisfied with the excuse "Well, God must have some reason for it," one would have become a pathetic spin doctor, a toady who knows on which side his bread is buttered. One thus becomes an accomplice. One sells one's soul in order to save it.

In the *Left Behind* books, God is like a bad parent: "I'll give you something to cry *about!*" Besides, the whole thing commits the distribution fallacy: has God been trying to get through to *these* sinners for thousands of years, or just sinners in general? If the latter, why beat up on these particular sinners so badly?

Again, Tsion Ben-Judah assures us that "all twenty-one judgments that have come from heaven . . . have been God's desperate last attempts to get man's attention" (*Glorious Appearing*).[68] Here is the persuasion God of Process theology, but with a baseball bat. In the end, what is this kind of submission and obedience worth? God may have bludgeoned people into submission, but he is not likely to have changed any hearts. Every knee may bow, and he may have wrung a confession of fealty from every creature in heaven, on earth, and under the earth, but will they not hate him the more for it? Is not the only way truly to defeat an enemy to relieve him of his enmity? Does God say to the human race, "Come, let us reason together" and then damn them to Gehenna if they don't see it his way? Winston Smith (in George Orwell's *1984*) was finally persuaded to obey and even to love Big Brother, but it was only because his natural fear of torture bade him believe that maintaining his integrity was a luxury he could no longer afford. Is that how God works? "Why should anyone obey the commandments of this divine lawgiver? How are they distinguished from commands given by a human tyrant? He is stronger than I am. He can destroy me. But is not that destruction more to be feared which would follow the submission of one's personality centre to a strange will?" (Tillich).[69]

WHAT'S THE DIFFERENCE BETWEEN NICOLAE AND JESUS?

Traditionally, as we saw in chapter 3, the Antichrist is supposed to imitate the Messiah, or Jesus Christ. But it is disturbing that, in the *Left Behind* books, it appears to be the other way around: Jesus looks like a copy of Nicolae Carpathia! Again and again, we behold some imperious demand or maniacal arrogation ascribed to Carpathia, only to find

Jesus emulating him later (whether Jesus is actually on stage, as in the last book, or just described in the theology of one of the good guys). For instance, Carpathia's resurrection thunder and lightning show and his mad declarations of being the sole divinity are hardly different from those attributed to Jehovah and Jesus. There is no critique in principle, just a conflict of brand loyalty. The born-again reader is supposed to take umbrage at the audacity of some jerk like Carpathia fulminating about his godhood—just because he's not actually God. But it is entirely appropriate for the one who *is* God to fulminate and threaten unbelievers with damnation if they do not submit to his Lordship. They don't seem to see that it is precisely such self-magnification, such ego inflation that renders a potential Christ an Antichrist instead. It is power corruption, and whoever exhibits it reduces himself to an idol and a false Christ.

Jenkins envisions the millennium as a thousand years of doting on Jesus. "You're going to find that He is all that matters now" (*Glorious Appearing*).[70] "Jesus was all that mattered any more."[71] How is this monomaniacal fixation in principle different from the fawning servility Carpathia exacted from his flunkies? Is it only that he was supposed to be a bad guy and Jesus is supposed to be a good guy? Is there nothing disturbing about it otherwise? It is this very demand for adoration that made Carpathia a villain. Has Jesus overturned the throne of Antichrist—or merely usurped it for himself? Why does Jesus appear as such a megalomaniac in the Gospel of John (the main place he makes such grandiose claims on his own behalf)? D. F. Strauss explained it.[72] The fourth evangelist has taken the paeans to Jesus by his worshipers and translated them from the second-person (praise heaped on Jesus) to the first-person (self-praise by Jesus). His Jesus is the fictive concatenation of Christian devotion. He is made to say of himself what Christians say of him. In this way, the text becomes an object of pious meditation. The devout reader of John's Gospel does not in the first instance imagine a historical Jesus saying such things of himself; intuitively the reader knows that is not the point. The mischief begins with the wretched scheming of apologists, who feel that if they can vindicate such epiphanic statements as actual "claims" of the historical Jesus, then they can use sophisms like the Trilemma argument to swindle the unwary into converting. In the process they create a Jesus who repels faith by boasting intolerably about himself—just like Nicolae Carpathia.

Hattie tearfully testifies to the long-suffering love shown her by the born-again Christians: "You all wanted to love me the way God loved me, and that was whether I agreed with you or not" (*The Mark*).[73] That's the way God loved her? Not Jehovah, surely? He sounds more like Carpathia, "the egomaniac who murders those who disagree with him" (*The Mark*).[74] Nor is this some caricature of Jenkins's Jesus. After all, what is going to happen to you if you don't accept Jesus' grandiose claims? You're headed for punishment far worse than Nicolae could dish out.

An even more blatant parallel occurs again and again. Jenkins underlines what bitter mockery it is when Carpathia and his minions claim that his subjects have a free choice as to whether they will take the mark of the Beast. Some choice—if the alternative is the guillotine! Carpathia says: "I have come to give life! But to the one who chooses to place his loyalty elsewhere? Well, he has chosen death. What could be so stark, so clear, so black-and-white?" (*Desecration*).[75] But can anyone miss the exact parallel to the fundamentalist ultimatum: "Love Jesus—or else!"? Leon Fortunato (the False Prophet) lowers the boom: "Woe and beware to the enemies of the lord of this globe who would thumb their noses in the face of the most high!" (*The Mark*).[76] But if we didn't know from the typography (no capitals for "lord" and "most high"), we would surely think he means Jesus. For the returned Elijah says the same thing about him: "To reject Jesus as Messiah is to spit in the face of almighty God. He will not be mocked" (*Soul Harvest*).[77] Of course, the real Elijah of the Bible never says anything of the kind. But even if he had, he'd have been wrong. He'd have been committing the bifurcation fallacy, so beloved of fundamentalist apologetics. No fair-minded person would believe that you either accept "Jesus" (i.e., what Christian theology says about him) or you are angrily blaspheming God. Would a fair-minded

God think so? Muslims esteem Jesus more highly than the Prophet Muhammad in some respects but believe Jesus was raptured to heaven before he could be crucified. They may be wrong, but are they simply "spitting in the face of God"? Was Gandhi, who embraced Jesus' ethics but didn't feel the need to abandon his cherished Hinduism, spitting in the face of God? Are those Jews who today esteem Jesus as a prophet of Israel? Of course not. At the most, they are mistaken theologically. Now it may be that God will decide to *treat* them as if they were spitting in his face, but then this God would be the one Whitehead disdained: "It is, of course, the figure of an Oriental despot, with his inane and barbaric vanity. Such a conception is an insult to God."[78] "'The choice you make this day,' the golden image roared, 'is between life and death! Beware, you who would resist the revelation of your true and living god, who resurrected himself from the dead! You who are foolish enough to cling to your outdated, impotent mythologies, cast off the chains of the past or you shall surely die! Your risen ruler and king has spoken!'" (*Desecration*).[79] Jehovah, no? "They had made their choices, yes, but did they *really* know what they were choosing? It wasn't between loyalty and death; it was between heaven and hell, eternal life or eternal damnation" (*The Mark*).[80] Doesn't seem to bother God! Or at least his self-appointed sales force, who are constantly telling us how people who decline to become born-again Christians have *chosen* to go to hell. Of course they have not. Even as they are headed for hell, it is going to come as a nasty surprise. There is no sense in which one can truly say anybody chose hell. No, even if they arrive there screaming, their wretched lot will have been imposed upon them as a Draconian punishment, extrinsically. But that is to make God into Hitler, and the clever evangelist/apologist doesn't want to admit that, so he tells us God is only letting the poor damned souls have their way! Can't blame him for that, can you? Such sleazy, phony rhetoric only convinces outsiders to have nothing to do with any religion that twists the truth in such a manner. It is bad enough to have a God who comports himself like the devil, but to deny it, too!? It just shows a complete lack of integrity. It shows you know it's wrong, and that you just don't care.

Buck stepped closer. "Alex, listen to yourself. You just sent more than a dozen women to their deaths because they don't share Nicolae Carpathia's faith. And you call *them* intolerant? . . . Whatever happened to freedom?"

"We've still got freedom, Jack [Buck]," Alex spat. "These people can decide for themselves whether they want to live or die." (*The Mark*)[81]

Jenkins can see the farce such a gun-to-the-head proposition makes of "free choice" when somebody else forces it on us. But when Christian evangelists do so, with their threats of hellfire for those who don't embrace the "love" of Jesus, it somehow looks different.

"Those who die by the blade choose this for themselves. Nicolae is not willing that any should perish but that all should be loyal and committed to him" (*Remnant*).[82] One can only hope that born-again readers of the *Left Behind* series will begin to recognize their own outrageous rhetoric in the mouth of the Antichrist and the False Prophet and realize there are better examples to follow.

JESUS IS THE BIBLE

The prize for dud climaxes goes to . . . *Glorious Appearing* by Tim LaHaye and Jerry Jenkins! When Jesus gets back, all he does is quote the Bible! Like we needed him for that! It's just like the analogous scene in 3 Nephi in the Book of Mormon. The returned Jesus is just a Bible-quoting statue—like the talking statue of Carpathia! As always for fundamentalism, "Jesus" is just the Bible with a face on it.

Isn't it high time for the imperfect to yield to the perfect, as in 1 Corinthians 13:19? Prophecy, disparate words of knowledge, even scripture, itself so often a collection of fragmentary and ambiguous hints: are all these not merely treasured hints of what one might expect when the Word of God himself appears, when we shall know as we are known? But it doesn't happen. It's all a big set-up for nothing. Jesus, as

Jenkins paints him, turns out to be no more than some moving man-
nequin in a Mormon tourist center, mechanically mouthing prere-
corded scripture quotes.

It's just like Derrida says, the final, definitive disclosure of meaning,
the Parousia of the Word, is simply never going to happen. It cannot
happen, because of the endless deferring character of language.
Thanks to its indeterminacy, we can never arrive at a final truth. As the
"apophatic" theology of the Eastern churches tells us, we may at best
peel away layer after layer of illusion and misunderstanding, but we
will never get to a clear vision of the Truth. It is like the North Star:
we navigate *by its light*, but we never imagine we will *get to it*. Nor is that
even the point. Likewise, the point of the Messiah as a theological concept is that he is always *coming*, never arriving. For the moment he does,
he becomes a false Messiah; he enters history, and that is not his proper
place. He can only exist as Messiah in the future. Thus Messiah is the
bearer of hope. When someone arrives in the present and announces
himself the Messiah, he forfeits any possibility that he is. For we do not
hope for what we see.

It is not for lack of imagination that Jenkins's Jesus is just the Bible
with a face on it. No, Jenkins is being quite faithful to his tradition, for
in evangelical Christianity, that's what Jesus is: the Bible. He is no more
than their favorite character in a sacred novel. Look at the "proofs"
offered by apologists like Benjamin B. Warfield and John Warwick
Montgomery. They seem to have to do with Jesus, but he turns out to
be merely a support to prop up the Bible, their *real* savior. First, Jesus
claimed to be God's son, and that he would prove by rising from the
dead (though no one can point to any specific Gospel verse saying precisely this). Second, Jesus did rise, vindicating his claim. Third, now
that we recognize him as the Son of God, everything else he said must
be accepted as true, too. Fourth, he set his stamp of approval on the Old
Testament and authorized the New Testament in advance when he predicted the coming of the Paraclete to remind the disciples of what he
had taught and to teach them further truths. Thus Jesus plays a role vis-
à-vis the Bible that John the Baptist played for him: the forerunner, not

the ultimate authority itself. Thus, when the Evangelical Jesus appears, all he can do is parrot scripture.

I'LL BET YOU SAY THAT TO ALL THE GIRLS

It appears that Jenkins's apocalyptic climax is revelatory after all: it unwittingly lays bare some of the most important self-contradictions of evangelical theology and piety. And here is another. Has it ever occurred to you that the Risen Jesus, still retaining his genuine humanity, cannot possibly be listening to the prayers of all billion Christians at the same time? He cannot conceivably be participating in a "personal relationship" with all of them simultaneously. Rising from the dead does not change that. Being one with the Father cannot change that. If we are still talking about a human person analogous to us, even though lifted above the frailty of the flesh, he simply cannot be devoting his attention to many people at once. Don't you see? You are implicitly imposing such limits on your Jesus concept the instant you start using language like "personal relationship." Jesus isn't the Internet or the Field of Creative Intelligence.

Well, now Jenkins has to put the evangelical cards on the table (even though they don't play cards): he's got to somehow depict the joyful reunion between all those avid, eager Christians and the personal savior for whom they long. How does he do it? His first attempt is unintentionally comical. When the huge crowd of believers hear Jesus going on and on quoting scripture, they hear him add their names, simultaneously and at the same juncture, as if he were addressing each of them privately (notwithstanding the utterly inappropriate context, as if a copy of the US Constitution had your name in it). They are so delighted: Jesus is personalizing it! But of course he's *not*: it is only a stinking form letter. That's pretty lame. But from there Jenkins spins off into rank heresy:

> As Rayford seemed to walk on air back to his place among the throng, something deep within him understood that as personal as that had

been, Jesus was bestowing the same love and attention on everyone present. He suddenly became aware that Mac and Abdullah were also returning to the crowd, tears streaming, body language evidencing that they had also been with the Master.... As Rayford looked around, he could see from every face that each person had personally encountered Jesus. (*Glorious Appearing*)[83]

This is a blatantly Gnostic motif: simultaneously Jesus appears differently to different people. He has no true, intrinsic form. It is called *docetism*: the only *apparent* physical objectivity of Jesus. Like the Olympian gods, he can appear in any form at will because he is a deity unhindered by the constraints of the flesh. Here are two examples from second-century documents. In the first, the Acts of Peter, Peter has assembled the consecrated widows of a local congregation and urged them to seek the Lord Jesus in prayerful meditation.

Peter said: "Tell us what you saw." And they said, "We saw an old man of such beauty that we are not able to describe to you." But others said, "We saw a young man;" and others, "We saw a boy touching our eyes delicately, and so were our eyes opened." Peter therefore magnified the Lord, saying, "You only are the Lord God, and what sort of lips would we need to give you due praise? And how can we give you thanks proportionate to your mercy? Therefore, brethren, as I told you only a little while ago, God is always greater than our thoughts, even as we have learned of these aged widows, how they beheld the Lord in diverse forms." (Acts of Peter 21)

In the second, from the Acts of John, the aged apostle recounts the moment Jesus summoned him and his brother James into his service.

For once he had called Peter and Andrew, who were brothers, he comes next to me and my brother James, saying, "I need you! Come to me!" And my brother, on hearing it, said, "John—this child standing on shore and calling us! What can he want?" And I said, "What child?" And he replied, "That one, motioning to us!" And I answered, "We have kept watch at sea too long, my brother! You are not seeing straight! Can't you see it is a man standing there? Handsome, light-skinned, and smiling?" But he said to me, "Him I do not see, my brother. But let us go to shore, and we will learn what it is he wants of us." And so when we had docked the boat, we saw him helping us secure the boat. And when we left there, inclined to follow him, I saw him this time as largely bald but with a thick and curling beard, while James saw him as a youth with only fuzz on his cheeks. So we were both uneasy and confused. What we saw: what could it mean? (Acts of John 88–89)

I want to say that, naturally, Jenkins does not intend a docetic portrayal of Jesus, but actually I think he does. He might have thought twice had anybody pointed out the heretical implications of what he wrote, but surely he *was* aiming at some sort of depiction in which Jesus so far transcended human limitations that he could talk to untold numbers, individually, all at once. He is saying, as CBS news anchor Harry Reasoner once did in a Christmas essay, that, "[l]ike beauty, Jesus Christ is in the eye of the beholder." And that's docetism: no objective Jesus. Without intending it, Jenkins has demonstrated that the business about every Christian having a "personal relationship with Jesus Christ" is and must be an illusion. And remember, it was because they lacked this illusion that most of humanity was left behind to face the terrors of the Tribulation in the first place.

NOTES

1. Tzvetan Todorov, *The Fantastic: A Structural Approach to a Literary Genre*, trans. Richard Howard (Ithaca, NY: Cornell University Press, 1975), p. 69.

2. Edmund D. Cohen, "Review of the *Left Behind* Tribulation Novels: *Turner Diaries* Lite," *Free Inquiry* 21, no. 2.

3. Tim LaHaye and Jerry B. Jenkins, *Left Behind: A Novel of the Earth's Last Days* (Wheaton, IL: Tyndale House, 1995), p. 110.

4. Jürgen Moltmann, *The Crucified God: The Cross of Christ as the Foundation and Criticism of Christian Theology*, trans. R. A. Wilson and John Bowden (New York: Harper & Row, 1974), p. 84: "Christian theology must show how far the Christian confession of faith in Jesus is true as seen from outside, and must demonstrate that it is relevant to the present-day understanding of reality and the present-day dispute about the truth of God and the righteousness of man and the world. For the title 'Christ' has never been used by faith only to say who Jesus was in his own person, but to express his dominion, future and significance with regard to God, men and the world."

5. Todorov, *The Fantastic*, pp. 24–57.

6. Such stories would include some of John Dickson Carr's detective stories, Arthur Conan Doyle's *The Hound of the Baskervilles*, and pulp novels including the adventures of Doc Savage and the only apparently supernatural horror stories in the "Weird Menace" subgenre. The *Scooby Doo* cartoons take this approach as well: what seems to be a ghost, a monster, or an alien, is always merely a mundane crook with some imagination.

7. LaHaye and Jenkins, *Left Behind*, pp. 116–17.

8. LaHaye and Jenkins, *The Mark: The Beast Rules the World* (Wheaton, IL: Tyndale House, 2000), p. 146.

9. Ibid., p. 339.

10. LaHaye and Jenkins, *Assassins: Assignment: Jerusalem, Target: Antichrist* (Wheaton, IL: Tyndale House, 1999), p. 327.

11. LaHaye and Jenkins, *The Mark*, pp. 138–39.

12. Jeff Prewitt figured this out for me. E-mail to the author, November 19, 2006.

13. Carl Gustav Jung, *Psychology and Religion* (New Haven, CT: Yale University Press, 1938), pp. 76–77.

14. LaHaye and Jenkins, *Apollyon: The Destroyer Unleashed* (Wheaton, IL: Tyndale House, 1999), p. 105.

15. Cf. LaHaye and Jenkins, *Soul Harvest: The World Takes Sides* (Wheaton, IL: Tyndale House, 1998), pp. 213–14. In LaHaye and Jenkins, *Nicolae: The Rise of Antichrist* (Wheaton, IL: Tyndale House, 1997), p. 359–60, liberal theology and toleration are set forth in a reasonable manner. The only thing that "refutes" it is that it is placed in the mouth of the False Prophet! Like the closing scene in a Jack Chick tract where the demon unmasks.

16. LaHaye and Jenkins, *The Indwelling: The Beast Takes Possession* (Wheaton, IL: Tyndale House, 2000), p. 85.

17. John Warwick Montgomery, *Principalities and Powers: A New Look at the World of the Occult*, rev. ed. (New York: Pyramid Books, 1975), p. 22; Watchman Nee, *The Latent Power of the Soul* (New York: Christian Fellowship Publishers, 1972).

18. Cf. LaHaye and Jenkins, *Apollyon*, p. 140.

19. LaHaye and Jenkins, *Assassins*, p. 366.

20. LaHaye and Jenkins, *Armageddon: The Cosmic Battle of the Ages* (Wheaton, IL: Tyndale House, 2003), pp. 281, 285.

21. LaHaye and Jenkins, *Glorious Appearing: The End of Days* (Wheaton, IL: Tyndale House, 2004), p. 71.

22. LaHaye and Jenkins, *The Mark*, pp. 310–12.

23. See also LaHaye and Jenkins, *Apollyon*, p. 100.

24. LaHaye and Jenkins, *Glorious Appearing*, p. 194.

25. Paul Tillich, *Systematic Theology. Volume III: Life and the Spirit; History and the Kingdom of God* (Chicago: University of Chicago Press, 1963), p. 408.

26. LaHaye and Jenkins, *Glorious Appearing*, p. 178.

27. LaHaye and Jenkins, *The Mark*, p. 117.

28. Ibid., p. 291.

29. Ibid., p. 358.

30. Dietrich Bonhoeffer, *Letters and Papers from Prison* (New York: Macmillan, 1962), p. 163.

31. LaHaye and Jenkins, *The Remnant: On the Brink of Armageddon* (Wheaton, IL: Tyndale House, 2002), pp. 343–44.

32. LaHaye and Jenkins, *Armageddon*, p. 281.

33. Ibid., p. 245.

34. LaHaye and Jenkins, *Soul Harvest*, p. 244.

35. Ernest W. Angley, *Raptured: A Novel on the Second Coming of the Lord* (Old Tappan, NJ: Fleming H. Revell Company, 1950), p. 228.

36. LaHaye and Jenkins, *Glorious Appearing*, p. 370.

37. LaHaye and Jenkins, *Apollyon*, pp. 322, 343.

38. Lucien Price, *Dialogues of Alfred North Whitehead* (Boston: Little, Brown, 1954), p. 277.

39. This passage is actually quoted in LaHaye and Jenkins, *Armageddon*, p. 275.

40. LaHaye and Jenkins, *Left Behind*, p. 237.

41. LaHaye and Jenkins, *The Mark*, p. 196.

42. LaHaye and Jenkins, *The Remnant*, p. 275.

43. LaHaye and Jenkins, *Tribulation Force: The Continuing Drama of Those Left Behind* (Wheaton, IL: Tyndale House, 1996), p. 158.

44. Paul Tillich, "The Depth of Existence," in Tillich, *The Shaking of the Foundations* (New York: Scribner's, 1948), p. 62.

45. LaHaye and Jenkins, *Apollyon*, p. 128.

46. LaHaye and Jenkins, *The Remnant*, p. 228.

47. LaHaye and Jenkins, *Armageddon*, p. 294.

48. C. S. Lewis, *Mere Christianity* (New York: Macmillan, 1952), p. 56. We find it also in Carol Balizet, *The Seven Last Years* (Grand Rapids, MI: Baker Book House/Chosen Books, 1978), p. 226.

49. LaHaye and Jenkins, *Soul Harvest*, p. 329. The whole passage is a rich vein of nonsense. And he is plain wrong that a delusion of grandeur on the part of a teacher cancels everything he has said. That's the ad hominem fallacy.

50. LaHaye and Jenkins, *The Mark*, pp. 373–74.

51. James Barr, *Fundamentalism* (Philadelphia: Westminster Press, 1977), p. 46: "Fundamentalist interpretation does not take the Bible literally, but varies between taking it literally and taking it non-literally. This variation is made necessary by the real guiding principle of fundamentalist interpretation, namely that one must ensure that the Bible is inerrant, without error. Inerrancy is maintained only by constantly altering the mode of interpretation, and in particular by abandoning the literal sense as soon as it would be an embarrassment to the view of inerrancy held."

52. LaHaye and Jenkins, *Tribulation Force*, p. 67.

53. Ibid., p. 70.

54. LaHaye and Jenkins, *Apollyon*, p. 315.

55. Ibid., p. 318.

56. LaHaye and Jenkins, *Desecration: Antichrist Takes the Throne* (Wheaton, IL: Tyndale House, 2001), p. 42.

57. Ibid.

58. LaHaye and Jenkins, *The Mark*, p. 142.

59. LaHaye and Jenkins, *Assassins*, p. 330.

60. LaHaye and Jenkins, *The Mark*, p. 147.

61. LaHaye and Jenkins, *Tribulation Force*, p. 236; *Soul Harvest*, p. 318.

62. LaHaye and Jenkins, *Assassins*, p. 146.

63. LaHaye and Jenkins, *Apollyon*, p. 157; cf. 303, 330.

64. LaHaye and Jenkins, *Assassins*, p. 241.

65. LaHaye and Jenkins, *Armageddon*, p. 18.

66. Ibid., p. 280.

67. Ibid.

68. LaHaye and Jenkins, *Glorious Appearing*, p. 103.

69. Paul Tillich, *Love, Power, and Justice: Ontological Analyses and Ethical Applications* (New York: Oxford University Press/Galaxy Books, 1960), p. 76.

70. LaHaye and Jenkins, *Glorious Appearing*, p. 397.

71. Ibid.

72. David Friedrich Strauss, *The Life of Jesus for the People*, trans. anon., 2nd ed., vol. 1 (London: Williams and Norgate, 1879), pp. 272–74.

73. LaHaye and Jenkins, *The Mark*, p. 173.

74. Ibid., p. 320.

75. LaHaye and Jenkins, *Desecration*, pp. 33–34. See also David Dolan, *The End of Days* (Springfield, MO: 21st Century Press, 2003), pp. 162, 187.

76. LaHaye and Jenkins, *The Mark*, p. 202.

77. LaHaye and Jenkins, *Soul Harvest*, p. 376; cf. LaHaye and Jenkins, *The Indwelling*, p. 186.

78. Price, *Dialogues of Alfred North Whitehead*, p. 277.

79. LaHaye and Jenkins, *Desecration*, p. 87.

80. LaHaye and Jenkins, *The Mark*, p. 298.

81. Ibid., pp. 316–17.

82. LaHaye and Jenkins, *The Remnant*, p. 322

83. LaHaye and Jenkins, *Glorious Appearing*, p. 299.

CONCLUSION

The Eschaton

"How many are there who ever remember that the openly appointed time for the second coming of Jesus has long passed by, and that consequently one of the mainstays of Christianity is shown to be utterly worthless?"

—Hermann Samuel Reimarus,
On the Intention of Jesus and His Disciples[1]

W hat an irony! The *Left Behind* series allows born-again readers to gloat over the poor saps who failed to heed their annoying, Jehovah's Witness-style warnings about the coming of the Antichrist, the Tribulation, and the Rapture. The majority of the world's population is envisioned as being abandoned to the Auschwitz of the End Times simply for their failure to embrace a set of religious jargon ("I have a relationship with Jesus Christ as my personal savior"). The ultimate revenge fantasy in which the true believer says: "Boy, won't *you* be chagrinned, Mr. Sophisticated Nonbeliever, when my bumper sticker prophecy comes true and you're left holding the bag! If you're lucky, maybe God will let you jump on the train after it's left the station," as the heroic Rafe Steele, a refugee from 1970s *Airport* movies, does. The lesson of *Left Behind* is a warning to repent of the sin of critical thinking, which the fundamentalist, eager for people to embrace the Gospel of irrational nonsense, equates with "intellectual pride."

And the irony is that, if anyone has been "left behind," it is the legion of smirking born-again Christians. It's not that the Rapture came and they missed it. It is that the Rapture was scheduled for a particular time—and it never happened. The New Testament never promised the Rapture would come *someday* in the sweet by-and-by. No, there was *a statute of limitations* on the thing. It was scheduled for the end of the first century. Writer after writer of the New Testament plainly says so. The abject failure of the promise ought to make as much of a laughingstock of such faith as it does when the Jehovah's Witnesses miss deadline after deadline for Armageddon and fundamentalists lead the guffawing. But the fundamentalists don't realize it. They have been willingly gulled and lulled by a set of absurd text-twisting harmonizations of the verses that set the date ("This generation shall not pass away until . . ."). They have repressed the trauma of the failure of the Parousia (the Second Coming of Christ) and, as Freud could have predicted, they have inherited a whole host of neurotic symptoms, not the least of which is a repeating loop of dysfunctional behavior whereby they continue to set themselves up for failure by projecting ever-new Rapture deadlines and smarting when they pass uneventfully. The psychologically sound thing to do would be to face the traumatic truth head on and get past it: grow up, "be mature in your thinking" (1 Cor. 14:37), and get used to the fact that as individuals and as a nation we must do our best to think through the geopolitical and ecological crises facing us. We have and deserve no fairy-tale promise that angels will save us and torment the bad guys (who might even be *us*) and that God will toss out this world and give us a brand-new one. No, this is the only world we have, or will ever have, and we need to take responsibility for it. This is the only history we will ever have, and it is up to us to try to make a positive difference in it. No supernatural beings are going to do it for us. And we are only playing at concern for the events of our day when we ask of any news report, "What does this portend for Bible prophecy?"

In truth, it is born-again fundamentalist Christians who have been tragically left behind. Jesus left them at the altar nineteen centuries ago. In the Gospel of Thomas, the bemused disciples ask Jesus when the kingdom of God will arrive. He informs them that what they expect has already come, they just do not recognize it (saying 51). But it is worse than that. What they expect will *never* come. So instead of putting everything on hold until it comes, they had best forget about the coming and get on with business. Think of the Synoptic parable in which the head of the house is about to leave for a trip and assigns his slaves each his duties. Jesus warns it is important for each slave to do his best to discharge his duty lest, when the master returns, the servant be caught in the act and severely punished. But don't you see? The real danger is that something may happen to the master. He may never return. And that increases the gravity of the slaves' responsibility a hundredfold. If the household is left to them, they'd better realize they have no one else to blame but themselves if things break down for lack of vigilant maintenance. Their chief responsibility is to themselves and not to another. This is the lesson that Christians, left behind by a failed promise long ago, need desperately to learn.

NOTE

1. Hermann Samuel Reimarus, *Reimarus: Fragments*, ed. Charles H. Talbert, trans. Ralph S. Fraser, Lives of Jesus series (Philadelphia: Fortress Press, 1970), pp. 227–28.

APPENDIX 1

Wastin' Away in Millenniumville

"Such conceptions as grinding to powder the teeth of the sinners, or stars whose privy members are like those of horses, do not figure prominently in the teaching of our Lord."

—T. Francis Glasson, *The Second Advent*[1]

I t was another beautiful day in Jerusalem. It was always a beautiful day in Jerusalem. How far was it into the Millennium? Rayford had lost track. Actually, he was *hoping* he would lose track. Maybe that way time would seem to accelerate. As it was, he felt like he had once felt in nightmares that saw him in the cockpit of a commercial airliner (how long ago *that* seemed!) and trying to come up to takeoff speed. But he couldn't seem to do it, and he would very shortly be out of usable runway. The dreams would always end before he crashed the plane, and he had never had the faintest idea what they meant. Probably nothing. He wondered what the feeling meant *these* days.

As he sat there on the tiled patio of his own private mansion, he found himself thinking of going back into the air. Now that most of the pieces were picked up from the carnage of the Tribulation, both from the chaos inflicted by Nicolae Carpathia, the erstwhile Antichrist, and that rained on the earth by God, civilization was being rebuilt yet again. Seemed like the Tribulation had been one long process of smashing down and rebuilding, so things didn't feel like they had changed much. But at least now there were no foot-long bugs with human faces trying to fly up your butt. At least now there weren't phantom missiles spewing out of the Beast's gunships and passing through your plane like holographic projections. Rayford had more than once asked himself how he knew that's *not* what those strangely insubstantial shells had been? But he had banished the thought as soon as it had occurred to him. You never knew who might be listening to your innermost thoughts these days. At least Carpathia hadn't been able to do *that*.

They would soon be needing pilots to ferry materials and people, pretty much like the old days before the Disappearances, before the Rapture. True, the elite, the martyrs of the Tribulation, like his beloved Chloe and her husband, Buck, had little need for any mundane conveyance. They were able to travel on foot with superhuman speed. There seemed to be no place they could not reach in moments. Which sort of meant they didn't bother anymore, since it hadn't taken them but a few hours to cover the whole earth several times over, and to see any sight they had ever dreamt of seeing. Rayford had been "lucky" enough to make it alive through the Tribulation to witness the Second Coming (or was it the Third? Depended on whether you counted the Rapture as a separate coming) with his original blood flowing through his veins. But that meant he was one of the second-classers now. A mere mortal, albeit he was destined to last out the Millennium unless some accident cut him down. Would he age—and *stay* old for a thousand years? That would be a lot of fun, wouldn't it? Without your teeth? Or control of your bladder? Maybe threescore and ten wasn't such a bad idea. He didn't rightly know what would happen to him once he died. Would there be another resurrection after the Millennium? If so, would he be cooling his heels somewhere off in a now-empty heaven till then? Well, one thing's for sure: they wouldn't be needing pilots up there.

There might not be much to do here in a world with no challenges left. But there was nonetheless quite a bit to get used to. He had two wives, alive again! It was weird to see them both, and his romantic feelings for each clashed with the other. But then he couldn't touch either one of them! They were "daughters of the resurrection, not to be given in marriage." But he wasn't a son of the resurrection. Just a "Tribulation saint" who made it through alone. He thought of seeking out female companionship among some of the other survivors, who were still flesh and blood like him. But he wasn't getting any younger, and all the women his age were agog over Jesus, whom they saw daily on TV (which meant pretty much FOX News. No more Global Community CNN—or anything else). He had thought his first wife, Irene, a bit nutty because she was in church every hour of the week its doors were ajar. But that was nothing compared to this!

Oh, Rayford loved Jesus, too. But actually having him there, as the head of state, as a concrete historical figure? It was almost disappointing. For the first time he thought how few people back in the first century AD would have had any personal contact with Jesus. Maybe twelve? Only now did it occur to him how Jesus had once sought privacy off the beaten track in Tyre and Sidon, hoping nobody would know to look for him there. And he kept the crowd at arm's length to such a degree he had to ask the disciples who the people thought he was! Some of them didn't even know he wasn't John the Baptist! Oh sure, he could still close his eyes and pretend Jesus was in his heart speaking to him, like he used to, but it seemed sort of silly now, when he realized Jesus was in the rebuilt palace of the Davidic kings up on Mount Zion.

In fact, Rayford began to notice, wasn't that Jesus on the TV again now? Yes, he thought, as he retreated into the den to get out of the merciless sun. Jesus was in the middle of a press conference. Someone was asking the Lord when they could expect to have the power restored in the villages up in Galilee. His answer? "It is not for you to know the times and seasons the Father has set by his own authority." That sounded familiar. Someone else asked why food distribution had not yet reached certain far-flung Buddhist and Hindu districts where Carpathia's long arms had never reached, with the result that the people weren't Christians but didn't have the damning mark of the Beast either. Didn't they deserve some consideration from the new regime? What was Jesus' position on that? "Between us and them a great chasm has been fixed, in order that those who would pass from here to there may not be able, and none may cross from there to us." Wow! thought Rayford, that seemed kind of cold. But, hey, it was the King of kings talking. It might not sound fair to mere mortals, but God must have his reasons.

Suddenly the TV went off, seemingly by itself. And then he felt the rush of wind and noticed his old friend and mentor Tsion Ben-Judah was standing there and had shut off the set. "I hope you don't mind, Rayford?"

"No, I guess not. It's nothing I haven't heard before. It never is. And when are you going to take off that stupid-looking costume?"

"What's the matter? Don't you think it suits me?" Actually it did. Tsion, one of the resurrectees, had been restored to the physique of his youth, and, like the rest of them, he could run at phenomenal speeds, certainly a surprise bonus the Bible never hinted at. Even as a man of advancing middle age as he was during the Tribulation, Tsion had been no slouch and took care to stay fit and spry. But now here he was, wearing the costume of the comic book superhero the Flash.

"So it's a little affectation I picked up! Harmless, if you ask me."

"Yeah, I guess as long as the world has been turned into one big daycare center, we might as well play. So, Tsion, what else have you been doing with your time these days?"

Tsion sat down in the overstuffed chair Rayford indicated, and as his friend went to the fridge to get him some lemonade, the once-wizened rabbi answered him, "To tell you the truth, I've been getting out the old books and studying them again."

"What, you mean your Greek New Testament, your Hebrew Bible? Stuff like that? Why? What do you need that stuff for? Now you've got the real thing—right there on TV! No more hunting for clues."

"Old habits are hard to break, I guess. No, listen, Rayford, I . . ."

There was another of those abrupt gusts of wind out of nowhere, stirring the pages of the magazines, the only ones now published, *Christianity Today, Moody Monthly, Christian Life, Time.* This time, it was Chang. He was dressed in a common jogging suit.

"Nice outfit!" he quipped, observing Tsion's skin-tight, red and gold suit. They all laughed. "Hope you gents don't mind my butting in like this, but I'm on break from the computer lab." Chang's talents were much in demand up in Zion. Now, once again, there was a one-world government, and it had to work better than the jury-rigged network Carpathia had slapped together. It had been as tenuous and fragile as a dusty old cobweb. Rayford, Tsion, and Chang knew that all too well, as they had taken advantage of the system's inefficiency for years in order to undermine it. But the Jesus administration was doing a much better job of it, as might be expected. Couldn't Jesus, the almighty Son of God, simply make everything happen by telling it to? Presumably yes, but that would be treating him as some sort of supercomputer, and that was beneath his divine dignity. So his sanctified fans took care of daily operations. Besides, it gave them something to do.

Rayford fetched a second lemonade and brought it to his new arrival. "So they're keeping you pretty busy these days, eh, Chang?"

"Yeah, man, it's great to feel useful. Especially since I'm not much good to Naomi anymore. You know, 'sons of the resurrection' and all that. So far I find I can stand it okay, but there are times. . . . And then I just get busy on the computer."

"But there's no more porn sites!" Rayford said, and all three men laughed guiltily, and, as if it was rehearsed, reflexively looked over their shoulders. Was anyone listening? Their laughter faded into nervous chuckling.

"Explain something to me, genius," Rayford asked Chang. "How come you can run at amazing speeds, like the Flash here, but I can't? I mean, Tsion was dead and then raised from the dead. But you weren't. Neither was I, but you can keep up with him, and I'd have a heart attack if I tried!"

Chang frowned. "I wish I had an answer for you, Rayford. I've thought about that, too. But then so much of this is confusing. Almost as if somebody designed the whole scenario from an inconsistent theoretical model."

"Right," interjected Tsion, not looking at either of his friends, but straight ahead, as if deep in thought. "Almost as if someone were trying to piece together the various different Bible passages that don't really fit together, and then make them real."

"Huh?" Rayford's jaw dropped. "I can't believe I'm hearing this! You've never talked about the Bible that way before!"

"That's true, my friend. But then I had never scrutinized it so closely before."

"What do you mean?" asked Chang. He had the sort of leading tone that implied he suspected he and Tsion might be thinking along the same lines.

"I was just telling Ray that I've been filling my time with my old hobby: scripture study. The thing is, I was speeding around Europe, curious to see how much of the old architecture was still standing after Carpathia's rampages and all the trumpet plagues, and I stopped at one or two of the old German universities, Tübingen and Göttingen, and I checked out their libraries. Most of the books survived, miraculously. There I saw dusty old tomes by scholars I had never heard of. Baur, Bultmann, Wellhausen, Strauss. I must have read reams of the stuff. I don't really know how long I was at it, because this new speed seemed to rub off on my reading. I suppose I absorbed a goodly amount of it quickly."

Rayford interposed: "I don't remember Reverend Bruce ever mentioning any of those names. You say they were biblical scholars?"

"Yes, Rayford, and very great ones. The more I read, the more I found myself feeling like the Emmaus disciples: my heart began to burn within me as the scriptures became a whole new book to me."

"I don't get you, Tsion. After all, what more could they tell a man who's seen the Bible literally come to life all around him? What good could the guesswork of these old writers do you?"

"Well, friend Rayford, I'll tell you this: there are many worlds. We are living in one right now, and it is a far different one from the world we lived in for those seven terrible years. And both are very, very different from the one we lived in prior to that. Unimaginably different. In the same way, the text of scripture is a world in itself. As with any book, when you begin reading it, you are transported into that world, the one the writer has created in your imagination, and for a while you forget the world you came from. The world you will return to when you close the book. And you start tracing out the logic inherent in that world on the page. It was that world within the text that the old scholars made clearer to me. It was as if I had been playing a game by the wrong rules, the rules of another game. Naturally it skewed the results."

Chang said, "So you're saying you realized you'd been wrong on . . . like what? Surely not anything all that important, right?"

"My friends, I'm not sure we should go any further in this vein. You know how our Lord said, 'I tell you the truth, men shall give account of every idle word they speak'?" Again, Tsion looked around with a hint of fear on his usually jovial face.

Chang took the floor. "You don't have to worry about that. Though your instincts are right on target. I fixed everything."

Rayford's feeling of mild confusion was now turning into genuine alarm. "You fixed *what?*"

"It's the same sort of thing I used to do when I worked in New Babylon for the bad guys. I never thought I'd have to do this sort of stuff again. But I was poking around in the system. I had to. I mean, I was searching for bugs, hunting down viruses, straightening out glitches. And I found things, programs and such, that obviously nobody ever intended me to find. Just like the old days. I talked to David, and he'd found them, too. He'd been afraid to tell anybody."

Rayford was sitting back in his chair now, a hand over his forehead, as if trying to fend off a migraine. "I really don't like the sound of this, Chang! I'm not sure I want to hear any more."

"Too late, now, Rayford. For all of us. Go on, Chang. Then I'll tell you both what I found."

"Okay. First, have you fellows noticed that Jesus hasn't made mental contact with you in the last few days?"

In chorus, both men gasped, "Yes!"

"You have David and me to blame for that. We discovered that somehow, somewhere since the Glorious Appearing, each of us has been outfitted with some kind of implant, a chip or something, tuned to receive subtle broadcast signals. Feelings of reassurance, words of comfort from Jesus. You know, inspirational greeting card stuff. Mostly Bible paraphrases. You know how, when you pray, even when you ask specific questions, that's about all you get for an answer?"

Rayford had a sinking feeling. "Yeah. I told myself I was just too much of a babe in Christ to be able to handle anything heavier."

"Well," Chang went on, "apparently there's a *reason* they want you to 'become as a little child.' It makes things a lot easier for certain people. And the same chip enables surveillance on your thoughts. Actually thought *patterns*. Alpha, Beta, etc."

"Like *now*, you mean?"

"Yes, Rayford, but, like I said, it's cool. You don't have to worry, because David and I altered the programming of the chips in the three of us, David, and a few others. If they monitor you, and it's only sporadic for everybody, all they'll tap into is a repeating loop of Alpha waves, which they'll think is either praising Jesus or 'the peace that passeth understanding.' But I want to hear more from you, Tsion. What were you saying?"

"Something that is starting to make more sense to me now! You know how I devoted some years, at the request of the Israeli government, to messianic prophecy? I have never pretended to be a biblical specialist. Languages ancient and modern were my forte. So I was able to read the original sources with great fluency. But I was really something of a stranger in a strange land. I took my cues from scholars that Christian missionaries had suggested to me, like Afred Edersheim, himself a Jew who converted to Christianity. That was premature of me. I found myself seduced by the sense he made of the scriptures, because he was able to fit all manner of confusing fragments into a larger pattern. That pattern was Christian theology, as I now see. But it had little to do with the intent of the old prophets. This Wellhausen, on the other hand, he took the ancient texts on their own terms and laid bare the underlying ways of thinking, showed the legendary nature of the whole thing. I tell you, it was a revelation."

"But what about Jesus as the Messiah of the prophets?" Rayford asked, unable to credit what he seemed to be hearing. "You can't be backing away from what you said on international TV! I mean, you've seen for yourself that Jesus is the Son of David. . . !"

"Have I, Rayford? God forgive me, but I have seen many things, including Nicolae Carpathia raising himself from the dead. That was pretty convincing at the time, too. I can only tell you that, if the prophetic scriptures mean anything at all, this man who is ruling over us in Jerusalem, if he is a man at all, is not the Messiah of Israel."

Chang remained silent, as if hearing bad news he had feared. Rayford, on the other hand, was on the verge of hysteria, torn between weeping and laughing. And his head was pounding like the drum in a slave galley. "So you mean Jesus isn't the Messiah? Are you saying he is . . . uh, something greater?"

Chang answered the question. "If I'm right, that isn't either the Messiah or Jesus sitting on that throne in Jerusalem. Doesn't it strike you that he never says much besides Bible quotes? I'm thinking our savior is a fancy computer effect. I don't know who's in charge up there on Mount Zion."

"No! This is nonsense!" Rayford protested. "You can't tell me I didn't meet my Lord and Savior! He called me by name! He told me he loved me!"

Chang was even-tempered. You could tell he'd already passed through the same set of reactions. "He told me the same stuff, Ray. He told everybody the same thing. Doesn't *that* strike you as odd? Now ask yourself, what would account for that?"

Rayford wasn't silent long. "A hypnosis chip. Broadcasting the same signal, just filling in the different names. Amazingly complex, but easily imaginable."

"What about the speed? And the other heightened abilities we have, Chang?" Tsion asked. He had the tone of a student asking how some operation was accomplished, not that of a skeptic thinking he had stumped someone.

Chang answered, "I haven't figured that one out yet. But I'm beginning to think there is some sort of induced hallucination involved, as when the witches of old times thought they were riding broomsticks through the skies. They were taking some drug. Maybe we are being fed some such substance in the food they provide us. I don't know to what end. It might have some military use."

"But the fire . . ." Rayford was searching for counterevidence. He was not sure he was any longer trying to refute Chang, maybe only trying to get him to explain everything. "How'd we survive getting nuked that time at Petra? You walked through the flames without singing a hair—just like me!"

"Actually, Ray, that's one of the easiest to explain. It was more like a light show. Remember, we didn't even feel any heat?"

"How could I be so stupid?" Rayford asked himself, but aloud.

"It's the same for all of us," Tsion said, putting his hand on Rayford's broad shoulder. "In the end, we believe pretty much what we want to believe. Even if it leads to martyrdom, that gives our lives the ultimate meaning."

"But look at you, Tsion! You can't deny you've been rejuvenated!"

"It's not a question of the facts, my friend. The question is what to *make* of the facts. And I'm still trying to figure that one out."

Rayford had risen to his feet again and walked over to the picture window. He looked out but saw nothing except the kaleidoscope of images in his seething mind. "I don't have the dimmest idea how I'm going to broach all this to Chloe and Buck."

A new voice joined the conversation. In the hallway stood his daughter and her husband, Chloe and Buck. "We're already up to speed."

Rayford ran to embrace the both of them, as if he hadn't seen them in years. Of course he had, but given the state of uncertainty he had become lost in during the past half hour, he latched onto them like an anchor. "What tipped you two off?"

Buck laughed. "If you must know, it was the command not to have sex with your wife if you were among the resurrectees, the 'sons of the resurrection.'"

Chloe blushed, then chuckled. Then she added, "For me it was the sickening feeling I got when I saw Jesus basically wash his hands of all those boor bastards who had taken the mark of the Beast like frightened children. I thought of the hymn I used to love, 'Jesus, thou art all compassion. Pure unbounded love thou art.' What a crock."

"Yes," Tsion commented, "I admit I had a moment's distress at that. I'm ashamed it was *only* a moment. I guess I was too busy being glad I wasn't *one* of them!"

"Well, if it isn't 'gentle Jesus, meek and mild,'" Chang asked, "who *is* it? Whose game are we playing?"

"Isn't it obvious?" Rayford asked with a returning sense of the determination that had marked him in the old days, before the "Sabbath rest," the enforced idleness of the Millennium. "Consider the big picture. We are dealing with someone who demands unquestioning worship. Who wants to be adored as the savior. Someone who will brook no dissent, no 'heresy.' Someone who rules the whole world from Jerusalem. One who deems himself a god on earth and destroys those who don't believe it. Who speaks to the world through a false image. Remind you of anyone?"

Chloe's turn. "Faked his death, didn't he?"

"Simple for him," agreed Chang.

"Well," said Rayford, with a mix of resignation and rising invigoration, "you boys and girls ready to go into action again? How does the name 'Millennium Force' sound to you?"

They all rose to their feet, ready to shout their acclamation—until they heard a noise at the door. It was Kenny, an adolescent now, who had grown up swiftly during these opening years of the Millennial period. Chloe was surprised to see him and said, "Kenny, honey! What are you doing out? Your father and I . . ."

"Are betraying Jesus," he finished the sentence for her. "It's as I thought. Officers?"

Into the room crowded an arresting party, all in black uniforms, led by the man they had known as Gabriel. "Come along peaceably now. The Potentate has much to discuss with you."

NOTE

1. T. Francis Glasson, *The Second Advent: The Origin of the New Testament Doctrine*, 2nd rev. ed. (London: Epworth Press, 1947), p. 41. To be fair, Glasson was making a serious point, contrasting the absurd excesses of some of the noncanonical apocalypses with the relatively restrained imagery ascribed to Jesus, for example, in the Synoptic Apocalypse. But I think it's pretty damn funny.

APPENDIX 2

Yet More Christian Apocalypse Novels

I know that if I were the reader of this book, I would be eager to see, as I perused the two chapters on Antichrist novels written by Christian authors, if my favorite was included. I would be slightly annoyed if it was not. And yet, as the writer, I realize all too well that I have already given too much space to these books. But then that's what appendices are for. If you have had enough of evangelical End Times novels, feel free to skip to the bibliography—you might actually find that more enjoyable! But if you are still curious about these strange and interesting books, then read on. Let's see if I can get to your favorite.

THEY SAW THE SECOND COMING, BUT NOT THE THIRD

Doug Clark was or perhaps still is the host of a television program called *Amazing Prophecy*. In it he pursues an odd-seeming array of interests: Bible prophecy, economics, and politics. He wrote a book called *How to Survive the Money Crash*, but that is not the one to be discussed here. But it almost could be, because all of the same ideas are represented in another book called *They Saw the Second Coming* (1979). Clark has something of a feel for the political and economic realities that might ensue in the End Times based on the standard fundamentalist biblical projections. As one might guess, the immediate future he once wrote about looks out of date now, such as a reference to the Antichrist's girlfriend relaxing while listening to an eight-track tape, the technological counterpart to a leisure suit. But there is very little such anachronism. Reading Clark's novel has a bit of the feel of reading *The Third World War* or something in that genre: speculative futurism, just this side of hard science fiction. His scenario of how the Beast might use computers to dominate the world economy seems fairly convincing. He doesn't just tell us that the Antichrist did it, period. We get more the feeling that events are unfolding via their own inner logic, and that the biblical seers had simply observed it in advance. By contrast, most other Christian apocalypse novels create the impression that the events are happening with no inner gravity or motivation; they're just being propped up like ducks in a shooting gallery to fulfill one prophecy after another. Clark is at his best describing apocalyptic warfare: the massing and migration of unthinkably vast armies across the continents, the dreaded rain of nuclear bombs, the decimation of the human race as if it were mosquitoes being gassed.

Given Clark's interest in financial survivalism in the face of coming monetary disasters, it should come as no surprise that he is one of our few posttribulationist authors. He seems to feel that real Christians don't pray to be spared the Tribulation; rather, they get ready to weather it—in style! Most of his main characters have lucrative careers as high-society psychiatrists, chiropractors, and so on. Their danger from the Antichrist comes primarily from existing in high-enough social echelons that they may not be able to avoid compromise with him. They have the resources to plan strikes against him and his technology as well as to fortify their own survivalist hideaways during his reign. They are canny enough, like Clark himself, not to depend on the cheap cyber-currency introduced by the Beast. The message comes through loud and clear: buy up gold and silver coins; they'll never go out of style.

One thing Clark's novel shows about the literary use of the Secret Rapture (which of course it *doesn't* use): it packs a more powerful punch than the posttribulation version. If LaHaye and Jenkins are right, the sight of heaps of clothes and empty drivers' seats should scare the hell out of you because it means you're stuck enduring the horrors of the

Antichrist's reign. But if you see your buddies disappear as Jesus is coming back to open the millennium, what the heck—so you're "doomed" to live in an earthly paradise for hundreds of years even if you don't repent, but there's plenty of time to repent anyhow! It's almost like just missing the beginning of a movie you want to see—so what? There'll be another showing soon enough!

They Saw the Second Coming may be plotted out rather easily. The action concerns three sets of interlocking or interrelated families who trade members through the course of the story. The action proceeds along one long vertical/temporal axis, a generational story recounted from memory, then taken up again in the story's present and extending to its conclusion. This trajectory begins with the desperate gambit of a couple of young Jews (Sarah and Moishe, later to be husband and wife) from a Nazi massacre of Jews in Poland. They undergo an odyssey of survival, eventually relocating to Israel, where they pass relaxing decades raising a family. Terror begins to intrude with the shadow of Palestinian violence, itself the adumbration of the soon-coming Antichrist who will turn Hitler-like ferocity on the Jews, forcing them to flee again, this time to the familiar (to us readers!) rock city of ancient Petra. This family has become in-laws with another as one of their soldier sons has married the daughter of a rabbi, and all finally flee together.

The second axis is a horizontal, geographic one, and along it we may plot the course of another pair of related families, this one the wealthy family of chiropractor Steven Scott and that of psychiatrist Raymond MacDonald. Their two wives are sisters. While the Scotts have a young son and daughter, the MacDonalds have an adult daughter, Tonya Rae, who is a technician and a beautiful escort assigned for the (chaste) charming of clients and dignitaries. Other than this, the families function as literary doubles. The Scotts begin as born-again Christians, while the MacDonalds are pushovers and soon come to share the faith. Savvy to Bible prophecy, Steve moves his family from London to South Lake Tahoe, where they construct a cushy lodge in which to wait out the Tribulation in style. The geographical trajectory, then, is the relocation of the Scotts from England to the United States, where they function as the reader's window on the degeneration of American society during the Tribulation. The worst that happens to them is a running gun battle with motorcycle thugs, an exciting sequence. The MacDonalds represents the shadow of the Scotts back in England, their branch office there.

The third "family" is a figurative one, a third collection of related characters. This one consists of the Antichrist and his cohorts. The Antichrist himself is a Greek diplomat and businessman called Stanos Papilos. Yes, it works out neatly to the number value 666, as author Clark points out, besides having the added bonus of suggesting "Satan's pupil." Stanos improbably assumes the presidency of a broad federation of the Common Market and the United States. After a massive invasion of Israel by a juggernaut of soldiery from Russia, Africa, and the Arab States, a great earthquake decimates all these countries and destroys the conquerors, leaving the wrecked nations as Stanos's booty. He restores order to the world with the powers of a seemingly benevolent dictatorship. Soon he announces his intention to move his offices from Rome to Jerusalem, for no real reason (except that, on Clark's interpretation of prophecy, he has to). He does not even own Israel when he moves there! But soon, in defiance of any rational motivation, he seizes the rebuilt temple and converts it into a condo. Jews rebel at this, naturally, and he turns on them. In the meantime, legions of Jews have converted to fundamentalist Protestantism, er, I mean "Completed Judaism." Stanos declares open season on both Orthodox and Christian Jews. Why? For all his verisimilitude in describing military matters, Clark fails to impart any plausibility to the evil wrought by Stanos. Of course, he's only up to such hijinks because, as Clark says once or twice, he's possessed—but by the author, not by the devil.

The two Jewish families become related near the start of the book when one's daughter marries the other's son. Later on we have a negative counterpart, as beautiful Tonya Rae meets Stanos at a corporate social event, dances the night away with him, and impulsively agrees to join his payroll in his planned Jerusalem office. And naturally they become an item. His subsequent nastiness extinguishes her affections, but she sleeps with him as long as she has to in order to carry through a plan she works out between her father (who warned her not to date the Antichrist!) and one of Stanos's bodyguards, to whom Tonya begins to warm. The three of them wire the world supercomputer to blow up, and they take it on the lam. Bingo: the daughter is extricated from the "family" of the Antichrist and restored to the Christian family, all of whom are reunited at the Rapture after Armageddon.

On the whole, one must say the narrative is well written, with plenty of convincing real-world texture. The occasional action scenes are believable. And the climax, the description of the figure of the returning Christ bathed in otherworldly radiance is spun out at risky but effective length in suitably extravagant prose verging on poetry. As a teenage fundamentalist expecting the Second Coming, I always for some reason pictured the returning Jesus as a giant, filling the skies. That is the way Clark pictures him, too, as it turns out. He also gives him jet-black hair, golden skin, and eyes that flash black when preparing to unleash death rays. All in all, just what one ought by rights to expect in an apocalyptic pulp novel!

BAD MOON RISING

In the introduction to his End Times novel *Blood Moon* (1996), Hal Lindsey, notorious author of *The Late Great Planet Earth*, trumpets the fact that this is his very first nonfiction book. Some might doubt that claim. Oh, it's not that *Blood Moon* isn't a piece of fiction. It's just that his other score of prophecy books seem equally sealed off from reality. And, for a novel, this one is way too heavy in terms of exposition. The twenty-first-century action is periodically interrupted by short chapters depicting passages from Genesis, Jeremiah, and even Islamic history, all in a barely narrated form. They are little more than Living Bible paraphrases and expansions of the underlying texts, and the Islamic history (the episode of Muhammad ascending to power in

Yathrib, or Medina) is erroneous: he was invited in to tip the balance of power between feuding factions and he was given the rule of the city in return for his success. According to Lindsey, Muhammad just shows up in Yathrib one day on an evangelistic mission, wins over the Arab majority, and soon thereafter massacres Jews who won't accept Islam. But these vignettes, accurate or inaccurate, are entirely beside the point. Mostly they do not even provide historical parallels by way of foreshadowing for the End Time events. They serve only to break up the main story.

And it's not much of a story to break up. Much as in *They Saw the Second Coming*, the action revolves around four groups of two or three characters. There are three good Americans, left behind in the wake of the pretribulation Rapture. They are kicking themselves because they did not heed the warnings of "saved relatives" who had suggested they read a book called *The Late Great Planet Earth* by a fellow named Hal Lindsey, who we must suppose had been raptured, too, leaving his Porsche to career driverless off the road. (Oh, what fun it would have been to see Lindsey himself cast as the False Prophet!) These three procrastinators are Congressional Medal of Honor winner Jeremy Armstrong (whose battlefield valor counts as nothing without a "personal relationship with Christ" in Lindsey's cultic scheme of things), his old army buddy Zeke Charlton (who is gradually drawn into the service of the Antichrist), and the Maureen O'Hara look-alike Erin . . . O'Hara! They all work for the United Nations, which has grown to become a world government encompassing Europe and America (the latter now a second-rate power, having suffered economic collapse due to the national debt), with a more tenuous hold on the Middle Eastern states. As the sinister nature of the secretary general, one Gianfranco Carlo, becomes clearer, the three depart his employ one by one.

The second trio is a team of Israeli military officers (don't worry—they will eventually become born-again Christians): Captain Isaac Barak and General Ariel Oved, plus a later addition, Sergeant Joshua Schwartz. They do not trust the UN's guarantees of security for Israel and take steps to prepare a secret antimissile system in case of a

Muslim attack, rightly suspecting that the UN would be only too happy to let such a thing happen. They prove to be exactly right. Turning aside a terrorist nuke, they save Tel Aviv, but not before the Israeli prime minister launches a retaliatory strike that vaporizes Damascus (though Syria had nothing to do with it). Standing revealed, the Israeli patriots are barred from their formerly secret facility by UN troops who mean to guarantee it is not used again. When an impending Russian nuclear attack is discovered, Barak, Oved, and Schwartz have to shoot up the UN troops to regain access to the antimissile bunker. They turn aside seventeen of the score of nukes, saving Israel from annihilation—and becoming state criminals in the process! They flee to underground safety in an abandoned bomb shelter for the duration of the book, hearing nuclear shells exploding and endless columns of Russian and Chinese armies marching overhead as Armageddon unfolds. A brief reconnaissance foray embroils them in an exciting battle with UN helicopter gunships, but this, too, they survive. This subplot is by far the most interesting part of the book.

The third group are the trigger-happy terrorists who launched the nuke. Lindsey variously calls them the Sword of Islam and the Flame of Islam. Their loose-cannon leader is the wily Ishmael Muhammad, a direct descendant (and modern-day stand-in for) the Prophet Muhammad, assisted by his compatriot Nayaf Haddad. Ishmael Muhammad proves to be quite as bad a story-stalling expository windbag as Lindsey himself.

The fourth trio is an unholy trinity. Secretary General Carlo is the Antichrist as Endtyrant (who of course gets assassinated, rises from the dead, and is possessed by Satan), Pope John Paul III, and Prophet Elijah ben-David, who is either the president or the prime minister of Israel (Lindsey cannot seem to decide which) and who is also popularly hailed as the Jewish Messiah. As we have seen in our chapter on the Antichrist, this is the historic prototype of the "second Beast," the Antichrist as False Messiah. We are not surprised to see both figures in a novel based on the book of Revelation. What is unexpected is the presence of the antipope. This character occurs so frequently in Antichrist novels, though, he seems to have become a fixture, so Lindsey makes him a second False Prophet. By the way, Lindsey is no Catholic-basher; he concedes that John Paul II was probably a "true believer," unlike his namesake. Keep in mind that, until fairly recently, most Protestants believed not that the Antichrist might have his own counterfeit pope but that the actual pope of the Roman Catholic Church was the Antichrist! Compared to this bigotry, Lindsey and his cohorts sound like ecumenical liberals.

The novel contains the raw material for a genuine story of three-dimensional characters, at least in the first group of characters, Jeremy, Zeke, and Erin. Lindsey builds up to a developing romance between Jeremy and Erin, but it happens too soon and is immediately put into suspended animation as Jeremy is transferred to Israel, where, not surprisingly, he teams up with Barak, Oved, and Schwartz, becoming a colorless and interchangeable fourth among them. Sure, he pines for Erin and says how much he misses her, but their final postapocalyptic reunion is pretty perfunctory, despite the fact that Lindsey tells us how good the sex was. Similarly, there is good potential for an emotional rift between Jeremy and Zeke when the latter seems to sell out his integrity to become Carlo's Himmler, in charge of the persecution of uncooperative evangelicals. But Jeremy splits to Israel, and we hear no more of Zeke until he wanders into Erin's underground Christian commune, repentant and looking for God's forgiveness. It is all pretty abortive.

And yet let it not be said that Lindsey has no imagination. There are scenes in which Barak, Oved, and Jeremy receive ghostlike angelic apparitions, then more subtle assurances directly from Christ or God. The best of these is when, struggling with anxiety in the middle of the night, Jeremy picks up the ringing telephone, hears nothing but hangs on until he hears, or thinks he hears, a whispered "I will return soon. Fear not." All right, Hal! That is a nice moment: eerie, as a contact from the supernatural world ought to be, as Rod Serling knew.

The authors of apocalyptic novels often do not seem to know what to do with the return of Jesus, which is pretty disappointing, since, of course, this is the moment to which the whole story drives. Lindsey first drops the ball, having Jesus appear in the sky in as perfunctory a scene description as those in which he shows Jeremy or General Oved walk into a room. But he makes up for it in the ensuing scenes in which he is unafraid to experiment with Jesus as a genuine fictional character. There are no sudden authorial kid gloves, and the result is pretty effective. Jesus kicks butt! His showdown with the impotent but defiant Satan is very good. He exorcizes the devil from the possessed form of Secretary General Carlo, and the stripped-off corpse rapidly decomposes like a vampire in a Hammer film. Satan appears not as an angel of light but as a black, horned, goat-hoofed, leather-winged monster. He defiantly mocks Jesus, "Well, what's our next move, sonny boy?" After stashing Satan in the Bottomless Pit (presumably without cable television, which a liberal Methodist Jesus would surely have allowed, at least PBS), Lindsey's Jesus finds the antipope cowering in the farthest recesses of the temple, where the pontiff starts making with the excuses. But Jesus, merciful as he may be, is no bleeding heart to be suckered by reminders that he *has* to be forgiving. He pitches the bastard into the pit without a pang.

Lindsey finesses the merciless destruction of the unbelievers by painting them as still rebellious. They're like the thief who's sorry he'll be going to jail but not particularly sorry that he stole the watch—a description similar to that used by Rhett Butler of Scarlet O'Hara (that *name* again!). We just are not shown what would happen if Jesus encountered the Dalai Lama or Mahatma Gandhi. Would he send *them* down the chute to hell? Lindsey doesn't tell us, and I for one do not want to know.

Muhammad and Islam do not come off very well in this decidedly anti-ecumenical tale. It is obvious in Lindsey's other works (especially *Satan Is Alive and Well on Planet Earth*) that he sees no essential distinction between non-Christian faiths and raw, baby-butchering Satanism. For him, if it isn't fundamentalist Christianity, it is satanic. In *Blood Moon*, we get a flashback to the childhood of Muhammad, and it turns out he was demon-possessed even as a kid. And, sure enough, Jesus has a final showdown with terrorist boss Ishmael Muhammad, his modern-day counterpart.

> "This is my holy city!" thundered Jesus in perfect Arabic. "How dare you attempt to defile it?"
>
> Muhammad strode to the front of his column. He yelled out in defiance, "Who are you?"
>
> "I am the Lord thy God," Jesus said, "Who are you?"
>
> "I am sent here on a mission from Allah to reclaim this city," said Muhammad. "I recognize no God but Allah and Muhammad is his one true prophet."
>
> "You are a blasphemer and a murderer," said Jesus. "Get on your knees and beg for forgiveness for all you have done to wreak havoc and death in this world." (p. 313)

Instead, Muhammad draws a gun on Jesus—but finds it difficult to fire with his skin melting and his eyeballs bursting like stepped-on grapes. In our day, one cannot quite take offense at such depictions of Islamist terrorists. One might relish the prospect of a few well-aimed thunderbolts at certain jihadist posteriors.

Ironically, however, it is the liberal reader (if Hal somehow has any) who may be tempted to regard Lindsey as a prophet after all. Remember, this book was published in 1996 and speculated on developments in the twenty-first century. The World Trade Center disaster was five years in the future. But Lindsey depicts the Antichrist imposing the totalitarian system of the mark of the Beast as a security measure (p. 213): "He used as his excuse the 'war on terrorism'"!

Just as we find in the LaHaye/Jenkins finale, *Glorious Appearing*, the Bible has lost none of its central importance even after the Second Coming of Christ. Lindsey's Jesus tells his people to keep on reading that Bible. But that just cannot be! Here Jesus Christ, the living Word of God, has appeared. It is the ultimate Parousia of Truth, which will allow us to know as we are known. In the face of this revelation all fragments of knowledge and prophecy must wither away like a baby's picture books in the wake of a postgraduate education. And we must still read the Bible, full of contradictions and ambiguities? Surely the Buddhist parable is right: once we have poled our way across the river to the farther shore of Enlightenment, we can have no further use for the raft! Or to paraphrase Galatians, if we still need the Bible, then Christ returned in vain. It just goes to prove, as if further proof were required, that fundamentalism is not so much Christ-centered, as it likes to claim, but rather Bible-centered.

But perhaps there is even more to it. Maybe there is a built-in limitation that stops our apocalyptic novelists from making the leap from walking by faith in the Bible to walking by the light of the Lamb. They are bound by the same restriction that binds participants in actual messianic movements. Imagine their inevitable predicament: they have anticipated the passing away of history as we know it, its dissipation like the morning mist with the rising of the messianic sun. The kingdoms of this world will have become the kingdom of our Lord and of his Christ. There will be no more temple, because God will henceforth make his dwelling among mortals. And the ostensible Messiah steps onto the stage of history. And history does not end. It never does. In Paul Tillich's terms, the world of finitude is beset by ambiguities, especially including the lack of clarity of truth. That is what necessitates faith under the conditions of this age. But the Messiah is expected to bring in a new age whereupon all will be made clear. And it is not. He leaves again, is succeeded by a new dynasty, replaced by an all-too-human vicar who is stuck poring over an ambiguous scripture (even if a new one), the same as the rest of us. The final Truth has been deferred yet again! Colossians 2:17 boasts that Christianity replaced the mere shadow of Judaism with the substance of Jesus Christ, but did Christianity do any more than substitute new doctrines and rituals for old ones? People are not freed from sinning. They just have a different set of hoops to jump through to get forgiveness. If historical messiahs cannot create a qualitatively new world for their followers, how can a mere novelist be expected to jump beyond the inherent limitations of this finite, ambiguous world? The Buddhists are right: there is about as much chance of describing that world of Blessed Otherness *before entering it* as there is of a frog conveying to a tadpole what it is like to breathe air and hop around on land. Ultimately, the apocalyptic genre just cannot succeed. But that's okay. That's the way it is with all religious symbols: they can only point to the reality, not describe it.

DAY OF INSANITY

William A. Stanmeyer's *Day of Iniquity: A Prophetic Novel of the End Times* (1999) is one of the rare Roman Catholic entries in our field. But that fact makes less difference than one might expect. Here, too, one is warned that a true Christian is one who cultivates "a personal relationship with Jesus Christ" (it's even placed in quotation marks in the text!). In this we see the result of the single greatest, albeit unsung, ecumenical advance (if one wants to call it that) in modern Christian history. In February 1967 a group of Duquesne University faculty organized a weekend student retreat to pray and to discuss *The Cross and the Switchblade* by Assemblies of God urban evangelist David Wilkerson. This event ignited the Catholic Charismatic, or Catholic Pentecostal, Movement. Subsequently, parish evangelism everywhere in the American Church has included revivalism, personal conversionism, in its education program. Once Roman Catholics assimilated to this all-important tenet of fundamentalist Protestantism, the demise of the old Protestant-Catholic enmity was ensured. Protestants, especially fundamentalists, were still not too wild about worshiping the Virgin Mary, but in many quarters this antipathy seemed to drop back to the level of a secondary objection, say, the kind of qualm Baptists had about Presbyterian infant baptism: it stuck in your craw, but you could live with it.

An interesting difference between Protestant and Catholic treatments of eschatological themes is the Catholic reliance not just upon the obscure texts of scripture, but also on the (sometimes even more obscure!) predictions of monks, nuns, anorexics, and fanatics (in other words, the usual gang of suspects) ranging from the Middle Ages to today's fervid conventicles of sectarians who fancy themselves more

Catholic than the pope. Yet even here the difference is not so great as might be imagined, since Protestants, too, have larded the prophetic scenario with plenty of their own innovations, not least the unwieldy apparatus of dispensational theology, which has produced the pretribulation Rapture out of exegetical thin air. In light of that, what's an extra comet or two? Or Mary kicking Satan's blistered butt?

Speaking of Mariology/Mariolatry, *Day of Iniquity* opens right up with a dose of it. We see Mary in heaven, approaching the throne of the Heavenly Father. She offers to him a blue orb, which, like a crystal ball, depicts the flashing, passing sights of Catholics praying, doing penance, resisting temptations, whatnot, down on earth. In return for these pieties (implying a bizarre quantification of sin and righteousness right out of the Dark Ages, if you ask me), she seeks a favor. Will Jehovah please allow that Pope John Paul II may continue to live on through at least the beginning of the Tribulation? God grants the boon, and we see the towering, shining form of Michael the archangel dispatched to watch over him. John Paul II? Living to see the End Time Tribulation? Well, can't win 'em all, I guess.

Stanmeyer's *Day of Iniquity* is a particularly good example of the distinction Rudolf Bultmann drew between theology and mythology. What is the difference? Mythology depicts the Transcendent in objectifying terms. For instance, God, who infinitely transcends our order of being, is depicted as a being basically like us and as merely living vertically far above us in space. Or, as Tillich would say, myth drags down the Ultimate into the immanent, worldly realm of cause and effect, as if God were one more cause in a series. God, properly considered Being itself (as per the whole sweep of historic Christian theology, Eastern and Western), is reduced to the status of *a being*, even if it is the supreme being. Stanmeyer's opening scene, a kind of equivalent to the heavenly prologue of the book of Job, portrays heavenly entities as earthly beings, actors in the same story and in the same sense as human characters to whom we will shortly be introduced, including investigative reporter Pat Greene and Father Michael Kanek. The ensuing Armageddon (as in all these books—I do not mean to pick on Stanmeyer in particular) will be in principle no different from, say, the *JLA* miniseries *Paradise Lost*, in which the angel Zauriel, in disfavor because he has fallen in love with the earthly woman he had been assigned to watch over, calls in the Justice League to help turn back a palace revolution in heaven. We are treated to the exciting spectacle of the Martian Manhunter and Green Lantern slugging it out with bull- and eagle-headed angels right out of Ezekiel's vision! Those who objectify divine powers as mundane players in our novels are inviting us to take their apocalypses no more seriously than the parallel comic books. In the same way, the encounter between Satan and the returned Jesus in Hal Lindsey's *Blood Moon* is pretty much indistinguishable from such a scene between Loki and Thor in Marvel Comics. What can top this line, or this level, of theological discourse, from *Day of Iniquity*? "God the Father authorized the Blessed Mother to deal with this satellite" (p. 155). Is this great pulp theology, or *what*?

Again: I happen to love such comics and pulp fiction, as well as such End Times novels, so I'm not wagging the finger. It's just that, if, as Mr. Stanmeyer assures his readers in the introduction to the novel, you believe that angels and demons are invisibly brushing past you running their errands every day, you are verging perilously close to the cultist Exidor on the old *Mork and Mindy* show. Every once in a while, the gaunt, robed figure would recoil with no apparent cause and yell, "Stop tickling me!"

I suppose it is inevitable by now that the author of such a book as this will seek to buttress his theological credibility with a short course in (futile) apologetics:

> [I]f you're going to believe in *any* God, he had decided [with all the theological acumen of a college freshman], the Christian one was the only one that made any sense. Hell, this Jesus person was so . . . *concrete*. Here's a fellow, he had come to realize, who goes around doing *practical* things like changing whole jugs of water into wine . . . feeding 5,000 hungry men . . . walking on water . . . curing people with leprosy . . . giving sight to the blind . . . raising a man from the dead and then *predicting* and actually *doing* it for *Himself!* How could anyone

make that stuff up? Those Apostle guys were just not that bright. And besides, they had all been willing to *die* for their testimony, which most people living in the same city as their killers had ample ways to check out. If the stories were a bunch of lies, everybody would know it, and most of the disciples would have cracked under torture within a couple of days—they wouldn't have conquered the whole damn Roman Empire in a few hundred years. (p. 10)

Well, need I say it? Just about everything's wrong with this. First, one might venture that Jewish and Islamic God-concepts, unburdened as they are with the Brand X arithmetic of the Trinity, might qualify as "making better sense" (if that matters in the case of hypothetical realities far beyond human ken) than Christian theism. Second, notice the minor profanity: rhetoric to make these specious arguments sound like they are impressive to an unbiased outsider, not only to the pious, holy scapular-wearing devotee who authored these words. Third, how "practical" is it to create hundreds of gallons of wine for a feast where everyone is already, as the host points out (John 2:10), smashed? Is walking on water "practical"? Impressive, yes, but is it an alternate mode of travel Jesus invented? And if we are counting practicality as a criterion of true miracles, wouldn't it have been much more practical for Jesus to have invented a cure for leprosy, blindness, and so on, than just to heal one man (or a few)? If he had done that, we might have had some proof that he had come from outside the time stream, from a divine realm where no mists of ignorance obscured such medical secrets. Then we would have known we were not just reading culture-bound fantasies. Who could have made that stuff up, you know, the stuff of the Gospels? Well, ask any of the spinners of similar tales in contemporary healing religions and hero cults.

Fourth, did Jesus predict his own resurrection? I guess it's safe to say Stanmeyer has never studied redaction criticism. The only such prediction appears in Matthew 12:40, where, as comparison with Mark 8:11–12, Matthew's source, reveals, the prediction has been gratuitously added by the later evangelist. Fifth, did Jesus rise from the dead? That is hardly a piece of evidence for something else when it remains a storm center of controversy and doubt in its own right. Sixth, it is cute to appeal to the thickheadedness of the disciples when it is handy for apologetics' sake, but Stanmeyer takes quite a different tone when appealing to them as the patrons and guarantors of the authority of the pope and the bishops (p. 21). I think they used to call it *casuistry*. Seventh, how can we appeal to the courage of the apostles to die as martyrs as a way to prove they hadn't been making it all up? In fact, we don't know how any of them died. The famous martyrdoms of Peter, Paul, and others occur only in fabulous apocryphal texts of the second century, which no historian otherwise credits with any historical value at all. Besides, all fundamentalists, whether Protestant or Catholic, have no trouble at all believing that Mormon founder Joseph Smith made up his whole story of discovering the golden plates with an angel's guidance—and yet he died for his faith. Eighth, the stories of Jesus told by the earliest preachers may indeed have been debunked by their contemporaries. Even the Gospels record critics' opinions that Jesus was a sorcerer, a drunk, a glutton, and a madman. It's just that Jesus' fans were no more willing to believe in these criticisms than modern followers of the discredited Peter Popoff, Guru Maharaj Ji, Jim Bakker, Jimmy Swaggart, or Bhagwan Shree Rajneesh. In any case, the Gospels were written after the fall of Jerusalem when all of Jesus' contemporaries were safely dead. Ninth, it was not the immediate followers of Jesus who took over the Roman Empire but later generations who had no way of knowing whether any of the Gospel tales were true. And, tenth, the dramatic expansion of Christianity no more proves its truth than the even more astonishing spread of Islam and Mormonism vouches for their veracity.

The fundamentalist Protestant reader may be egging on the intratextual apologist—until the same arguments are used to defend the authenticity of the Marian apparitions at Fatima! And the Protestant, who can see through such sophistry in such a case, had best start taking a second look at the cases where he thinks the same arguments are convincing, for example, for the resurrection of Jesus.

The most ironic thing of all, however, must be the fact that, while Stanmeyer scoffs at the very notion of early Christians making up miracle stories about Jesus, he himself feels no qualms about creating completely fictitious supernatural adventures about Pope John Paul II within the latter's lifetime! "Oh," he (or a reader) might object, "but everybody realizes this is edifying fiction, that it's not to be taken for history!" Yeah, and how do you know the Gospel writers wouldn't have said the same thing?

Does Stanmeyer think it's heresy to theorize that Paul and Peter did not pen some of the epistles attributed to them? He does the same damn thing when he creates a "Last Testament" letter from John Paul II to be delivered to all loyal bishops once he is replaced by a counterfeit pope. In this fictive document, written by Stanmeyer, remember, while John Paul II was still alive, the pope is made a crackpot creationist railing against evolution. And this at the very time the *real* John Paul, the "historical John Paul," was publicly repudiating creationism and calling evolution "no mere theory."

Similarly, Stanmeyer derides as heresy the notion that early Christians fabricated the sayings they ascribed to Jesus (p. 57), and yet on the very same page he unwittingly provides a perfect example of the reasoning that led Bultmann and others to posit exactly this. "More than once, those bothersome one-liners that Jesus sprinkled into His public life kept popping into his mind: '*What does it profit a man if he gain the whole world but lose his immortal soul?* and '*I would have you hot or cold, but the lukewarm I will spew out of My mouth*'" (p. 57). Two things to notice: first, Stanmeyer has unconsciously embellished the first saying (Mark 8:36), which does not use the word "immortal" and may thus not be considering the issue of life after death at all. Second, more seriously, the other saying is a slight contraction of Revelation 3:15b–16, which is presented as an oracle from the ascended Christ, through his angel, to John the Revelator on the Isle of Patmos near the end of the first century. It does not purport to be a saying of the historical Jesus; that is, it is not a saying from his earthly ministry. Stanmeyer has forgotten where he read the saying and simply assumed the earthly Jesus said it. That is just what Bultmann said must have happened in numerous cases when the early Christians ascribed indifferently to Jesus remembered sayings from his earthly days and recent revelations through Christian prophets like John on Patmos. They had no way of telling the difference and, not being historians, no reason to try. There is nothing insidious here, as Stanmeyer thinks. He actually says that liberal Catholics embrace such critical judgments by means of satanic hypnosis! "Such thoughts were subtly inserted into his mind by an invisible being assigned to shadow him" (p. 58). Stop tickling me!

This book, for all its schoolboy apologetics, swerves between paranoia and superstition. As to the paranoia: "John didn't much care for television news. It was canned, the doctored product reflecting a truncated world view of elitist commentators and 'anchormen' who were high paid propagandists for secular humanism" (p. 106). What, they're not even real "anchormen"? At any rate, the good Catholic characters prefer to get their news analysis from sectarian flysheets with titles like *McAlvaney Intelligence Advisor* and *Remnant Review* and books of modern prophecy transcripts like "Sadie Jaramillo's *THE GREAT SIGN: Messages and Visions of Final Warnings*" (p. 107). This is not very far from the demented plunge undertaken by Johnny Smith's mother in *The Dead Zone*. She had delved into a bizarre netherworld of fanatical booklets and poorly printed tabloids filled with revelations from various angels and UFOs.

Once the Antichrist gets busy preparing for his takeover, the pope vanishes into hiding, and the bad guys fake his death, electing one of their own as the new antipope, a no-good theological liberal. The Satanized Church draws up a *hit list* of conservative Catholics (even laypeople!). One of them is John de Santo, a former fighter pilot and now commercial aviator. He is rescued by angelic intervention when a bunch of Germans stationed at a launching platform in northern Indiana try to take him out with a surface-to-air missile! Just for saying the Rosary and believing in Transubstantiation! And why are there German troops stationed in the United States (along with other foreign nationals)? The Antichrist has smuggled them in to pave the way for an international takeover. How does anyone know this? You guessed it: pretty much the same way presidential candidate Pat Robertson "knew" there were still Soviet missiles in Cuba. Uneducated Stratolounger seers uttered these prophetic bulletins, and they're more credible than the networks.

So much for the paranoia; now for the superstition. The characters conclude that the severe weather of recent years "is part of the punishment for our sins" (p. 107). The author likes to compare the innate moral sense we ought to have to the gyroscope in an airplane, which tells the pilot when he is not flying right even when, according to all other impressions, he is. Well, we need the same thing when it comes to religion. The minute we start explaining inclement weather as a sign of Zeus's disfavor, we have kissed scientific thinking good-bye and returned to the superstitions of Cro-Magnon man who cringed at the storm and sought to mollify his totems with blood sacrifice. So much for the smug intellectual pretensions of Catholicism the author tries to hide behind.

His writing, one has to admit, is better by a thousand times than that of genre pioneer Salem Kirban, though that is pretty faint praise. We find some mixed metaphors that call a momentary halt to the narrative flow: "the warp and woof of much science fiction . . . was pockmarked with fantastic essays about life on . . . these planets" (p. 84). Other times, Stanmeyer tries to simulate natural conversation, generally successfully, but sometimes with a labored self-consciousness, especially between men and women: "Hey, buster, thanks for the compliment, but flattery will get you not one inch farther than your honorable intentions" (p. 220). Nobody talks like this. And if one did, we would have him committed. Or try this one on for size: "On one condition: you bring Talkmeister-the-Bonbon-Supplier along. Every *Directed Study* course I teach has to have at least two students in the class" (p. 54). Okay, even if you knew what the sickeningly cutesy language is referring to, if somebody said something like this in real life, you'd have no choice but to slug him.

The novel seems to reach out to Protestant evangelicals who may have picked up the book by mistake, thinking it one of theirs. And it eventually tries to set them straight vis-à-vis the Rapture: there's not going to be one: "The Rapture, . . . as most Evangelicals understand it, does not really appear in Scripture. In my opinion, they take texts that refer to the Second Coming of Christ and invent what can only be called an Intermediate Coming, which thus adds a Third Coming, a final one" (p. 221). Bingo! (Pardon the expression.)

But the grassroots Catholicism of seers and oracles on display in this book has its own unscriptural equivalent to the Rapture, namely, the Warning. Perhaps the advantage of the Warning over the Rapture is that no one even pretends the Warning is a scriptural idea, coming as it does from the utterances of rec-room sibyls and suburban stigmatics. What is the Warning? Reminiscent of the eponymous scene from the Ray Bradbury science fiction classic *The Day the Earth Stood Still*, the Warning is a sudden worldwide suspension of all motion, even the passage of time, as each and every individual witnesses a private review his or her own moral failures hosted by a peeved Divine Voice. This is perhaps the most effective sequence in the novel, as one character witnesses her life of sins as if on an episode of *Biography*, including eerie rebukes and plaints from the daughter she aborted. Only in the vision, she sees her growing up as she *would have* been. Then she sees herself descending a flight of stairs to what appears to be a smelting furnace, only she knows it is hell, and she is aging and fraying with every downward step. Will she repent before it is too late?

Though this interruption, this sacred visitation, has happened to everyone in the world, the secular humanist TV networks downplay, rationalize, and pooh-pooh the whole thing, as they do the Rapture in Protestant novels of this kind. But the message does get through to many, and they promptly turn from their sins. And some of those "sins" will bring most non-Catholic readers up short in surprise. One of my favorite Johnny Hart "B.C." cartoons gives the *Wiley's Dictionary* definition of "mishmash" as what happens when a guy is too hung over to attend church the next morning. Stanmeyer's God considers missing mass a serious offense against the Divine Dignity. A pouting Jehovah rebukes a Catholic backslider: *"Mass is not a fashion show . . . I came to you expecting love, but you didn't even show Me courtesy . . ."* (pp. 177–78, italics and ellipses in the original). Stanmeyer represents that kind of excessive Roman Catholic devotion in which worship has itself become the object of worship. An even more creepy, mutant specimen of Catholic hothouse piety: in their Warning visions, priests "felt the pain they inflicted on Jesus in the Eucharist for hiding Him in little boxes on plain walls in tiny rooms instead of enthroning Him in a golden tabernacle where the people would be motivated to pray to Him" (p. 184). Let me get this straight: we are talking about the pitiful sorrows of *wafers of bread in a box?* That is some weird, wild stuff.

But it gets weirder: a devout Catholic FBI agent finds himself walking through the wreckage of a defiled chapel he used to attend, now in ruins thanks to rioting pagan thugs. He is dismayed at the blasphemous sight of three eucharistic wafers lying on the floor, and just then the hooligans return, armed. That the three hosts may not be further dishonored, the agent bursts into action, firing on the thugs and getting shot as he makes a dash for it, scooping up each wafer and gulping it down just in time—before he falls dead. In Mark 2:25–28, Jesus cites the example of David violating the sanctity of the reserved sacrament (the "show bread") in order to satisfy the hunger of his famished men. How far (in the wrong direction) we have come when it is worth sacrificing one's life to preserve the dignity of three wafers.

Hoo boy, but Stanmeyer hates those liberals! They are those who "had given their heart to the whore of new age Modernism" (p. 184). We learn that modernist theologian "Franz Jung" (Hans Küng), decredentialed by John Paul II, is a likely choice for promotion in the new regime of the antipope. On the other hand, one of Stanmeyer's heroes is "Rendoll Berry" (Randall Terry), a radical antiabortionist and avowed theocrat. The arrogant Terry was quoted in the *Fort Wayne (IN) News Sentinel* (August 16, 1993) as telling his minions: "Our goal is a Christian nation. . . . We have a biblical duty, we are called by God to conquer this country. We don't want equal time. We don't want plu-

ralism. . . . Theocracy means God rules. I've got a hot flash. God rules."
Well, isn't that special.

Then again, maybe there is something to the "private messages"
Stanmeyer and his characters have been soaking up. Keep in mind, *Day
of Iniquity* was written in the year 1999. It still anticipates the apocalyptic
possibilities of Y2K, which of course actually came to nothing. But then
Stanmeyer has the president order a unilateral attack on Saddam Hussein's Iraq. The fact that it is the first unprovoked American invasion of
another country sparks both domestic and international outrage and the
isolation of America. Following the invasion, America undergoes four
synchronized terrorist strikes in New York, Chicago, Atlanta, and Los
Angeles. These provide the excuse for the president to impose martial
law for the sake of domestic security. Despite the protests of civil liber-
tarians of all stripes, constitutional liberties swiftly erode, and not by
accident: the whole thing, including the bombings, was a scheme of the
Antichrist, the chairman of the Council of Europe, to whom the American president has sold out. It all sounds eerily familiar! But Stanmeyer's
luck (or prophetic afflatus) runs out at last: in his scenario, Saddam pre-
vails, nuking two of our warships and crippling all future war efforts,
softening up all the nations for the Antichrist's dominion.

Finally, just as we have seen how LaHaye and Jenkins, as well as
Lindsey, cannot see past the Bible even once the Living Word himself
has appeared, we must note that Stanmeyer is such an ardent papist that
he cannot imagine a day when a pope will no longer be necessary.
Though he never depicts the return of Jesus (whose place as mediator
and savior is almost entirely usurped in this book by his mother), he
does have a concluding scene set in the post-Parousia paradise. And the
big climax is that one of the book's heroes, Father Michael Kanek, the
last surviving bishop secretly appointed by John Paul II, has now been
named pope. John Paul was eventually martyred and so is unavailable
for the job. But, uh, wait a minute! Isn't the pope supposed to be "the
vicar of Christ on earth," his earthly stand-in while Christ is away in
heaven? Then what the heck do we need a pope for when Jesus himself
has returned in person?! It's exactly analogous to Lindsey and the

Protestants with the Bible. For the Protestant fundamentalist, the Bible is the vicar of Christ. And when Christ himself returns, they still prefer the Bible! Stanmeyer still prefers the pope. Now there's a Catholic for you!

EIGHT TOO MANY

Yes, *Eight Books Opened* is subsidy published, and that's no surprise. One hopes Larry Hawk Williams, a minister in the Pentecostal denomination the Church of God in Christ, did not have to spend too much to have his "novel of the second coming of Christ" printed, given the awful editing job they did for him. Caesar, Gandhi, and Buddha all misspelled on the same page? Then there's "Adolph" for "Adolf" Hitler and "diefy" for "deify." "Now" becomes "not" at a crucial point. But why go on?

This book barely fits into our purview, as it concerns the Final Judgment scene itself, not the End Times, the Tribulation, the Antichrist, and so on. Well, maybe the author deemed that a burned-over district. In any case, the bulk of this book is the backstories of eight people facing the Judgment Seat of the not-very-merciful Messiah. There are sob stories and soap operas aplenty. And only two of the eight make it to heaven. One is a young minister ("Hawk Riley," a surrogate for the author, I'm guessing) who had to wade hip-deep through muddy rivers of slander and discrimination for years to carry out his unsung ministry. The other is a bloodthirsty Ku Klux Klan hooligan who is brought to repentance in a racially integrated tent meeting. But the caricatures are so outrageous that Williams somehow manages to make you feel he's being unfair to the Klan! Nonetheless, that remains the only poignant or striking of the eight fictive biographies, all of which are basically summarized, not recounted naturalistically.

Reverend Williams detests homosexuality, viewing it in medieval terms. I disagree with those who believe homosexuality is immoral, but I do not automatically deem their opinion "homophobia." Yet what else can one call the hysterical approach of Williams?

> Ernest was in awe. John had just come in from playing basketball and was clad in a tee shirt and shorts. Ernest looked at him and fell in love. Ernest didn't know it then, but an evil spirit, a dark, black, hideous demon had just entered him. It filled his heart with vile, ugly thoughts. Thoughts that were in opposition to all that GOD had commanded. It had roamed the earth since the days of Sodom, seeking a new host body. Ernest's soul accepted it gladly. (p. 79)

Naturally Ernest goes on to become a well-known media advocate for "the gay agenda." He is finally murdered in bed, his throat slit by his lover. I guess that's what's liable to happen to you gay demoniacs, so wise up!

Reverend Ike and the Prosperity Gospel come in for a drubbing as well. When an aspiring religious con artist seeks out the notorious "Reverend Mike" for some professional tips, his new mentor places him under the tutelage of his own patron, one Leon Matthison. Author Williams cannot quite decide just what sort of bad guy he wants Matthison to be, how thickly he wants to tar the Prosperity Gospel he is blaming on Matthison. "Matthison is a Satanist" (p. 169). "Leon Matthison was a well known spiritist and new age preacher. He was an advocate of the extermination of the organized church and organized religion, and pushed for a religion based on secular humanism. He consorted with witches and warlocks and was a willing tool of satan [*sic*]" (p. 172). Except for the Satan business, he almost sounds like the whole Unitarian Universalist Association rolled into one! But it's hard to imagine a single individual holding all these opinions and allegiances at once. This shotgun attack on heresies, which we find in Hal Lindsey and many others, simply denotes that Pentecostals and fundamentalists see the whole world around them as so many slight variations on a theme, "rival" products manufactured by the same company side by side on the same shelf: if they're not with us they're against us, and that's all we need to know!

Despite the occasional flashes of descriptive imagination, which are most likely what caused someone to tell Williams he could write in the first place, *Eight Books Opened* is bad writing and bad theology.

ALL AGOG

Baptist pastor Ted Duncan's trilogy *A Snowball's Chance* (1980, repr., 2001), *Aaron's Rod* (2003), and *Gog's Revenge* (2004) has the distinction of being the first apocalyptic series published after the LaHaye/Jenkins opus *Left Behind*. In minor ways Duncan's series sets out to correct its longer rival theologically. For instance, Duncan has only the children of raptured fundamentalists disappear along with them, not all babies, explaining in an appendix that scripture never promises a free ride to the offspring of the damned. And the saints are not caught up nude, as in *Left Behind* and most of the other books in which their clothes are left in suddenly emptied heaps. Duncan skewers LaHaye and Jenkins by having the wily Antichrist argue that the disappearance of millions could not have been the Rapture because no empty suits were left behind, while many infants were! Take *that*, LaHaye and Jenkins! More seriously, Duncan opts for a Tribulation of only three and a half years, equating the Tribulation proper with what LaHaye deems the *Great* Tribulation, the second, violent half when the Antichrist has revealed his true colors. Duncan also adopts the stricter version of Tribulation soteriology: no one who had the chance to accept the evangelical message before the Rapture is going to have another chance afterward. It's not that some of them won't *want* to. No, God will no longer supply the powerful conviction of the Spirit, which Duncan imagines him dispensing to the converted with virtually Calvinistic sovereignty— whether the convert wants it or not. But once the Christ is replaced by the Antichrist, one will try in vain to pray the sinner's prayer at the back of the *Four Spiritual Laws* booklet.

Unless, of course, one is a Jew. A good dispensationalist, Duncan has the machinery crank up to usher in a new dispensation, one in which the old "prophetic time clock" starts up again, and Jews assume their old position at the center of the salvific stage. So we see Orthodox Jews converting to Protestant fundamentalism left and right once their exegetical judgment has been raptured away. As in *Left Behind*, we witness the silly spectacle of Jews, who know much better, getting gulled by the Holy Spirit into accepting absurd, grossly anticontextual proof texts for Jesus being the promised Messiah of Israel. One can see the grotesque effects of trying to make born-again Christian devotionalism the natural outgrowth of Judaic messianism in cringingly awful passages like these, describing the thoughts of newly Jesus-converted Orthodox Jews: "[A]fter spending time in prayer with his newly accepted Messiah, Aaron took advantage of the time alone" (p. 58). "Jesus of Nazareth is the Messiah of Israel [Saul confessed]. I know that now. But I want Him as my own Messiah. Son, tell me what I need to do" (p. 101).

Duncan's faith in divine sovereignty comes in handy, making his story perhaps a bit too easy to tell. Too often he moves the action along by divine (authorial) fiat. If he wants a crowd to follow somebody they don't know, one of God's agents, he simply has God mysteriously move them to do so. The heroes suddenly know what they must do next because God has inspired the knowledge. Unlikely prospects get converted because God decides they will. Other authors face a bit more of a challenge: they have to supply narrative motivation. Any author wants to have something happen for the sake of the plot, but he has to convince us that his characters have their own reasons for wanting it to happen as well. Otherwise it is not much of a story. Think how lame the biblical story of Joseph (a masterpiece!) would be without the scene of Joseph finally revealing to his brothers, "You meant it for evil, but God meant it for good." Duncan's story suffers somewhat from the lack of character motivation. Everything is deus ex machina, interventions of the writer from offstage.

The same issue occurs in a more fundamental sense in all novels that try to flesh out the End Times scenario of the Bible. We are assured that everything is under control despite all the chaotic appearances: God has unleashed some of the chaos in punishment on the human race, but the rest of it, too fiendish to ascribe to God's will, he has merely allowed on the part of Satan and the demons who apparently wish they could do even more evil! God (seemingly arbitrarily) protects 144,000 of his special agents from all harm during the Tribulation, but others he sends like sheep to the slaughter. This much all our novelist-theologians are stuck with: the Bible makes it so. But that is only to say the biblical writers themselves were in the same tight spot: ancient seers or modern novelists, both were stuck depicting an epic battle to the death that turns out to be a sham, since God could have won the thing in the first round with one divine hand tied behind him! Why did he let the whole bloody mess continue? There is a tension in the texts that stems ultimately from the unstable theology underlying them. Back in chapter 1, I suggested that Jews eagerly adopted what they could of Zoroastrian dualism, positing Satan as an evil opponent of Yahve, so as to blame all evil on the former, absolving the latter. The cosmic warfare of the apocalyptic worldview is part and parcel of this dualism. But at just the same time Jews were trying to secure the newly minted doctrine of monotheism, so they couldn't make Satan an equal and opposite deity as Zoroastrians made their antigod Ahriman. The result was an adversary to God who was far from being God's equal and thus was no real foe. He was just on a long leash, and that leash was in reality a long coil of rope with which Satan should eventually hang himself. There was never any chance Satan could have won. But, to avoid seeming to blame God for evil, adversity and misfortune were heaped on Satan as soon as they raised their ugly heads. It is thus the logical conflict between a dualistic theodicy and the assertion of monotheistic sovereignty that created the charade character of Revelation and of novels based on it.

Aaron's Rod centers on a young Orthodox Jew, converted at the Rapture, who has been inducted into the ranks of God's 144,000 witnesses, spreading the Gospel among fellow Jews (and some others) during the Tribulation. Aaron Muller had been one of a group of college chums who had been pulled into a criminal intrigue surrounding the mob fixing the outcome of college basketball games in the first book of the trilogy, *A Snowball's Chance*. As that book is strictly preliminary to the eschatological action that begins only in *Aaron's Rod*, I have elected to skip it here. Suffice it to say that Aaron had proven his worth in fundamentalist eyes in the first volume by helping blow up the Dome of the

Rock in Jerusalem so that the Jewish temple might be erected in its place. He takes center stage in *Aaron's Rod*. He is a good choice for a focal character, but (perhaps inevitably) Duncan borrows too many pop culture associations in providing detail for Aaron's character. A guardian angel leads him to fashion a rod that works miracles like that of Moses' brother Aaron in the Exodus. Beyond this, Aaron Muller finds he possesses new physical strength, endurance, and agility to aid him in his upcoming struggle with the Antichrist and his hordes. In other words, Aaron has become Buffy the Vampire Slayer. At one point he bluffs his way past a group of guards using the same Jedi mind trick Obi-wan Kenobi uses in *Star Wars*. And then Duncan rubs it in by having a delighted onlooker quote *Star Wars* chapter and verse! You know, if one insists on comparing the Rapture with getting "beamed up" on *Star Trek* (which Duncan does quite often), one is asking the reader to take this allegedly biblically based preachment about as seriously.

One thing about the elite fraternity of 144,000 of which Aaron is a part: they are celibate. "It is these who have not defiled themselves with women, for they are virgins" (Rev. 14:4). Aaron has a girlfriend whom he loves, but during the Tribulation, while he is off rescuing new Christians (whom he has put in danger by converting them in the first place!), he can do no more than give her a kiss maybe once a year. In light of this we must take a second, Freudian look at his weapon of choice: a *wooden staff* from which he fires off flame jets to consume the bad guys. It's called sublimation; get used to it.

The one disturbing element of Duncan's eschatological expectation is his way of handling the problem of evil and suffering. How can those redeemed and delivered by divine grace from the horrors of the Tribulation (and hell to follow) possibly experience the bliss of heaven, knowing too well of the grueling suffering of unsaved loved ones? Such a consideration might incline one to posit a doctrine of universal salvation: for God to "wipe away every tear" would then mean that no one will be suffering, and thus no one will be suffering *over* that suffering. But no. Duncan's perverse solution is to atrophy the compassion of the saved. They will simply cease to give a flying frack about their old friends and their relatives, and this Duncan calls a superior, enlightened state of mind.

> Great multitudes were absent from their gathering [at the Rapture]—those who had failed to place their confidence in the finished work of Jesus Christ. But it didn't diminish their joy. That fact would have broken their mortal hearts in their former state of existence, but it was accepted without the slightest difficulty by their now enlightened minds. They were able to see things as God sees them. They were able to praise Him for His infinite mercy and grace manifested toward themselves as believers; with equal enthusiasm, they were able to praise Him for His infinite wrath and judgment visited upon those who had rejected His truth. [I'll bet Eva Braun felt the same way about Auschwitz.]
>
> The Bible study saints [a group from the previous book] were well aware of the absence of Tony D'Angelo, but it didn't devastate them. Pastor Bobby, who had wept and prayed for his conversion, and who had been emotionally devastated by his determined refusal to accept Christ, now accepted the young man's fate with calm resignation as being the will of his perfect and just Heavenly Father.
>
> The same was true of Scott Graham, who had been Tony's best friend. He had agonized over his friend's unbelief during the two brief days of his own experience [before the Rapture] as a born-again Christian, but now Tony's absence did not weigh upon his heart at all.
>
> Something else had also radically changed in his emotional makeup. Before the rapture he had been hopelessly in love with Candace Mercer, and she with him. Especially after his conversion, they had been flooded with romantic feelings toward each other.... But now, Scott and Candy loved each other with an even greater love, yet with one that had been transformed. They loved each other in exactly the same way as they loved each and every one of the other saints of God. Gone were all thoughts of romance and the desires for sexual union.... These emotions belonged to their former lives ... to their lives as spiritual children ... and now they had come of age. (pp. 22–23)

This description reminds one of nothing so much as a scene in the classic movie *Invasion of the Body Snatchers*, in which a man's friends, whose minds have already been taken over by space aliens, try to persuade the hero and his girlfriend that they are being foolish to resist yielding to the alien intelligence. The transformation, they insist, is nothing to fear. One retains one's memories and personality, only without intense emotions such as love. Good riddance, eh? One only wishes evangelical readers might take a second look at a passage like this and see the moral repugnance of their religion as others see it.

AN ADEQUATE ANTICHRIST

Ted Duncan's Antichrist (Constantine Kurios Augustus) stands in the tradition of Damien Thorn and Lucien Apleon as well as Jenkins's Nicolae Carpathia: he was supernaturally, demonically conceived, and with the proper Gothic trappings of torch-lit, bloody ritual. If there was a devil, would he have any interest in such theatrics? Hard to say, but since the devil is by nature little more than a bit of Gothicism himself, it is unwise to separate him from it. Constantine aspires to the imperial throne of a Revived Roman Empire (and even calls it that, as if he had borrowed it directly from some fundamentalist book on biblical prophecy!). It is based on a United States of Europe, which he expands into a World Federation of Nations. He is a raging spoiled brat of a man, made remotely interesting only by the same element we see in *Damien: Omen II*, namely, he is merely part of a larger plan and is by no means the originator of it. Catechized in the belief that he is Lucifer's Son, he accepts it by faith until his resurrection (Aaron Muller kills him, but it doesn't take). From that point on, faith gives way to sight, and he *knows* himself to be the Son of the god of this world.

One red herring presents itself: Duncan's version of the image of the Beast, which is made to speak and given the semblance of life (Rev. 13:14–15), is a computerized android duplicate of Constantine Augustus. Gifted with artificial intelligence, it is almost a mechanical clone, a second self. One half expects it to eventuate that Constantine did not come back to life after getting skewered through the throat with a bayonet; what if, instead, his awakening three days later was another clone-droid coming online, with all of his memories? But no. That would be "unscriptural," in other words, too original.

At any rate, Duncan provides the Antichrist Constantine with his own "personal savior" in the form of a demon posing as the shade of the emperor Marcus Aurelius, who imparts military advice to the fledgling Beast. The saber-rattling leader of Russia, Gregor Galinikov (whom we meet in Duncan's third volume, *Gog's Revenge*), is one of Constantine's major rivals and something of a would-be Antichrist himself. In fact his Norwegian mother, a spiritist, gave him the middle name Odin at the instruction of that god himself. You know, a guy with a set of initials like that just might wind up with a certain nickname! It has all the verisimilitude of a shaggy dog story.

Naturally, Galinikov's spirit guide "Odin" is just another impostor demon. Fundamentalist Protestants do not believe in spiritualist mediums (and rightly so), but they cannot seem to leave it as a matter of fraud and imposture on the part of greedy showmen. No, they are gullible enough to believe the mediums are in touch with genuine supernatural entities, but since the fundamentalist creed leaves no natural place for ghosts and shades, they are identified with demons, a handy catch-all category for any Brand X spiritual phenomena. Thus Marcus Aurelius and Odin are demons masquerading. Fair enough, one supposes. After all, the novel is the work of a fundamentalist minister; he has every right to set the action within his preferred cognitive universe. But there are a couple of strange snags. Why pick the noble and enlightened Stoic Marcus Aurelius as a warmongering devil? That philosopher-statesman is remembered less for his military campaigns than for his devotional manual *The Meditations*, in which no reader, ancient or modern, can fail to find edification. It is sort of like making the ghost of the saintly Robert E. Lee into the counselor for Hitler. Similarly, Odin was not the Norse god of war. Duncan has his pantheon mixed up here. Tiu (for whom we name Tuesday) was the Norse war deity, not Odin (or Wotan, honored in our Wednesday). The latter was a kind of divine magician, as well as king of immortals.

It is hard enough to depict the End Times events leading up to the consummation of all things. Most of our writers have trouble bringing it off convincingly. But how much harder, as we have seen, is it to depict the wonders of the end itself? Here imagination usually trails off, though not after a miserably unsuccessful attempt or two. Duncan anticipates the eschatological denouement when he shows a penultimate heavenly reunion of Tribulation martyrs. "Each life was examined, and rewards were either granted or withheld.... [M]any humble and obscure saints received manifold rewards, and were assured of positions of great responsibility in the age to come" (p. 289). This one receives "decoration," that one a martyr's crown (p. 290). What does any of this mean? Are we to picture people parading around celestial streets in their medals and pompous finery, like the Beatles on the cover of *Sergeant Pepper*? And are we to imagine "humble saints" wielding judicial authority over hard-nosed sinners who managed to survive Armageddon to make it into the Millennial Kingdom? I think of a sweet old Pentecostal lady I once knew who every week would slowly rise to her feet in church to enunciate the same tongues utterance in brittle tones—she is going to hold court over unregenerate thugs and fallen angels? Some meek Baptist sales clerk is going to be in charge of his own planet? And "rewards"? What *kind* of rewards, pray tell? Seventy-two virgins? Big-screen TVs? Cadillacs? Lots of money? To buy *what*? Has Christianity degenerated into some kind of cargo cult? Or does Duncan think Jesus will plug electrodes into the pleasure centers of the brains of the saved and then zap them with high-voltage jolts of orgasmic ecstasy? I doubt if he has anything in particular in mind at all. And that is because there *is* nothing much *to* have in mind. Heavenly rewards? In the immortal words of George Costanza, "It's just something you say."

It only gets more comical when Duncan reaches the Parousia itself. Like the Lone Ranger, Jesus is mounted on a white stallion, ready to ride. And all the dead evangelicals are with him (which pretty much ought to leave out anybody up to the seventeenth century, when this kind of Christianity was invented). "In front of them rode Pastor Bobby Davis . . . Bruce and Florence Graham joined the triumphant brigade, as did the saved members of the UCLA basketball team, and the saints from the Antioch Baptist Church in Compton" (p. 186). It is an eschatological vista worthy of Milton or Handel, is it not? Or perhaps of a rubber cell.

BUTTLOAD OF PROPHECY

Judging by the cover blurbs from Rush Limbaugh, Sean Hannity, Tim LaHaye, and others, you'd think Joel C. Rosenberg's *The Ezekiel Option* was the greatest piece of fiction Tyndale House had published since *The Living Bible.* It is another post–*Left Behind* novel and, like Tim Duncan's books, actually mentions the LaHaye/Jenkins series. It's an infinite regress: in the narrative universe of *The Ezekiel Option,* the *Left Behind* series heralded the End Times, which "actually" commence in *The Ezekiel Option.* So maybe the reader of *The Ezekiel Option* will find it plausible that the events of the novel he is reading might happen in his own reality, too! (Not likely.)

Rosenberg's novel is a sequel to his earlier book *The Last Jihad* (2002) and leads into a sequel of its own, *The Copper Scroll* (2006). Like them, it is a geopolitical techno-thriller. All the books deal with political intrigue in the Middle East and feature the continuing characters Jonathan Bennett, presidential adviser, and Erin McCoy, beautiful gun-toting CIA operative, both born-again Christians. But *The Ezekiel Option* is the only one so far in which End Times events begin to happen. *The Copper Scroll* cools things down a bit before the Antichrist is to take the stage in a subsequent volume. In *The Ezekiel Option* we witness the abortive invasion of Israel by Gog (Russia led by neo-czar Yuri Gogolov) and the ensuing smithereening of Israel's foes. That pretty much brings us up to the point where *Left Behind* starts.

This is the kind of book that political junkies like to read on the plane. Some folks idolize movie and TV stars; they can't get enough of their performances and find their private lives equally entertaining, so they read about them in the tabloids. In the same way, these techno-thrillers are for people for whom CNN and FOX News are not enough. They would like to see international events progress at a more rapid pace than they do on cable news, and in these books they may pretend they are following such developments as they are "breaking" rapid-fire. The good ones feed the reader just enough soap opera about the main characters to make one try to care about them and just enough resume about secondary characters to make them more than names. There are endless, constant references to weapons systems, communications technology, and political savvy, all aimed at making the reader feel he is a fly on the walls of the corridors of power. It takes a lot of research for the author either to master the requisite knowledge or to give the impression that he has. Likely enough, it's all bluff. But who cares? Is it a good read?

The Ezekiel Option, I say, is such a book. But it offers two variations on the usual themes. First, the soap opera is widened to include pietistic evangelical witnessing, which seems the more incongruous the better the surrounding techno-prose is rendered. It is as if the narrative stopped for "a word from our sponsor, Tyndale House Christian Publishers" and then went on with the espionage. The occasional pitches to give your life to the precious Lord Jesus are jarring, harder to take seriously for being embedded in an otherwise secular, violent novel, not easier, as if the profane intrigue were sugar helping the spiritual medicine go down, which is probably what Rosenberg intended. Second, the "tech" lore served up to the reader includes massive doses of pseudo-scholarly claptrap about Bible prophecy. Owlish experts initiate the secret agents (and with them the reader) into out-of-context, anachronistic Bible citations applied to current events via ventriloquism. We are within spitting range of Dan Brown's *The Da Vinci Code* when we read Dr. Eliezer Mordechai, retired head of the Mossad and a born-again Christian, soberly citing quacks like LaHaye, Hal Lindsey, Dwight Pentecost, and *The New Scofield Reference Bible*. It is like listening to Professor Lee Teabing miseducating the protagonists of *The Da*

Vinci Code in the nonsense of books like *Holy Blood, Holy Grail* and *The Templar Revelation*. The very notion that the prophet Ezekiel, in the seventh century BCE, issued prophecies, not to his contemporaries, to whom they might have had some relevance, but way over their heads, targeting events two and a half millennia later is just plain silly, the fantasy of Bible fans who don't want to admit much of the Bible is a long-irrelevant museum piece. To run the old texts through the sausage grinder of fundamentalist hermeneutics and highly dubious etymologies and to have enough confidence in the result to shape nuclear defense policy on it is just preposterous.

And this leads us to the most disturbing element of the book. The combination of behind-the-scenes political realism and endorsements by well-known right-wing political analysts on the one hand with hack prophecy-belief on the other raises the chilling specter that some hyperconservatives, if they attained political power, might actually base foreign policy on some fringe reading of obscure Bible prophecies. For them, as C. S. Lewis once said in another connection, "myth would become fact" and Doomsday prophecy would become self-fulfilling.

BIBLIOGRAPHY

NONFICTION

Alnor, William M. *Soothsayers of the Second Coming.* Old Tappan, NJ: Fleming H. Revell, 1989.

Anderson, C. LeRoy. *Joseph Morris and the Morrisites.* Logan: Utah State University Press, 1981.

Barker, Margaret. *The Great Angel: A Study of Israel's Second God.* Louisville, KY: Westminster/John Knox Press, 1992.

Berger, Peter L. *The Sacred Canopy: Elements of a Sociological Theory of Religion.* Garden City, NY: Doubleday Anchor, 1969.

Berger, Peter L., and Thomas Luckmann. *The Social Construction of Reality: A Treatise in the Sociology of Knowledge.* Garden City, NY: Doubleday Anchor, 1967.

Bonhoeffer, Dietrich. *The Cost of Discipleship.* Translated by Reginald H. Fuller with Irmgard Booth. London: SCM Press, 1949. 2nd ed., 1959.

———. *Letters and Papers from Prison.* New York: Macmillan, 1962.

Bousset, Wilhelm. *The Antichrist Legend: A Chapter in Christian and Jewish Folklore.* Translated by A. H. Keane. London: Hutchinson and Co., 1896. Reprint, New York: AMS Press, n.d.

———. *Kyrios Christos: A History of the Belief in Christ from the Beginnings of Christianity to Irenaeus.* Translated by John E. Steely. New York: Abingdon Press, 1970. Originally published, 1913.

Bultmann, Rudolf. "New Testament and Mythology." In *Kerygma and Myth: A Theological Debate,* edited by Hans Werner Bartsch and translated by Reginald H. Fuller. New York: Harper & Row, 1961, pp. 1–44.

Carroll, Robert P. *When Prophecy Failed: Cognitive Dissonance in the Prophetic Traditions of the Old Testament.* New York: Seabury Press, 1979.

Charles, R. H. *Eschatology: The Doctrine of a Future Life in Israel, Judaism, and Christianity. A Critical History.* New York: Schocken Books, 1963.

Cohen, Edmund D. "Review of the *Left Behind* Tribulation Novels: *Turner Diaries* Lite." *Free Inquiry* 21, no. 2.

Cohn, Norman. *Cosmos, Chaos and the World to Come: The Ancient Roots of Apocalyptic Faith.* New Haven, CT: Yale University Press, 1993.

Colani, Timothee. "The Little Apocalypse of Mark 13." Translated by Nancy Wilson. *Journal of Higher Criticism* 10, no. 1 (Spring 2003): 41–47. Excerpted from Colani, *Jesus-Christ et les croyances messianiques de son temps,* 1864, pp. 201–14.

Collins, John J. *The Apocalyptic Imagination: An Introduction to the Jewish Matrix of Christianity.* New York: Crossroad, 1989.

Currie, David B. *Born Fundamentalist, Born Again Catholic.* San Francisco: Ignatius Press, 1996.

Detering, Hermann. "The Synoptic Apocalypse (Mar 13 par): A Document from the Time of Bar Kochba." *Journal of Higher Criticism* 7, no. 2 (Fall 2000): 161–210.

Dobschütz, Ernst von. *The Eschatology of the Gospels.* London: Hodder and Stoughton, 1910.

Dodd, C. H. *The Parables of the Kingdom.* Rev. ed. New York: Scribner's, 1961.

Eliade, Mircea. *Cosmos and History: The Myth of the Eternal Return.* Translated by Willard R. Trask. New York: Harper & Row, 1959.

Engnell, Ivan. *Studies in Divine Kingship: Critical Essays on the Old Testament.* Nashville: Vanderbilt University Press, 1969.

Festinger, Leon. *A Theory of Cognitive Dissonance.* Stanford, CA: Stanford University Press, 1962.

Festinger, Leon, Henry W. Riecken, and Stanley Schachter. *When Prophecy Fails: A Social and Psychological Study of a Modern Group that Predicted the Destruction of the World.* New York: Harper & Row, 1964.

Fowler, Robert M. *Let the Reader Understand: Reader-Response Criticism and the Gospel of Mark.* Minneapolis: Augsburg Fortress, 1991.

Fuller, Robert. *Naming the Antichrist: The History of an American Obsession.* New York: Oxford University Press, 1995.

Gager, John G. *Kingdom and Community: The Social World of Early Christianity.* Prentice-Hall Studies in Religion series. Englewood Cliffs, NJ: Prentice-Hall, 1975.

Girard, Rene. *Violence and the Sacred.* Translated by Patrick Gregory. Baltimore: Johns Hopkins University Press, 1977.

Glasson, T. Francis. *The Second Advent: The Origin of the New Testament Doctrine.* 2nd rev. ed. London: Epworth Press, 1947.

Godwin, Joscelyn. *The Theosophical Enlightenment.* Albany: State University of New York Press, 1994.

Goldziher, Ignaz. *Mythology among the Hebrews and Its Historical Development.* Translated by Russell Martineau, 1877. Reprint, New York: Cooper Square Publishers, 1967.

Goulder, Michael D. *The Psalms of Asaph and the Pentateuch.* Studies in the Psalter, III. *Journal for the Study of the Old Testament* supplement series 233. Sheffield, England: Sheffield Academic Press, 1996.

Graves, Robert, and Raphael Patai. *Hebrew Myths: The Book of Genesis.* New York: Greenwich House, 1983.

Gunkel, Hermann. *Creation and Chaos in the Primeval Era and the Eschaton.* Translated by K. William Whitney Jr. Grand Rapids, MI: Eerdmans, 2006.

———. *An Introduction to the Psalms: The Genres of the Religious Lyrics of Israel.* Edited by Joachim Begrich. Translated by James D. Nogalski. Mercer Library of Biblical Studies. Macon, GA: Mercer University Press, 1998.

Guy, H. A. *The New Testament Doctrine of the "Last Things": A Study of Eschatology.* New York: Oxford University Press, 1948.

Hanson, Paul D. *The Dawn of Apocalyptic: The Historical and Sociological Roots of Jewish Apocalyptic Eschatology.* Philadelphia: Fortress Press, 1975.

Himmelfarb, Martha. *Ascent to Heaven in Jewish and Christian Apocalypses.* New York: Oxford University Press, 1993.

Hooker, Morna D. *Jesus and the Servant: The Influence of the Servant Concept of Deutero-Isaiah in the New Testament.* London: SCM Press, 1959.

Jackson, Hugh Latimer. *The Eschatology of Jesus.* London: Macmillan, 1913.

Jenks, Gregory C. *The Origins and Early Development of the Antichrist Myth.* Beihefte zur Zeitschrift für die neutestamentliche Wissenschaft und die Kunde der älteren Kirche Band 59. Berlin/New York: Walter de Gruyter, 1991.

Jeremias, Joachim. *The Eucharistic Words of Jesus.* Translated by Arnold Ehrhardt. Oxford: Basil Blackwell, 1955.

———. *The Parables of Jesus.* 2nd rev. ed. New York: Scribner's, 1972.

Judah, J. Stillson. *The History and Philosophy of the Metaphysical Movements in America.* Philadelphia: Westminster Press, 1967.

Jung, Carl Gustav. *Psychology and Religion.* New Haven, CT: Yale University Press, 1938.

Kaufmann, Walter. *The Faith of a Heretic.* Garden City, NY: Doubleday Anchor, 1963.

Keating, Karl. *Catholicism and Fundamentalism: The Attack on "Romanism" by "Bible Christians."* San Francisco: Ignatius Press, 1988.

Knox, Ronald A. *Enthusiasm: A Chapter in the History of Religion with Special Reference to the XVII and XVIII Centuries.* New York: Oxford University Press, 1950.

Kramer, Werner. *Christ, Lord, Son of God.* Translated by Brian Hardy. Studies in Biblical Theology, no. 50. Naperville, IL: Alec R. Allenson, 1966.

Lewis, C. S. *Mere Christianity.* New York: Macmillan, 1952.

————. "Myth Became Fact." In *God in the Dock: Essays on Theology and Ethics,* edited by Walter Hooper Lewis, 63–67. Grand Rapids, MI: Eerdmans, 1970.

Lifton, Robert J. *Boundaries: Psychological Man in Revolution.* New York: Random House/Vintage Books, 1970.

Lindsey, Hal, with C. C. Carlson. *The Late Great Planet Earth.* New York: Bantam Books, 1973.

Longenecker, Richard. *Biblical Exegesis in the Apostolic Period.* Eerdmans, 1975.

Lüling, Günter. "Preconditions for the Scholarly Criticism of the Koran and Islam, with Some Autobiographical Remarks." *Journal of Higher Criticism* 3, no. 1 (Spring 1996): 73–109.

Malina, Bruce J. *On the Genre and Message of Revelation: Star Visions and Sky Journeys.* Peabody, MA: Hendrickson, 1995.

McGinn, Bernard. *Antichrist: Two Thousand Years of the Human Fascination with Evil.* San Francisco: HarperSanFrancisco, 1994.

Mettinger, Tryggve N. D. *In Search of God: The Meaning and Message of the Everlasting Names.* Translated by Frederick H. Cryer. Philadelphia: Fortress Press, 1988.

Moltmann, Jürgen. *The Crucified God: The Cross of Christ as the Foundation and Criticism of Christian Theology.* Translated by R. A. Wilson and John Bowden. New York: Harper & Row, 1974.

Montgomery, John Warwick. *Principalities and Powers: A New Look at the World of the Occult.* Rev. ed. New York: Pyramid Books; Minneapolis: Bethany Fellowship, 1975.

Moore, A. L. *The Parousia in the New Testament.* Supplements to Novum Testamentum. Vol. XIII. Leiden: E. J. Brill, 1966.

Mowinckel, Sigmund. *He That Cometh: The Messiah Concept in the Old Testament and Later Judaism.* Translated by G. W. Anderson. New York: Abingdon Press, 1954.

————. *The Psalms in Israel's Worship*. Translated by D. R. Ap-Thomas. New York: Abingdon Press, 1962.

Nee, Watchman. *The Latent Power of the Soul*. New York: Christian Fellowship Publishers, 1972.

Nelson, William. *Fact or Fiction? The Dilemma of the Renaissance Storyteller*. Cambridge, MA: Harvard University Press, 1973.

Perrin, Norman. "Mark 14:62: The End Product of a Christian Pesher Tradition?" In Perrin, *A Modern Pilgrimage in New Testament Christology*, 10–18. Philadelphia: Fortress Press, 1974.

Pink, Arthur W. *The Antichrist*. Bible Truth Depot, 1923. Reprint, Minneapolis: Klock & Klock, 1979.

Price, Lucien. *Dialogues of Alfred North Whitehead*. Boston: Little, Brown, 1954.

Price, Robert M. *The Incredible Shrinking Son of Man*. Amherst, NY: Prometheus Books, 2003.

Price, Walter K. *The Coming Antichrist*. Neptune, NJ: Loizeaux Brothers, 1974; 2nd ed., 1985.

Reimarus, Hermann Samuel. *Reimarus: Fragments*. Edited by Charles H. Talbert and translated by Ralph S. Fraser. Lives of Jesus series. Philadelphia: Fortress Press, 1970.

Ringgren, Helmer. *The Messiah in the Old Testament*. Studies in Biblical Theology, no. 18. London: SCM Press, 1956.

Robinson, James M., ed. *The Nag Hammadi Library*. 3rd rev. ed. San Francisco: Harper & Row, 1988.

Robinson, John A. T. *Jesus and His Coming*. Philadelphia: Westminster Press, 1957. 2nd ed., 1979.

Rowland, Christopher. *The Open Heaven: A Study of Apocalyptic in Judaism and Early Christianity*. London: SPCK, 1984.

Russell, J. Stuart. *The Parousia: A Study of the New Testament Doctrine of Our Lord's Second Coming*. London: T. Fisher Unwin, 1887. Reprint, Grand Rapids, MI: Baker Book House, 1983.

Ryle, John Charles. *Holiness: Its Nature, Hindrances, Difficulties, and Roots*. Greensboro, NC: Homiletic Press, 1956.

Scheler, Max. *Ressentiment*. Translated by Lewis B. Coser and William W. Holdheim. Milwaukee, WI: Marquette University Press, 1994.

Schmithals, Walter. *The Apocalyptic Movement: Introduction and Interpretation*. Translated by John E. Steely. New York: Abingdon Press, 1975.

Schreck, Alan. *Catholic and Christian: An Explanation of Commonly Misunderstood Catholic Beliefs.* Ann Arbor, MI: Servant Books, 1984.

Schweitzer, Albert. *The Mystery of the Kingdom of God: The Secret of Jesus' Messiahship and Passion.* Translated by Walter Lowrie, 1914. Reprint, New York: Schocken Books, 1964.

Scott, E. F. *The Kingdom and the Messiah.* Edinburgh: T. & T. Clark, 1911.

Sharman, Henry Burton. *Son of Man and Kingdom of God: A Critical Study.* New York: Harper & Brothers, 1943.

————. *The Teaching of Jesus about the Future according to the Synoptic Gospels.* Chicago: University of Chicago Press, 1909.

Smith, Jonathan Z. "Wisdom and Apocalyptic." Chap. 3 in *Map Is Not Territory: Studies in the History of Religions.* Chicago: University of Chicago Press, 1993.

Smith, Mark S. *The Early History of God: Yahweh and the Other Deities in Ancient Israel.* San Francisco: HarperSanFrancisco, 1990.

————. *The Origins of Biblical Monotheism: Israel's Polytheistic Background and the Ugaritic Texts.* New York: Oxford University Press, 2001.

Stendahl, Krister. *The School of St. Matthew and Its Use of the Old Testament.* Philadelphia: Fortress Press, 1968.

Stone, Jon R., ed. *Expecting Armageddon: Essential Readings in Failed Prophecy.* New York: Routledge, 2000.

Strauss, David Friedrich. *The Life of Jesus for the People.* 2nd ed. Translated by anonymous. London: Williams and Norgate, 1879.

Tillich, Paul. *Dynamics of Faith.* New York: Harper & Row, 1957.

————. "The Depth of Existence." In Tillich, *The Shaking of the Foundations,* 52–63. New York: Scribner's, 1948.

————. *Love, Power, and Justice: Ontological Analyses and Ethical Applications.* New York: Oxford University Press/Galaxy Books, 1960.

————. *Systematic Theology. Volume III: Life and the Spirit; History and the Kingdom of God.* Chicago: University of Chicago Press, 1963.

————. *What Is Religion?* Edited and translated by James Luther Adams. New York: Harper & Row, 1969.

Todorov, Tzvetan. *The Fantastic: A Structural Approach to a Literary Genre.* Translated by Richard Howard. Ithaca, NY: Cornell University Press, 1975.

————. *The Poetics of Prose.* Translated by Richard Howard. Ithaca, NY: Cornell University Press, 1977.

Torrey, R. A. *Difficulties in the Bible: Alleged Errors and Contradictions.* Chicago: Moody Press, n.d.

von Rad, Gerhard. *Old Testament Theology Volume II: The Theology of Israel's Prophetic Traditions.* Translated by D. M. G. Stalker. New York: Harper & Row, 1965.

Wakeman, Mary K. *God's Battle with the Monster: A Study in Biblical Imagery.* Leiden, Netherlands: E. J. Brill, 1973.

Walvoord, John F. *The Rapture Question.* Rev. ed. Grand Rapids, MI: Zondervan Publishing, 1979.

Washington, Peter. *Madame Blavatsky's Baboon: A History of the Mystics, Mediums, and Misfits Who Brought Spiritualism to America.* New York: Schocken Books, 1995.

Webb, James. *The Occult Underground.* LaSalle, IL: Open Court, 1988.

Widengren, Geo. "Early Hebrew Myths and Their Interpretation." In S. H. Hooke, *Myth, Ritual, and Kingship: Essays on the Theory and Practice of Kingship in the Ancient Near East and in Israel,* 149–203. New York: Oxford University Press, 1958.

———. *Mesopotamian Elements in Manichaeism: (King and Saviour II) Studies in Manichaean, Mandaean, and Syrian-Gnostic Religion.* Uppsala Universitets Arsskrift 1946:3. Uppsala, Sweden: A. B. Lundequistska Bokhandeln, 1946.

Wilson, Dwight. *Armageddon Now! The Premillenarian Response to Russia and Israel since 1917.* Grand Rapids, MI: Baker Book House, 1977.

Wittgenstein, Ludwig. *Lectures and Conversations on Aesthetics, Psychology and Religious Belief.* Edited by Cyril Barrett. Berkeley and Los Angeles: University of California Press, 1966.

Zaehner, R. C. *The Teaching of the Magi: A Compendium of Zoroastrian Beliefs.* New York: Oxford University Press, 1976.

FICTION

Allnut, Frank. *The Peacemaker.* Van Nuys, CA: Bible Voice, 1978.

Angley, Ernest. *Raptured: A Novel on the Second Coming of the Lord.* Old Tappan, NJ: Fleming H. Revell Company, 1950.

Balizet, Carol. *The Seven Last Years.* Grand Rapids, MI: Baker Book House/Chosen Books, 1978.

BeauSeigneur, James. *Acts of God: The Christ Clone Trilogy, Book Three.* New York: Warner Books, 1988. Reprint, 2004.

————. *Birth of an Age: The Christ Clone Trilogy, Book Two.* New York: Warner Books, 1988. Reprint, 2004.

————. *In His Image: Book One of the Christ Clone Trilogy.* New York: Warner Books, 1988. Reprint, 2003.

Benson, Robert Hugh. *Lord of the World.* Charlotte: Saint Benedict Press, 2006.

Bernhard, Harvey, and Joseph Howard. *Damien: Omen II.* New York: New American Library, 1978.

Betzer, Dan. *The Beast: A Novel of the Future World Dictator.* LaFayette, LA: Prescott Press, 1985.

Burroughs, Joseph Birkbeck. *Titan, Son of Saturn: The Coming World Emperor. A Story of the Other Christ.* Oberlin: Emeth Publishers, 1914.

Chapman, Graham, John Cleese, Terry Gilliam, Eric Idle, Terry Jones, and Michael Palin. *Monty Python's The Life of Brian (of Nazareth).* New York: Ace Books, 1979.

Clark, Doug. *They Saw the Second Coming.* Irvine, CA: Harvest House Publishers, 1979.

Cohen, Gary G. *Civilization's Last Hurrah.* Chicago: Moody Press, 1974. Reprinted as *The Horsemen Are Coming,* 1979.

Dolan, David. *The End of Days.* Springfield, MO: 21st Century Press, 2003.

Dostoyevsky, Fyodor. *The Grand Inquisitor.* Translated by David McDuff. New York: Penguin Books, 1995.

Duncan, Ted. *Aaron's Rod.* Enumclaw, WA: Pleasant Word, 2003.

————. *Gog's Revenge.* Enumclaw, WA: Pleasant Word, 2004.

Gruhn, Carrie E. *A Trumpet in Zion.* Chicago: Moody Press, 1951. Reprinted as *The Lost City,* 1969.

King, Stephen. *The Dead Zone.* New York: New American Library, 1980.

————. *The Stand.* New York: New American Library, 1980.

————. "Survivor Type." In *Terrors,* edited by Charles L. Grant. Chicago: Playboy Press, 1982.

Kirban, Salem. *666.* Wheaton, IL: Tyndale House, 1970.

Kuttner, Henry. "A Cross of Centuries." In *Star of Stars,* edited by Frederik Pohl, 130–44. New York: Ballantine Books, 1960.

LaHaye, Tim, and Jerry B. Jenkins. *Apollyon: The Destroyer Unleashed.* Wheaton, IL: Tyndale House, 1999.

————. *Armageddon: The Cosmic Battle of the Ages.* Wheaton, IL: Tyndale House, 2003.

————. *Assassins: Assignment: Jerusalem, Target: Antichrist.* Wheaton, IL: Tyndale House, 1999.

————. *Desecration: Antichrist Takes the Throne.* Wheaton, IL: Tyndale House, 2001.

————. *Glorious Appearing: The End of Days.* Wheaton, IL: Tyndale House, 2004.

————. *The Indwelling: The Beast Takes Possession.* Wheaton, IL: Tyndale House, 2000.

————. *Left Behind: A Novel of the Earth's Last Days.* Wheaton, IL: Tyndale House, 1995.

————. *The Mark: The Beast Rules the World.* Wheaton, IL: Tyndale House, 2000.

————. *Nicolae: The Rise of Antichrist.* Wheaton, IL: Tyndale House, 1997.

————. *The Remnant: On the Brink of Armageddon.* Wheaton, IL: Tyndale House, 2002.

————. *Soul Harvest: The World Takes Sides.* Wheaton, IL: Tyndale House, 1998.

————. *Tribulation Force: The Continuing Drama of Those Left Behind.* Wheaton, IL: Tyndale House, 1996.

Lee, Christopher, ed. *Christopher Lee's Treasury of Terror.* New York: Pyramid Books, 1966.

Levin, Ira. *Rosemary's Baby.* New York: Random House, 1967.

————. *Son of Rosemary: The Sequel to Rosemary's Baby.* New York: E. P. Dutton, 1997.

Lindsey, Hal. *Blood Moon.* Palos Verdes, CA: Western Front Publishing, 1996.

Lumley, Brian. *Demogorgon.* London: Grafton Books, 1987.

McCammon, Robert R. *Baal.* New York: Avon Books, 1978.

McGill, Gordon. *The Final Conflict: Omen III.* New York: New American Library, 1980.

————. *Omen IV: Armageddon 2000.* New York: New American Library, 1982.

————. *Omen V: The Abomination.* New York: Time Warner, 1990.

Meier, Paul. *The Third Millennium.* Nashville: Thomas Nelson, 1993.

Monteleone, Thomas F. *The Blood of the Lamb.* New York: Tor Books, 1992.

————. *The Reckoning.* New York: Tor Books, 1999.

Musser, Joe. *Behold a Pale Horse.* Grand Rapids, MI: Zondervan Publishing, 1970.

Patterson, James. *Virgin*. New York: Bantam Books, 1981.

Robertson, Pat. *The End of the Age*. Dallas: Word Publishing, 1996.

Rosenberg, Joel C. *The Ezekiel Option*. Wheaton, IL: Tyndale House, 2005.

Seltzer, David. *The Omen*. New York: New American Library, 1976.

Shirley, John, and Kevin Brodbin. *Constantine*. New York: Pocket Books, 2005.

Stanmeyer, William A. *Day of Iniquity: A Prophetic Novel of the End Times*. Herndon, VA: St. Dominic's Media, 1999.

Watson, Sydney. *In the Twinkling of an Eye*. 1910. Reprint, Los Angeles: Biola, 1921. Reprint, Old Tappan, NJ: Fleming H. Revell Company, 1933.

———. *The Mark of the Beast*. 1911. Reprint, Los Angeles: Biola, 1921. Reprint, Old Tappan, NJ: Fleming H. Revell Company, 1933.

Williams, Larry Hawk. *Eight Books Opened: A Novel of the Second Coming of Christ*. Lincoln: iUniverse.com, Inc., 2001.

INDEX

SCRIPTURE INDEX
(Canonical and Noncanonical)